WOULD POETRY DISAPPEAR?

WOULD POETRY DISAPPEAR?

*American Verse and the
Crisis of Modernity*

JOHN TIMBERMAN NEWCOMB

THE OHIO STATE UNIVERSITY PRESS

Columbus

Copyright © 2004 by The Ohio State University.
All rights reserved.

Newcomb, John Timberman.
    Would poetry disappear? : American verse and the crisis of modernity / John Timberman Newcomb.
        p. cm.
Includes bibliographical references and index.
    ISBN 0-8142-0958-0 (alk. paper) — ISBN 0-8142-5124-2 (pbk. : alk. paper) — ISBN 0-8142-9035-3 (CD Rom)
    1. American poetry—20th century—History and criticism. 2. Modernism (Literature)—United States. 3. American poetry—History and criticism—Theory, etc. 4. Poetry—Authorship—Psychological aspects. 5. Poets, American—20th century —Psychology. 6. Alienation (Social psychology) in literature. 7. Anxiety in literature. I. Title.

    PS310.M57 N49 2004
    811'.509112—dc22
                    2003023446

Text and jacket design by Jennifer Forsythe.
Type set in Palatino.
Printed by Thomson-Shore, Inc.

The paper used in this publication meets the minimum requirements of the American National Standard for Information Sciences—Permanence of Paper for Printed Library Materials. ANSI Z39.48-1992.

9 8 7 6 5 4 3 2 1

**To the memory of two turn-of-the-century families,
my grandparents:**
Charles Milton Newcomb (1882–1956)
Bertha Harrison Newcomb (1884–1968)
Don Timberman (1892–1976)
Helen Swartz Timberman (1898–1982)

And, of course,
to Lori

CONTENTS

ACKNOWLEDGMENTS

This book has been an odyssey to write. The journey has made a lot more sense because of the following people, and it gives me great pleasure to acknowledge them.

Initial thanks must go to two superb scholars of American poetry, Frank Lentricchia and the late Bernard Duffey, who first showed me that turn-of-the-century verse was so worth reading; and to the inimitable Barbara Herrnstein Smith, who showed me what "worth reading" might mean.

Very big thanks are due to Bruce Michelson and Robert Dale Parker, who read large chunks of the manuscript and gave suggestions both encouraging and exacting. Nina Baym brought her formidable attention to bear on the prospectus, for which I'm grateful. Bill Maxwell and Julia Walker offered positive comment on the introduction, while Janet Lyon enabled me to present a part of the book at a very timely moment. Conversations with Gardner Rogers, Leon Chai, Ann Abbott Barbieri, Philip Graham, Rick Powers, Gillen Wood, Merrill Schleier, Stephen Kern, and Cheryl Walker have meant much. Anyone who works on modern American poetry today owes a great debt to Cary Nelson; mine is greater than most, and not only because it includes so many delicious turkey dinners.

Researching this book was a true pleasure, thanks to the libraries and staffs of Duke University, West Chester University, Indiana University, the University of Delaware and above all the University of Illinois at Urbana-Champaign, from which Gene Rinkel, Madeline Gibson, Bill Brockman, and Barbara Jones are due particular thanks. The staff overseeing the wonderful Lester S. Levy Collection of Sheet Music at the

Milton S. Eisenhower Library of Johns Hopkins was a model of helpfulness. Those of the Newberry Library, the Regenstein Library of the University of Chicago, the Museum of the City of New York, and the New York Historical Society helped greatly as well. I'm grateful to the National Endowment for the Humanities and to West Chester University for multiple grants allowing me to travel to collections. The Campus Research Board at the University of Illinois Urbana-Champaign supplied a generous grant for illustrations. In these times of crisis in academic publishing, the Ohio State University Press, personified by Heather Lee Miller and Eugene O'Connor, has been exemplary from beginning to end.

I'm grateful for these fine colleagues and scholars, formerly and presently of West Chester University's English Department, who showed that it could be done: Michael W. Brooks, Carol Shloss, Christopher Buckley, Cheryl Wanko, Carolyn Sorisio, Anne Herzog, and Robert Fletcher (who also helped with multiple versions of the prospectus). I'll always be grateful to C. Ruth Sabol for putting so much faith in me. The world has been made friendlier by Luanne Smith, Chuck Bauerlein, Bill Lalicker, John Thomas Kelly, Karen Fitts, and the much-missed Alan France. Kristina Brooks helped me grasp the importance of Alice Dunbar-Nelson's work. So many students have inspired me over the past dozen years that I can't come close to naming them all, but I certainly must thank Andy Thomas, Chris Corbo, Amy Murray, John Dixon, Juliet McCarter Latham, David Amadio, and John Kerrigan. Fine scholars and colleagues, Paul Maltby and Lynette McGrath have also been the greatest of friends, helping me to get through difficult times, and enjoy good ones. And so has my best bud Michael Peich, who stuns and amazes me with his industry, his enthusiasms, his good taste, and his martinis (while Dianne Peich amazes me by putting up with us in such good humor).

Far-flung friends have given me lots of help, even when they didn't always know it. Thanks to Suzanne Churchill, Christopher Breu, Celena Kusch, Miranda Hickman, and Alyson Tischler, my little Modernist Studies circle, for their seriousness and their jocularity. David Chinitz and Mark Morrisson helped at key moments as well. David Jarraway and Leonard Diepeveen have been ideal colleagues and steadfast friends. Adam McKible's friendship is a great deal more than academic.

My exceptional family provides me so many examples of good lives. All my cool cousins continue to delight me, and Dick and Lois Humphrey keep me amused. My aunt Eleanor Newcomb Rice has offered advice and wisdom, photos and news clippings, volumes of verse and framed poems. Telling me the story of my grandfather's friendship with Edmund Vance Cooke, she inspired the dedication to my grandparents who, each in a different way, gave me something I truly treasure: a love of the past. My brother Christopher Newcomb inspires me with his dedication to his family, parishioners, and patients. I'm prouder of Chris, his wife, Amanda, and their kids, Kaelea and Daniel, than I've ever been able to tell them. My mom, Jane Timberman Newcomb, keeps on keeping on, making her world and mine a better place. And my dear dad, Charles Elwyn Newcomb, wasn't able to keep on, but lives in the hearts of all who loved him.

Everything I accomplish finally comes from, and returns to, Lori Humphrey Newcomb. Our continuing adventure now spans three books, four states, five cars, six homes, nine jobs, nineteen years, and countless acts of love and support. May it never end.

LIST OF ILLUSTRATIONS

INTRODUCTION

From 1890 to 1910, as the United States hurtled into cultural modernity, American poetry underwent a serious crisis that many diagnosed as fatal. For the previous half century, the genre enjoyed a period of canonical prominence that had placed volumes of verse in nearly every middle-class parlor. But soon after 1890, poets, editors, publishers, and readers discovered they could no longer take this comfortable prominence for granted. Confronting the sudden inadequacy of existing accounts of poetry's value, they found they had two choices: either reimagine poetry's uses in a culture of dime novels, vaudeville halls, and nickelodeons, or watch it disappear. Over the next two decades they generated a debate about cultural value dominated by anxiety and suspicion toward tradition, convention, and orthodoxy. Indeed, they were so skeptical even of their own iconoclasm that they could seldom support verse experimenting with new forms and themes. Two powerful convictions—that the dominant genteel traditions of American poetry were moribund, and that no new directions were viable—formed an impasse that threatened to paralyze aspiring writers and to bring the production of American poetry to a halt. Yet I argue in this book that without undergoing this often lacerating phase of anxiety, disillusionment, and seeming futility, poetry in the United States could not have become modern. The period between 1890 and 1910 was crucial to the emergence of twentieth-century poetry's dominant paradigms of cultural value, which adopted such "modern" qualities as uncertainty, marginality, and irony as central to artistic achievement. Participants in the vigorous "New Poetry" movement that emerged after 1910, while retaining this skepticism toward received ideas and conventional strategies, would rediscover a conviction in the value of their calling. But it was their "lost" predecessors of the previous two decades who first broke the ground, struggling to use verse to articulate the ambiguous meanings of their own modernity.

My inquiry into American poetry, like any study of how cultural value is posited, maintained, and changed, takes up the analytic challenge outlined by Barbara Herrnstein Smith's seminal *Contingencies of Value*. Like Smith, I treat the activity of evaluation as a central constituent of literary studies, as accessible to analysis and as needful of interpretation as the concept of meaning has been. Smith's rigorously theoretical work invites historical application by emphasizing the multiple, shifting, and context-specific variables that affect patterns of evaluation. In this book I have sought to remain aware of the irreducible contingency of cultural value by being equally skeptical of two forms of disparagement common in the era I discuss: repudiations of elite forms, because they are valued by only a small percentage of the populace; and dismissals of the genres used by millions, because they don't embody the best that has been thought and said. My analysis assumes that both elite and mass-marketed texts have their uses, their particular virtues and strengths, and their notable limitations. Both are compromised by their entanglement with capitalist ideology production; on occasion both challenge such ideologies. In this book I hope to suggest that the shifting value of each might be best understood by examining the points of contact between them.

My approach synthesizes Smith's evaluative relativism with Jerome McGann's redefinition of the literary work not as a thing or object but "as a complex event in socio-historical space" generated by "an interactive network of productive people and forces" (*Beauty of Inflections* 5, 10). My methodology, which might be called "value-history," aims to describe the discursive networks in which these texts, people, and forces, inevitably implicated in the histories and ideologies of their times (and ours), interact to produce cultural value. The task of value-history in this study is to analyze the ideological formations, structures of feeling, and institutional practices through which the value of verse writing was constructed in the United States a century ago. Between 1890 and 1910 these processes were especially urgent and illuminating, because to a great many people, poetry's very existence was in serious question.

I divide this discourse of value into two interdependent categories of text: (1) the verses produced by Americans during these years, which articulate more or less explicitly the conditions of their own creation; and (2) a myriad other forms of writing (including but not limited to criticism, reviews, editorials, manifestos, anthologies, textbooks, parodies, fiction, biographies, private letters, cartoons, songs) that posited, denied, and contested poetry's value in the nation's homes, public squares, periodicals, classrooms, and bookstores. Like McGann, Richard Brodhead has proposed that we understand surrounding discourses of value as integral to the nature and function of literary texts: "A work of writing comes to its particular form of existence in interaction with the network of relations that surround it: in any actual instances, writing orients itself in or against some understanding of what writing is, does, and is good for that is culturally composed and derived" (*Cultures of Letters* 8).

Each major section of the book examines these reciprocal categories to describe how and why turn-of-the-century Americans believed, and often despaired of believing, that poetry could be of continued value to their modern world. Part 1 traces the construction of a national ideology of poetic value in the decades before 1890, focusing on the reception and poetics of the nation's first literary canon, the so-called Fireside poets, whose increasingly inhibiting shadow dominated U.S. cultural institutions beyond the end of the century. Part 2 mounts an analysis of what American poetry was thought to be "good for"—or no good for—between 1890 and 1910. This account of the genre in crisis provides an interpretive framework for part 3, which reads turn-of-the-century verse through its "particular forms" as they voice and challenge the period's troublesome evaluative dynamics.

AMERICAN POETRY ELSEWHERE

The time frame of this study goes against the grain of traditional "modernist" scholarship, which often assumes that on or about October 1, 1912, American poetry changed with Ezra Pound's first appearance in *Poetry: A Magazine of Verse,* and that little of interest, other than Whitman and Dickinson, had happened before that. No matter that the decisive dynamics of cultural modernity in America had all emerged by 1900, nor that recent historicist scholarship has shown turn-of-the-century American prose writers vividly registering the experiential and ideological shifts that define urban-industrial modernity. Cary Nelson's seminal assertion that "We no longer know the history of the poetry of the first half of this century" (*Repression* 4) applies, if anything, even more comprehensively to the verse produced between 1890 and 1910, which generations of American literature scholars have been told possesses neither historical nor aesthetic significance. Our "impoverished memory" (Nelson, *Revolutionary* 68) of this era is a dubious legacy of the New Critical paradigm of value under which modern poetry was institutionalized in the mid-century academy, reduced to the narrow formation of "high modernism."[1] New Criticism's will to ahistoricity rendered unpalatable, or even unreadable, whatever relationships turn-of-the-century texts posited between the genre of poetry and the condition of modernity. Its fetish for stylistic originality meant that the traditional forms and meters used in most turn-of-the-century poems rendered them insufficiently "modernist."[2]

This criterion of stylistic originality has often enforced powerfully antimodern accounts of the history of American poetry, in which a few writers gain access to the valorizing term "modernism" by rejecting modernity for some "world elsewhere," in Richard Poirier's well-known phrase. The theory of literary value advanced in Poirier's influential 1966 book of that name frames its subject in uncompromising fashion: "American literature is a struggle with already existing literary, social, and historical organizations for power over environment and over language itself" (ix). Poirier's argument identifies the best American literature by its radical disconnection from the "prison" of historical "reality" (29). This paradigm of value confines the canonical American text within an idealized self-created realm based on stylistic uniqueness. This equation is made explicit by the full title of Poirier's book—*A World Elsewhere: The Place of Style in American Literature*—and by this passage from the preface: "The great works of American literature are alive with the effort to stabilize certain feelings and attitudes that have, as it were, no place in the world, no place at all except a writer's style can give them one" (ix). Thus modernism becomes a narrative of embattlement in which titanic individuals seek a breakthrough in style and voice dramatic enough to propel their work beyond the reach of a materialist modernity that reduces everything else to commodity status.

Similar assumptions still undergird the chronological and aesthetic boundaries of much American poetry scholarship. I make this claim well aware that high modernism and New Criticism have been critiqued philosophically and politically (not least by Poirier himself), and that in recent years exciting historicist work has demonstrated how American literary forms can be situated in a range of complex relation to modernity, from abject accommodation to corrosive critique to utopian idealism.[3] Still, a remarkably small proportion of New Americanist scholarship deals with poetry. Though by now few would openly argue that the most valuable verse must escape the dispiriting realm of modernity for a realm of aestheticist detachment, this premise nonetheless lingers in choices made and not made, particularly in the tendency of many scholarly projects to define a historicized American literature as fiction, or at least prose, making poetry into something less than an afterthought.[4]

This severance of poetry from the main contemporary currents of American literature studies has been noted by several scholars, but remains mostly unredressed. Joseph Harrington reminds us that much verse of the early twentieth century was "popular, narrative, and conventional in its representational strategies" ("Why American Poetry" 508). Why is such verse not as valuable to New Americanist practice as previously devalued prose texts and genres? Harrington argues that verse "remains barely visible to critics of American literature because they read poems (if they read them) through the social form of 'poetry' institutionalized 50 years ago" in the disciplinary norms of New Criticism (508). It appears that New Americanism's own "disciplinary unconscious" (Pease 3) sustains a powerful complex of formalist assumptions about poetry that implicitly privilege stylistic density over transparency, emotional opacity over directness, and disillusioned cynicism over idealism.

This subterranean formalism creates a generic double standard in which prose works of vastly varying linguistic sophistication and stylistic distinctiveness are admired—as they should be—while verse texts that come across as sentimental in tone, transparent in theme, or conventional in form, are ignored or scorned. Where poetry is concerned, we are still influenced by an "ethic of difficulty-based machismo" that Leonard Diepeveen sees as foundational to the construction of high-modernist literary value ("Difficult Pleasures"). Harrington proposes that at its most extreme, this self-contradictory practice threatens to eradicate poetry from "American literature" as the field is now being reinscribed under historicist paradigms. Ultimately this absence may be as damaging to New Americanism as to poetry, since it confutes the movement's disciplinary mission to imbricate literature into a historical field defined by political struggle and ideological contestation. Poetry is nearly always the genre claimed to exemplify "the literary" in exactly the sense that New Americanism contests this concept: as a privileged realm separate from history and politics. If a disciplinary movement holding these premises does not demonstrate that this most "literary" of genres is as susceptible to historical imbrication as any other sort of text, then its claim to have situated literature into history will never be realized.

Though this critique still needs to be made, I'm happy to acknowledge fine recent scholarship reasserting American poetry's productive relations to history and politics. Work by Cheryl Walker, Nina Baym, Joanne Dobson, Paula Bennett, and Suzanne Clark, among others, has rethought the boundaries, scope, and uses of nineteenth- and early twentieth-century American women's poetry, loosing the *sentimental* from long-standing pejorative baggage and proposing it instead as a productive category of writing we can study and evaluate differentially, as we do *romantic* or *realist* texts (Dobson, "Reclaiming Sentimental Literature" 283).[5] Recent investigations of American left culture, extending the project initiated by Nelson's *Repression and Recovery,* augur radical (and overdue) changes in the canonical shape of American poetry after 1910.[6] The following chapters will demonstrate that these emerging critical movements have shaped my account of turn-of-the-century poetry at many points.

So far, however, the years between 1890 and 1910 have fallen between these two revisionist paths, which have remained largely within the traditional periodizing strategies of American poetic history, in focusing either on the middle third of the nineteenth century or the interwar years of the twentieth. The canons have changed (from Longfellow/Whittier to Whitman/Poe to Dickinson/Sigourney; from Eliot/Pound to Stevens/Williams to whom—Loy/Hughes?), but the periods have remained the same.[7] These surprisingly tenacious chronological divisions make a productive reading of turn-of-the-century verse difficult, but not impossible. My analysis refreshes this verse by placing it in the evaluative contexts of its production and initial reception, and by measuring not its unfitness for conventionally conceived "modernism," but its engagement with modernity. At various points my argument interrogates the lingering tendency of much Americanist scholarship to treat sentimental and hortatory verses as meretricious subliterary performances rather than as complex and productive deployments of discursive conventions "emerging from a shared cultural/aesthetic impetus at a particular historical moment" (Dobson, "Reclaiming" 265). I seek finally to show that turn-of-the-century verse tropes its times with such variety and intensity that it must be seen as a key moment in the nation's poetry, dramatizing the epochal transition between genteel and modern paradigms of cultural value, and rearticulating the genre's possible uses in a world of million-selling novels, daily newspapers, and hit songs. In its broadest implications, my work joins many of the studies cited above in reconfiguring what is meant by the phrase "modern American poetry." Instead of the great stylistic divide before and after 1912 that has long framed, and perhaps limited, our scholarly work, "modern poetry" might mean, first and foremost, poetry addressing the conditions of modernity.[8]

Many qualities I associate with this modern poetry will no doubt sound familiar: an impulse to resist or challenge traditions; a tendency to measure literary value through the creation of distinctive forms and unique authorial voices; an affinity for irony, historical awareness, and self-reflexivity; an ambivalent attraction to other cultural genres and disciplines; an interest in articulating oppositional political positions; and above all, deep engagement, however anxious or oppositional, with the conditions of modern life. I certainly don't mean these attributes as prescriptive litmus tests a text must pass to be considered "modern," but as a flexible cluster of characteristics traceable across a vast body of verse (in innumerably varied styles) written after 1890. As I conceive the term, such early-twentieth-century poets as Carl Sandburg, Edna St. Vincent Millay, Claude McKay, Amy Lowell, and Langston Hughes (and for that matter, Harriet Monroe, Stephen Vincent Benét, and even Joyce Kilmer) are fully as modern as Ezra Pound, T. S. Eliot, Wallace Stevens, Hart Crane, and Marianne Moore. To claim all these poets are equally modern does not imply that their "modern-ities" are all necessarily of the same type, or their poetry of the same quality or value. These are questions that must be pursued case by case. But the only poems I would exclude from considering as "modern" altogether are those seeking to pretend that urban-industrial modernity never existed at all. There were a vast number of such poems produced up through the first half of the twentieth century (and later?) by writers both well-known and unknown. But even here, I've sometimes found that verses attempting such pretense can still illuminate conditions of modern culture in their very strategies of evasion and repression. Nor would I rule out a priori any poem from being modern because of its author, genre, or site of publication. At various points in this book, I look at verses from popular magazines, advertisements, pop songs, and political protest movements, as well as more "literary" venues. All of these warrant further intensive study as productive genres of modern verse.

In this study, when I describe texts or attitudes of the 1890s and 1900s as "modern," I see them departing from prevailing genteel conventions, and deploying some attitude, image, or representational strategy more typical of the "New Poetry" after 1912.[9] Paula Bennett has used the term "protomodernism" in this way, to describe late-nineteenth-century women poets who "moved toward a poetry of obliqueness and doubt" that challenged prevailing genteel idealism ("Not Just Filler" 207). I'll use "modern" instead, because I want to avoid privileging "modernism" as any sort of a teleological destination, and also because the key poets of this study, born between 1860 and 1880, were barely older than most of those who were central in the New Poetry. If this seems ambiguous, it's an ambiguity calculated to keep in mind the peculiar generational dynamics of the 1910s, in which long-excluded middle-aged writers assumed crucial positions in an emerging avant-garde. Edgar Lee Masters, Amy Lowell, Robert Frost, Vachel Lindsay, Carl Sandburg, Wallace Stevens, born between 1868 and 1879, were chronological contemporaries of Stephen Crane, William Vaughn Moody, Edwin Arlington Robinson, Paul Laurence Dunbar, Trumbull Stickney, Alice Dunbar-Nelson, and Francis Brooks, born between 1867 and 1875. My argument makes this latter group the first moderns of American poetry. Most of them did not even live to see 1912, and thus have seldom been seriously considered in relation to conventional "modernism." But without them, their contemporaries could not have made the New Poetry as vigorous as it became.

WHAT'S SO GREAT ABOUT THE GREAT DIVIDE?

In this book "modernity" describes the epochal material, social, and cultural forces that during the nineteenth century transformed the United States from a relatively homogeneous Christian agricultural society into a multicultural industrial powerhouse dominated by secular values. T. J. Clark and others have proposed reading major artistic movements since Romanticism as often contradictory responses to these processes of secularization and capitalist modernization (7-8). I concur with this, but I see more productive ambiguity in modernization's effects than does Clark's bleak (though magnificent) account of the intertwined decline of modernism and utopian socialism in *Farewell to an Idea*. With Marshall Berman I treat modernity as a paradoxical and conflicted condition in which we "find ourselves in an environment that promises us adventure, power, joy, growth, transformation of ourselves and the world—and, at the same time, that threatens to destroy everything we have, everything we know, everything we are" (15).

In my account of American poetry the central event of cultural modernity was the emergence of the mechanized metropolis, which catalyzed a paradoxical and productive set of social dynamics in the later nineteenth century. Urbanizing and technologizing conditions of experience made possible unprecedented geographical, emotional, economic, and social mobility; yet these new freedoms were achieved by displacing traditional anchoring communities of work, home, family, and religion with networks of more impersonal economic interaction. For Berman, the increasing physical mobility of modern metropolitan life in Western Europe through the nineteenth century shattered long-standing class stratifications and dramatically increased class consciousness, with a rich variety of consequences (150-55). In the United States, with its weaker traditions of social stratification, the growth of the industrialized metropolis, massive immigration, and the postwar emergence of big capitalism initially increased suspicion and disdain across classes. This climate of polarization was a significant factor in American poetry's turn-of-the-century crisis of modernity, as an embattled elite tried to use the genre to enforce rigid categories of cultural legitimation and distinction, in Pierre Bourdieu's sense.[10] However, the continued impact of these forces of modern heterogeneity prevented this climate of distinction from becoming fully naturalized, and generated a contested and multivalent discourse on social marginality that inflected American poetry beginning in the 1890s.

As Clark suggests, one of modernity's defining paradigm shifts pertains to cultural value. Societies can be designated modern by their turn away from measuring value through reverence of past precedent or tradition and by their "pursuit" instead "of a projected future—of goods, pleasures, freedoms, forms of control over nature, or infinities of information" (7). The entanglement of these emergent conceptions of value with ideologies of market capitalism produces another decisive contradiction of cultural modernity. As more people can afford an enlarging array of goods, activities, and pleasures, they are induced to construct their identities around personal economies based on accumulation of material objects, which support capitalist systems of manufacture, distribution, and advertising. Analogously, the individual's relationship to knowledge becomes a paradoxical bargain in which an incredible wealth of knowledge is made available but largely through mass-marketed systems of information, authority, and entertainment whose reliability and beneficence are (or should be) in constant question. These shifts in the relations between macroeconomic forces and cultural value augured radical changes for a genre as tradition-bound and financially tenuous as poetry. Chapter 1 shows that for a time after 1840, the growth of capitalist cultural institutions aided American poetry, as modernized systems of publishing, marketing, and distribution enlarged the audience for an emerging national canon of poets. But by 1890 this delicate balance had spun out of control as voracious market imperatives demanded more immediate and spectacular returns than poetry could usually generate, and as dramatically increasing demand for leisure activities gave rise to new cultural forms competing for the public's coin and allegiance. It is no coincidence that poetry's crisis of value erupted in this gap between its desertion by mainstream cultural economies and the invention of

alternative modern forms of publication—above all, the little magazine—that better addressed the genre's distinctive requirements and
attractions.

Although modernity's liberating and restricting dynamics are always
shifting in proportional importance depending on specific circumstances, both are defining aspects of modern experience, and both are
crucial to my analysis of American poetry. In insisting upon this, I am
contesting the polarization that Berman describes as typifying twentieth-
century writing about modernity:

> Our nineteenth-century thinkers were simultaneously enthusiasts and ene-
> mies of modern life, wrestling inexhaustibly with its ambiguities and con-
> tradictions; their self-ironies and inner tensions were a primary source of
> their creative power. Their twentieth-century successors have lurched far
> more toward rigid polarities and flat totalizations. Modernity is either
> embraced with a blind and uncritical enthusiasm, or else condemned with
> a neo-Olympian remoteness and contempt; in either case, it is conceived as
> a closed monolith, incapable of being shaped or changed by modern men.
> Open visions of modern life have been supplanted by closed ones,
> Both/And by Either/Or. (24)

At the turn of the century, the most compelling accounts of poetry's
value, and the strongest American verses, sought to engage modernity's
defining contradictions as sources of creative power. To reexamine the
enabling aspects of these contradictory engagements, long obscured by
high modernism's Olympian disdain for modernization, will help us
construct accounts of American poetry more responsive to the heterogeneous textures of modern life.

Though as Berman notes, the crippling polarity of "cultural despair"
and "modernolatry" often bisects conventional left-right political divisions (169-70), the former is usually associated with elite or "literary" culture, the latter with mass culture. Like Richard Ohmann, I take the emergence of the genres we term "mass culture" as "a development of world-
historical importance" (31)—indeed, as one of the decisive consequences
of the modern condition. And I view American poetry beginning in the
1890s as being consistently inflected by this development. Andreas
Huyssen's revision of the relationship between modernism and mass culture pertains to my position: "Contrary to the claims of champions of the
autonomy of art, contrary also to the ideologists of textuality, the realities
of modern life and the ominous expansion of mass culture throughout
the social realm are always already inscribed into the articulation of

aesthetic modernism. Mass culture has always been the subtext of the modernist project" (47). But Huyssen's use of the singular "modernist project" risks equating a particular formation (typically, high modernism) with the entire culture of the modern period.

I also question Huyssen's claim that "What has to be put in question is the presumably adversary relationship of the modernist aesthetic to the myth and ideology of modernization and progress, which it ostensibly rejects in its fixation upon the eternal and timeless power of the poetic word" (56). Here Huyssen usefully reframes this relationship away from simplistic opposition but interprets this as exposing a dirty secret, one so unmentionable that all of modernism becomes a "reaction formation" (54) defined by its need to repress involvement in "the processes and pressures of the same mundane modernization it so ostensibly repudiates" (56). When Huyssen refers to "the subterranean collusion of modernism with the myth of modernization" (56), he circumscribes his position within an evaluative paradigm of elitist high culture, able to see mass culture's emergence only as "ominous," the promises of modernization only as delusive and debilitating. Such a conclusion veers toward the "flat totalizations" Berman objects to.

This book uses a less global and more contingent approach to exploring the relative value of elite and mass culture as "twin and inseparable forms of the fission of aesthetic production under late capitalism," as Fredric Jameson puts it (14). As we investigate multiple "modernist projects" that use mass culture quite differently from high modernism's uses of it, we'll find this means not just considering how individual writers of the high canon echoed, borrowed from, or parodied mass culture, illuminating as such studies can be. It also means investigating how forms of mass culture inflected traditionally elite genres such as poetry, even if such inquiry means taking seriously the sort of verse we were taught to regard as worthless doggerel—an assertion put to the test in chapter 2 when I discuss a poem advertising canned baked beans.

I propose that American poetry's engagement with mass culture has been not deviously collusive, but often exuberant and powerfully energizing. The mass-culture verse genres that challenged poetry's elite status in the 1890s generated energy by appropriating conventions of genteel verse for use in forms more relevant to the actual textures of modern life. During those same years, Americans who were still committed to literary poetry were forced to acknowledge the obsolescence of its existing cultural functions and worked to reimagine its possible uses, often by adapting or parodying conventions of mass culture. It was no accident that American poetry was rejuvenated in the 1910s when a vast range of poets immersed themselves in the defining textures, settings, and discourses of modern urban experience.[11] But as the final chapter of this book details, even in the 1890s and 1900s some American verse writers—Stephen Crane above all—began to draw upon forms of mass culture for conceptual, structural, and even ethical models. These attempts to reformulate poetry's value exhibit plenty of anxiety and antagonism toward mass culture, but in their strongest and most self-aware works, anxiety and antagonism generate valuable *resistance* to modernity's dispiriting aspects. This resistance is the opposite of the genteel desire to *escape* modernity altogether. Of course not all such forms of engaged resistance are equally valuable, but engagement in some form is surely prerequisite to any meaningful contribution that literature might make to modern social life.

THEMATICS OF VALUE

In the book's interpretive sections, I foreground the tendency in turn-of-the-century American poems—from the perfumed effusions of rarefied aestheticist circles to the hastily composed light verses of mass-circulation magazines—to ruminate upon their own status, function, or value. This quality contrasts strikingly to American verses written after 1910, which exhibit far less need to investigate or justify the conditions of their own existence. To chart these articulations, I have drawn upon the "thematics of writing" underlying Michael Fried's brilliant deconstructive reading of Stephen Crane's prose, which argues that "Crane's relentlessly metaphorical style" continually explores "the multifarious aspects of . . . the scene of writing" (98, 120). This choice is not arbitrary, since Crane is the central poet of my analysis, the one most intensely engaged with turn-of-the-century American modernity. Fried sees such recurrent Crane images as "disfigured upturned faces with open unseeing eyes" troping "the blank page on which the action of inscription takes place," and providing an intricate self-reflexive level of signification even in his most historically embedded and occasional writings (99-100). My interpretive approach could be called a "thematics of value," charting the ways that turn-of-the-century verses trope the conditions of their own production and reception. Sometimes these self-reflexive moments thematize the physical act of inscription, but they may also evoke the activity of reading, either individual or communal; explore the psychosocial economies of creating poetic writing; portray books or poems as material commodities or cultural icons; articulate their own conflicted relationship to past canons; measure poetry against such popular genres as newspapers, fiction, and song; or ponder poetry's capacity to intervene in the realms of politics and history.

In tracing the ways that American poems offer reflexive commentary on their own value, the last thing I want is to imply a closed circle of self-reference—that poetry always talks about itself and not much else. My goal is the opposite: to show that when such texts problematize the premises of their own value or valuelessness, they are grappling with far-reaching issues, particularly the changing relationship between traditionally elite genres and the forms of modern mass culture. When poems voice anxieties about their own ephemerality, for example, they don't merely bemoan their misfortune but also struggle to comprehend unstable modern dynamics of cultural permanence and change. When they portray the poet as an outcast wandering the margins of society, as a vast number of turn-of-the-century verses do, they may (or may fail to) appropriate key conceptual polarities such as center and margin in order to challenge existing aesthetic and social hierarchies. Poems such as Robinson's that exploit disparities between traditional styles and modern subjects offer new ways for artistic "form" to embody social "content." Poems parodying or critiquing forms of mass culture may advance perspectives of intelligent resistance to repressively polarized responses to modernity (elitist dismissal or blind acceptance). These are the sorts of interpretive premises historicism uses productively with American prose texts but has seldom tried with the nation's rich reservoir of poetry.

It's not enough simply to say that we ought to read a different kind of modern poetry because it was politically or morally well-intentioned. Our understanding of poetry's value has been profoundly shaped by the formalist lineage of New Criticism and American deconstruction that showed how to read such poets as Stevens, Eliot, Moore, and Hart Crane with the subtlety their work deserves. But at the same time, imperatives of aesthetic craft and conceptual depth need not mean that we can appreciate only those same poets and their work. It is premature—drastically so—to assume that the interpretive skills we use to read modernist titans must fail when applied to poets writing with different premises and priorities. Yet this is not only assumed all the time, but also taken for granted that such "failure" clinches the inferiority of those latter poets. In my view, all that such disclaimers demonstrate is that the strategies critics honed to read Eliot in 1940 with such revelatory force that they transformed the canonical outlines of American literature—the somewhat different ones used to read Pound in 1950, Stevens in 1960, and Williams in 1970—are overdue for further retooling. Richly contextual approaches can, and must, be adapted to the concerns of modern American poets—and not just the few greats vetted by high modernism, but also those who used "popular, narrative, and conventional" forms to garner sizable audiences and exert powerful influence on the nation's culture. The work of Cary Nelson, Alan Wald, Walter Kalaidjian, Mark Van Wienen, Michael Thurston, Nancy Berke, Joseph Harrington, Robert Shulman, Rita Barnard, and others has reasserted American verse after 1910 as a discourse that engages modernity rather than trying to repudiate it. My analysis extends the reach of their work by showing how a range of turn-of-the-century poets fit into this developing narrative of modern American poetry.

Some readers may perceive a few—or most—of the verses I discuss as lacking sufficient aesthetic value. I would gently urge them not to turn away too quickly, but to examine their own interpretive and evaluative premises, as historicists have done while working with once denigrated prose works. The rigorously relativistic model of literary evaluation advanced by Smith in *Contingencies of Value* and Jane Tompkins in *Sensational Designs,* among others, treats the value and meaning of texts not as intrinsic to them, but as dependent on complex contextual variables. This relativist position has become widely professed, if not predominant, in current Americanist practice. Those who claim to hold it must accept the corollary that verse dismissed as lacking aesthetic value by New Critical high modernism might become significant or even crucial within historicist paradigms. Yet this process will not happen instantaneously or easily: these poems need a chance to breathe, to show us what they can do, before we close the book on them for another hundred years.

I have opened many musty volumes since I began this study and am happy I did so. After completing a dissertation and book on Wallace Stevens, I knew I was no longer interested in projects on single authors. My quarrel was not with Stevens (far from it), but with modernist criticism's "incredibly narrow focus on a select group of seminal careers," as Kalaidjian puts it (2). I therefore resolved to explore a wide range of American verses that grapple with questions of cultural value, regardless of whatever canonical or non-canonical baggage they currently carry. Originally my discussion of turn-of-the-century work was conceived as a prefatory chapter in a study of early-twentieth-century American poets' engagement with urban-industrial modernity (my next major project). But I found so much of interest before 1910 that I wound up with an entire book. My enthusiasm was piqued by the almost complete lack of recent critical material on turn-of-the-century verse. As I read these poets whose names I had usually heard spoken in tones of condescension or even ridicule, I had the liberating sense that some of my high-modernist preconceptions were falling away. I also developed deep respect for their often brave and ingenious responses to the excruciating conditions in which they found themselves. Reading them, I felt the surprised pleasure one feels upon discovering old but fresh currency in a discarded coat. If this metaphor seems crassly materialistic, it is intentionally so, since the turn-of-the-century poems that speak to me most are those willing to acknowledge their own ambiguous embeddedness in a stubbornly material and irreversibly modern world. I hope that upon encountering this body of verse in a sympathetic yet open-eyed analysis, others will find more to say about these poets, and will carry on excavating the still undervalued riches of modern American poetry.

PART 1
Consensus

1

LOOKING BACKWARD FROM 1890

Antimodernity in Canonical American Poetry

E merging in the 1840s and peaking in the decade after the Civil War, an influential model of poetic value conferred canonical status on a half-dozen American-born poets—William Cullen Bryant (1794–1878), Ralph Waldo Emerson (1803–1882), Henry Wadsworth Longfellow (1807–1882), John Greenleaf Whittier (1807–1892), Oliver Wendell Holmes (1809–1894), and James Russell Lowell (1819–1891). These writers have been given various names: the New England poets, the Schoolroom poets, the Fireside poets. I use the latter because of its enormous resonance with their ideological functions in nineteenth-century America. A few of their contemporaries enjoyed periods of greater popularity; still others would be canonized by twentieth-century readers. In today's academy the Fireside poets generate less interest than female literary professionals such as Frances Osgood, Sarah Josepha Hale, Lydia Sigourney, Elizabeth Oakes Smith, and Lydia Maria Child, who commanded great influence in the middle of the century but later fell into neglect. As the term "canonical poetry" in my chapter title is meant to acknowledge, the construction of the Fireside writers as *the* central American poets excluded a great deal. Recent scholarship by Nina Baym, Paula Bennett, and others has demonstrated that nineteenth-century American verse was a much richer and more varied discourse than most histories have admitted, featuring sentimental verse with a wide range of cultural and emotional functions; challenging explorations of women's consciousness by Emily Dickinson, Sarah Piatt, and many others; poems by such pioneering African American figures as Frances Harper; and verse of great tonal and ideological variety dealing with contemporary political issues, particularly abolition.

I have no interest whatsoever in claiming the Fireside writers' aesthetic, political, or ethical superiority to other poets of the period. My focus on this canon should not be taken as any kind of endorsement of its exclusivity. On the contrary, I see my critique of the damaging effects of this exclusivity complementing the efforts of scholars recovering alternative verse traditions devalued for so many decades. But I frankly found it impossible to understand turn-of-the-century American poetry without describing the antimodern genteel hegemony that the period's young writers chafed against. It was the six Fireside writers, and no one else, who were constructed as the icons of a national poetic canon after the Civil War. By the 1890s the complexity and variety of American poetry had been mostly reduced to a single canonical narrative focused upon them.[1] Even in decline this genteel model and its exemplary poets dominated the nation's elite literary institutions and set the evaluative terms for American verse. The Fireside canon's dominance left young poets with virtually no reservoir of imagery, voice, or subject matter through which they might articulate a productive relation between their modernizing culture and their own verse.

The dramatic ascent and lingering decline of the Fireside poets' reputations reveals much about nineteenth-century literary practice in the United States, particularly as a form of resistance against the nation's spectacular modernization. For the readers who lavished extraordinary devotion upon them through the second half of the century, these writers offered emotional anchorage in a time of growing social instability and moral relativism. Their work articulated a distinctive antimodern account of literary value, claiming independence from local and material contingencies and insisting on fidelity to established traditions, formal conventions, and universal moral laws.[2] But as I'll propose through readings of several key texts, the recipe of nostalgia, domesticity, pastoralism, and formal conventionality that defined Fireside poetics could not sustain a viable account of poetry's value in a condition of accelerating modernization. Refusing to address the depersonalized textures of experience in which Americans were coming to dwell, eventually turning away from political comment, the Fireside poets looked backward as the United States sped forward. Yet as a new century approached, they paradoxically remained so dominant in the nation's literary culture that their great age registered as the obsolescence of the entire genre of poetry. By 1900 these converging evaluative circumstances had thrown poetry in America into a crisis so severe that many felt it could not recover but would simply wither away in the baffling crosscurrents of modern times.

VALUE AND THE INDIVIDUAL TALENT

As their sobriquet implies, these six poets were ubiquitous in the middle-class American household in the century's second half (their volumes "found almost by every fire-side," as it was said of Longfellow in 1865 ["Evangeline" 77]).[3] Their birthdays became occasions of celebration in public schools; their names topped the compilations of "Best American Books" and "Our Forty Immortals" that proliferated after 1880; their benevolent bearded visages gazed from mantels in hundreds of thousands of middle-class parlors. It probably could go without saying that they were the earliest literary inductees into the Hall of Fame for Great Americans. As all these markers of individual distinction imply, the Fireside poets were the earliest beneficiaries of the argument that the United States needed its own great authors. Their status as star national writers was ironic on a number of levels, especially since they consistently rejected arguments in favor of a distinct American culture. Their espousal of the nostalgic virtues of childhood, family, and small-town life was also paradoxical, since they were backed by an increasingly sophisticated cultural establishment and boomed by a publishing industry's value-making machinery that was state-of-the-art for its day. Yet this contradiction was crucial to their appeal to readers who desired a poetry transcending venal realms of nationality and economics to reinforce moral virtues that were increasingly menaced in the nation's headlong rush into urban modernity.

We can trace the emergence of this first American poetic canon to the professionalizing climate of the later 1830s and 1840s, when notions of literary authorship were consolidating within a national frame of reference. Before 1835, as William Charvat notes, most who called themselves publishers were "primarily retail booksellers" in a "predominantly local" industry (169), and no American literary magazine had ever attained a strongly national profile. The chaos of copyright law meant that poems published in magazines or newspapers could be "clipped" with impunity by other publications, which often mangled the text or misidentified the author.[4] Perhaps the most popular anthology of the antebellum era, Rufus W. Griswold's *The Poets and Poetry of America* (1842; reprinted eleven times by 1849), documented what we can call the final precanonical moment in the nation's literary history. Griswold cast a wide but shallow net, evenhandedly representing more than 150 writers, few of whom were "poets by profession. Law, politics, medicine, and journalism were their common occupations; versification, a pastime" (Wortham 278–79). The six writers who would soon form the first national poetic canon occupied 59 of its 544 pages, roughly 11 percent of the book—hardly a dominant showing.

During this professionalizing moment, some high-toned American magazines clung to the trappings of amateur models of authorship, but amateurism's residual attractions counted for little against the forces constructing the author-as-celebrity as the locus of modern literary value.[5] By the end of the 1840s the institutional outlines of a national culture were taking shape, and a period of substantial canonical coalescence had begun. It was no coincidence that *Graham's Magazine* and Louis Godey's *Lady's Book,* the first magazines to achieve large national circulation (in the early 1840s), were also "among the first to permit, even encourage, authors to sign their real names" (Tebbel and Zuckerman 31). George Graham began using well-known contributors as advertising, unabashedly trumpeting their names on the cover of his magazine (Mott, *History of American Magazines,* 546; Tebbel and Zuckerman 31). Ronald Zboray notes that by the 1840s new technologies of stereotyping and electrotyping had begun to shift book marketing practices toward "in-depth, long-term advertising campaigns" designed "to boost not only the sales of a particular work but also the author's celebrity, in the hopes that previous works by that author might be sold" (189). These trends all contributed to the emergence of star authors such as Longfellow. In 1836, just before his thirtieth birthday, Longfellow had taken up the most prestigious academic position in American letters, the Smith professorship of Modern Languages and Literatures at Harvard, and as Matthew Gartner details, began the "invention of himself as a poet" after a lengthy hiatus from verse writing (59–60). Urged by the publisher to allow his name to appear on the title page of *Voices of the Night,* which was issued for the Christmas season in 1839, the initially diffident Longfellow found himself with a "best-seller": the first edition of nearly one thousand was gone within three weeks, and over the next twenty years it would sell forty-three thousand copies (Hart 73). By 1842 *Graham's* had tendered him a standing offer of fifty dollars per poem, with a guarantee of at least one purchase each month (Charvat 109). Six years after moving to Harvard, he had produced several popular works, including "A Psalm of Life," *Hyperion,* and "The Village Blacksmith," that made him perhaps the most famous verse writer in America.[6]

If by 1850 an economic basis for the American author had been established, in the two decades that followed, a national genteel culture was consolidated institutionally. The ascendancy of the Fireside writers was central to this consolidation, which largely took place in another new type of magazine, to some extent modeled on both *Graham's* and the *Lady's Book*. These "quality magazines," including *Harper's* (founded 1850), *Putnam's* (1853), the *Atlantic Monthly* (1857), *Lippincott's* (1868), and *Scribner's* (1870, to become the *Century* in 1881), quickly came to carry the ideological standard of American genteel culture. Nearly all of them had direct financial links to major book publishing firms, encouraging ideological homogeneity across the nation's most prominent literary institutions. Their devotion to the Fireside canon would set a tone for American genteel culture into the 1910s: earnest, high-minded, distrustful of difference and nonconformity, seeking to employ literature, particularly poetry, to stabilize and perpetuate universal moral values.

The institutional epicenter of this genteel culture was the *Atlantic Monthly*, which forthrightly espoused the Fireside poets' values and provided a remunerative space for their work. But it has seldom been emphasized how fully the *Atlantic* was conceived as *their* magazine. Fewer than a dozen men attended the initial meetings to discuss the project in the spring of 1857, among them Emerson, Longfellow, Lowell, and Holmes (Howe 13–21). The first issue, in November 1857, featured work by all four of them and Whittier. Lowell became the magazine's editor, accepting on the condition that Holmes, who had proposed the name *Atlantic Monthly*, be designated as "the first contributor" (Howe 18). The magazine's purchase in late 1859 by the prestigious Boston firm Ticknor and Fields, which already had published books by four of the Fireside poets, completed a triple alliance extending from authorial composition through periodical appearance to book publication. Even the easing out of Lowell as editor in 1861 in favor of James T. Fields meant little disruption in this tight circuit of literary production. Fields took full advantage of his dual role by promoting his firm's books in the magazine, through advertising, reviews, and strategically timed features, making the *Atlantic* into a powerful "Fame-dispensing Organ," in Holmes's jocular phrasing (qtd. Austin 74).[7] Charvat concludes that by the time of Fields's retirement in 1871, "Ticknor and Fields publications had become the core of the American canon of classics" (187). The core of the firm's list was the work of the Fireside poets. This seamless mutual sponsorship between author, magazine, and publisher (which eventually became Houghton Mifflin) continued uninterrupted for the rest of their lives.

ACROSS THE UNIVERSE

Their preferential access to the nation's leading cultural institutions notwithstanding, the Fireside poets were not foisted upon an unwilling public. Their ascent to canonicity, and their long hold on American literary institutions, suggests that they embodied a model of cultural value that resonated powerfully with readers of the era. In contrast to the twentieth-century's attraction to literature's oppositional capacities, nineteenth-century genteel culture sought a literature that, if not always explicitly Christian, was "inherently religiocentric" (Buell 108).[8] In his 1881 essay "Character, and What Comes of It," *Scribners'* editor Josiah Gilbert Holland elaborated a moralistic account of poetry's value in terms of its "service" in domestic and religious realms: "The further art is removed from ministry, . . . the more illegitimate it does become. Pyrotechny attracts many eyes, and may excite a great deal of wonder and admiration, but when we talk about the value of fire, we only think of its service in the furnace and on the hearth" ("Character" 469). Holland's premise that "Above all other things in the world, character has supreme value" led effortlessly into praise of "Our own Bryant, and Longfellow, and Whittier, and Holmes, and Lowell," who were "all men of character, and the outcome of their art is as hearty and healthy as a mountain wind" (469). Genteel readers treasured the implicit invitation in Fireside poetry to join this community of good character, as the telling modifier "Our own" reveals.

Warren Susman has elaborated the centrality of this term "character" in dominant nineteenth-century accounts of ethical behavior that took "self-control" as the quality most "essential for the maintenance of the social order" (214). Holland's validation of the Fireside poets' good character also functioned as an attack on their most pyrotechnic contemporaries, Poe and Whitman, who exemplified the dangers of uncontrolled individuality divorced from communal "ministry."[9] Holland reiterated the era's prevalent condemnation of Poe as a man of corrupt character: "It is only necessary to know . . . that he was a man of weak will . . .—a dissipated man—a man of morbid feeling—a self-loving man . . .—to know that he could never write a poem . . . that possessed any intrinsic value whatsoever" ("Character" 469). "A man of talent without principle" (Duyckinck 254), Poe lacked self-control, causing him to flout traditions he should revere, to put his own gratification above his readers' edification. Likewise, respondents to the first editions of *Leaves of Grass* were affronted by Whitman's refusal of self-censorship, which led some to consign him to a level of animal or brutish subhuman existence: Whitman "calls his free speech the true utterance of a *man:* we, who may have been misdirected by civilisation, call it the expression of a *beast*" ("Review" [*Critic* (London)] 32; italics in original). To the genteel sensibility, speech "free" from self-control was inevitably licentious, animalistic speech.[10]

Whitman's and Poe's use of distinctive forms that bespoke the unmistakable identity of their creators clashed with the demand for a poetics of moralistic self-control and provided further evidence of their corrupt self-absorption. Poe's poems, disfigured by an "extreme artificiality" that offered only "cunning skill in construction, and displays of artistic force which have no merit but their ingenuity," confounded the genteel need for a close identification between moral and aesthetic value (Ripley 248). In contrast to the unimpeachable rectitude of the Fireside poets, he failed to satisfy "universal principles of taste" (247). Early reviewers of Whitman reacted even more violently to his self-aggrandizing repudiation of time-honored poetic forms. Charles Dana linked the formal uniqueness of his poems, "shaped on no pre-existent model" but "out of the author's brain," to a "coarse and defiant" independence, and in the next sentence, to a moral failing that made the poet's language "too frequently reckless and indecent" (3). Lowell commented of Whitman in 1855, "When a man aims at originality he acknowledges himself consciously unoriginal," precluding a "capacity for great things" ("Letter Extracts" 7), while Charles Eliot Norton linked Whitman's formal originality to his questionable moral character, concluding that because he had gratified his own scorn for convention before the moral health of his reader, *Leaves of Grass* was "not to be read aloud to a mixed audience" (5). An often-repeated anecdote, as irresistible as it is unverifiable, has a scandalized Whittier banishing Whitman from the familial scene of canonical poetry by throwing a copy of *Leaves of Grass* into his own fireplace (Shi 32, Wagenknecht 20, Leary 82).[11]

Nearly all mid-century genteel commentators would have scoffed at the notion of Poe and Whitman as exemplary American writers.[12] Yet convention-bound notions of American poetic value created their own problem. The moralistic paradigm of value, demanding the subordination of personality to conventional practices and normative ethics, threatened to inhibit the emergence of American writers distinctive enough to realize a national culture, as Lawrence Buell notes: "The American writer was both marginalized and pedestalized—both useless (as measured by the materialistic scale of priorities in a developing nation) and, at the same time, a national necessity (as the symptom of complete cultural emergence). The writer was charged with the responsibility of finding an American voice for a still colonialized culture not disposed to recognize or value that voice—a problem especially oppressive for the poet, given the fact that the British poetic tradition was more imposing than that of the novel" (117).

To legions of American readers before 1890, the Fireside poets successfully negotiated this contradiction. In contrast to the ungoverned idiosyncrasy of Poe and Whitman, their social marginality as poets was countered by wide popularity, indisputable moral probity, and eminent achievement in the material world. They answered the need for individual distinction while also functioning as a coherent community whose like-mindedness provided self-reinforcing evidence of its sound values. Readers perceived their "philanthropic" force (Whipple 514) as a collective more powerful than the sum of its parts, and often equated their personal character to the value of their work. As Holland put it, "Knowing any one of these men is to know that their work is good" ("Character" 469). Under genteel evaluative premises, this phrase resonated with two powerful interdependent meanings: it *is good* (possesses value) because it *is good for* those who read it.

A major part of the Fireside poets' appeal in a rapidly modernizing society came from their unabashed claims of access to moral and aesthetic universals. These abiding universalist commitments appeared as early as 1825 in Bryant's rejection of an American poetry based on indigenous contemporary actualities ("the roots used to signify canals, railroads, and steamboats" [*Prose Writings* 1:34]), because such a language would quickly become obsolete. From the mid-1830s they elaborated a universalist poetics conceived against the prevailing rhetoric of literary nationalism. Though in his early "Defence of Poetry" (1832) Longfellow had given some lip service to nationalism (69), he quickly lost enthusiasm, arriving in his 1849 novel, *Kavanagh*, at a pointedly anti-nationalist position "guided by an overruling belief in tradition, in the permanence of the literary canon" (Beach, *Politics* 38–40; see also Vanderbilt 73–74).[13] The young Emerson had famously asserted in 1837 that Americans had "listened too long to the courtly muses of Europe" ("American Scholar" 113).[14] Thus his shift away from nationalism almost immediately thereafter augured the emergence of a universalist hegemony of genteel culture. Finding himself unwilling to accept that all cultural value should be treated as relative, "determined not by the inherent properties of an object but by extrinsic factors such as opinion and desire" (Gilmore 22), Emerson too embraced the value of poetry as intrinsic, universal, and capable of transcending all cultural circumstance.

The increasingly militant universalism of genteel culture by the later 1840s was exemplified by James Russell Lowell's powerful review of *Kavanagh* in the *North American Review,* which deployed a set of assertions about literary value that became linchpins of genteel poetics and dominated the nation's elite cultural institutions through the end of the century.[15] Lowell opened with some satiric mimicry of the nationalist-relativist position, holding that since "the form of an author's work is entirely determined by the shape of his skull, and that in turn by the peculiar configuration of his native territory, perhaps a new system of criticism should be framed . . . [in which a lack] of sublimity would be inexcusable in a native of the mountains, and sameness in one from a diversified region, while flatness could not fairly be objected to a dweller on the prairies, nor could eminent originality be demanded of a writer bred where the surface of the country was only hilly or moderately uneven . . . "[16] (198).

For Lowell, the uselessness of a self-conscious national literature had been demonstrated by the miserable failure of Joel Barlow, who had "made the lowest bid for the construction of our epos, got the contract, and delivered in due season the *Columbiad,* concerning which we can only regret that it had not been entitled to a still higher praise of nationality by being written in one of the proposed new [American] languages" (which speakers of genuine English would luckily be unable to read) (203). Lowell's construction metaphors reinforced his antimodern satire, insinuating that the nationalist position failed because it attempted to apply preposterous utilitarian criteria to the creation of art, which properly existed outside worldly standards. Against the extremism of his straw nationalist, Lowell's own rhetoric of intrinsic value sounded like sweet reason: "it is barely possible that the *power* of a book resides in the book itself" (200; italics in original). Like Bryant, he argued that poetry concerned with the contingencies of life would be limited to "jokes, anecdotes, and allusions of such purely local character that a majority of the company are shut out from all approach to an understanding of them" (208). Lowell thus concluded that a relativist criterion such as nationality was nothing but a "treacherous antiseptic" for literature, which would survive "not because of its nationality, but in spite of it" (202). This universalism dovetailed with Lowell's emphasis on the rarity and inexplicability of genius, producing a canonical scarcity theory that would exert a stranglehold over American poetry at century's end. He found Americans foolish to compare this country's literature to older ones whose mediocrities time had winnowed away (197). The natural pattern of even the greatest literatures was for "years of scarcity, downright famine even, . . . between every full harvest. . . . What a length of stalk between Chaucer and Spenser, and again between Milton and Wordsworth" (201). Much like Eliot seventy years later in "Tradition and the Individual Talent," Lowell defined literary value in terms of an unbroken chain of sacralized genius, the "selecter list of English poets" (205). Through this "apostolic succession," transcending distances of time and geography, we were privileged "to see the *vitai lampada* passed thus from consecrated hand to hand" (207). I call this enormously influential formulation a "genius model," which defines literary value not just by the rarity of genius, but by the "impassable gulf between genius, which only deals with the true, and that imitative faculty which patiently and exactly reproduces the actual" (207). The absolute barrier Lowell posited between the genius and the yeoman writer would descend into Poundian high modernism, though it would be vigorously contested by contemporaries such as Harriet Monroe, who argued instead for the thoroughgoing interdependence of "genius" with its surroundings.[17]

Lowell's scarcity theory of genius advanced another presumption influencing American evaluative practice well into the next century: the notion that the greatest literature was independent of external circumstances. We can call this tendency "evaluative Darwinism," in which literature of the highest value emerged through a kind of natural selection, was impervious to unfavorable circumstances, and could not be cultivated into existence, but only awaited. For Lowell, attempts at encouragement, especially the puffery of the nationalist camp, had led to a damaging unwillingness to allow mediocrity to wither naturally: "We watered so freely, and sheltered so carefully, as to make a soil too damp and shaded for any thing but mushrooms; wondered a little why no oaks came up, and ended by voting the mushroom an oak, an American variety" (203).[18] To give too much aid and comfort to the tender shoots in the cultural soil would produce only motley "mushrooms," ephemeral, grotesque, and likely unwholesome. As I will demonstrate later, this Darwinian genius model of value was severely inadequate to the sprawling and often chaotic cultural scene of American modernity. In the short term it might have been easier to watch and wait patiently for some single great figure rather than remaining open to the variously imagined goals and methods of a host of aspiring creators. But in the longer term this mystification of genius greatly exacerbated American poetry's turn-of-the-century crisis by undermining virtually every activist avenue that might have challenged and altered the obsolescing practices of genteel verse writing.

For the Fireside writers and their readers, poetry best confirmed moral universals through "images of reconciliation and harmony of feeling," which Bernard Duffey has termed "fictions of coherence" (xii). The trope that best conveyed this harmonious coherence was analogy, as Bryant described it in 1826: "analogies and correspondences . . . between the things of the moral and of the natural world" evoke "images of visible beauty and majesty" and infuse "moral sentiment into natural objects" (*Prose Writings* 19). The inherent wholesomeness of this analogical relation derived from the "purity and innocence in the appearances of Nature," which became almost impossible "to pervert . . . into an excitement of the bad passions of the soul" (19).

This analogical-universalist paradigm of value underlies the dogged formal conventionality of the Fireside poets that so exasperated modernist readers. For these poets, the forms on the page could evoke an unalterable realm of spirit unavailable elsewhere in the mutable modernizing world. If, as one reviewer put it, "An unjust measure in verse" was *"prima facie* evidence of a jarring note in the soul of the poem" ("Review" [*Crayon*] 29), then a poem's formal regularity could be read as a reassuring sign of a spiritual universe with everything in its proper place.[19] Longfellow earned special approbation for the formal gloss and regularity of his work, in which "The most fastidious taste and the most delicate ear will seek in vain . . . for a halting stanza, a harsh line, an imperfect rhyme or an ill-chosen epithet" ("Henry Wadsworth Longfellow" 8). An early assertion of his canonical importance, published anonymously in *Graham's* in 1843, prescribed just this sort of formal regularity in verse to readers beset by the jarring forces of modernity:

> The peculiar literary qualities of [Longfellow's] poetry, its grace, its delicacy, its sweetness of versification, its ideal and imaginative beauty, especially commend it to the very class of minds which are most in need of that moral tonic which it prescribes and administers; we mean those minds . . . jangled into harsh discord by the touch of pain, which, from their fastidiousness, are in peril of becoming selfish both in their joy and their sorrow, and which must borrow those moral weapons which are forged in the armory of Truth, in order to aid them against the assaults of time. ("Henry Wadsworth Longfellow" 8)

Modern minds (whose exemplar is clearly Poe), jangled by the world's discord and their own hyperfastidious natures, lose themselves in "consuming passions which waste the heart" (9). But Longfellow's formal grace offers a weapon against "assaults of time"—an evocative phrase for the fragmenting psychic effects of modernization and moral relativism. Such poets are thus "benefactors of their race," offering their readers moments that "lift the soul upward from earth and enable it to commune with Heaven" (9).

Over the next half century of accelerating modernization, the relative innocence of this moralized analogical paradigm hardened into an exclusionary rhetoric of genteel class distinction. In an 1877 essay exemplifying this reactionary late phase, Josiah Gilbert Holland used Bryant's analogical argument to rail against the encroachments of modernity. Opening the books of many contemporary authors was "like opening the front door of a third-rate boarding house," redolent of "the stale and mixed exhalations of inelegant living" ("Old Cabinet" 867). Not content to employ this flamboyant metaphor of distinction merely as a metaphor, Holland went on to assert that "the modern boarding-house is directly responsible" for this "vulgarity," which he "identified with the murmur of crowded dining-rooms, and all that is dreary and demoralising in beds and tables, stools and candlesticks which have been bought at a sale of steamboat furniture" (867). Finally Holland extended his analogy into the arena of poetic form: "Yes, even poems; for, just as there is a musical and, as we must say, a well-bred way of arranging the nouns and adjectives, and even the vowels and consonants in a poem, so there is a common and boarding-house way of using them" (867). Such classist accounts of value remained accessible, even pervasive, in the century's last quarter, because the Fireside poets still seemed to exemplify a "well-bred way" of verse writing in America.

Like the forces of nature in their poems, the Fireside poets themselves became reassuring evidence of the continuity and coherence of a benevolent cosmic order. The analogical function of their canonicity is vividly demonstrated in a commemorative verse to Longfellow, published on the centenary of his birth in 1907 by Thomas Bailey Aldrich (1836–1907), a well-known poet of the next generation, and editor of the *Atlantic* between 1881 and 1890. Aldrich's "Longfellow" turns upon an analogy between the poet and the natural world: "Above his grave the grass and snow / Their soft antiphonal strophes write." Just as the eternal verities of nature write strophes for our edification, Longfellow has become a "Belovèd presence," holding "time and chance at bay," leaving his "thought / Imprinted on some deathless page," giving voice to the emotional life of his readers:

> . . . now as then
> Thou standest by the hearths of men.

Their fireside joys and griefs are thine;
Thou speakest to them of their dead;
They listen and are comforted
They break the bread and pour the wine
Of life with thee, as in those days
Men saw thee passing on the street
Beneath the elms. (289)

These lines evoke well the Fireside poets' multifarious significance in genteel America. Integral to the everyday life of the middle classes, they were tellers of gently fantastic tales, counselors in the ways of the world, and surrogate ministers and grandfathers, capable of providing both an evening's amusing entertainment and urgently needed spiritual consolation.

In the decades after the Civil War, their paterfamilial presences so personified virtuous literary value that admirers largely suspended critical judgment in favor of iconic adulation. This adulation came even from those not committed to genteel models of cultural value, like Edward Bok, dynamic editor of the *Ladies' Home Journal* and one of the most vocal turn-of-the-century advocates of commercialized mass culture. Yet Bok's reminiscence of his starry-eyed teenage tour of literary Boston in 1881 treats the Fireside poets as ageless, otherworldly presences who incarnate the moral substance of a vanishing nostalgized world. In a remarkable section of his autobiography, Bok describes being conveyed seamlessly from one kind genteel eminence to another, from Holmes to Longfellow to Wendell Phillips to Phillips Brooks to Louisa Alcott to Emerson to Charles Francis Adams (*Americanization* 34–60). The sole obstacle in his swath through greater Boston is Emerson's distressing senility, which Bok dwells on at some length—but only because at the last minute Emerson rallies enough to autograph a book and thank him for visiting, showing that the Fireside writers cannot belie their innate good character even in dotage (56–59). The feature of genteel Boston that emerges most forcefully in Bok's account is its coherence: its members know each other intimately, interact with one another in perfect comfort, and live so proximately and respond so accessibly that Bok can visit them all within three days. Longfellow and Holmes in particular come across as secular saints, humble about their accomplishments, preternaturally considerate of their young visitor. In a typical example, as Bok leaves Holmes's house for Longfellow's in a horse-car, he tries to pay, only to be told by the conductor, "Doctor Holmes paid me your fare, and I'm going to keep that nickel if I lose my job for it" (40). Like saints, their possessions, the very things they touch, become objects of reverence, conveying healthful spiritual meaning.[20]

The greatest impression of all is made by Longfellow, whom Bok describes as "the man around whose head the boy's youthful reading had cast a kind of halo" (41).[21] Upon meeting the poet, Bok extends and literalizes this fancy: "when he saw the head itself he had a feeling that he could see the halo" (41). Bok's use of the halo to portray Longfellow evokes Marshall Berman's analysis of the image in *All That Is Solid Melts into Air.* For Berman, Baudelaire's prose poem "The Loss of a Halo" (1865) from *Paris Spleen* constitutes an "archetypal modern scene" (155), a chance encounter on the urban boulevard between an ordinary person and an artist whom he (the speaker, not Baudelaire) exalts as "the eater of ambrosia, the drinker of quintessences" (qtd. 155). Baudelaire's irony is that, having seen his halo jostled to the macadam, the artist concludes he is better off without it. Instead of exalted separation, he seeks indistinguishability from "ordinary mortals" [*simples mortels*], so that he can indulge his baser desires and throw himself "into every kind of filth" [*me liver à la crapule*] (qtd. Berman 156)—a revelation that enlightens his "ordinary" interlocutor about the changing role of the artist in modernity. Bok's self-presentation exactly identifies him as this ordinary mortal, but Baudelaire's sardonic dissonance is unthinkable in his archetypal genteel scene. Bok encounters nothing to shake his understanding of genteel art's exalted status, and indeed finds it reconfirmed by every new acquaintance he makes in Boston. If, as Berman argues, "The Loss of a Halo" establishes a possible discursive trajectory in which "the history of modernization and the history of modernism fuse into one" (157), then Bok's account of Longfellow's securely situated halo helps us understand the deeply agoraphobic function of the Fireside poets in their later years. They shrank from the frenetic urban street ("with death galloping . . . from every side," as Baudelaire puts it), as they refused the incoherent modernity it emblematized. Their devoted readers endorsed those refusals, believing that poetry must use its good offices to construct a finer world in the ideal.

Bok's remembrance was written forty years after the events, showing that the Fireside poets' high-minded community of character shaped accounts of the value of literature, poetry above all, well into the twentieth century. To an extent never achieved before in this country—and, it's safe to say, never since—they embodied an integrated understanding of cultural value, in which broad popularity and individual quality were not in conflict, as we assume they must be, but combined coherently into the same "reverend feet" who "walk in far celestial ways," yet still hover reassuringly about the hearth (Aldrich 289). While dissenting contemporaries Poe, Whitman, and Baudelaire were exploring the benefits and risks of discarding their halos on the modern boulevard, the Fireside poets' admirers were polishing theirs in the comfort of the middle-class parlor.

IRONIES IN THE FIRE

The Fireside poets' affirming balance between domestic and worldly, individual and communal, did not mean that their poetry accurately reflected its times. As James H. Justus remarks, in their work "the play of reasonableness, charity, and respect for the homely virtues . . . is so emphatic not because those virtues were emphatic in American life but because they were not" (149). In his account of American publishing in the mid-nineteenth century, Ronald Zboray has proposed that emerging institutions of national culture carried a similarly compensatory function: "As economic development disrupted local community life, the publisher presided over the partial transference of community spirit to the world of literature. Wearing the familiar, comforting mask of the humble artisan printer, the publisher offered through print a new national community" (197). For a time, even more than these publishers, the Fireside poets spoke so resonantly to their readers' needs that they became a "national community"—a canon—of literature. Like all canons, this was a manufactured cultural coherence, made psychologically necessary by the same double-edged changes in American life that made it technologically possible.

But its defensive character produced structural contradictions that eventually undermined its force and left Americans without a viable account of poetry in an inexorably modernizing world. By examining the anxieties Fireside poetry sought to assuage, and the often ironic effects of their strategies of evasion and repression, we'll make better sense of the crisis in American poetry catalyzed by their decline after 1890.

A central irony in the canonicity of these six male writers is that it came while American poetry, by some influential accounts, was being "feminized." If, as Christopher Wilson remarks, the act of reading was seen as "the archetypically private endeavor" at a moment when "the public realm struck many as impersonal, chaotic, even debilitating" ("Rhetoric" 41), then the reading of poetry in particular seemed destined to become exclusive to domestic experience. Why then did the women who ostensibly ruled the domestic realm not take charge of poetry and its canons? Several mid-century female poets commanded an audience at least as large as that of the Fireside poets. Yet even at that moment of greatest prominence, gender-based evaluative conventions were widely deployed to contain female reputations whose high public profiles challenged the ideology of separate spheres. Most male custodians of poetry resisted work by women that did not reconfirm an essentialized contrast of male and female natures. In various commemorations of Frances Osgood after her untimely death in 1850, for example, Griswold offered a separatist model of literary value based on universal gender binaries. Osgood was worthy because "she had no need to travel beyond the legitimate sphere of woman's observation," unlike some female writers who had "quit their sphere" for the realms of "rude or ignoble passion" ("Frances Sargent Osgood" 29).[22]

As these metaphors of spatial restriction and self-silencing imply, female poets could expect the favor of the genteel establishment only by maintaining the "attitude of the amateur" (Walker, *Nightingale's Burden* 56)—even as some of them supported themselves and their families through their work. The case of Elizabeth Oakes Smith demanded elaborate argumentative gymnastics by Griswold as he negotiated contradictory stereotypes of female duty. Though Oakes Smith had previously published some anonymous verses, "a shrinking and sensitive modesty forbade her appearing as an author" until the "embarrassed affairs" of her husband "impelled" her to take up a pen. Though "she did not hesitate, like a true woman, to sacrifice feeling to duty, yet some of her most beautiful prose writings still continue to appear under *Nommes de Plumes,* with which her truly feminine spirit avoids identification" (*Poetry and Poets of America* 379). Oakes Smith springs unhesitatingly into the publishing fray to provide food for her children, proving her true womanhood; yet still she clings to public anonymity, proving her true femininity! The anthologist Caroline May walked a similar tightrope in describing Lydia Sigourney's early life. Claiming that Sigourney "was distinguished for the ease with which she acquired knowledge, and for her unceasing devotion to study," May hastened to add that "she loved domestic employments; and was as industrious in her attention to them, as in her favorite studies" (76–77).

These strategies of containment gradually effaced the complexities of popular female poets' work, and they came to function as archetypes of the poet feminized or infantilized. May noted Osgood's "almost childish playfulness" and described her verse as "sparkling little epigrammatic little poems," akin to "jewels on a ball-dress" (382, 381), while Sarah Hale characterized Osgood as a tuneful but mindless canary, who "never required study or encouragement; she poured out her strains as the birds carol" (qtd. DeJong 269). This stereotype of the spontaneous canary poetess has been contested by recent scholarship, such as Joanne Dobson's revision of Osgood as both a sentimental poet writing of flowers, children, and death, and a sophisticated adept of literary "roguishness" whose delighted friends likened her to Circe—in other words, no angel ("Sex, Wit, and Sentiment" 632). Yet Dobson notes that Osgood's "witty, sexy, and cosmopolitan poems" remained unpublished through the nineteenth century, and the "angelic sentimentalist" became her dominant persona soon after her death (633, 645). Despite their professional accomplishments and their personal strength in the face of daunting resistance, the popular mid-century female poets were mostly diminished into domestic angels after the Civil War. By 1876, when Edwin Whipple wrote of Osgood's work as having "the thinness of substance which often accompanies quickness of sensibility and activity of fancy," and concluded that the reader leaves her work "with but few thoughts in his head" (531), her reputation had been cemented in the marginal position that most female poets would occupy in the canons of American verse for the next century. As Baym and others have shown, the circle of domestic affections does not accurately represent what they wrote, but by and large it was what they became known by.

This problematic maleness of nineteenth-century poetic canons also suggests that the "separate-spheres" paradigm may never have been adequate to understanding the production of American literary forms, especially poetry.[23] As various scholars have shown, female writers and readers did play a central role in the production of poetry, particularly in the middle of the nineteenth century. The first page of Nina Baym's *American Women Writers and the Work of History* (1995) states the case in no uncertain terms: in the "extensive writing about history" they produced between 1790 and 1860, American women, including poets, were continually "demolishing whatever imaginative and intellectual boundaries their culture may have been trying to maintain between domestic and public worlds" (1). In her study of Sarah Josepha Hale, longtime literary editor of Godey's *Lady's Book,* Patricia Okker lists more than six hundred American women involved in editing periodicals in the nineteenth century (6, 170–220). While not denying the prevalence of separatist rhetoric, these revisionist formulations emphasize its disjunction from the realities of American cultural experience and often follow Linda Kerber in treating the separate spheres as "a trope" (39), a discursive strategy having complex effects, variously inhibiting, empowering, and compensatory.

Kerber proposes a largely compensatory explanation for the profusion of separatist rhetoric in a period when the forces of modernity were challenging traditional gender assumptions and boundaries: "the noise we hear about separate spheres may be the shattering of an old order and the realignment of its fragments" (22). The effects of modernization can also account for the shift from "republican" to more binarized high-Victorian ideologies of gender by about 1850. The earlier model of republican gender relations took the advancement, education, and relative equality of women as crucial to the future prosperity of the republic. For example, in Sarah J. Hale's 1827 novel of rural New England, *Northwood*, the family business (farming) is inseparable from its domestic space; men and women work side by side and share the responsibilities of child rearing (Okker 43–44). But further into the century, the capitalist work world became more complex and impersonal, work space and home space separated, and more men daily ventured away from their roles as hands-on parents and domestic actors. This created a need for a compensatory private realm sheltering a stable set of moral values, a need addressed by an increasingly rigid "canon of domesticity" that harnessed these broad social changes to "a specific set of sex-roles" (Cott 67). The middle-class cult of domesticity, the pedestalization of the angel in the house, and the fetishization of the fireside—all can be read as defensive reactions to the modernizing forces that were weakening Americans' emotional investments in clan, community, and church. Cresting at the century's midpoint, the canons of genteel domesticity offered adherents a counterforce against their growing alienation from values, beliefs, and practices once understood as immutable, now perceived as notably unstable. Genteel poetry was at the very center of this compensatory formation.

If revisions of the separate-spheres paradigm have established that nineteenth-century American women were "important social actors within various public arenas" (Park and Wald 611), the complementary conclusion that men remained important domestic actors has traditionally been less disputed but also less thoroughly explored. It was not only poetry by women that dealt with "the whole sweet circle of the domestic affections," in Lydia Sigourney's famous phrase (qtd. Walker, *Nightingale's Burden* 24). The verse of the male Fireside poets demonstrates an intense, if often evasive, engagement with the culture of domesticity, and resonates with anxieties over the emotional consequences of modernization. My analysis of Fireside poetry in terms of its domestic functions should not be taken as an endorsement of a gender-based separate-spheres paradigm. In fact, I'm deeply suspicious of any notion that poetry by women must possess one set of attributes, poetry by men another. But this is not to say that a perceived gap between public and private life didn't (and doesn't) have a shaping impact on cultural value in the United States. For me, the engine driving this separation is not gender essentialism but social distinction: the emergence through the second half of the nineteenth century of a suburbanized (or at least antiurban) middle class, whose domestic culture was defined by its disengagement from social heterogeneity that it located in the modern industrial city. The men and women of this class canonized the Fireside poets as the repository of their nostalgic desires for a lost simplicity and clarity of experience.

Even Sarah J. Hale, leading ideologist of separate spheres and canny explorer of its empowering aspects for women, felt the need to reaffirm male access to the domestic. In the 1833 essay "True Genius Always at Home," she portrayed literary genius in terms of a domestic figure who "constructs a domain of his own; and no man is so truly at home as in his own abode. He draws around him a hallowed circle, and in it he moves, and lives, and breathes. The scenes are his own, the atmosphere is his own, every thing within it is his own. Others may wander there, and gaze and admire, but they must still acknowledge that it is his. He only, as its rightful possessor, can stand within it with the proud consciousness that he is *at home*" (italics in original; qtd. Okker 104). Okker asserts that Hale's use of domestic metaphors "implicitly creates a feminine definition of genius" (104). This may be so, but the explicitly male genius Hale describes is studded with markers of acquisitiveness, pride in ownership, and the desire to provoke envy in others—all of which run counter to conventional notions of a domestic realm ennobled by the morally superior female.

Hale also figures prominently in Amy Kaplan's analysis of domesticity and imperialism, through her construction of a "traveling domesticity" that functioned "in contradictory circuits both to expand and contract the boundaries of home and nation" (583). The poet of the home place Hale describes in this passage may not travel, but he does rearrange boundaries. Like Stevens's jar in Tennessee, this *genius loci*, once situated, takes dominion everywhere and forces the surrounding "scenes" and the very atmosphere into forms of his "own." Hale's formulation, written in the formative moment of nineteenth-century American expansionism, does not critique this arrogation so much as hallow it, authorizing the domestic male artist as benevolent imperialist, his mission to define a "domain" in which he will be admired as a source of moral enlightenment. The distinctive combination of homely familiarity

and patriarchal self-assertion that defined her "genius poet" also under-
lay the canonical authority of the Fireside poets.

What drove this need to preserve male access to the domestic, particularly in poetry? Despite its declining status as a vehicle of public discourse, the genre was still entangled with emotionally resonant images
of stability, coherence, and moral improvement. Therefore, in a highly
patriarchal culture, the notion that poetry might be ceded to exclusive
female control provoked substantial anxiety. Through the second half of
the nineteenth century, one can trace a long, gradual, losing battle
against *the perception* of American poetry's feminization.[24] For a time, the
poetry of the Fireside writers palliated anxieties over the declining efficacy of literature in a market-dominated culture. By being successful
actors both at the domestic hearth and in the modern world, these poets
managed the "problem" of poetry's feminization for their readers. In fact
they were immensely capable participants in the world of the modern
marketplace; yet in their verse they embraced premodern values without
apology. Each projected a strongly patriarchal, quasi-religious persona
Duffey calls "a father-interpreter of his world," advocating the virtues of
stability, tradition, and continuity in a "voice that carried authority and
conviction to his hearers" (43). Because they obviously inhabited the
domestic realm of their own free will, they reaffirmed its value to male
readers fearful of choosing between their masculinity and their emotional lives.[25]

Around this balancing act was constructed a category of domestic
male poet that dominated canonical poetry in America from the Civil
War through the end of the century. We can trace its evolution through
the years of the Fireside writers' ascendancy. In 1852 the manly sentiment they exemplified was still not under full rhetorical control, as this
evaluation of Longfellow makes clear:

> [His work] throws into verse the feelings, moods, and fancies of the
> young or female mind of genius, not the mature cogitation of pro-
> found philosophy. . . . [To] "build" up poems slowly and solidly, as
> though he were piling pyramids, is neither his aim nor his attain-
> ment. He gathers, on the contrary, roses and lilies, . . . and wreathes
> them into chaplets for the brow and neck of the beautiful. His
> poetry is that of sentiment, rather than of thought. But the senti-
> ment is never false, nor strained, nor mawkish. It is always mild,
> generally manly, and sometimes it approaches the sublime. It
> touches both the female part of man's mind and the masculine part
> of women's. (Gilfillan 44)

The most bookish and elegant of the Fireside writers, Longfellow was particularly vulnerable to imputations of effeminacy or sentimentality. Here, the critic's discomfort with these qualities leads to a dangerous characterization of the poet as effete flower gatherer rather than builder of solid architectonic structures like pyramids—dangerous because it threatens to repudiate the most prominent male writer of the day in terms that question the potency of the entire genre. But George Gilfillan's unease with Longfellow's ostensible effeminacy is ultimately outweighed by his anxiety over the rigid separation of gender spheres, and he takes pains to recuperate "sentiment" as a quality that offers men access to femininity, women to masculinity, healing the wounding separation between them.

Later in the canonical heyday of the Fireside writers, this strategic recuperation of poetry as a balance of manliness and sentiment became more fully assimilated to genteel-elite models of literary value, as this 1875 appreciation of Lowell's works: "Nobody is less inclined than Mr. Lowell to bring his feelings to the poetical market, and to pet and dandle his private griefs in order to gain applause from the outside world, and therefore the sentiment, when it comes, is the more impressive because the more unmistakably genuine. The sweetest of smiles are those which come upon the sternest faces; and a sob in the voice of a manly speaker is incomparably more affecting than a whole torrent of hysterical blubbering" (F. T. 394). Although we can detect lingering anxiety over poetry's imputed feminization in the reference to the "hysterical blubbering" of less manly sentimentality, this writer professes smug contempt of these, rather than fear. Still, this sentimentality can be celebrated only by assuming readers' concurrence about Lowell's patriarchal authority (as one of the "sternest faces"). Lowell so deftly balances reason and emotion, self-control and sensitivity, that "His thorough truthfulness and manliness" becomes "his most unfailing charm" (F. T. 394). Here a writer's tonal skills—the ability to gauge an appropriate level of emotional expressiveness, and to resist superfluous display—coalesce into the patriarchal virtue of "truthfulness and manliness," a phrase that curiously is given a singular verb, as though manliness is truth, truth manly. For such readers the Fireside poets navigated the polarizations of separate-spheres discourse and thus controlled the threatening effects of feminization anxiety.

But finally, this containment was illusory and counterproductive, since the Fireside poets addressed the separate-spheres paradigm only by capitulating to its central dichotomy, succeeding in domestic and public realms only by rigidly segregating them from one another. All six forged "conspicuously public lives" in the worldly realms of journalism, academe, medicine, and politics (Justus 148).[26] They were also among the first American beneficiaries of the modern commodification of the literary work. Charvat calls Longfellow "the first American writer to make a living from poetry," and concludes that he was responsible for the dramatic increase in the rates American magazines paid for verse in the 1840s (158).[27] Longfellow's canny policy of purchasing the stereotype plates of his books, from which he then sold the rights to print, almost doubled his financial returns over conventional royalty arrangements and protected him from the whims or dishonesty of publishers (159). The other Fireside poets did astonishingly well for themselves also. An 1899 article by Theodore Dreiser noted with admiration that after Bryant's death in 1878, the poet's interest in the *Evening Post* fetched more than $400,000 ("Home of William Cullen Bryant" 94). The total value of Bryant's assets approached one million dollars (McLean 14). Even the Quaker Whittier, born into the humblest circumstances of the Fireside writers, left an estate worth more than $133,000 in 1892 (Wagenknecht 55).

But the more success these poets enjoyed in the world, the more completely they effaced worldly arenas of achievement from their verse. As they used it to preserve life's noblest elements against an impure, ignoble world, poetry became "Unreadable in the broad daylight of the marketplace" (Wortham 286). As early as 1826 Bryant had located poetry's value in its distance from that daylight world, from "all that disgusts, all that tasks and fatigues the understanding, and all matters which are too trivial and common to excite any emotion whatsoever" (*Prose Writings* 13). The dichotomization of experience in their lives and work had less to do with gender binaries than with oppositions between work and home, between the industrializing city and an antiurban realm variously imagined as countryside, forest, and village. In his 1832 "Defence of Poetry," ostensibly a discussion of Sidney's text but actually an account of poetry's value for his own era, Longfellow theorized this division, offering a myth of poetry's origin "amid the scenes of pastoral life, and the quiet and repose of a golden age" (66). What Longfellow calls "the soft melancholy of the groves" (a bookish pastoral cliché singularly inapt to the deep and wild North American forests) makes possible a consoling emotional "retirement" conducive "to the musings of the poetic mind" (66). For Longfellow, poetry's value is inextricable from its ability to create these idealized realms removed from the daylight marketplace of the modern city. Likewise, Bryant's engagement with the natural sublime, which made him such a source of inspiration to the Hudson River painters, could not be allowed free rein, but had always to be defensively circumscribed in scope and power, producing a "piously domesticated wildness" meant to imply the "spiritual election" of poets, readers, and the nation itself (R. Wilson 120–24).

If in nineteenth-century genteel literature, countryside and forest evoked a preindustrial past as refuge, the village housed a more recent but no less antimodern past. As Buell has shown, New England writers deployed an elaborate "roster of conventional motifs" such as ancient trees, and a typology of familiar village characters (favoring such qualities as "simple, thrifty industriousness"), in order to contain the threat of uncontrollable cultural change (306). This iconography was drawn from a "preindustrial reality" that was waning during the heyday of the Fireside poets, but Buell points out that in many villages it was doing so "at a pace . . . sufficiently gradual to permit the onlooker to picture them in terms of the old order that was passing, rather than the new order that was coming to pass" (308). In other words, the village allowed its observers exactly what the chaotic, convulsively changing industrial city denied them: the melancholy luxury of nostalgia. Adam McKible describes nostalgia as "an ideological production of pleasures that makes the incommensurable tolerable," refashioning the past as an emotionally resonant counterforce against a "disordered, contradictory present" (59). In the nostalgic writings of the Fireside poets, oppositions between past and present keep the discomfitures of modern urban experience at a tolerable distance, or displace them into more palatable forms.

Like their embrace of universalism over ethical relativism and cultural nationalism, the Fireside poets' self-censoring of the particulars of industrial expansion, urbanization, and social dislocation developed gradually over their earlier careers. Longfellow's 1837 review of James Grant's book *The Great Metropolis* shows he was still capable of evoking the excitement of the modernizing city with a young Romantic's enthusiasm, but it also shows him experimenting with strategies for containing or repudiating the uncontrollable aspects of urban modernity. Longfellow first expounds upon his "affection" for cities such as London, where he finds a pleasant excitement in being among a crowd and comes to feel "that life is not a dream but a reality" (*Outre-Mer and Driftwood* 367). At times his evocation of urbanity approaches Whitman in sentiment (though not of course in style): in cities "we see ourselves in others" and "become acquainted with the motley, many-sided life of man" (368). Each inhabitant possesses a distinct history and each "a human heart, whose fibres are woven into the great web of human sympathies;

and none so small that, when he dies, some of the mysterious meshes are not broken" (367–68). And yet, even here, in the midst of his open-hearted appreciation of "the greatest works of [human] handicraft," Longfellow yearns to convert the modern city into a fantasy of pastoral shelter. Just one paragraph after asserting that in cities "we learn to look the world in the face," to "shake hands with stern realities," he celebrates escaping from the "deafening" din of urban thoroughfares into by-lanes, through which one may "emerge into little green squares" dominated by "great trees," where "no sound of living thing is heard, save the voice of a bird or child" (369). From there he is quickly drawn to even less urban aspects of the metropolis, great parks "where you may lose yourself in green alleys, and dream you are in the country" (369). Thus to lose oneself in "dream," so soon after finding value in "reality," became a defining goal of Fireside poetics. Most of their mature verse would completely eradicate the defining sites of modernity—above all, the industrial city. The young Longfellow's contradictory treatment of the metropolis shows with exceptional clarity this desire to withdraw from those sites even while paying lip service to their value.

In the second half of their careers, the Fireside poets were inexorably drawn to various iconographies of nostalgic community. Their works increasingly placed human unhappiness within historical or legendary frames and excluded almost everything identifiable as part of modern life: in Longfellow's case, "no factory workers, no businessmen, no salesmen, no staple-crop farmers, no slaves (after 1842)—only blacksmiths, cobblers, and other holdovers from the images of an agrarian-handicraft economy" (Charvat 141–42). The substitution of village for city allowed Longfellow to divert urgent questions concerning the ethics of masculine endeavor into highly contained and reassuring forms. In "Nuremberg," "The Building of the Ship," "Keramos," and above all, "The Village Blacksmith," Longfellow uses "master craftsmen dedicated to excellence in their tradition-governed work" (Gartner 62) as preindustrial embodiments of masculine virtue. This mythography also includes the poet, who is thereby recuperated into "a worker" benefiting the community (62). But this ingenious symbolic concatenation works only in a premodern context of unalienated labor. A great strength of Fireside poetics had been its dual portrayal of poetry as transformative agent of the spiritualized imagination and, equally, as everyday contributor to the social weal. But increasingly that balance could be maintained only through nostalgic settings that kept a stubborn distance from the depersonalizing forces of actual late-century life. This resolutely agoraphobic poetics, admitting so little of the texture of modern American experience, ensured both Longfellow's "immediate success and his long-run failure" (Charvat 142). Similar assertions could be made for all the Fireside poets.

The Fireside writers' insistence on poetry's pastoral character was firmly within Romantic convention. Indeed, the cultural elite of nineteenth-century America was almost unanimous in deploring the industrial city, opposed only by a few figures like Whitman and William James, whose voices "did not compete with the antiurban roar produced by Jefferson, Emerson, Thoreau, Hawthorne, Melville, Poe, Henry Adams, Henry James, and William Dean Howells" (White and White 2). But unlike their prose-writing counterparts, the Fireside poets generated no productive engagements from this antipathy—no "Bartleby," no "Man of the Crowd," no *American Scene*, no *Hazard of New Fortunes*. They claimed that "pastoral discourse is . . . a universally positive or redemptive force which in itself can right the injustices done by man in his social, urban environment" (Beach, *Politics* 121). But their almost total unwillingness to deal with the urban in their work implied serious unease with pastoral poetry's capacity to redeem the soul from the encroachments of modernity. Ultimately their refusal to accept the idea that poetry should, or could, grapple with the sources and effects of modern emotional dispossession not only damaged their own reputations, but seriously undermined poetry's place in American life.

The few exceptions to their refusal of urban subject matter, like Bryant's "The Crowded Street" (1843), exhibit a compulsion to impose moral coherence, whether earned or not. This poem's speaker surveys an "ever-shifting train" of walkers in the street and concludes that the city is a space defined by structural incoherence: "Each, where his tasks or pleasures call, / They pass, and heed each other not" (318–19). For Bryant, modern city life is defined above all by its fragmentation. This generalized sense of modernity's alienating effects is not finally separable from more specific anxieties over the city's growing cross-class and multiethnic heterogeneity. Bryant's alienated city dwellers "heed each other not" because they don't speak a common language, possess the same skin color, or value the same cultural heritage. In 1843 he is still able to counter the city's threatening otherness by invoking the deity who (ostensibly) effaces all such difference: "There is who heeds, who holds them all, / In His large love and boundless thought." This standard-issue Christian affirmation of the penultimate stanza drives the poem's final lines inexorably into pastoral, as if urban imagery is altogether incapable of representing the coherence Bryant requires:

> These struggling tides of life that seem
> In wayward, aimless course to tend,
> Are eddies of the mighty stream
> That rolls to its appointed end. (*Poetical Works* 320)

If Bryant's flight from street to stream enforced the genteel conviction that poetry and modernity were fundamentally antithetical, so too did his habitual choice of subject matter. Christopher Beach notes that although Bryant resided in New York City for over fifty years, he wrote only one other poem that deals directly with urban life (*Politics* 118).[28] In most Fireside verse, the city registered only as a lurking source of oppression, containable through an intense focus on a bygone pastoral realm. Bryant and his fellows stubbornly clung to the pastoral, making poetry the vehicle of their refusal to inhabit the modern world.

ACTS OF ENCLOSURE

Bryant's image of God sheltering humankind "in His large love and boundless thought," as a parent's arms would hold a child, is one of many such metaphoric spaces of enclosure in Fireside verse. Converting unbounded, uncontrollable spaces into demarcated and manageable ones, such images of shelter almost always promise escape from the worldly and the modern. The manufacture of these distinctive spaces began with the earliest major Fireside poem, Bryant's "Thanatopsis" (1815–1817), which ends by advising its addressee to "approach thy grave / Like one who wraps the drapery of his couch / About him, and lies down to pleasant dreams" (*Poetical Works* 20). For the next seventy-five years, Fireside verse routinely analogized these spaces of shelter to all its favorite topics—God, nature, memory, love, family, even the nation. In "Nature" (1876), for example, Longfellow sketched nature as "a fond mother," who "when the day is o'er, / Leads by the hand her little child to bed" (*Complete Poetical Works* 3:207). There was a special fascination with analogically laden natural enclosures like the "nest of bending reeds" in Emerson's "Threnody" (1847) (*Complete Poetical Works* 138). Personified animals shared in the benefits of this analogical shelter, like Bryant's famed waterfowl, whose "toil shall soon end" when "reeds shall bend, / Soon, o'er thy sheltered nest" ("To a Waterfowl" [1818], *Poetical Works* 27). The inevitable conclusion of all this analogical shelter was a consoling portrayal of death, as in "Thanatopsis"; in Holmes's "Under the Violets" (1859), where the beloved's grave is sheltered by "gray old trees of hugest limb / [that] Shall wheel their circling shadows round / To make the scorching sunlight dim" (*Complete Poetical Works* 163); and in Lowell's "The First Snow-Fall" (revised 1855), whose speaker kisses his little daughter, who "could not know / That *my* kiss was given to her sister, / Folded close under deepening snow" (*Complete Poetical Works* 292; italics in original).

These analogies of enclosure buttressed Fireside agoraphobia by reasserting the endangered view "that life has a measure of coherence and can be fulfilled within a recognizable set of boundaries" (McMartin 98). We can usefully contextualize these analogies through Amy Kaplan's linkage of the nineteenth-century culture of domesticity to "the process of domestication," in which the domestic "contains within itself those wild or foreign elements that must be tamed," and "monitors the borders between the civilized and the savage" (582). Kaplan deals with domestic culture's containment of racial and ethnic foreignness, but I propose that oppositions between domestic and foreign, inside and outside, often carry a temporal valence as well, troping modernity as an alien Other that must be sealed off from the psychic space of nostalgic domesticity. In innumerable Fireside poems, images of familiarity, restriction, enclosure, and home associate the domestic with a premodern past of stable boundaries maintained by a comprehensible and immanent deity. In contrast, the unfamiliar, the mobile, the crowded, the spatially unbounded, all imply the heterogeneity and depersonalization of the modern city. As the depredatory forces of modernity grow more obtrusive through the nineteenth century, it becomes all the more urgent that poetry maintain this monitoring posture. The rigid strictures of tone, form, and subject matter imposed by late genteel commentators (described in detail in chapter 3) can be interpreted as attempts to regulate "savage" modern elements from the genre—as if that could somehow eradicate them from American experience.

Whittier's well-loved verse "The Barefoot Boy" (1855) deploys several key topoi of Fireside verse to synthesize these analogical images of shelter with intense nostalgia for more elemental experience. The barefoot boy is blessed in living "hand in hand," "face to face" with Nature (*Complete Poetical Works* 396). The lessons imparted to him—

> How the tortoise bears his shell,
> How the woodchuck digs his cell,
> And the ground-mole sinks his well,
> How the robin feeds her young,
> How the oriole's nest is hung

—all script the natural world as a space of sheltering innocence that can be recaptured by remembering "boyhood's painless play." Nowhere in the poem do we find the opposite numbers of barefoot boys, the shod adults of the urbanizing nineteenth century, losing touch with past, family, and nature. Conspicuous by their absence, they were the poem's implied readers and those who made it popular. Such Fireside classics as "The Barefoot Boy," like the bifurcated lives of their idolized creators, consoled these modern readers that they could have it both ways. Poetry could inhabit a comfortable nook of their existence, promising their continuing "enclosure in a world of fixed moral ideas" (McMartin 100). Ironically, however, by effacing the modernity of everyday American life, Fireside poetics implicitly accommodated the worldly travails of its readers by declining to raise a disapproving gaze no matter how ruthless their striving.[29]

The most resonant of these sheltering spaces, which both embodied the favorite topics of Fireside poetry (family, home, God, memory) and identified the main site of its consumption, was the domestic hearth itself. The fireplace was central to the analogical basis of Victorian domestic culture, in which the middle-class home was "designed to be read like a book whose symbolic meanings would be almost self-evident" (C. Clark 114). Like the architectural features and decorative objects surrounding the bourgeois hearth, Fireside verse evoked a realm of spiritual enrichment seemingly unavailable elsewhere, offering escape from the fetters of the world and the assaults of time, encouraging the subject "not to aspire but to dwell in Memory and Hope," as Justus puts it (156).[30] This escapist function is theorized in Emerson's "The Snow-Storm," (1841), where all signifiers of worldly activity—"sled and traveller," "the courier's feet," even "friends"—are "shut out," as "the house-mates sit / Around the radiant fireplace, enclosed / In a tumultuous privacy of storm" (*Complete Poetical Works* 43). Twenty-five years later Whittier used these lines as an epigraph to his own fireside idyll, *Snow-Bound.* The analogical linkage between familial hearth and divine source was made plain by Whittier's second epigraph, taken from Agrippa's *Occult Philosophy:* "As the Spirits of Darkness be stronger in the dark, so Good Spirits which be Angels of Light are augmented not only by the Divine light of the Sun, but also by our common Wood Fire: and as the celestial Fire drives away dark spirits, so also this our Fire of Wood does the same" (7). The Fireside poets sought to make these spaces of shelter into outward and visible reassurances of an inward spiritual plenitude. To readers they provided an imaginative space protected and isolated from the depredatory daylight world, offering renewed validation of individual and communal identity, and access to emotional intimacy with like-minded companions (including God), all within an ethos of physical privacy and class homogeneity.

The iconography of the genteel fireside also articulated an urgently desired but increasingly burdensome link to long-venerated but now fragile cultural traditions. This problematic relation was addressed directly in Lowell's "A Winter-Evening Hymn to My Fire" (1854), which portrays the fireside as the only means of preserving the nation's collective cultural memory. Remarking to the fire that "with thee I love to read / Our brave old poets," Lowell's speaker cherishes a sense of cultural continuity: "'T was by thy flicker" that "The English Muse" "conned / The fireside wisdom that enrings / With light from heaven familiar things" (*Poetical Works* 321). In one efficient stroke Lowell defines his tradition to be English (no surprise there) and to be immanent in the material objects of the genteel household. But it's still startling to realize his admission that without the fireside's spiritualizing aura, these poetic traditions would be moribund:

> at thy touch how stirs
> Life in the withered words! how swift recede
> Time's shadows! and how glows again
> Through its dead mass the incandescent verse. (321)

Without the domesticated fire's unique ambience of fancy, solitude, comfort, and leisure, the work of past poets is a withered and dead mass—a valueless commodity—in a modern world without heritage or inspiration.

Like most Fireside verse, Lowell's poem maintains a relentless rhetoric of affirmation, but in heaving the entire burden of maintaining cultural traditions onto a symbol of bourgeois domesticity, it bespeaks barely suppressed desperation. The hearthside imagery of Longfellow's moving poem "The Fire of Driftwood" (1848) departs from conventional affirmation to demonstrate how precariously this analogical poetics depended on the material functions of bourgeois domesticity. Here two old friends, painfully aware that "Their lives thenceforth have separate ends / And never can be one again," sit in a drafty "farm-house old," overlooking a desolate beachscape. The spurts and dyings of their fitful conversation remind the speaker of the flames in a beach fire "Built of the wreck of stranded ships" (*Poetical Works* 3:269). The driftwood fire, whether real or imagined by the speaker, contrasts pointedly to the absence of fire in the "damp and cold" house, in which "Our voices only broke the gloom" (268). The analogical method remains in place, all too firmly: "They were indeed too much akin, / The driftwood fire without that burned, / The thoughts that burned and glowed within" (269). But not only has the method lost its consolatory power, it has become oppressive because its connection to middle-class comfort has been severed.

There was good reason for the unease imperfectly repressed in "A Winter-Evening Hymn" and left clearly audible in "The Fire of Driftwood." Even as the canon of poets named for the fireside emerged in the middle third of the century, the fireside as embodiment of familial "trust, interdependence, and safety" (H. Green 98) was undergoing problematic shifts in significance. Gaslight replaced firelight in the houses of affluent urbanites in the 1830s, and by the end of that decade "even modest artisans' households in cities and country villages were adopting stoves" rather than relying on the open hearth for heat (Larkin 138, 141). Gas stoves, and then the advent of central furnaces after the Civil War, did not eliminate the hearth from middle-class homes, but they did change it from practical necessity to decorative ornament. To late-century manuals of middle-class domesticity such as Clarence Cook's *The House Beautiful* (1881), hearths that were "gas-fired or installed without any intention of use for heat" (H. Green 98) were distinctly perturbing, since they implied a falseness to the fireside's once inviolate connotations of bourgeois respectability.[31] To many, the shift from the comfortable family room with working fireplace to a more formally and fashionably decorated parlor had deleterious effects on health, family, and community relations. Harriet Beecher Stowe's satiric 1864 story "The Ravages of a Carpet" decried the "darkened solitude" of the new parlor with "a grate always shut up, and a hole in the floor" to warm the room (20). This space repelled the family and alienated visiting friends, in contrast to the bright, lively room into which all the old furnishings had been moved, where "the old brass andirons glistened and the wood-fire crackled" (21). Such lampoons of pretentious living spaces with nonfunctional fireplaces only registered their prevalence. Indeed, building practices had shifted so thoroughly away from fireplaces even by 1881 that Cook grimly pronounced "the hearth-stone" a "dead institution" in the face of the furnace, "the devil's last, best gift to man" (111).

Ironically, it was in this obsolescent phase that the hearth fire was canonized as a genteel "deity of home," "the last representative" of the ancient household gods Lares and Penates; like an ancestor, "too much honor and remembrance cannot be given to it," as Harriet Prescott Spofford insisted in 1877 (233). No longer needed as a practical heat source, the hearth became an uplifting site of nostalgic display, "the truest household inspiration" (Stowe 7), or "the modern and the medieval household altar" (Spofford 233), upon which material icons loomed ever larger as markers of identity, taste, and social standing. In her 1877 manual of home decoration, Spofford remarked, "A room without any mantel has not the dignity of a tent" (233), presumably because it possessed no space for such analogical display. From the decorative mantel above the nonfunctional fireplace, the next step in design modernization was the mantel alone with no pretense of a hearth, whose only conceivable function was to hold "artful bric-a-brac" as signs of the owner's culture and taste (Roberts 48). In 1902 the disapproving Edith Wharton and Ogden Codman noted that voracious demand for mantels as bric-a-brac shelves had led to gratuitous "enlargement of the whole chimney-piece," exemplifying the "general decline of taste" of the century's second half (82–83).

As mantel displaced fireplace as the locus of symbolic value, the connotations of that value shifted decisively toward the past. The functional heat of the fire was replaced by the warm glow of family memories, in portraits, photographs, letters, and heirlooms displayed on mantels whose elaborate decorations worked to stifle anxieties of familial or spiritual poverty. This was a highly patriarchal past, as one mantel manufacturer's catalog made clear around 1900: "The thought that creates a fireplace is first of all ancestral. It means you have a father and a home" (qtd. C. Clark 114). Here, as with Sarah Hale's description of the "genius at home," the source of domestic authority was constructed as male. Stowe's comments on the significance of the fireplace, while half facetious in tone, also emphasized its links to a patriarchal national past: "Would our Revolutionary fathers have gone barefooted and bleeding over snows to defend air-tight stoves and cooking ranges?" Indeed not, for it was the fireplace that "made their hearts warm and bright with a thousand reflected memories." Synthesizing the religious and political dimensions of this iconography, Stowe concluded that the fireplace was "an altar of patriotism" (7). Mantels were ornamented not just with family portraits, but also with likenesses of admired cultural icons, including the six Fireside poets themselves, especially after a series of frontispiece engravings by Timothy Cole and Wyatt Eaton in *Scribner's* in 1878 and 1879 placed their images in hundreds of thousands of middle-class parlors. These engravings were issued alongside long, laudatory essays by well-known writers, illustrated by scenes from the poets' boyhoods, depictions of their homes, and other markers of intimate connection to their readers. It would be hard to overestimate the force of this iconography of pious domestic virtue upon young Americans growing up in bourgeois households over the next half century. One of them, Richmond Croom Beatty, began his 1942 biography of Lowell by sardonically recalling: "I can remember the seven of them [including Hawthorne], done impartially in sepia, framed above the large mahogany bookcase in the back hall. . . . Here, I was given to understand, was American Literature" (vii).

But if the Fireside poets loomed large in the childhood of future modernists, that very domination sowed resentment and rebellion. Told to "strive to be good and great, as they had been," Beatty and his contemporaries "dutifully read their books" but later yearned to question and debunk "the peculiar dispensation" that "made them, exclusively, into . . . our 'army of unalterable law'" (vii). This last phrase quotes T. S. Eliot's "Cousin Nancy" (1917), which itself borrows from George Meredith's sonnet "Lucifer in Starlight" (1883). Its progress over those sixty years can be used to measure the growth of modern skepticism toward genteel traditions representing themselves as sanctified and immutable. For the raging but impotent Lucifer of Meredith's poem, the army of unalterable stars arrayed across the sky reasserts the impregnability of divine authority, and his continued subservience (182–83). "Cousin Nancy," frisky with avant-garde iconoclasm, ironizes the phrase to lampoon Eliot's canonical ancestors ("Matthew and Waldo") as ossified figures staring blankly from their "glazen shelves," redundant "guardians" of a faith whose very unalterability has doomed it to irrelevance (*Prufrock* 34). In 1942 Beatty comfortably assumes his contemporaries' knowledge of Eliot's poem and uses it to evoke their consensual repudiation of nineteenth-century genteel values.

In 1879, the same year of the *Scribner's* frontispieces, the publication of Henry T. Coates's monumental anthology *The Fireside Encyclopedia of Poetry* culminated the domestic ideology of genteel poetry. Coates's brief preface located the project wholly within the comforting ethos of the bourgeois hearth from conception (it was begun "to while away the long winter evenings, which threatened to hang heavy on the Editor's hands"), to consumption (his aim has been to create "a welcome companion at every FIRESIDE" [v; caps in original]). The anthology began with three thematic sections, "Poems of Home and the Fireside," "Poems of Infancy and Childhood," and "Poems of Memory and Retrospection," that neatly reinforced the prevailing associations of the fireside with a less complicated premodern experience evoked through nostalgic memories of childhood.

Coates's compendium also linked the nostalgizing of the fireplace to the growing climate of cultural distinction in the century's final decades. His choices reflected the dramatic narrowing of the canons of American poetry since the wide-open selections of Griswold's pioneering anthology of 1842. Griswold had featured more than one hundred poets born after Bryant in 1794. Other than the Fireside six, just twenty-eight of these poets appeared in *The Fireside Encyclopedia,* with only fifty-four (mostly brief) poems. The six claimed sixty-four poems. For Griswold they had warranted 11 percent of the total space given to their contemporaries; for Coates it was almost 60 percent. Since the *Encyclopedia* also included British poets from Elizabethan times onward, the Fireside writers' prominence asserted that they were the (only) Americans worthy of those past greats. They had become icons proclaiming the legitimacy and maturity of American literary culture, no longer so easily disparaged as a bastard of the British. Much as family pictures ameliorated anxieties over growing social rootlessness, these grandfatherly visages gazing from mantels reassured genteel Americans that they possessed a lineage and a home even in the proliferating disjunctions of modernity.

But the intense nostalgia of their verse ensured that this American heritage would be framed and valued in antimodern terms. All the most resonant connotations of the domestic hearth—ease, consolation, comfort, familiarity—dictated against formal innovation, linguistic eccentricity, moral ambiguity, and political dissent. These poets' deployment of emotionally potent subjects such as family, childhood, memory, and God prioritized for American poetry a particular set of ideological functions that obfuscated the nineteenth-century bourgeoisie's seizure of the sites of capitalist endeavor and validated their accelerating retreat after the Civil War from the heterogeneous metropolis into the privacy of single-family houses in suburban enclaves. In the disparity between the escapist domesticity of this poetics and the worldly lives of the Fireside writers and their readers, we can detect the shift of separate-spheres ideology into perhaps its most salient twentieth-century form, which Marshall Berman refers to as the modernized pastoral: "a spatially and socially segmented world—people here, traffic there; work here, homes there; rich here, poor there; barriers of grass and concrete in between, where haloes could begin to grow around people's heads once again" (168). In "The Barefoot Boy," "The Village Blacksmith," and many other central Fireside works, the open wood fire stood in for the gas furnace, the countryside or village for the middle-class suburb, as idealized counterforces against the despoiling modern scene—nostalgic substitutions at once psychologically poignant and ideologically expedient.

REGIONS OF REPOSE

Deeply invested in the lures of nostalgia, the canonicity of the Fireside poets ultimately became not only paradoxical but paralyzing. Despite their dominant cultural position over several decades, these writers suffered from persistent and sometimes disabling doubt that their own verse—and American poetry generally—could stand up to past canons or speak to a modern condition of explosive change. Its enormous argumentative vigor notwithstanding, even Lowell's universalist account of poetic value in the *Kavanagh* review betrayed anxiety over the future value of "American literature": "It may not be our destiny to produce a great literature, as, indeed, our genius seems to find its kindliest development in practicalizing simpler and more perfect forms of social organization. We have . . . a continent to subdue with the plough and the railroad, before we are at leisure for aesthetics" (Review of *Kavanagh* 209). The Fireside poets' unease with the present and future value of American poetry flared especially when they dealt with the act of writing, the functions of genius, and the effects of tradition. If genius was such an overwhelming and yet rare phenomenon, surely America seemed to have little chance of witnessing it and none of cultivating it. And what could their own poetic ambitions amount to?

This anxiety ranged from Holmes's frank, good-natured pessimism about his future reputation in the 1872 "Epilogue to the Breakfast-Table Series," to more grinding anxieties of inadequacy in Whittier and Longfellow that demonstrate the oppressive effects of genius models of literary value. In "An Autograph" (1868), Whittier likens his poetry to a frosty pane of glass on which he has written his name, or alternatively, as "sands by waves o'errun" (*Complete Poetical Works* 413). The distance between these metaphors and the conventional Romantic topos of the poem as monument, urn, or other long-lasting object is profound. However ironically, monumental Romantic ruins, epitomized by Shelley's statue of Ozymandias, assert a faith in their own immutability that Whittier's self-consciously ephemeral images lack. The "waves of time" and melting frost of his posterity will usher in a "shadow vast, / The silence that shall last!" in which "I and all who know / And love me vanish so." Here, conceding that he hopes to "leave some faint echo still" in future canons, despite the "wiser and better names" whose claims will fail, Whittier acknowledges the Fireside poets' troubled relationship to tradition.

In the "Proem" that introduced his first collected edition (1847), Whittier's anxiety about his work's future value is even less controlled, edging into agonistic self-delusion. Measuring his attainments against "the old melodious lays / Which softly melt the ages through" (by Spenser, Sidney, Milton, and Marvell), the poet concedes that he has tried "vainly" "to breathe their marvellous notes" into an inhospitable culture ("frozen clime"), hampered by deficient education ("the harshness of an untaught ear"), and insufficient leisure that produced "jarring words of one whose rhyme / Beat often Labor's hurried time" (*Complete Poetical Works* 1). Too insistent in denying that these deficiencies worry him, Whittier reveals that the canon has become a source of discouragement and shame. The vigor of past works, "sprinkling our noon of time with freshest morning dew," merely reveals his "lack" of "the seer-like power to show / The secrets of the heart and mind." Denied these more complete poetic attainments, Whittier offers a compensatory set of ethical values he wishes might be "as deep and strong / As theirs":

> Yet here at least an earnest sense
> Of human right and weal is shown;
> A hate of tyranny intense,
> And hearty in its vehemence,
> As if my brother's pain and sorrow were my own.

But the poet's failure to overcome his agonistic relationship to canonical poetry emerges in the aggressively clumsy and tin-eared texture of the poem. Limiting ourselves to the five lines quoted above, we find a clumsy passive construction ("Yet here . . . is shown"); the stuttering phrase "hate of tyranny" rather than the more mellifluous "hatred"; the rhyme-dictated redundancy of "hate . . . intense . . . in its vehemence"; the choice of the incongruously cheerful adjective "hearty" to modify "hate"; and the plodding iambs of the whole passage. Having conceded the aesthetic laurels to past canonical poets, Whittier uneasily redefines poetic value away from aesthetic criteria toward those of moral righteousness. He feels this need urgently enough to allow this execrable verse to headline, and thus undermine, his entire collected oeuvre.

In "The Day Is Done," Longfellow offered perhaps the most revealing expression of ambivalence toward canonical tradition, signaling his awareness of its metacritical character by placing it as the proem to his 1844 volume *The Waif*. If, as Thomas Wortham suggests, this poem catches "the spirit and the tone of these poets' popular appeal" (284), their appeal was unlikely to withstand the mounting challenges of modernization.

Come, read to me some poem,
Some simple and heartfelt lay,
That shall soothe this restless feeling,
And banish the thoughts of day.

Not from the grand old masters,
Not from the bards sublime,
Whose distant footsteps echo
Through the corridors of Time.

For, like strains of martial music,
Their mighty thoughts suggest
Life's endless toil and endeavor
And to-night I long for rest.

Read from some humbler poet,
Whose songs gushed from his heart,
As showers from the clouds of summer,
Or tears from the eyelids start;

Who, through long days of labor,
And nights devoid of ease,
Still heard in his soul the music
Of wonderful melodies. (*Poetical Works* 1:246–47)

Here the footsteps of "sublime" greats, although exasperatingly inaccessible, still echo oppressively through Time. Far from providing respite from the tribulations of mundane existence, glorious past poetry is identified with "corridors," a word redolent of the restrictive and impersonal arrangements of modern urban space: offices, factories, crowded streets, apartment buildings, railway carriages, steamboats. But the claustrophobic oppression of these past canons might, like "the thoughts of day," be "banished" by the "simple and heartfelt lay" of "some humbler poet," whose very anonymity soothes rather than threatens, and whose verse produces in the listener "the benediction / That follows after prayer" (1:247). Longfellow defines American poets here not as the mighty strivers of the canon, but as domesticated figures of meager ambition just getting through the day. Despite his protestation that this was desirable, such creatures measure up poorly against past genius. Ultimately "The Day Is Done" demonstrates that even the most celebrated American poet of the century feared there could be no profitable connection between contemporary verse and past canons.

Before the war the Fireside poets had been important spokesmen on sociopolitical issues, especially abolition (Kramer 352–54); but after 1860 they retreated as a group into agoraphobic escapism. Two landmarks of nineteenth-century canonical poetry, each composed in the shadow of the war, initiated their fervently nostalgic and retrograde late phase, which would catalyze American poetry's turn-of-the-century crisis. Longfellow's *Tales of a Wayside Inn* (1860–1873) and Whittier's *Snow-Bound* (1866) use the topos of fireside storytelling as both metaphor and actual setting for recovering the sense of community threatened by modernity. A wayside hostelry might seem a more appropriate setting for a modern narrative of physical mobility and emotional transience, but Longfellow's prelude takes up that challenge, establishing this community as defiantly antiurban and antimodern. The opening lines of *Tales of a Wayside Inn* oppose the "meadows bare and brown" of a bleak autumn night to the inn's welcoming windows that "Gleamed red with fire-light through the leaves / Of woodbine, hanging from the eaves / Their crimson curtains rent and thin" (*Poetical Works* 4:13). However thin, the woodbine "curtains" clinging to the building's exterior provide a classic Fireside image of shelter, fusing the natural and the domestic. Across the road where "panting teams" still carry passengers as in olden times, an active farm celebrates preindustrial labor. The inn's geographical remoteness, where "no noisy railway speeds," makes it a nostalgic "region of repose" featuring various markers of bourgeois domesticity, such as "chimneys huge, and tiled and tall," and an "old spinet" in the parlor. As a structure "Built in the old Colonial day," the inn evokes an American cultural heritage that is powerfully mythicized, yet at least in some places, still materially present.

This "place of slumber and of dreams" provides a setting for an idealized impromptu community in which people of far-flung origins sit "around the fireside at their ease" (15), telling in turn their enthralling tales. The fireside itself is the centerpiece and source of their inspiration, "shedding over all / The splendor of its ruddy glow." Longfellow spends two dozen lines of the prelude describing the play of the firelight on various parts of the parlor. Its glimmering creates an aura of benedictory immanence on every surface, gently caressing the face of a long-dead princess portrayed upon the wall, bronzing the rough wood rafters, creating "inaudible melodies" on the spinet, repainting the landlord's faded blazon a "livelier red" (15). But most of all, the firelight creates a kind of poetry:

And, flashing on the window-pane,
Emblazoned with its light and shade
The jovial rhymes, that still remain,
Writ near a century ago. . . . (15)

This hearth fire writes old rhymes upon the windowpane, like Lowell's fire in "A Winter-Evening Hymn," enlivening a cultural heritage otherwise in danger of falling into desuetude. In "An Autograph," Whittier had imagined his verse as written in ice upon a windowpane, implying both frigidity and ephemerality; here Longfellow more forcefully, if evasively, invests the hearth fire with the power to inscribe a continued meaning and value for poetry.

The genteel investment of antimodern nostalgia and pastoral domesticity into the bourgeois fireside culminated in Whittier's *Snow-Bound*, published in the war-weary year of 1866 to success "instant and sustained" (Duffey 55). Describing the renewal of familial bonds in the face of severe challenge, *Snow-Bound* offers a "microcosm . . . of a still largely homogeneous America, though one that also felt strains being put upon it calling for renewed dedication" (Duffey 54). In typical Fireside fashion, however, those contemporary strains were radically distanced. Rather than acknowledging any of the forces of modernizing America, especially the war that had torn many families viciously apart, Whittier framed his narrative as a nostalgic memory of his childhood and deflected the source of strain by analogizing it into a force of nature, the snowstorm. This substitution initiates a series of ingenious antimodern displacements that assert poetry's ability to recapture a lost world of emotional integration. *Snow-Bound* is punctuated by reminders of the distance between the time of the poet's childhood and the time of its writing, as Whittier laments the loss of family members who once gathered around the fireside:

O Time and Change! with hair as gray
As was my sire's that winter day,
How strange it seems, with so much gone
Of life and love, to still live on!
Ah, brother! only I and thou
Are left of all that circle now,—
The dear home faces whereupon
That fitful firelight paled and shone.
Henceforward, listen as we will,
The voices of that hearth are still. . . . (19–20)

Thus the snowstorm is displaced by an even more universalized nemesis, death. Unlike the shrinking sentiments of "The Day Is Done," *Snow-Bound* advances its antimodern poetics as a positive redemptive agency, claiming to have death's match in the power of nostalgic memory, which is apotheosized as the "Angel of the backward look" (50).

In Fireside poetics it matters little what one looks at, only that one look backward. Ultimately the oppressive element in the symbolic logic of *Snow-Bound* is not the snowstorm, or even death: it is routinized, depersonalized modernity. In fact, the snowstorm's sublimity disrupts this soul-crushing everyday world and offers spiritual renewal. When the family goes outside after the snow stops, they look "upon a world unknown, / On nothing we could call our own" (12). This estrangement releases the imagination, as "The old familiar sights of ours / Took marvellous shapes; strange domes and towers / Rose up where sty or corn-crib stood." Such a mundane object as the "well-curb" now has "a Chinese roof," while the "long sweep" (the pole used to lower a bucket into a well) is seen "in its slant splendor" "to tell / Of Pisa's leaning miracle" (12–13). As the long, silent day draws toward night, this unfamiliarity threatens to become alienating but is contained by the lighting of the evening fire, which Whittier dwells upon for twenty-three lines (16–17). As the fire catches, "the old, rude-furnished room / Burst, flower-like, into rosy bloom" (16). Embodying qualities that reflect the character of God—love, empathy, shelter—the fire transforms the snow's oppressive featurelessness into a consoling reconfirmation of spiritual community: "radiant with a mimic flame / Outside the sparkling drift became." The fire in Longfellow's wayside inn had gotten as far as the window; Whittier's goes much further, transforming the snow from a metaphor or even agent of death into a mirror of the benedictory powers of domestic life. At this moment of radiant mimicry, the imagination, no longer alienating, is domesticated into the family circle, and they while away the evening telling stories of all types—mournful, outlandish, uplifting, blood-curdling. Whittier compares these tales to the "warming" capacity of the fire, so that "Forgotten was the outside cold, / The bitter wind unheeded blew" (28). The value of imaginative constructions—tales told around the family fireside, verses by the Fireside poets—is to create a sheltering space for the auditor/reader, who is thereby allowed to forget about the uncontrollable forces howling beyond the hearth's sanctified circle. By equating the fire's heat with the spiritual warmth offered by these narratives, Whittier articulates the quintessential Fireside metaphor of poetic value.

The last pages of *Snow-Bound* theorize a deeply agoraphobic escapism, as Whittier prescribes poetry as a form of therapy for his own loss-weary spirit:

> Yet, haply, in some lull of life,
> Some Truce of God which breaks its strife,
> The worldling's eyes shall gather dew,
> Dreaming in throngful city ways
> Of winter joys his boyhood knew. (51–52)

The reader is then proffered the invitation implicit in so much Fireside poetry, to "Sit with me by the homestead hearth, / And stretch the hands of memory forth / To warm them at the wood-fire's blaze," a process of nostalgic recollection that will yield, in the poem's final line, "the benediction of the air" (52). Here the reader is assumed to be, like the author, a "worldling" weary of urban throngs, in urgent need of spiritual refreshment. Hands, the vehicles of action in the daylight world, are numbed by its frigid impersonality but can yet be warmed by Fireside poetry. By calling them "hands of memory," Whittier identifies nostalgic familial consciousness as the path to spiritual benediction. Further, since hands are also the vehicles of writing, he has ingeniously thematized poetry's value as its ability to revivify the realms of memory and tradition for the displaced worldling of modernity.

This metaphoric equation of the hearth fire with the imaginative material of poetry can be found in early and very late texts by the Fireside writers, suggesting its centrality in American genteel poetics for almost half a century. Longfellow's "Curfew" (1845) consists of two parallel sections of equal length: the first describes extinguishing the fire at the end of the evening; the second the laying aside of the book being read (or written?) by the speaker. Longfellow ensures that this analogical parallel cannot be overlooked by describing the book's "fancies" as being "Like coals in the ashes, / They darken and die" (*Poetical Works* 1:264). "Curfew" is an apt title not just because the word derives from the Old French *cuevrefeu* (cover fire), but because it evokes the Fireside writers' willingness to allow their imaginative practices to be regulated, even behind closed doors, by external social convention. At the late edge of the Fireside era, Holmes's short verse "At My Fireside" (1888) employs an almost identical analogy of the hearth fire with the material of poetry, this time to meditate morosely on old age and "the spoils of years gone by" (269). The poet's once vigorous creative impulse is now troped as "drift-wood brands that glimmering lie, / Before the ashes hide the fire." "At My Fireside" functioned as an unofficial proem to Holmes's 1888 volume, which was entitled *Before the Curfew*. Its use of the fire as setting and metaphor evokes not only "Curfew" but Lowell's "A Winter-Evening Hymn to My Fireside" and Longfellow's "The Fire of Driftwood," all written almost half a century before. In these intertextual resonances, Holmes's little verse offered one last demonstration of the Fireside canon's striking coherence—or put another way, its generic homogeneity and unwillingness to change with its times.

The account of poetic value enacted by such poems, promising sanctuary from the encroachments of modernity, was embraced by readers of the century's third quarter. But the defensive maneuverings of "The Day Is Done" and even *Snow-Bound* were ultimately unequal to the forces they resisted: "Nostalgia reenchants," as Fred Davis notes, but "only for a while until the inexorable processes of historical change exhaust that past which offered momentary shelter" (116). Given the defining qualities of late-nineteenth-century American experience—accelerating urbanization, immigration, and industrialization—the relief offered by the Fireside poets from headache-inducing canonical footsteps, from the insomniac restlessness of modern life, and certainly from dry-eye, was an increasingly feeble palliative. Their genteel poetics of value, stubbornly refusing to acknowledge that verse must accept and even enact the changes wrought by modernity, drove American poetry from cultural centrality into what Raymond Williams calls a "residual" formation (*Marxism and Literature* 122), housing the resistance of a particular group to unwelcome social changes, here the emergence of a commercialized mass culture catering to a heterogeneous urban populace. As the century drew toward its close, these forces dislodged American poetry from its comfortable inglenook and threw its future into serious jeopardy. The following chapters outline the genre's exile between 1890 and 1910, and describe its varied and surprising fortunes in the wilderness.

PART 2
Crisis

2

INVASION OF THE TINSEL RHYMESTERS

Poetry, Mass Culture,
"Nineteen Hundred and Now"

From the early 1890s through 1910, impoverished by
exhausted accounts of its value that made it increasingly
irrelevant to turn-of-the-century modernity, assailed by the impact of
emerging forms of mass culture, poetry in America underwent a serious
crisis. This crisis was at once imaginary and real. It was imagined in the
sense that the actual volume of verse published in the United States during the 1890s and 1900s may have actually increased over previous
decades, part of an ongoing expansion in the periodical and book publishing industries. Paula Bennett has rightly taken issue with the rhetoric
of poetry's turn-of-the-century decline as it sometimes functions in histories of modernism to aggrandize writers of the 1910s by maximizing
stylistic contrasts to their precursors, and to devalue the impact of nineteenth-century women poets on the American literary scene ("Not Just
Filler" 202–04). It is certainly no coincidence that prophecies of poetry's
doom proliferated concurrently with a desire and power to write among
marginalized social groups—African Americans, immigrants, men and
women involved in labor movements and radical politics. Adherents of
the genteel elite often used the rhetoric of decline as a strategy of distinction against growing cultural heterogeneity, apparently preferring to
allow poetry to wither altogether rather than allow it to become more
responsive to the heterogeneous conditions of modernity.

Still, poetry's turn-of-the-century crisis cannot be dismissed entirely as a retrospective construction of high modernism, or as a snobbish stratagem to keep the unwashed outside the gates. After all, growing access to print, both throughout the population and among the socially marginalized, had been a long-range development of modernity for centuries and would continue in other forms, regardless of whether poetry existed to house it. In a sense it hardly matters how many individuals continued to write and publish verse in the United States during the 1890s and 1900s if almost all this work remained unread or disparaged. Indeed, before 1910 the profusion of poetry publication was often perversely interpreted as a damaging state of overproduction, and the economic unviability of verse had become a truism throughout the publishing industry. During these two decades a vast range of people, spanning the entire ideological spectrum of American literary culture, became convinced that poetry had entered a crisis that would either transform or destroy it. Most of them, their creative lives and sometimes their livelihoods invested in poetry's fortunes, had little to gain and much to lose from this development. They simply found no way of evading the conclusion that poetry was declining, even dying. In this respect, the forms of modern culture are not unlike stock markets: if enough people come to believe that poetry is losing its value, and behave as if it were true, then it effectively becomes the case.

Commentaries of the 1890s insistently demonstrate that previously effectual accounts of poetry's value had broken down, and few sources of institutional or intellectual support existed through which new ones could be generated. The canons of mainstream American verse were dominated by the Fireside writers, but this genteel consensus increasingly registered as inhibiting rather than enabling, a "national umbrella / Of perished celebrities," as Amy Lowell would later put it, underneath which "the air's somewhat stifling" (*Critical Fable* 15). Anxieties over the value of American poetry, in mid-century still sufficiently manageable to allow the Fireside poets each a copious lifetime's worth of writing, would bulk so large by 1900 that they threatened to paralyze the younger generations of poets. At the same time, an emerging mass culture underwritten by corporate capitalism was elaborating a rhetoric of anti-intellectual skepticism toward the supposedly feminized or infantilized forms of elite culture. Though they shared little common ground, the partisans of genteel antimodernity and those of philistine modernity concurred in two ways: both saw their own understanding of cultural value as utterly incommensurate with the other's; and both viewed poetry as the genre that best crystallized that incommensurability. As discourses of mass culture grew more secure institutionally and bolder rhetorically, the disdainful genteel elite withdrew further into its upholstered ghetto, merely increasing the other's opinion of its irrelevance and obsolescence. Neither position offered a viable account of poetry's value in a condition of accelerating modernity.

Part 2 demonstrates the dynamics of this polarized evaluative climate, proposing that American poetry's continued value was most clearly demonstrable on the relatively few occasions when commentators challenged the binary of elite and mass culture and explored their points of interdependence. Chapter 2 sketches the emergence in the 1890s of two genres whose runaway success exacerbated poetry's crisis: mass-magazine verse and million-selling popular songs. Yet my analysis concludes that poetry and these forms of mass culture had more to offer one another than either could often admit. The third chapter examines the discourse of poetic value in the United States between 1890 and 1910 as a series of paradoxical formulations traceable to two simultaneous and irreconcilable responses: a conviction that the forms, attitudes, and canons dominating the genre were obsolete or exhausted; and a reflexive distrust of efforts to rejuvenate poetry through innovation in form or iconoclasm of attitude. This impasse created a corrosive evaluative climate that threatened to eradicate poetry from American culture.

It's worth noting that if "crisis" implies threat, it also implies opportunity. The turn-of-the-century rhetoric of decline does not fit so well when applied to alternative cultural formations—organized labor movements, feminist cells, radical populist political organizations, anti-imperialist agitators—that found verse an empowering vehicle to articulate and disseminate their views.[1] Yet if these alternative sites of verse, less invested in poetry's transcendent literariness, its Romantic-individualist heritage, its disdain for the mundane, perceived no crisis, this only reconfirms my assertion that the state of crisis perceived in more "literary" venues derived from widespread unwillingness to allow verse to address the actual conditions of modern American life. Those who discerned opportunity in this crisis need not have assumed that American poetry must inevitably wither away. But they did see that it must change.

GIANTS IN PHILISTIA

In part 1 I argued that American genteel culture had been defined by its reaction against modernity even before such hugely popular exercises in pastoral nostalgia as Longfellow's *Tales of a Wayside Inn* and Whittier's *Snow-Bound* consolidated the Fireside poets' canonicity just after the Civil War. The Fireside poets' wholesale withdrawal into nostalgia after 1865 exacerbated American poetry's tendency to deny any relationship with the modern scene. In the century's last decades, in keeping with its increasingly residual status, American genteel culture turned "much more narrowly elitist and reactionary" (Brodhead, "Literature and Culture" 476), and its custodians increasingly employed poetry to buttress elite culture against what they saw as an irredeemably commercialized and vulgarized world.[2] Agoraphobic genteel culture was hardening into an openly elitist formation that linked modernity's depredations to various nonelite groups—rustic Midwestern peasantry, vulgar nouveau riche, unwashed urban mob—as usurpers of standards and despoilers of taste. As massive immigration and emerging genres of popular culture eroded clear class boundaries and created modernized cultural marketplaces accessible to a larger and more heterogeneous group of Americans, many of those unwilling to face these democratizing forces clung to the "noble art" of poetry as their preferred vehicle of distinction.

The urgency of adapting poetry to shore up crumbling cultural boundaries caused some adherents to forfeit the humane ideals of their ostensibly superior social model. This 1893 remark by Charles Moore is typical: "Compared with the drill and discipline of poetry, prose has the disorder of a mob, or at least the non-coherent movement of the procession of life in a city street" ("Future" 770). Though Moore quickly backed away from the metaphorics of the "mob," his comments register late genteel culture's distrustful association between nonelite prose forms and the heterogeneous social fabric of urban modernity. Mobilized to carry this ideological standard, poetry had to remain uncontaminated by the poisonous leveling of class privilege that modernity seemed to augur. Hence Moore's worry (in a different article) that "If the plain people get it thoroughly established in their heads that they are as good subjects for literature as kings and heroes and poets, that pumpkin-pies and pitchforks and blue-jean blouses are just as important as wit and philosophy and divine exaltation," then American verse would be reduced to commonplace banality ("In Regard" 218). Poetry's proper role, it seemed, was to encourage plain people to consent cheerfully to their lot in life (a life with plenty of pumpkin pie but not, apparently, wit, philosophy, or exaltation). As such, the genre was one of the "overlooked" but crucial "antiseptics of society and the conservative forces of government," as Richard Watson Gilder sternly remarked in the *Century* in 1900 ("On the Reading of Poetry" 961). Such commentators relied on poetry to uphold "The beauty of simplicity and the supremacy of the ideal" against a condition of cultural entropy in which "the increasing number of new fortunes is giving to life and society a noticeable air of vulgar luxury" (960).

For many, indeed, poetry was virtually the only literary weapon left in the struggle to conserve aesthetic value against a septic erosion of standards that threatened to plunge all existing cultural authority into mediocrity or anarchy. They sought to maintain a view of poetry as "a complete organism with volition and power" [Moore, "Future" 770–71]), against what Ronald Martin calls a modern "universe of force" promulgated by the popular novel, the newspaper, and other forms of commercialized prose. Though poetry's genteel defenders seldom celebrated the universe-of-force worldview, they often unwittingly reinforced the structure of assumption that made it seem so formidable. Charles Moore's 1893 essay "The Future of Poetry," for example, depended on a universe-of-force paradigm in which "Man-kind is on a long march and must discard all superfluous *impedimenta* and content itself with what is easiest carried" (770). When Moore likened prose to "a blind force" (771), he was ironically furthering "the uninhibited extension" of "scientific theories of force, conservation, development, and evolution" to virtually any and every cultural application, an ideological campaign led by Herbert Spencer and his American disciples (R. Martin 33). The theory of literary value advanced decades earlier by James Russell Lowell and others, which assumed that true poets would be winnowed from pretenders by an unfathomable evolutionary process, had now gained a quasi-scientific theoretical basis that would be deployed on a variety of fronts, none of them to poetry's benefit.

Those who embraced poetry to resist these despoiling forces saw its refusal of the modern everyday, its conjuring of an ideal world elsewhere, as crucial to its value. So they largely eschewed morally complex or ambiguous themes and rejected attempts to engage with contemporary settings, subjects, and issues. In much late genteel discourse, poetry was defined, sometimes wholly defensively, in opposition to a more compendious category of "real life." Even Moore's ostensible desire to think about poetry's uses in the "long march" of modernity was defeated by his overriding need to maintain the genre's association with ideality, which ultimately rendered it incommensurable with the modern world: "Nearly all great poetry . . . [has] sought out remote times and places so that its divine make-believe might have an air of possibility" ("Future" 773). In contrast, verse set in familiar or contemporary times and places, irredeemably linked to the material, the mundane, the modern, lost its power to beguile and thrill. In *Poet-Lore* in 1904, suspicions of topical and modern subjects were theorized into prohibitions by a young critic, Oscar W. Firkins, who asserted that "poetical matter is but a small part of the real or imaginable life" and proceeded to anatomize five categories of what "the poetical" could not include: "the repulsive" (including the rude, clumsy, grotesque, coarse, foul, brutal, ugly, and rank); "the arid" (the plain, homely, dull, mean, trivial, but also the technical, general, and abstract); "the humorous"; "the utilitarian" (industrial, economic, commercial, legal, political); and finally, "the conventional" (77–79). Eighty years earlier, in the first formulations of Fireside poetics, William Cullen Bryant had made some similar exclusions (*Prose Writings* 13), but had not found it necessary to go into this excruciating level of detail, or to admit that "the contents of this list are large and rich," comprising "Three-fourths perhaps of all that men observe" (Firkins 79). All these things were what poetry wasn't; Firkins never managed to say what, if anything, poetry might actually be.

This genteel rear guard brandished poetry against "the mighty forces that make for the vulgarization of life" (Thomas 511), incarnated by forms of mass culture that were waging an increasingly aggressive campaign for the allegiance of the American public. In 1904, the *Dial,* one of the most prominent bastions of reactionary gentility, diagnosed the contemporary "Rejection of Poetry" by endorsing the views of British Poet Laureate Alfred Austin as he condemned mass culture's debasement of public taste: "Among the causes assigned for our modern 'alienation of taste from the higher, more serious, more intellectual poetry' are the prevalence of novel-reading, the newspaper habit, and the standards set by the popular stage." The novel "completely ruins 'the taste for mental food of a more delicate and sustaining kind,'" while reading newspapers "is bound to dull the literary sense and coarsen the intellectual tastes" ("Rejection of Poetry" 354). Though no doubt the poet laureate and the young African American Paul Laurence Dunbar had little enough in common, Dunbar's "The Poet" (1903) articulated similar anxieties at the apparently unequal struggle of poetry against emergent forms of mass culture, describing a noble poet who "From some high peak, nigh yet remote, / . . . voiced the world's absorbing beat" (*Complete Poems* 191). Not interested in hearing about its own nobility, "The world" instead "turned to praise / A jingle in a broken tongue." Was Dunbar consciously exploiting the common twentieth-century usage of "jingle" to mean a meretriciously memorable advertising slogan or melody? Even if not, he was participating in the pattern of usage that created that pejorative terminology.[3]

Dunbar's cynical formulation suggested what the turn-of-the-century "craze" for fictional best-sellers also seemed to imply: that the entire locus of cultural value was shifting toward mass-market genres. As Ferris Greenslet put it in 1899, "there are giants in Philistia, and within the last two years we have beheld the edifying spectacle of prose Goliaths selling their hundreds of thousands" ("Propaganda" 44). This formulation replaced the hallowed figures of true literature with monstrous "giants" of philistine mass culture, oppressing American culture with wholly commodified forms of prose. In this paradigm the imaginative art of reading was turning into the utilitarian act of skimming, with all the attenuation of intellectual and emotional depth that the term implies (Wilson, "Rhetoric" 41).[4]

Disturbed that books were being treated as infinitely reproducible and quickly disposable commodities, some commentators portrayed the consumption of mass-culture genres as a pernicious addiction, as in this 1901 remark by Kate Douglas Wiggin (a pioneer of the children's literature movement who would publish *Rebecca of Sunnybrook Farm* two years later): "If you find a twelve-year-old boy addicted to juveniles, you may as well give the poor little creature up. . . . [H]e will never know the Faerie Queene or the Red Cross Knight, Don Quixote, Hector or Ajax; Dante and Goethe will be sealed oracles to him until the end of time. . . . He drank too long and too deeply of nursery pap, and his literary appetite and digestion are both weakened beyond cure" (871–72). Even if we assume a degree of satirical exaggeration on Wiggin's part, it's difficult not to read the passage as an attempt, like the founding of "Children's Literature" as a professionalized discipline, to wrest children's canons away from mass-market forces that elite culture found difficult to control.

Such reactionary assertions of poetry as an exclusive art form of timeless purity were no longer capable of alleviating doubts about the effectuality of elite culture. Genteel critiques of mass culture's ostensible intellectual reductiveness were often undermined by their own lack of rigor, as in this 1898 comment on the fiction versus poetry debate by Calvin Thomas: "Take any one of the myriads who read novels, but eschew poetry, inquire into the grounds of his preference, and you will probably get an answer equivalent to this: 'Poetry is too hard reading. It demands greater alertness and concentration, hurrying one from image to image and compelling one to think, to visualize, perhaps even to parse. On the other hand, the prose tale adapts itself more readily to a lethargic condition of the mind, whether this result from fatigue or from a natural ineptitude for cerebral effort.'" (510). Carried off by his rhetoric, Thomas fails to note the unlikelihood that these myriads would impute their preference for fiction over poetry to their own cerebral ineptitude. However ludicrous its logic, this comment is typical of the deviousness of turn-of-the-century decline rhetoric: it masquerades as serious analysis of the merits of various literary genres, but is little more than knee-jerk elite condemnation of supposedly degraded mass culture.

Such feebly reasoned defensiveness only confirmed the views of those inclined to deride poetry as an obsolete and frivolous genre, "a sign of school-girlishness" (W. Clarke 32). Typical of the philistinism from which genteel commentators recoiled was the newspaper editor and proprietor who remarked in 1888: "If . . . a member of my staff wrote verse, I wouldn't have the public know it for a good deal of money. . . . Any child can write poetry. A journalist, to be a success, must let such stuff alone. No; there is no distinction between verse and poetry; it's all alike; it's all slush" (qtd. W. Clarke 32). This editor was not alone in viewing poetry as disqualifying its aspirants from productive adult life in the modern world. Elizabeth Waddell sardonically posited a modern hierarchy of genres in which a young writer might produce juvenilia in verse but then would be "promoted" to prose forms—articles, short stories, and ultimately, the "seventh-heaven of novel authorship." As the author declined into senility, the sequence would be replicated in reverse, the less fortunate writers "relaps[ing]" all the way back to the "second-childhood and mere oblivion of poetry-writing" (Waddell 150–51).

At its most extreme, the rhetorical pressure exerted by philistine mass culture threatened to flatten out all possible gradations and varieties of cultural value into a single instrumentalist duality: useful/useless. This reductiveness reached its nadir in an 1899 article in *Lippincott's*, "Will Poetry Disappear?" by H. E. Warner. Warner answered his question in the affirmative, advancing a ruthlessly utilitarian account of modernity in which "The mind and heart of man have been made the subjects of scientific study and reduced to their places in the iron-bound and law-governed system" (287). Warner's Social-Darwinist bent emerged in the phylogenic analogy between the evolution of a culture and the life cycle of an organism. He saw poetry as having an important cultural function only at an early stage of development, "when the emotional is at its height." Later, "poetry concerns itself with domestic life and relations, with the arts of peace, with the picturesque and scholarly elements of life, or with mere decoration" (285). Now, viewed from the perspective of fully evolved industrialized modernity, poetry became only a prop "to the childhood of the individual as well as to the infancy of the nations" (284). Though phrased in infantilizing terms, Warner's condescension is related to contemporaneous complaints that American elite culture had been feminized and therefore enfeebled: poetry "starts inquiries and asks a multitude of questions, as a child does, but prose answers them. It is wayward, capricious, passionate, and unreasonable. Its purpose may be called selfish. Beauty or pleasure it seeks, but never use" (286). In Warner's philistine modernity, American poetry's very integration into domestic life, until recently understood as a main source of its value, was now read as evidence of its imminent obsolescence. Conversely, a culture demonstrated its maturity by concerning itself "more and more with the practical, the material, and the definite," meaning that the "sources of the inspiration of poetry have been removed" (285). This was the phase that American culture had just entered, and poetry's manifest senescence was therefore not to be regretted, but welcomed as a sign of progress.

Warner's characterization of poetry reveals the close relation between the rhetoric of evaluative Darwinism and turn-of-the-century strategies for what Judy Hilkey calls the "legitimation of the new industrial order" (6). For Warner, poetry's "indirect and suggestive method and . . . its artificial restraints of rhythm and rhyme" render it unable "to compete where analysis, examination, research, and exact expression are needed" (Warner 287). Likewise, poetry is unfit to expand into emerging modern subjects: "there are some [subjects] which poetry has never approached; or, if it has, its effort has been met with the most dismal failure. Mathematics, the sciences, theology, biography—in fact the entire domain of exact thought and exact statement—is closed to poetry" (286). Here culture becomes an arena of economic expansion among competing expressive methods, in which poetry is at a crippling disadvantage due to the restraints of trade intrinsic to it.

Such utilitarian arguments were prevalent at the turn of the century and were taken very seriously. Their effects were dramatized by Stephen Leacock's essay "The Passing of Poetry" and its reception by one contemporary reader in *Canadian Magazine* in 1906. Leacock proposes facetiously that poetry is unnecessary because prose communicates the same ideas with greater efficiency. His "argument" culminates in a hilarious juxtaposition between some sentimental lines from Burns about "the return of a cottage labourer to his home on Saturday night" to enjoy a "'cheerfu' supper'" and recitation from "'The big ha' Bible, ance his father's pride'"; and the police news of the Dumfries *Chronicle* for October 3, 1905, which reads, "the prisoner had returned to his domicile at the usual hour, and, after partaking of a hearty meal, had seated himself at an oaken settle, for the *ostensible purpose of reading the Bible.* It was while so occupied that his arrest was effected" (73; Leacock's italics). Leacock's deadpan conclusion is that "the two accounts are almost identical," "[w]ith the trifling exception that Burns omits all mention of the arrest, for which . . . the whole tenor of the poem gives ample warrant" (73). The final paragraph suggests the author's satiric attitude by hinting at "remedial legislation, or application of the criminal law," evoking Swift's "A Modest Proposal," but he finally decides to leave poets to the workings of "inevitable natural evolution" (73).

Reading a century later, we conclude that the Canadian humorist did not actually believe that "The poet is destined to become extinct" (71), and we take this work as a lampoon of the complacent chronocentrism, the ham-handed cultural Darwinism, and the fetishization of "common sense" typifying the utilitarian position. But in 1906 this satiric performance provoked a deadly earnest response by Susan E. Cameron, suggesting how threatening utilitarian and Darwinist positions had become to anxious advocates of poetry. Despite acknowledging Leacock's piece as "a delightful *jeu d'esprit,*" Cameron could not let his contentions, however facetious, go unchallenged, and particularly attacked his "parallel passages in verse and prose" as "not parallel at all and hence not valuable as illustrations to the subject at hand" (507)—as if that incongruity were not the whole point of his joke.

As the Leacock/Cameron exchange indicates, dismissals of literary writing and dire predictions of poetry's future were not limited to some philistine splinter of American mass culture. They were echoed with startling frequency through the 1890s and 1900s by a rhetoric of anxiety and desperation throughout the precincts of genteel culture. Often the purveyors of this rhetoric were so riven by anxiety that their attempts to assert poetry's continued value unwittingly revealed why it was in such straits. For example, in "Have We Still Need of Poetry?" Calvin Thomas earnestly set out to reject the damaging notion that poetry was no more than "frivolous play" (505), but then articulated its value in this way: "If the poet, with his bagatelles of fancy, can beguile us now and then to forget the awful burden of our responsibility for the world's welfare, we should bless him as a benefactor, instead of chiding him for his frivolity" (509). Beguiling bagatelles stood little chance—and why should they?—against the burden of responsibility for the world's welfare, which the Boks and Warners of the era were more than willing to accept. On the academic front, the advocacy of poetry could take on positively grotesque aspects. In *The Lost Art of Reading* (1903) Gerald Stanley Lee describes (but alas, does not cite) a recent article by the head of the University of Chicago's English Department that sought to correct Keats's faulty thought and versification, rewriting the last lines of "Ode on a Grecian Urn" thus: "Preaching this wisdom with thy cheerful mien: / Possessing beauty thou possessest all; / Pause at that goal, nor further push thy quest" (qtd. 128). Most striking about this bizarre "correction" is how it takes pithy and natural diction, which culminates in the notably conversational "that is all / Ye know on earth, and all ye need to know," and converts it into stiff and convoluted phrasing imaginable only in a book or lecture hall. If poetry's champions could do no better than this, then those like Warner, quite willing to consign poetry to the mausoleum of culture, would encounter little effective resistance.

The pressure of these mutually exclusive conceptions of elite and mass culture created a powerful evaluative impasse for poetry. Whether advancing elite or philistine positions, many commentaries reached the same conclusion: that poetry had little chance in an environment increasingly dominated by mass culture. This 1898 remark by F. L. Thompson in the *Dial* is a quintessential (if remarkably ill-phrased) expression of this binarized view of cultural modernity: "The strenuous clanking of the machinery of what constitutes the life of nearly all is too obstreperous for even musically attuned ears to distinguish delicate strains through" (287). These polarities were internalized even by young poets who desired greater relevance for their work. In a 1902 *Poet-Lore* article, Josephine Preston Peabody argued that contemporary verse must somehow bridge the widening chasm between Real and Ideal that defined modern life. Poetry, rigidly restricted to intoning the delicate strains of the Ideal, was now purely a marker of cultural elitism, "regarded with the respect due to a venerable tradition" like "the Sunday sermon" (59) but devoid of practical use and emotional resonance, likely to be lost amid the strenuous clanking of the Real world. But even as she diagnosed a "terrible exclusiveness . . . thrust upon Poetry" in which "the average man" assumes "that he is offensive to the Muses nine,—he and his household, his ox and his ass and everything that is his," Peabody resisted poetry's address to the everyday, the ordinary, the modern (58). Despite her desire to make poetry relevant, she was unable to shed the prevailing belief that poets had already been forced to value the modern too highly and ought to be allowed to drift back toward an idealized past. Ultimately Peabody could imagine modernity only as "the utter forgetfulness of whence and whither" (64), an endless present alienated from past traditions, hurtling heedlessly into an incomprehensible future.[5]

If poetry's champions could conceive modernity only as single-minded "glorification of the material and the present" (Peabody, "Modern

Life" 64), they could do little to stop the reductive evaluative norms of mass culture from superseding the outworn standards of the genteel elite. In this impasse, poetry could expect to face an inevitable decline in value, ending as "the rickety dream-child of neurotic aestheticism" (Greenslet, "Propaganda," 52). Two of those emerging forms of commercial culture, the mass-circulation magazine and the million-selling popular song, burst simultaneously upon the American scene during the momentous year of 1893. In the two decades that followed, they would forcefully challenge teetering genteel models of poetic value. Measuring their dwindling ranks against the millions who enjoyed these new genres, glum lovers of poetry worried that they were becoming nothing more than "an esoteric cult" (Greenslet, "Propaganda" 51). Such anxiety is understandable and forgivable; what is more difficult to forgive is their stubborn embrace of that stunting role, if the alternative were actually to engage with the realities of the modern condition.

STYLUS FOR SALE

The exodus of the American populace from country to city beginning around 1820 coincided with a series of technological advances enabling the inexpensive printing and marketing of publications on a massively expanded scale. First seen in the rise of large-circulation newspapers in the 1830s, these developments generated a dramatic increase in American magazine publication after the Civil War.[6] The key shift in magazine economics after 1880 was a downward expansion of markets through aggressive price slashing, so that "well-illustrated, well-edited general magazines brought their prices down" from thirty-five cents, some all the way to a nickel (Tebbel and Zuckerman 66). The advent of photoengraving made high-quality photographic illustration, once prohibitive, easily available even to precariously undercapitalized magazine ventures such as *McClure's,* which was initially backed by only seventy-three hundred dollars (H. Wilson 62). During the mid-1890s a group of periodicals commanding a staggering national circulation emerged. Taking advantage of new mass-production techniques, these publications sought to sell as many copies as possible, almost without regard for the price obtained for each one, in order to increase their advertising rates and revenues. The crucial year in the emergence of mass-circulation magazines was 1893. The appearance of S. S. McClure's magazine in June at fifteen cents a copy triggered a wave of price cutting, highlighted in October by Frank Munsey's radical experiment of dropping the price of his struggling publication from twenty-five cents to a dime, well below the production costs for a single copy. In the next six months *Munsey's* circulation shot from twenty thousand to more than two hundred thousand (Munsey, "The Publisher's Desk," 111). Within two years *McClure's, Munsey's,* and *Cosmopolitan* were all selling for a dime, and by 1900 they commanded a combined circulation of well over a million. Cyrus Curtis's *Ladies' Home Journal* was the first magazine to reach one million in circulation in 1903; in the same year Munsey reported his circulation as almost seven hundred thousand ("Impressions by the Way" [1903] 151).

This phenomenon represented a valuable cultural democratization, in that a hefty capital reserve was no longer needed to create an appealing product affordable by a larger and more heterogeneous public than the genteel "quality magazines" had been interested in attracting. The editors of mass magazines played this democratizing function for all it was worth. In an 1894 editorial, Munsey proclaimed, "there is no limit to the sales of MUNSEY'S," and asserted that his magazine "is within the reach of every one" ("Publisher's Desk" 111). In 1896, *McClure's,* whose circulation had grown from an initial 19,000 to 275,000 in three years, claimed as a badge of honor that it had been "founded practically without capital" ("Third Anniversary" 97). Celebrating ten years of "the Popular Priced Magazine" in 1903, Munsey evoked the country's trust-busting mood by characterizing his magazine as the "pioneer" that had first "broken through the dead line of monopoly" ("Impressions" [1903] 151). The often-used image of the monopoly smashed indicated a backlash against the repressive culture of the genteel elite and its chosen few poets, which I describe in detail in the next chapter. The ideological aspect of such pronouncements notwithstanding, these lavishly illustrated magazines had complex, interesting, and sometimes socially progressive effects. Given their omnivorous coverage of almost every notable social and cultural phenomenon of the period, they warrant greater attention from American cultural studies than they've received.

To the genteel "quality magazines," whose circulations had leveled off between one and two hundred thousand, the mass-circulation magazines represented a serious challenge.[7] This may seem odd to the casual reader of the twenty-first century, for whom the quality magazine and the mass magazine of the 1890s, with their heavy paper stock, small print, frequent and graceful illustrations, relatively lengthy features, and (mostly) decorously ghettoized advertising, resemble more than oppose one another. And indeed, as Theodore Greene shows, the qualities of behavior, success, and "character" celebrated by the mass magazines were not far removed from those upheld by the quality magazines

(72–109, especially 81). Furthermore, Christopher Wilson is certainly correct that the readership of this new category of periodical "remained firmly rooted in the middle class" ("Rhetoric" 44). But even if the conventional term "mass magazine" is something of a misnomer, it accurately captures the view of the late genteel elite that an alien entity had assailed its "most cherished power: the power to control the reading habits of the populace at large, and so to mold its sense of collective value" (Brodhead, "Literature and Culture" 476)—in other words, its hold over literary canonicity. The editorial establishment of the quality magazines reacted with predictable disdain to these challenges to its authority. In 1896 *Century* editor Richard Watson Gilder described the mass magazines as contributing to a general "vulgarizing of everything in life and letters and politics and religion" that "sickens the soul" (*Letters* 294), while his assistant, the genteel establishment's archreactionary Robert Underwood Johnson, hissed that the mass magazines were full of "revolutionary madness" while simultaneously dismissing them as merely "straining after effect" (Johnson 149).

This paradigm shift in magazine publishing had profound effects on American poetry, less in affecting the reputation of particular authors than in altering the cultural and economic status of the entire genre. What Richard Ohmann calls "the invention of the mind industry" in mass magazines and other contemporaneous sites represented an epochal shift in the relation of cultural products to their audiences. Such organs became "no longer dealers in their physical products," selling their wares to the public, but "dealers in groups of consumers" (Ohmann 31), offering their share of the public to advertisers. The mass-circulation magazines "had changed not just their price but the whole relation of the magazine to the economic realm," since, as "vehicles through which large-scale manufacturers could create and maintain markets for their commodities," they "now put verbal entertainment in the service of commercial interests" (Brodhead, "Literature and Culture" 475–76).[8]

Because poetry could seldom demonstrate appreciable effects on circulation or advertising revenues (as fiction could), mass magazines generally had little room for it. Though the content of genteel poetry offended few readers, the genre was ill-suited to the needs of mass-produced and consumed culture. In its ruminative and leisurely pace, in the attention to detail and nuance it demanded, and especially in its insistently stylized character, poetry resisted the reclassification of cultural forms as "inseparable from the circulation of commodities" that mass-culture ideologists attempted to enforce (Ohmann 39). Christopher Wilson has demonstrated that these mass magazines adapted principles of Taylorist scientific management, as well as advancing a rhetoric of realist style-lessness that "sought to acclimatize readers to a new social environment, [and] to 'naturalize' that environment by managing the reading process" ("Rhetoric" 48, 42). The editors of mass magazines repeatedly insisted on the insignificance of style, as in S. S. McClure's assertion that an author "can say the same thing in fifty different ways" (*My Autobiography* 196), or Edward Bok's insistence that "the message itself is of greater import than the manner in which it is said" (296). Bok described the whole notion of "literary style" as "a foolish phrase, since it often means nothing except a complicated method of expression which confuses rather than clarifies thought" (27). For him, the complication and confusion endemic to the quintessentially "literary" form of poetry were thus only undesirable obstacles to the relentless consumability of cultural products, which he coded as "clarity." Bok's ideology of mass-market realism converges seamlessly with the positivist economy of cultural value promulgated by H. E. Warner in "Will Poetry Disappear?" In Warner's happy, poetry-free future, inexorable demands for the virtues of scientific positivism will force fundamental changes in human language: "The spoken languages of the world may undergo some such change as stenography seems to be making in the writing of them. A new and wonderfully condensed form of expression may arise upon our present system, in which simple sounds, with few combinations, may take the place of our words, phrases, and sentences" (283). Warner's choice of stenography as a conceptual model for this evolution of language suggests the extent to which this "scientific" rejection of style was grounded in alienated forms of modern capitalist labor.

Yet the very persistence and vehemence of this rhetoric of styleless-ness support Wilson's conclusion that "The importation of a direct, forceful prose style" was actually crucial to this management of the reading process, "the first step in the managerial 'naturalization' of content" ("Rhetoric" 49).[9] For these ideologists of positivist mass culture, poetry was the literary form closest to pure style: arbitrary and arcane forms masking an emptiness of content. But if poetry were just the pointless nuisance they tried to imply, why the need to train the big guns of scientific positivism upon it in essays like "Will Poetry Disappear?" Perhaps we must posit that poetry's resistant potential came not from cultural centrality but from its very marginality. This marginal position, coupled with its still prestigious elite associations, paradoxically threatened to push it beyond the reach of the capitalist-realist managerial ideology that the mass magazines celebrated. The crucial question that the Boks and Warners were striving to preempt was this: in a linguistic condition defined by shorthand (and by the alienated activity it presupposes, the taking of dictation), in which ideologies of positivist realism driven by agendas of anti-intellectual consumerism sought to foreclose the discursive space of the "useless" humanities, might poetry still function as a locus of active resistance? Before 1910 that question remained barely accessible, broached by only a handful of commentators and some of the poems I discuss in part 3. Perhaps the greatest achievement of American poetry in the 1910s was to reopen it so vigorously.

In contrast to their attitude toward poetry, the mass-circulation magazines published fiction copiously. Their rise both manifested and fueled the enormous turn-of-the-century enlargement of fiction markets, a "craze" that was "denounced by pulpit and press but, nevertheless, resulted in the first million-copy sales for books" (Tebbel and Zuckerman 73). Unlike poetry, the continuously flowing structure of popular prose narrative lent itself perfectly to such new layout techniques as ad stripping, pioneered in the *Ladies' Home Journal* in 1896: "printing a continued story between columns of advertisements," which made "the story line an engine literally to drive the reader forward through consumeristic space" (Brodhead, "Literature and Culture" 476). Ohmann notes a characteristic tone—"casual, familiar, a bit coy" (28)—and a "stylistic mobility" among "a variety of registers and codes" (38) that magazine fiction shared with another seminal modern form concurrently being developed in the mass magazines and elsewhere—the advertisement. Ohmann deduces that the stylistic fluidity of magazine fiction encouraged in readers a sense of being "liberated . . . from any one class rhetoric" (38). Poetry, with its emphasis upon formal strictures, stylistic unity, and elevated moral tone, was the genre most clearly exemplifying the class-marked rhetoric from which such magazines strove to "liberate" their readers.

Even so, the uses of poetry in mass-circulation magazines did dramatize the desirability—and the difficulty—of adapting the genre to the stylistic and narrative imperatives of mass culture. The three mass-market periodicals of the 1890s and 1900s that aimed at the broadest spectrum of audience were *Munsey's, McClure's,* and the *Saturday Evening Post.* All three promoted a broadly positivist version of cultural modernity, in which poetry could hope to be little more than an ornament and could expect to be more likely an object of condescension and ridicule. But each magazine used and abused poetry in distinctive ways; their various forms of valuation and disparagement can help to chart complex changes in the genre's turn-of-the-century status. *Munsey's* employed verse extensively to fill up its pages and lend them a certain elevated tone, and this very profusion allowed, almost by accident, some acute explorations of poetry's possible uses in the modern condition. *McClure's* generally gave poetry short shrift but, when it seemed marketable, was willing to explore the genre's productive relations to emerging forms of realist fiction, and even its continuing power as a vehicle of social commentary. The *Post* offered by far the most corrosive treatment of poetry, using it to define and naturalize a repressive culture of capitalist middlebrowism, at the expense of intelligentsia and proletariat alike.

MUNSEY'S: ETCHINGS AND MODERNS

Though *Munsey's* has garnered almost no attention in literary histories, it may have printed more contemporary verse during the 1890s and 1900s than any other publication in the United States. After becoming a mass-circulation monthly in 1893, it published around 50 verses annually. About 10 more verses per issue were presented in a section called "Etchings." This is not to claim that 170 poems of significance appeared in the magazine every year: some of these pieces were but a few lines long, and most hewed to the paler gestures of homiletic genteel verse. By placing the bulk of its verse into "Etchings," *Munsey's* constructed poems in terms of pictorial representation and ascribed to them a certain miniaturist delicacy. Before 1895 the verses in "Etchings" were unsigned and often accompanied by illustrations. In this phase the "Etchings" sections also contained prose anecdotes, illustrated witticisms between courting couples, and humorous cartoons. Surrounding verse with articles, fiction, commentary, images, and ads, the magazine asserted a model of poetic value notably different from that of the Fireside canon, in which the corporate name "Munsey" replaced the absent name of the author. In this de-individualized discursive environment, the very notion of canonical authority was vulnerable to satiric attack, as in an 1894 "Etchings" entry that transforms the most intense scene of *Hamlet* into bumptious low comedy. A penciled illustration depicts a Good Samaritan half-carrying a drunken man back to his apartment doorstep, above which a woman leans out a window. This spectacle of working-class shiftlessness is rendered farcical by its caption, which quotes the line in which Hamlet uses his mother's two medallions to draw a searing contrast between her two husbands: "Look you now, here is your husband." The piece's irreverent treatment toward canonical authority is clinched by its mock-solemn title, "A Gem from Shakspere," which turns upside down the genteel notion that great literary works are valuable as ethical guides, instead asserting culture as a form of bricolage in which one may apply isolated fragments of the classics to scenarios from everyday life wildly disparate from their original contexts.

In 1895, perhaps in an effort to differentiate its appeal from its most direct competitor, *McClure's*, *Munsey's* made a somewhat greater commitment to poetry. "Etchings" became entirely a verse section and the illustrations were dropped, though poems scattered through the magazine were often still given some sort of pictorial punctuation. Although this basic format was maintained for the next dozen years, beginning in September 1903 the magazine quietly dropped all reference to verse in its volume indices, as if to propose that poetry was just a serendipitous pleasure taken as and if it came, capable of no sustained demand on the reader's interest.[10]

Behind the vapidity of much *Munsey's* verse, we can detect a deeply contradictory set of assumptions about poetry's value that reveals its changing status in the period. Two brief pieces by Tudor Jenks in volume 22 (1899–1900), "King and Minstrel" and "Immortality," are built around pious lip service to the claim that the creations of true artists are "deathless"—the key word in each poem—in contrast to the impermanence of worldly and kingly achievements:

> Sexton Time!—in vain you toll,
> Vainly gloomy echoes roll,
> For the theme once fitly sung
> Is deathless as the poet soul. ("King and Minstrel" 72)

The insistence of this genteel thematic convention is especially ironic, since both verses are clearly being used to fill up the bottom of pages and are printed in much smaller type than the features that precede them (a frivolously romantic short story and a celebration of wireless telegraphy, respectively). Readers could not have been wholly unaware of the disjunction between the grand claims such verses made for the genre of poetry and its obviously marginal status within the sites of mass culture. This same gap is explored by "The Tomes of Yesteryear," an unsigned verse printed in a "Literary Chat" section of *Munsey's* in 1903. A gloriously poetic past ("Once writing was a gallant trade, / When poetry was in its prime") has been replaced by canonical absence: "whether done in prose or rhyme, / Or whether with a blotted tear / Upon the faded leaves of time, / Where are the tomes of yesteryear?" (153). "Harp" and "troubadour" are "still" and asleep as "Our memories shorten more and more." The shortening of human memories evokes poetry's changing status in two senses: it describes how the accelerating scramble of modernity crowds the psychic space available for rumination and remembrance; and it measures the receding relevance of genteel poetry, so dependent on nostalgic memory for its coherence and emotional force. The poem's envoy, rather than urging some change upon the reader, offers only clipped platitude ("Brief are the days and art is long") that feebly echoes Fireside tradition (Longfellow's "A Psalm of Life" reads "Art is long, and Time is fleeting" [*Complete Poetical Works* 5]). This intentionally perfunctory envoy seems to concede that poetry can only wish that a few attention-deficient modern readers might "a moment linger here / Over the burden of the song." This song's "burden" is merely to ask repeatedly, without attempt at variation or answer, "Where are the tomes of yesteryear?"—and with one more such repetition the poem ends. Having discharged its burden in businesslike fashion, the poem authorizes the reader to move right along to the next item of "Literary Chat" (in this case, the much more interesting news that Sherlock Holmes is to be rejuvenated "to an admiring world" [153]).

"The Tomes of Yesteryear" is a slight piece, offering in pedestrian fashion a theme that more serious poets of the period would develop with greater skill and wit. But it does take a crucial step beyond the blinkered irrelevance of "King and Minstrel" by acknowledging its own problematic cultural status. In doing so it demonstrates the metathematic dimension that was almost as predominant in the pages of turn-of-the-century mass-magazine verse as in the rarefied contexts in which aesthetes such as Santayana and Crane published their poems. Indeed, much *Munsey's* verse, while conventional to the point of cliché in imagery, situation, and versification, is extraordinarily self-reflexive in tone, registering vivid awareness of the bewildered state of American poetic culture. This self-reflexive address to poetry's crisis shaped American verse in an intriguing variety of ways between 1890 and 1910, sometimes disabling, sometimes paradoxically affirming. In *Munsey's* the results of this self-consciousness were thoroughly mixed, ranging from pious hand-wringing over the unpoetic times, to derisive parodies of the conventional functions of verse, to more serious explorations of poetry's capacity to articulate the contradictory experience of modernity.

The least productive form of this self-reflexive impulse simply reiterated the "death of Pan" theme widespread in turn-of-the-century elite culture. "Apollo at the Plow" (*Munsey's*, 1894), by the young Edgar Lee Masters, offers a fairly unadulterated example of this agonistic stance, presenting a self-pitying Apollo, "plowing lorn and ruefully," "the Sampson of these grinding days" (158). This rather contemptible being asks forgiveness for his current weakness, comparing himself to a captive "'Mong ravin wolves within a prison cave" and admitting that he most craves "A deep repose, aye, even in the grave." All he can do is feebly implore the "Faithfulest and dearest of the friends I have" to remember him as he was; and perhaps "from thy memory / Ambition's shape will rise" and pass into him again. The poem exhibits no conviction that such a transformation could occur and ends with Apollo still plowing away, his harp "abandoned in the flowerless ways." The ambitious Masters would largely abandon poetry to plow other furrows (drama and law) for the next decade. Given this poem's lack of sensitivity to the comic possibilities of Apollo staggering along behind a plow, he was right to do so until he could shed his conventional agonistic earnestness and gain the satiric perspective that made *Spoon River Anthology* possible.

Such laments over the dormancy or imminent death of Pan were notably ironic in the pages of mass-circulation magazines, because the treatment of verse in those venues continually reinforced the notion that poetry was in decline. But it made a difference how such poems responded to the ironic valences inevitably hovering about them. Their differing levels of self-awareness dramatized the possible future trajectories of American verse. Would American verses refuse to acknowledge the gap between the claims conventionally made for poetry and its evident contemporary status, inviting readers to interpret this refusal as confirmation of the genre's fatal insularity and irrelevance? Or would they build such ironic awareness into their self-presentation, drawing energy from the contradiction rather than allowing it to enfeeble them, reasserting poetry's ability to engage such complex issues? "The Tomes of Yesteryear" offers at least hints of this enabling self-awareness. Other *Munsey's* verses, some of them apparently throwaway doggerel, pursue this enabling self-irony much further and accomplish more for the future of American verse than the pieties of "Immortality" and "King and Minstrel" or the ponderous self-pity of "Apollo at the Plow."

One of these unlikely accomplishments is the unsigned verse "Romance vs. Reality" (1894), which exploits a favorite theme of the mass-circulation magazines and of the American 1890s more generally: that romanticized descriptive conventions deserve debunking by clear-seeing partisans of reality. This piece amusingly implicates itself, and verse as a genre, in its critique of romance, playing with the common assumption that poetry's primary function is to hide unpleasant actualities or dress them up in beguiling forms. It offers a series of conventional "poetic" compliments to female beauty, "So exquisitely sweet / From the dark tresses of her hair / Down to her fairy feet" (92). But even before the poem becomes openly parodic, there is something off-kilter in the construction of these compliments in terms of artistic creation. The first three stanzas begin, "Full oft in verse I paint my Claire"; "I sing her charms by Venus given"; and "I tell how daintily she flits / A vision passing fair," as if the painting, singing, and telling, the performative process of complimenting, were more important than fidelity to the subject. And we must admire the sly adjective "passing," which in the poem's quasi-archaic tonality suggests *very* or *great,* as in "surpassing," but in a more contemporary idiom implies two very different meanings: either *transitory, cursory,* or *superficial* ("passing fancy"); or *pretending or appearing* ("passing as fair"). Sure enough, the fourth stanza turns away from fanciful falsehood to ask "Is all that beauty real?" The immediate answer is "Ah, no! In living truth, my Claire / Is scarce the bard's ideal." The final stanza amplifies this evaluation, averring that "Her face is plain as plain can be" and "Her temper corresponds"; yet she is still *his* Claire, since "she has millions two or three / In gilt edged stocks and bonds." In spite of its professions of decorative inutility, the genre of verse turns out to have a very material usefulness, in wooing Claire's millions into the speaker's tender embrace.

Other *Munsey's* verses lampoon the earnest conventionality of the genteel lyric tradition, proposing more lively satiric uses for the genre. "To Write a Summer Poem" (1894) details a formula for the love lyric, beginning with the amusingly crass directive, "First you get your atmosphere." Pursuing the tendency to pictorialize seen in much *Munsey's* verse, the speaker then pages through a series of artificial backdrops of nature as might be found in a portrait photographer's catalog or studio: "Have it limpid, soft, and clear; / Sandy beach or mountain high; / Trees and water; bright blue sky" (539). Whichever backdrop is chosen will silhouette "In the foreground lovers two"; but these lovers are ultimately just another species of atmosphere, props to be placed, framed, and ignored: "What they say or what they do, / *N' importe,* for the end is one; / And your summer poem's done." "Cupid Out of Practice" (1894) plays with another hackneyed convention of love poetry, Cupid's love-inducing arrows, with similarly comical results. Catching two likely prospects on the beach in moonlight, Cupid fears he is losing his "art," since he misses the couple four times in succession, instead piercing first two little fishes who are "married at high tide," then wedding "a lobster to a whale, / A sculpin to a flounder," and finally impaling "nose to tail" a hapless "bachelor bluefish" whose only mate is the arrow itself (541). The chaos Cupid generates before finally hitting his mark is not a dig at moonlight lovemaking, of course, but at conventional verse renderings of it. Such verses express the mass magazines' desire for the prestige still hovering around poetry; but at the same time, they cannot suppress their impatience with the more preposterous conventions (as they see them) that genteel poetry had come to entail.

Despite their often satiric air, *Munsey's* verses seldom come across as mean-spirited. Unlike the more corrosive presentation seen in the *Saturday Evening Post,* which seemed bent on stifling poetry's entire communicative function, *Munsey's* generally mingled its self-reflexive verses alongside more innocent ones. The overall effect of these verses is whimsically to destabilize genteel verse conventions, as in Charles Williams Barnes's 1896 verse "Fin de Siècle," which begins with ultraconventional imagery of Romantic love, a "shower" of rose petals on a "velvet lawn," punctuating the speaker's offer of love and matrimony to "Sylvia" as they sit in her "bower" (761). As he implores her to "give to me / Thy little hand to lead through life," Barnes's verse seems every inch the earnest Romantic profession of love, taking no chances as it treads painfully familiar ground. After a brief pause and silence, during which "all the world seemed gray," the speaker is rewarded for his fidelity to the role of ardent but proper suitor: Sylvia's joyful eyes turn to his, "And then, what I shall ne'er forget, / These words from her sweet lips." The poem has only ten syllables left to elevate it from the stale conventions of its genre, and Sylvia's answer to his proposal does so in surprising fashion: "You bet. / Why, here are both my hands, dear boy!" Barnes does not tell his readers how to feel about this startling invasion of slang, and casually direct gesture of affection, into the poet's bower of indirect and idealized discourse, other than to imply its contemporary typicality through his title. As Paula Bennett suggests of some late-century women's poetry ("Not Just Filler" 211–12), this sort of refusal to editorialize measures the distance between genteel inhibitions and a more unbuttoned modern sensibility that characterizes some of the era's strongest poems. Barnes here offers poetry not to enforce any ideological consistency or moral norms, but simply to record in memorable form some shift in the emotional and social landscape of the fin de siècle.

As the genteel consensus of Fireside poetry receded, and the turn of the century brought new technological marvels to celebrate, the verse in *Munsey's* turned somewhat away from Romantic conventionality, even from parodying it, to register more direct awareness of modernity. The results of this shift were aesthetically mixed and ideologically contradictory, but they usefully illuminate the stubbornly entrenched assumptions that exacerbated poetry's crisis. In March 1905, for example, *Munsey's* placed a poem called "A Song of City Traffic" on the final page of

"The Colossal City," Edgar Saltus's illustrated article on contemporary New York. A publication making such juxtapositions was clearly not uninterested in the possible relations between poetry and urban-industrial modernity. This article and another by Saltus in July can be linked to the magazine's move early in 1905 into the sensation of the New York skyline, the Flatiron Building.[11] "The Colossal City" is an intriguing jumble of impressions that alternates between two modes: (1) marveling at the enormous buildings and fortunes that had changed New York City from a "somnolent American port" into the quintessential city of twentieth-century modernity; and (2) foreseeing the bleak outcome of such rampant growth as "a City of the Homeless," consisting of desolate "mountain ranges of office and dry-goods buildings, with wind-swept, sunless ravines between" that offer "no shelter" (787, 789). Saltus predicts that the "perpetual house famine" required by the economics of New York City will be alleviated only partially by improved "rapid transit" and will produce wholesale flight to "league upon league" of "distressingly similar" suburban villas that will become the only spaces "really cherished" by millions of modern urbanites (790–91). Saltus foresees the next century of middle-class American urban experience pretty clearly but comes to no certain conclusion about the value of these epochal demographic shifts. His article neither buries nor praises the colossal city, but presents it as an "endless process of reconstruction" (790), the sort of ambivalent perception that Marshall Berman argues is quintessential to the experience of modernity (15).

Munsey's very willingness to place verse into modern urban contexts represented an advance over the genteel refusal to juxtapose the two. But Charles Hanson Towne's "A Song of City Traffic" lacks Saltus's sensitivity to the productive power of modernity's contradictions. Despite its Whitmanesque title, Towne's poem is mired in Romantic convention, constructing the city in antiurban terms drawn directly from Bryant's "The Crowded Street" and from Wordsworth before him. Indeed, Towne's likening of the "poor throngs of the great city" to drops within a "mighty stream" (793) flatly reiterates one of Bryant's central metaphors ("These struggling tides of life that seem / In wayward, aimless course to tend, / Are eddies of the mighty stream / That rolls to its appointed end" [Bryant, *Complete Poetical Works* 195]). Towne's comparison of the city's unending "procession" of "Coaches, wagons, hearses, engines, clanging cars, and thundering drays," to "a serpent long and sinuous," evokes another Romantic-genteel commonplace about modernization, the "machine in the garden" topos analyzed by Leo Marx. Towne's use of this topos, less nuanced than many of the writers Marx discusses, presents the industrial city as a poisonous, even demonic, affront to the Edenic American landscape. The second half of the poem addresses those in thrall to it: "When the brazen voice of traffic and the loud call of the mart, / Strangle all the hope within you, bruise your soul and break your heart, / Do you think of some far valley where life plays another part?" Though they "Miss the old, old beauty," still they "weep not" and will "join once more the foolish struggle" of "the city's tumult," which makes life nothing "but wounds and scars." The most problematic aspect of Towne's treatment of the city is the speaker's evasive position, which stunts his ability to empathize with these "poor throngs." The speaker says he has "watched them moving past" from an unspecified stationary point, but does not locate himself within the scene. This refusal to participate, to *be* part of the city rather than simply viewing it, suggests Towne's unwillingness to give up the privileged Romantic subject position of the observer who claims to understand all, yet remains apart from the miserable existence of an urban Other.[12]

I'm not seeking to revive the high-modernist claim that the mass-circulation magazine's celebration of capitalist modernity had stifled American poetry. Quite the contrary: Towne (1877–1949) might have achieved a richer view of his subject if he had entered more fully into *Munsey's* modernity, as Saltus's essay does. Towne's verse persistently gestured toward the modern city, most elaborately in the 1909 sequence *Manhattan.* But he was seldom able to escape the conventions of antiurban Romanticism dictating that verse about urban movement must prominently condemn the city's noise, dirt, disorder, and immorality. In "The Street Lamps" and "Night in Wall Street," both published in *Munsey's* in 1905, the city remains simply an unnatural place of "strife and awful turmoil" ("Night in Wall Street" 892). Ironically, despite defining the city by its concentration of elemental human desire and conflict, Towne leaves both poems devoid of human figures. He clings so stubbornly to the idealizing strictures of genteel verse that all his empathy is lavished absurdly on the street lamps, "Sad watchers of old sorrow and old sin," to whom he says "God pity you when darkness wanders in" ("Street Lamps" 629).

Apart from the danger of deficient empathy, some urban poems in *Munsey's* are stunted by their unwillingness to articulate the city's powerful allure. The magazine's pages offer abundant evidence of this allure, yet many of its poems refuse it altogether. If the throngs "miss the old, old, beauty" to be found outside the city, if "the loud call of the mart" will simply "strangle all [their] hope" ("Song of City Traffic" 793), why would they ever heed its call? This contradiction was dramatized most

HE walls of cliff-high buildings steeply crowd
　To shut away the light,
And all the panes are gray
　With their insistent shadowing; to-day
The morning masks as night,
　Scarcely a whit less dusky and grim-browed.

rapped creatures of the wild, we pine! Nay, see
　How roofs yield grudging space
To a faint, blue glimpse of sky
　That thrills to white flame—for the sun rides by
And with a royal grace
　Flings down our golden ransom—we are free!

　　　　　　　　　　　Grace Hodsdon Boutelle

Figure 1. *Valentine Sandberg, illustration to "A City Window" by Grace Hodsdon Boutelle. Munsey's, 1905. Courtesy of the University of Illinois Urbana-Champaign Library.*

compactly by *Munsey's* presentation of Grace Hodsdon Boutelle's "A City Window" in July 1905. This poem again deploys the conventional rhetoric of city as prison: "The walls of cliff-high buildings steeply crowd / To shut away the light" (407). The city turns morning into "dusky and grim-browed" night, its human inhabitants into "Trapped creatures of the wild," desperately grateful for any "faint, blue glimpse of sky," free only when the sun "rides by" at a certain angle and momentarily "Flings down our golden ransom." It is odd enough that such an indictment of the skyscraper city would come in the same issue as

Saltus's article "New York from the Flatiron" and within two months of Munsey's proud announcement that his magazine was moving into the skies. But even on the same page, this incongruity was brought into sharp focus by the illustration by Valentine Sandberg.

Sandberg offers an idealized rendition of the New York skyline that is densely built to be sure, but still leaves plenty of room for a brilliant clear sky. The skyline's sharp focus, clean lines, sunlit surfaces, and pleasing counterpoint of neoclassical, Beaux-Arts, and early modernist architectural shapes all assert that this city is no prison, but a breathtaking place of possibility. The continuity between the fluffy clouds and the white buildings implies a harmony between natural objects and human constructions. Though the lower portion of the frame exhibits some shadowing, its architectural lines are still sharply visible, clean, and beautiful. Moreover, it is the poem that blots out the lower half of the frame, as if implying that the only significant shadows in the image are cast by poetry's own unwillingness to enter into this vision of a modernity without boundaries. One can justly argue that the illustration is an ideologized version of the modern city; but so, in their own way, are Boutelle's poem, and Towne's as well. Neither illustration nor poems tell the whole story of urban modernity. Until American poetry could admit evidence of the city's magnetism into its bower, it would have difficulty speaking meaningfully to modern experience or addressing its own state of crisis.

In November 1903 Munsey's expressed a desire to make American verse relevant to modern life with a series of "Prizes for Topical Poems," designed to call forth verses "treating some subject of current interest in a humorous or satirical way" (320). A total of one hundred dollars (soon increased to $175) would be awarded monthly to the three winning poems, and, the editors emphasized, "Any other poem worthy of publication will be purchased at a fair price" ("Prizes for Topical Poems" 320). The terms of the contest ("humorous or satirical") discouraged deeply searching indictments of the shortcomings of modern American life. But from January through June 1904 Munsey's rewarded eighteen prize-winning verses dealing with such contemporary phenomena as the sensationalism of the newspaper press, the consequences of the Russo-Japanese War, the machinations behind the likely party tickets for the November elections, the ensnaring effects of rampant installment-plan buying, the piratical behavior of modern stock speculators, the class dynamics of bourgeois families and their domestic servants, the prevalence of plastic surgery among modern women, and the growing faddishness of American culture.

The staff of *Munsey's* was surprised and pleased (at least in theory) by the widespread interest in the competition. They supplied a running monthly total of submissions, which began at just under 1,000 and peaked at 1,623 ("Prize Topical Poems: The Result of the Competition for February" 727; "Prize Topical Poems: The Result of the Competition for April" 25), showing that even in the worst years of poetry's crisis, the nation contained vast reserves of poetic ambition. Despite the enormity of response to their contest, however, the editors became increasingly restive, and after six months they discontinued the series, complaining, "We have been disappointed . . . in the quality of most of the poems received" ("Prize Topical Poems: The Result of the Competition for May" 310). Whether this conclusion represented a genuine assessment of American verse writing or simply the exhaustion of a staff inundated by more than a thousand manuscripts a month, it made a deflating end to a significant experiment in contemporary American verse, one of the few mounted by anyone before 1912. Within two years, in April 1906, poetry's adjunct status in mass-circulation magazines was acknowledged by *Munsey's* in all but words, as the "Etchings" section (which at least carried connotations of something permanently marked on a readable surface) was replaced with the unambiguously ephemeral label "Light Verse." Some of the city poems I have discussed were still to be published in the magazine, but the failure of the Topical Poems contests and the shift to "Light Verse" marked the effective end of *Munsey's* efforts to sponsor a discourse of modern American poetry.

MCCLURE'S: PROFITING BY PROPHECY

McClure's, begun in 1893 and quickly growing into mass-circulation status, employed poetry more cavalierly overall than *Munsey's,* seldom investing it with much cultural or economic significance. In its first twelve years, the magazine generally published one or two poems per month, but even this paltry figure is misleading. *McClure's* clearly wished its verse to entail little risk and less cost; many of its featured poets had been around for dozens or hundreds of years, including Ben Jonson, William Wordsworth, Thomas Carew, W. S. Landor, Matthew Arnold, A. H. Clough, W. E. Henley (and Prime Minister Gladstone). But the magazine did exhibit occasional interest in reconceiving poetry for the world of modernity. Reflecting the enthusiasms of its founder, much of *McClure's* verse drew upon conventions of the genre fiction sweeping the country, particularly narratives of war, railroading, seafaring, gold mining, and other forms of masculine adventure.[13] In 1898 this interest in masculine travail was given focus by the Spanish-American War, and the dominant genre of *McClure's* verse became the histrionic celebration of martial adventure, typified by two of only five poems published in volume 15 (1900), Thomas Tracy Bouvé's "The Last Charge," and "Death in Battle" by Alfred Ollivant, who is identified as also the author of "Bob, Son of Battle," suggesting the formulaic expectations of mass-culture verse venues.[14] Both Bouvé and Ollivant plunged their readers into thickets of battle evoked through unabashed rhetorical bombast. "Death in Battle" begins: "His hand upon th' Impregnable, he blunders / Headlong in the cataract of War, / Blasted on by flaming-throated thunders, / Founders in the Deluge; sinks to soar, / Hugely borne upon Jehovah-handed surges" (96). Liberal capitalization, breathless exclamation marks, and highfalutin and archaic diction ("targe," "emulous," "guidon," "dragoons"), all indicate that no matter how gritty the subject matter, a certain elevated tone and distance from realism was expected in verse.[15]

Works such as these represent a late and rather debased form of the martial verse popular throughout the nineteenth century and exemplified by "The Charge of the Light Brigade." Judging by them, one might be tempted to conclude that *McClure's* offered nothing of value to American poetry in its crisis. But such an estimation would miss something significant. Exhibiting the omnivorous appetite for headline-grabbing material that characterizes both the best and worst elements of modern journalism, *McClure's* opted for currency over ideological consistency. As it sponsored these adolescent celebrations of imperial adventure and glorious battle, it was also publishing important essays by muckraking reform journalists, among them Hamlin Garland's scathing indictment of labor conditions in the steel industry, Lincoln Steffens's *Shame of the Cities,* Ida Tarbell's Standard Oil series, and Ray Stannard Baker's exposé of lynching. This climate of "ideological pluralism" (H. Wilson 111) allowed two productive modern functions for poetry in *McClure's:* as a form of realist-naturalist narrative, exemplified by Garland's two-part series "The Trail to the Golden North"; and as a vehicle for progressive social commentary, in "The Man with the Hoe" and other works by Edwin Markham.

"The Trail to the Golden North" (April-May 1899) was the product of Garland's journey by pack train through the gold fields of British Columbia and Alaska the previous summer. It consists of eight lyric and narrative sections describing aspects of the trip: the physical hardships, the many faces of nature from delightful to merciless, the psychology of the gold seekers, the mistreatment of horses, and the psychic consequences of such a life-altering journey. Its striking preface advances a realist poetics based on the principles that Garland (1860–1940) and others had begun to employ in American fiction. He informs his readers immediately that these poems derive not from fantasy or patched-together knowledge out of books, but from experiences he actually underwent; indeed, they "were written during the actual journey," some while "on horseback" (505). While he had also penned accounts of the journey in prose, "certain moods and scenes seemed to demand verse" (505). Garland never specifies exactly what determines these generic requirements, but he does imply that there are some experiences only reproducible or comprehensible through poetry, challenging the assertions of antistyle editors such as Edward Bok (and McClure himself) that poetry was just the tarting up of simple ideas into needlessly ornate form and arcane language. Garland concludes by noting that he left the poems "pretty nearly in their original bluff, rude form, in order that the flavor of the actualities of the trail should not be lost" (505). All in all, his preface forcefully asserts poetry's continued ability to capture the "actualities" of life as no other form of writing can.

Garland's preface also establishes the violent and disappointing character of the prospecting experience: "It led to failure at the end, and suicide and murder marked it with tragic dashes of red" (505). Many of the poems maintain this emphasis, drawing upon naturalist irony to evoke the enormous uncontrollable forces dominating the prospectors, who are beset equally by "relentless" nature and by internal compulsions that drive them on. The introductory poem, "The Golden Seekers," foregrounds the irony that their liberating repudiation of "hopeless" wage servitude comes only through their thralldom to far-fetched dreams of gold:

> "Once more I'm a man! I am free!
> No man is my master, I say.
> Tomorrow I fail, it may be—
> No matter, I'm freeman to-day."
>
> They go to a toil that is sure,
> To despair and hunger and cold;
> Their sickness no warning can cure,
> They are mad with a longing for gold. (505)

Garland constructs the eventual fate of these men within a naturalist framework of blind chance. Some "will sink by the way and be laid / In the frost of the desolate earth" as if they had never existed; others will return to a loved one, defeated and "Empty of hand as at birth." Refusing conventional idealizations, the poem provides no successful counterpart to these two dismal scenarios. Its coda acknowledges only the "gain" of the men's knowledge that "They have lived and have tossed." But there seems no question that the tossing "the gold of the dice" will be a losing proposition.

The other poems in the first installment of the sequence come nearer to celebrating the trip as an unforgettable life experience, proving a certain courage and manliness in its participants. But in the second group, published the following month, Garland returns to the meditative ambivalence of the first poem. The section called "Camp Fires" juxtaposes three imagistic glimpses of a pair of men in different stages of gold longing. In the first, two boys on a riverbank feed a poplar fire, dreaming of the adulthood that will allow them to "hunt gold towards the western sky" (65). The middle section offers a man in mid-search, who has put behind him the "quiet round of a farmer's life," resolving to "seek till I find—or till I die." He and his companion hunker down by their fire under a "limitless sky" with a "furnace glow," at the center of an enormous plain "as void as a polar floe." Garland uses the featurelessness and infinitude of the topography to undercut the man's resolution: in such a place, "seeking" inevitably seems endless and futile. In the final, strikingly bleak "Camp Fire," two men are dwarfed by "mighty mountains, cold and white / And stern as avarice," which "still hide their gold / Deep in wild cañons"—still more intimidating images of the search's futility. Despite their "spicy and cheering" pine fire, one despairing man cries to the mountains "'I'd rather have a boy with shining hair, / To bear my name, than all your share / Of earth's red gold.'" Garland shows him no more mercy than the mountains do, reporting tersely that he "died, a loveless, childless man, / Before the morning light began" (65).

This grim tone is the dominant one through to the sequence's end, as Garland describes the almost sentient cruelty of nature, the "mad" rushing of mountain streams, and the "ghosts of murdered horses," for whose suffering "men shall answer." The final poem, "The End of the Trail," describes arrival at an eerily peaceful terminus, where the speaker releases his horse and awaits the "last boat, the slow silent one." The fleeting moments of comradeship and accomplishment will now be dissipated in an endless sense of cosmic isolation: "We go each alone—no man with another, / Each into the gloom of the swift black flood." The final lines clinch the poem's naturalist modality, reminding us that "the powers that lead us / Shall govern the game to the end of the day" (67).

The realism of these *McClure's* poems represented a notable shift in Garland's approach to verse writing. As Joseph B. McCullough points out, in contrast to his tough-minded fiction, Garland had used verse, particularly in the 1893 volume *Prairie Poems,* to create a "different world" of nostalgic remembrance for "a nature unspoiled by humanity and uninterrupted by the often painful current affairs of the farmer" (170). But Garland now felt a very different need, to conjoin the two "worlds" of fiction and poetry into a clear-eyed examination of the complex phenomenon of the Western gold rush. This convergence was cemented by the form of his 1899 volume *The Trail of the Goldseekers,* which interspersed sections of prose and verse, as such later landmarks of modern poetry as *Cane* and *Spring and All* would do.

McClure, his ear always to the ground for literary sensations, was among the first to give national publicity to Edwin Markham's "The Man with the Hoe," which became "one of the anthems of the American labor movement" (Nelson, *Revolutionary* 15) and perhaps the best-known single poem in the world between 1890 and 1910. Markham (1852–1940) had first published the poem in Hearst's *San Francisco Examiner* on January 15, 1899, to immediate acclaim, which grew steadily over the next months. Though it had been reprinted in various newspapers, published in a lavish pamphlet on March 30 in San Francisco, and in a pirated New York edition that was quickly suppressed, the poem reached a truly national venue when *McClure's* printed it in the May issue. On May 27 Doubleday & McClure brought out *The Man with the Hoe and Other Poems,* a full volume of Markham's verse, which would reach a fourth printing by August. Doubleday & McClure would publish a revised edition with illustrations by Howard Pyle the following year (Shields 4–5). "The Man with the Hoe" was eventually translated into forty languages and reprinted perhaps ten thousand times in books and periodicals (Stidger 143). It remained prominent in commentaries and editorials long after its initial appearance, so much so in California that the *Examiner* ran a page every day for months featuring discussion of it (Stidger 151). It was widely quoted in sermons, political speeches, and public debates, and lauded by prominent figures from William James to William Jennings Bryan to future Vice President Thomas Marshall (Ferlazzo 281; Stidger 156, 160). Markham made a small fortune with the poem's worldwide success; undoubtedly McClure found it profitable as well. If poems of railroad and martial adventuring (and in a different way, Garland's naturalist narratives) had expressed the magazine's interest in situations of physical extremity and emotional strife, "The Man with the Hoe" added an important empathetic dimension to its ideological profile, which otherwise skirted Social-Darwinist callousness.

Expressing Markham's fervent synthesis of Christianity and Fourierist utopian socialism, "The Man with the Hoe" was a response in blank verse to Jean-François Millet's painting of a weary laborer leaning on his hoe in a dismal landscape of seemingly intractable soil. Cary Nelson argues that despite the sincerity of Markham's outrage, it is the poem's "relentless *othering* of the worker" that gave it "such remarkable cultural warrant" (*Revolutionary* 17). But despite a tendency to advocate "whirlwinds of rebellion" mostly in the abstract, the poem still succeeds in lodging a powerful protest against structurally entrenched social injustice. Its force depends upon a complex tonal balance of compassion, righteous indignation, and implied threat. Though he calls the laborer "A thing that grieves not and never hopes, / Stolid and stunned, a brother to the ox," Markham makes it impossible for the reader to blame the victim for his own dehumanization, turning the harshness of these descriptions into a rhetoric of interrogation: "Who made him dead to rapture and despair . . . ?" "Whose breath blew out the light within his brain?" (15). Markham also invests the man with a measure of agency by portraying him not as an aberration but as an exemplar, whose "dread shape" reveals all of "humanity betrayed, / Plundered, profaned, and disinherited." Markham seeks to create a "protest that is also prophecy" (16), an expression of dissent against worldly injustice transcending ineffectual hand-wringing and mindless antagonism, claiming for itself the moral authority of Judeo-Christian spiritual tradition.

From this point, Markham's rhetorically skilled questioning intensifies the hints of menace, ending with these lines:

> O masters, lords, and rulers in all lands,
> How will the Future reckon with this Man?
> How answer his brute question in that hour
> When whirlwinds of rebellion shake the world?
> How will it be with kingdoms and with kings—
> With those who shaped him to the thing he is—
> When this dumb Terror shall reply to God,
> After the silence of the centuries? (16)

Though Markham never fully gets past the "problematic curtailment of workers' agency" (Nelson, *Revolutionary* 22), the man balanced on the hoe remains ever poised on the brink of gaining such agency, a shaming reminder of all the world's injustice and a threat to those who foment it.

The poem leaves unanswered—but everywhere implied—the question of whether the man's "reply" will involve his hoe adapted to the function of a weapon. It evinces no doubt that eventually he "shall reply" in some form.

More than any poem of the era, "The Man with the Hoe" showed that poetry as social critique could still move a vast audience.[16] While not exactly typical of mass-market magazine verse, it demonstrated that venues of mass culture were not limited just to frivolous or formulaic pablum. The verses sprinkled through the pages of *Munsey's* and *McClure's* reflected the genre's tenuous cultural status, but they were not destroying poetry in America. Indeed, it's quite conceivable that they actually interested some new readers in verse. Not all their uses of verse were equally productive, nor did they lead directly or inevitably to the unbuttoned avant-gardist poetry of the 1910s, which would require a very different genre of periodical, the little magazine, barely a gleam in any American's eye in 1900. But in their puncturing of the inhibiting solemnities of the genteel tradition, *Munsey's* and *McClure's* did enlarge the social and rhetorical range of American verse and thus played some part in the formation of a poetics responsive to modernity.

THE *SATURDAY EVENING POST:* MANACLES OF THE MIDDLEBROW

The most threatening relationship between modern mass culture and turn-of-the-century poetry was asserted in the *Saturday Evening Post*, the quintessential success story of American magazine capitalism. The *Post* was virtually moribund when it was taken over in 1897 by Cyrus Curtis, who had just built the *Ladies' Home Journal* into the first publication to approach one million in circulation. Curtis used huge doses of nationwide advertising and giveaway issues to boost its feeble circulation; once that effort had succeeded, its revenues were driven almost entirely by advertising (Cohn 23–25).[17] From 1899, the editorial regime of George Horace Lorimer presided over the growth of the *Post's* circulation into the largest of any American magazine, topping two million in 1919 and nearing three million by 1929. More than just economic dominance in its market, the *Post* sought a defining cultural role in middle-class America. Claiming for itself a tortuous lineage from Ben Franklin, the ultimate American icon of commonsense practicality, the magazine embraced a "pervasive and often explicit class-consciousness" (Greene 181) that celebrated the middle class at the expense of both rich and poor. As

Lorimer grew older, his attitudes would become more repressively middlebrow, and the *Post* would proclaim itself the sworn enemy of "the intelligentsia" and anything that smacked of the foreign or avant-garde (Cohn 14).

The *Post*'s discursive manipulation of "the average American" prominently involved fiction, some, like the series "Letters from a Self-Made Merchant to His Son," written by Lorimer himself. Poetry was another matter. In its transitional phase in 1898–1899, the *Post* was still gesturing toward genteel poetry's domestic uses with a weekly series called "The Best Poems in the World," consisting of long-familiar material suitable for domestic consumption. The issues of January 1899 featured Burns ballads, a Thackeray poem, "The Sexton" by Park Benjamin (died 1864), Longfellow's "Paul Revere's Ride," and one tame verse by a living writer, James Whitcomb Riley's "The Elf-Child." Even before the arrival of Lorimer (whose name began appearing on the masthead on June 10), the *Post*'s philosophy of literary value was based on rigid cultural stratifications: to "give its readers not the best from the standpoint of the ultra-literary man, but such poems as appeal to all that is best in human nature" ("Best Poems" 445). Over the years this inverse relation between "ultra-literary man" and "human nature" would underlie the *Post*'s militant conflation of antielitism with anti-intellectualism. Though in January the magazine professed that "The Best Poems in the World" would continue "during the year 1899" (445), it was discontinued without explanation after the issue of February 4. This policy decision indicated that the *Post*'s coalescing commitment to an entrepreneurial modernity left little room for even the safest poetry.

While the new *Post* continued to publish some verse after 1899, poetry was not dignified with its own featured category such as "The Best Poems in the World" or "Etchings," but was scattered through issues with little consistency and not indexed anywhere. The magazine's celebration of modern middlebrowism was almost as antithetical to the earnest genteel Romanticism of Fireside culture as to the avant-garde; not for it the earnest effusions of "Death in Battle" or "Apollo at the Plow." In both tone and content, the *Post*'s verse refused to take poetry seriously and ridiculed those who did, as with Charles Battell Loomis's "Explanatory Lines to a Hen" of 1901, which inquires with mock solemnity, "Why has no poet turned his lyre to thee / O hen! producer of the tempting egg?" (7). Still, poetry was a key element in the *Post*'s campaign against the nineteenth-century genteel elite and its construction of an ideology of capitalist entreprenolatry. We can measure the corrosive effects of this campaign by looking at two verses published there in 1901,

Guy Wetmore Carryl's "The Babes in the Wood," and Paul Laurence Dunbar's "W'en the Colo'ed Ban' Comes Ma'chin' Down de Street." Different as their appeal and approach are from one another, both invited the primary target audience of the *Saturday Evening Post* to treat poetry as a self-parodic genre of the quaint and absurd that revealed the bankruptcy of genteel culture and the futility of any alternative to the *Post*'s repressively normative ethos of middle-class materialism.

"The Babes in the Wood" (January 1901) was the first in a series of parodic verses Carryl published in the *Post* during that year. Like most of the others, it lampooned the obsolete conventions of elite culture by synthesizing familiar topoi of nursery rhymes, fairy tales, and consolation verse, only to explode them all as ludicrous in the final stanzas. Two children, left a fortune by their expiring parent, are remanded to the care of an insidious uncle who, taking them into a wood, abandons them "seated on a gateway, / And took his own departure straightway" to await their own expiration, and his inheritance. Fanny Y. Cory's illustration to this poem depicts two forlorn infants seated precariously upon a gate, in good tugging-at-the-heartstrings fashion—but upon closer examination, we find their faces a bit cartoonish to take their plight entirely seriously. Having set up the conventional situation in deadpan fashion, Carryl soon invites readers to chuckle at its hackneyed sentimentalism: "For countless years their childish fears / Have made the reader pale, / For countless years the public's tears / Have started at the tale." Since readers "know full well / Their most pathetic fate" from countless similar poems, there is literally "No need to tell" (parodying the anthropomorphism of sillier genteel verse) "how with leaves each little dead breast / Was covered by a Robin Red Breast." Telling the very things it claims not to need to, the poem undercuts its own basis of existence. The effect, of course, is to urge readers to discard the childish and ludicrous sentiments that genteel poetry proffers, and to employ the genre instead to celebrate an ascendant ideology of hard-headed materialism. The young boy Paul happily exemplifies the *Post*'s modern values, summoning the strength to write a telling testament that indicts the culpable uncle: "Quite near to Paul was seen a small / White paper, neatly creased. / *'Because of lack of any merit, / B. Hyde,'* it said, *'we disinherit.'*" Even in his final extremity Paul has the proper equipment to discharge his fiduciary responsibilities and the wherewithal to do it neatly: that's the stuff readers of the *Saturday Evening Post* were expected to admire. The poem's coda administers the coup de grace upon the didactic piety of sentimental verse with an egregious but revealing pun:

> The Moral: If you deeply long
> To punish one who's done you wrong,
> Though in your lifetime fail you may,
> Where there's a will there's a way!

In the *Post*'s world, the only proper object of piety is financial rather than religious: why rely on God for justice when you can dispense it yourself through the swift sword of your last will?[18]

If the *Post* used Carryl's parodies to ridicule the stale conventions of genteel verse, it employed Dunbar's to patronize African American culture, which was especially ironic given Dunbar's foundational role in the emergence of that culture on a national level. "W'en the Colo'ed Ban' Comes Ma'chin' Down de Street," a description of an African American marching band, is a text capable of generating widely varying meanings in different contexts of reception, as recent commentators such as Henry Louis Gates and Joanne M. Braxton have suggested of Dunbar's work more generally.[19] African American readers of 1901 might well have derived an affirming sense of racial pride from the poem's comparison of the African American band to a Sousa-style white band: as Dunbar puts it, hearing the white band might "sometimes" produce "a ticklin' in yo' feet," "But de hea't goes into business fu' to he'p erlong de eah, / W'en de colo'ed band goes ma'chin' down de street" ("Band" 9). But one is still left with the uneasy perception that the editorship of the *Post* who printed the poem likely saw it as reconfirming standard racist-sentimental stereotypes; and that the *Post*'s white readership largely received it that way, especially when confronted by the lavish illustration the magazine supplied, which depicts the prancing drum major and "de piccaninnies crowdin' aroun' him," all marked by the exaggerated facial features and rolling eyes of the era's racist iconography. Such images were reinforced in the *Post* by frequent illustrations of African American servants in advertisements for Cream of Wheat, Knox's Gelatine, and other products.[20] The *Post*'s patronizing contextualization of Dunbar's poem was given further force by its placement in an issue featuring a long article, "West Point As It Was and Is," by General Charles King. Even if this juxtaposition was coincidental, it created a striking contrast between the gaudy costumes of the marching band in the illustration to the poem and the elegant cadet uniforms of full-fledged members of the American military, which were depicted in a line drawing on the opposite page (King 8).

The *Post* was surprisingly inventive and persistent in its deployment of verse to serve its entrepreneurial ideology. In August 1907, for example, poetry was featured on a bizarre page devoted to the activities and foibles of Wall Street magnates. There was first an account of E. C. Stedman's dual career in literature and finance, perfectly respectful but entitled (a bit pointedly?) "The Banker-Poet." Then came a Wall Street in-joke (so lame it's not worth the space of reproducing) concerning the supposedly "favorite poet" of the railroad king E. H. Harriman, who evaluates poems according to their relevance to his own business interests ("Harriman's Favorite Poet"). Presented alongside squibs describing J. P. Morgan's charitable response to a photographer seeking to document Native American life, and the vacation jaunts of various chief executives, these comments situated poetry into a world completely dominated by the values and activities of big business, to which it might lend a quaint but never foundational element of the "picturesque" ("Banker-Poet" 12).

What was the logical conclusion of the *Post*'s account of poetry? Like just about everything else in the magazine's world, poetry could be enlisted into the direct service of selling. The September 1907 ad for Snider Process Pork and Beans, one of many demonstrations of that function, offered a verse entitled "Filosofy of Beans" by the fictional farmer "Hiram Jones." Presumably a better bean farmer than he is a speller, "Jones" extols the virtues of Snider's canned beans over those that his wife still sometimes makes, which require almost a week of steeping, boiling, and baking. Homemade beans represent an unconscionably inefficient use of time and are "just *Awful*—/—On your digestion" to boot (31). But the Snider Process

> Makes 'em porous, mellow, tender,
> Digestible an' appetizin' as them
> 'Pies that Mother used to make'
> When we was girls and boys.

Despite all the surrounding valorization of efficient modern methods of production and distribution, the lure of the nostalgic still resonates here. The ad takes pains to neutralize this nostalgia in two ways, by insisting that the wholesome culinary pleasure of store-bought beans equals that of home-baked pies, and more subtly, by placing the phrase signifying lovable nostalgia ('Pies that mother used to make') under quotation marks, as if implying it's little more than an obligatory cliché. American farmers have begun to eat canned food, American poets have begun to advertise it: the *Post*'s modernity is disturbingly coherent in its replacement of preindustrial ethical and aesthetic values with those of modern corporate efficiency.

Also in 1907 the *Post* offered its most sustained attack on poetry's value in the modern world, Annulet Andrews's lengthy story "Narcissus the Near-Poet," serialized in July and August. Here the target is not genteel sentimentalism, but the ultramodern poetry of pseudo-intellectual highbrows. Sophie, a young woman from the country, comes to the metropolis hoping to find a direction for her energies and a way to support herself financially. Drifting into bohemian circles, she is warned by her faithful servant to avoid "thim long-haired animals what writes poetry or throws dynamite!" who supposedly populate the city (July 20, 1907, 3). Of course the narrative requires that she immediately become involved with such a person, Arthur Inness, alias Narcissus, the central figure in a "New Hedonist" school of verse, who fulfills every stereotype of the decadent feminized poet: "tall and slender, with exquisite, white, transparent skin, blue-veined on the temples, and great, yearning, black-lashed, langorous, violet eyes. His nose was long and slim and slightly aquiline; his lips scarlet, delicate, clear-cut; the expression of the mouth sweet and slightly satirical. A quantity of thick-curling, golden hair with the light shining on it made a nimbus about the luminous face" (July 20, 4). Less a human being than a "Burne-Jones ideal," Narcissus has made his flesh-and-blood person into artwork, while absurdly repudiating the actual world around him—he "makes a fairy-land out of everyday surroundings," as Andrews derisively puts it (July 20, 4, 5).

Narcissus turns out to be no bomb-throwing anarchist (too much energy and commitment needed), but someone equally unwholesome to impressionable personalities. He beguiles Sophie with his preening beauty and extravagant compliments, such as "in the fetid junk-shop of life—I found my perfect rose!" (July 20, 22), and they quickly marry, even though he claims not to believe in the institution. Of course, Narcissus is transparently in search of a meal ticket, and after their marriage he is often away, implying some never specified but evidently unsavory secret life. Sophie, settling into a sensible small-artisanal career as a designer of menus and invitations, comes to represent American normality beset by the poisonous influences of poets and bohemians. She eventually contracts diphtheria and lies near death as Narcissus makes one of his prodigal returns. Discovering her illness, he flies in terror and cravenly has his belongings moved out of their apartment without telling her. But in the *Post*'s universe, such perfidy cannot go unpunished, at least not when committed by anemic Bohemians. From the few moments he is exposed in the sickroom, he contracts the disease and quickly dies, while Sophie demonstrates her strength of character not just by conquering diphtheria, but by realizing that ultimately she desires neither Bohemian decadence or earnest social responsibility (exemplified by another male admirer), but a comfortable life of suburban convention: "My idea of love's realization lies in this dream of a cottage on a calm hill—a cottage white with green blinds and a garden fenced in with fresh-smelling white-washed palings" (Aug. 10, 28). Despite the wholesale stereotyping of the "near-poet," the story's main goal is to use poetry's reputation for effete pointlessness as a foil for defining a wholesome, plucky normality for modern America.

The *Post's* rejection of the conventions of nineteenth-century poetry, its piety and sentimentalism on the one hand, its decadence and worldly uselessness on the other, was not unrelated to modernist poets' critiques of their predecessors beginning in the 1910s. But as the 1907 publication of "In Nineteen Hundred and Now" by Edmund Vance Cooke made clear, the *Post* was totally uninterested in moving past that rejection toward an affirmative account of poetic value adequate to the twentieth century. Cooke's poem farcically reduced the canonical luminaries of English-language poetry to fodder for humorous rhyming couplets ("Shelley's a sealed-up book, and Byron / Is chiefly recalled as a masculine siren"). Poets, if remembered at all, were now noted for their other pursuits, like fiction (Scott, who "is forgiven his rhymes / Because of his tales of stirring times"), drama (Shakespeare, read less than seen on stage), even furniture design (Morris, whose "fame will wear / As a practical man who made a chair"). This poem concedes so little value to past canons that even Chaucer is forced to "own his tongue / Was the broken speech of the land when young." The speaker resolves ultimately to "throw the stylus away and set / Myself at the typewriter alphabet / To spell some message" that will penetrate the "rawhide skin" of contemporary audiences. To the poem's central question—"Then why should a poet make his bow / In the year of nineteen hundred and now?"—the *Post* has a smugly confident answer: don't bother.

While Cooke likely did not subscribe to the literal sentiments of the poem, whatever satiric purpose he intended was redefined by its appearance in the *Post;* in that context, it would hardly have provoked many readers to reconsider their attitudes toward poetry. Instead they would have read it as conceding what their Saturday-evening reading consistently encouraged them to believe: that poetry was a thing of the past, with no value in the alienated eternal present of "nineteen hundred and now." In the magazine's placing of these briefer verses in a section called "Sense and Nonsense," poetry became a species of humorous frivolity, redeemable into (common) sense only by lampooning its conventional role in an obsolete elite culture. Much more than its competitors, the *Saturday Evening Post* used poetry to advance an ideology of philistine modernity masquerading as commonsense camaraderie among Americans of wholesome normative values. Its readers were offered a modern Faustian bargain: a sense of self-validation within a mainstream national culture, in exchange for the self-alienating experience of taking dictation from the disembodied voices of corporate capitalism; or in Cooke's terms, their individual styli in exchange for mass-produced typewriters. The scorn heaped by the *Post* upon the quiescent literary elite of the 1900s would ultimately energize a poetic avant-garde far more radically antibourgeois than anything the magazine faced when it began its colonization of the American middlebrow. Until 1910, however, its ridicule would go largely uncontested.

"IT'S TOO SLOW FOR ME HERE"

Another frankly commercialized genre, the popular song, posed an even more forceful challenge to American poetry's status during these years. The song lyric instantly supplied most of the pleasures of poetry—memorability, verbal wit, rhythmic energy—as an alluring alternative to anyone beguiled by verse, yet disaffected from the inhibitions and pretensions of elite culture. Song sheets had been available for decades, but high prices (25 to 60 cents) had limited their circulation (Jackson 2). In the last decade of the century, costs dropped much as magazine prices were doing, and the consumption of songs exploded on a scale beyond anything literary poetry had achieved. The marketing of popular songs reached a truly mass scale in 1892–1893 with the stunning success of Charles K. Harris's "After the Ball," which would ultimately sell several million copies.[21] "After the Ball" was a watershed moment for American mass culture. In the two decades that followed, poetry's crisis was exacerbated by the surging popularity of two types of popular song: sentimental lyrics that resituated Fireside subject matter into mass-cultural contexts, and paeans to the pleasures of urban modernity that dismissed the genteel worldview as obsolete.

Since the middle of the century, hymns and sentimental consolation songs had served some of the same emotional and ideological functions as moralistic genteel verse.[22] Richard Jackson argues, for example, that myriad songs about death and angels served as "genteel devices to stimulate feeling among middle- and upper-class Victorians safely within their comfortably upholstered and gaslit homes" (29). But even in the genteel consensus before 1890, the economics of song production had begun to construct mass-cultural space as profoundly secular. As early as the 1860s, a hybrid form of consolation appeared in both hymn book and sheet music formats (Jackson 1–8). By the 1880s, mostly detached from the hymn book, secular songs were encroaching into the ideological and economic territory of genteel poetry, competing with its domestic functions, offering most of its nostalgic, pastoral pleasures, plus a catchy tune. One of the earliest classics of the modern popular song, "Love's Old Sweet Song" (1884; words by G. Clifton Bingham), presented purchasers with a compendium of Fireside images and attitudes, from the self-conscious nostalgia of its first line ("Once in the dear dead days beyond recall") to the hearthside setting of its sentimental chorus:

> Just a song at twilight, when the lights are low,
> And the flick'ring shadows softly come and go;
> Tho' the heart be weary, sad the day and long,
> Still to us at twilight comes Love's old song,
> Comes Love's old sweet song.

Similarly, Paul Dresser's "On the Banks of the Wabash, Far Away" (1897) begins with a characteristic Fireside fusion of nostalgic and pastoral ("Oftentimes my tho'ts revert to scenes of childhood, / Where I first received my lessons—Nature's school").[23] By the end of the first verse, the song has sounded the same mourning note for lost loved ones heard in *Snow-Bound:*

> But one thing is missing in the picture,
> Without her face it seems so incomplete,
> I long to see my mother in the doorway,
> As she stood there years ago, her boy to greet.

The second verse contains a quintessential phrase of Fireside-style nostalgia, "Long years have passed," which can also be found in "After the Ball."[24] These deployments of the sentimental placeholders of Fireside verse proposed to consumers that they could effortlessly transfer allegiance from elite to mass culture. "On the Banks of the Wabash," Dresser's greatest hit, was adopted as Indiana's state song in 1913, signaling a level of official institutional endorsement for mass-marketed commodities previously reserved for the products of elite culture.

Colonizing poetry's best-loved modes was just one of the challenges presented by popular song. Song also became a laboratory for developing a tone of jocular ridicule towards "elitist" culture that came to characterize much twentieth-century American popular culture. The 1893 number "The Poet's Morn" (words by Walter S. Bigelow, music by Charles Webber) revealed in its three short stanzas how poetry was viewed in the world of mass culture. Sardonically labeled "Allegro moderato—Grandioso," the song exploits a simple but humorous contrast between the poet's high-flown language and grandiose aspirations, and the embarrassingly mundane texture of his actual existence:

> The sun in martial splendor rose
> And put the shades of night to rout;
> I lightly leaped from my repose,
> I lightly leaped from my repose,
> I lightly leaped from my repose——
> And let the chickens out.

The poet is marshaling his lofty language in vain, since he really has nothing to say, an emptiness reinforced by the threefold repetition of each stanza's penultimate line. The final verse reiterates the infinite deferment of the poet's ambitions: "Ah, how Aurora's coursers speed! / Roll on, triumphant chariot, roll! / I'll follow on my wingèd steed—/ . . . / When I've put on the coal." For turn-of-the-century songwriters, many of them self-made cultural entrepreneurs well acquainted with coal scuttles and chicken coops, elite poetry meant little more than "gazing into space," a phrase used in the second stanza to describe the poet's typical posture.

"The Poet's Morn" was unusual among turn-of-the-century songs in directly lampooning the unworldliness and frivolity of genteel poetry. The more usual response was to reject genteel values for a very different conception of culture, inviting readers to do the same. In the 1890s the popular song underwent a decisive shift toward subject matter that celebrated ideologies of hedonist consumption and reflected the dramatic growth of leisure activities enjoyed in public spaces rather than at home, as poetry had generally been.[25] Many of these sites of modern leisure—dance halls, amusement parks, resorts, sporting events—offered opportunities for performing and hearing popular songs, and all provided subject matter for them. The originating song of American mass culture, "After the Ball," was itself associated with these developments in urban leisure, having been launched into its unprecedented popularity at the Columbian Exposition in Chicago, from which people from all parts of the country returned home with copies to play for their friends (G. Tompkins 747). As an 1895 article about the song phenomenon suggested, not

Figure 2. *Cairo Street, on the Midway. World's Columbian Exposition, Chicago, 1893. Author's collection.*

only song lyrics but the conditions of their production glamorized the racy charms of a modern world of leisure, temptation, risk, and windfall: "the element of speculation in [the songwriters'] calling . . . is, in its way, as fascinating as horse racing or dealing in stocks" (Jarrold 289). This emergent view of leisure made the poetry of genteel moral respectability seem stodgy and obsolete.

The Columbian Exposition provided subject matter for songs as well, though doubtless not the sort that its high-minded genteel organizers had in mind. Frank Briscoe's "On Midway Plaisance" (1893), written for and about the fairgoers, exhibits the inexorable pull of secular popular culture upon the song genre. The first verse disposes of the official exposition, as the speaker says wearily, "I hit the free lunch counters in the Agricultural Hall, / In the Lib'ral arts I looked at the junk in every stall, / Electricity, Machinery, watched the bands and fountains play." The music comments amusingly on the boredom that the speaker, and presumably listeners, felt at the edifications of the White City: the three lines just quoted are written to be sung in monotonous repeated notes, one per syllable (seventeen consecutive F sharps, followed by sixteen As and fourteen Bs). When the speaker is finally done with enlightened gentility and sings, "And then I buckled on my skates and headed for Midway," the vocal line becomes varied and sinuous, a palpable relief after the preceding melodic rigidity. In the four verses that follow, the speaker is enticed into one dubious encounter after another on the Midway, in the Javanese town, the "Moorish Palace," and before "an Alpine panorama or two"; and always he is lured by the promise of exotic beauties, who turn out to be "the belle Française from Paris, Ohio, / And the Russian belle from downtown, / and the Greek from Kalamazoo." As he recounts with cynical good nature the various ways in which "A wad it takes to see the fakes," the speaker remains conscious of both Midway's fakery and the genuine heterogeneity offered by its "motley crowd" ("The Arabs, Turks, the beauty show, / The Irish natives in Cairo, The old Johore of Bungalow").[26] Eventually arriving disoriented and exhausted at "Old Vienna" beer garden, he imbibes too much, "raise[s] a rumpus, sasse[s] a guard," and ends up in the drunk tank.

"On Midway Plaisance" happily participates in the Midway's tendency to "erotically charged commercialism" (Rydell 166) and never seriously questions the Orientalist stereotyping behind many of its "ethnographic" attractions, which have been analyzed exhaustively by Robert Rydell (157–69). But the song does resoundingly validate the spectacle of modern popular culture, as the speaker's catalogue of mock outrages to his decency is exploded by its final line, which demonstrates that despite all the moral chicanery and disconcerting social otherness he has encountered, his enthusiasm remains undampened: "And all night within the cooler did I think about Midway." Naming real Midway attractions, the song was no abstract meditation upon the idea of a world's fair, but an advertisement and a map for actual fairgoing. It promised listeners considering a possible expedition to Jackson Park that even in the worst-case scenario, winding up their visit incarcerated, they would have an unforgettable time—provided they didn't waste all their energies on the White City but concentrated them on the Midway.

The song craze that followed the success of "After the Ball" was peppered by a rhetoric of democratization claiming that mass markets had leveled the playing field, allowing people with little musical or economic capital to empower themselves as cultural entrepreneurs. This myth was easily supported by numerous stories of overnight success among songwriters (Dreiser, "Whence" 57–60). Indeed, in "The Birth and Growth of a Popular Song," Theodore Dreiser remarked whimsically that "almost every one has, at some time or other, ventured the task of writing a popular song . . . without knowing much or anything" of the

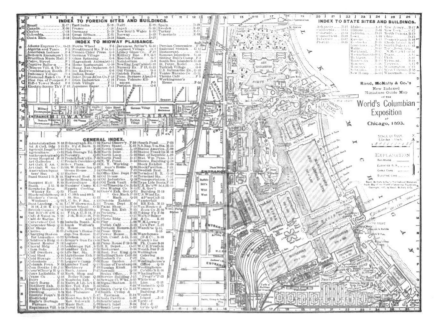

Figure 3. New Indexed Miniature Guide Map of the World's Columbian Exposition at Chicago, 1893. *Rand McNally, 1893. Author's collection.*

practical logistics of the business (19). Despite cautioning that failures far outnumbered successes, Dreiser ultimately reinforced this vision of democratized mass culture by claiming that the words of "On the Banks of the Wabash," on which he had collaborated with his brother, "were written in less than an hour" and the music in little more ("Birth and Growth" 19). Taken at face value, such a remark dangled that possibility in front of all literate Americans, even those exhausting themselves six days a week at some dismal job. They could always write songs on the seventh.

From the mid-1890s, popular songs took up a markedly secular cultural space, offering an alluring alternative to the restrictive parochialism of genteel culture. Many took liberties that Fireside verse didn't dream of, such as acknowledging changes in sexual mores as in "My Downtown Girl" (1905) and "Without a Wedding Ring" (1906). Others offered their listeners ways of comprehending momentous current events such as assassinations ("Our Martyred President" [1901]), disasters ("The Iroquois on Fire" [1904], "The Ruins of San Francisco" [1906]), and international conflicts ("Remember the *Maine*" [1898], "When America Is Captured by the Japs" [1905]). Whether these songs were cashing in on human misfortune or peddling world's fairs or Oldsmobiles, their exploitative aspects are obvious. But they shouldn't be dismissed merely as cynical rip-offs of the audiences that embraced them so eagerly. Relative to most poetry of the era, popular songs demonstrated a much more direct responsiveness to such key social dynamics of modernity as the changing position of women, the globalization of politics, the growing role of leisure and consumerism in American life, and the complex significance of machine-age technologies.

One very widespread subgenre of song, which included "After the Ball," invited readers to enjoy new forms of leisure, especially those involving notably freer public interaction between the sexes. Such songs celebrated strolling, cycling, or driving ("The Sidewalks of New York" [1894], "Bicycle Built for Two" [1892], and "In My Merry Oldsmobile" [1905]); trolley and even subway riding ("Hold Fast!" [1901], "On a Good Old Trolley Ride [1904], "Come Take a Ride Underground" [1904], "Take a Car" [1905]); going to music halls and nightclubs ("Waltz Me Around Again Willie" [1906], "Yip-I-Addy-I-Ay" [1908], "Take Me to the Cabaret" [1912]); to baseball games ("Take Me Out to the Ball Game" [1908] and many others); to amusement and picnic parks, fairs, and exhibitions ("Meet Me in St. Louis, Louis" [1904], "Wait Till the Sun Shines, Nellie" [1905], "With Mary Ann on a Merry-Go-Round" [1907]); and to the seashore ("Down at Rockaway," "Dreamland for Mine," and "Dear Old Luna Park" [all 1904], "On the Pier at Dreamland" [1906], "Meet Me on the Boardwalk, Dearie" [1909]). Like "On Midway Plaisance," these songs inform prospective audiences of the pleasures and accessibility of new forms of leisure, and literally invite them to see for themselves.

Will Dillon's "Take Me to the Cabaret" is a typical example of this invitational genre, beginning with a description aimed at those unfamiliar with this ultramodern site of fashionable leisure:

> Have you ever heard about the Cabaret,
> It's a big café where they sing and play.
> Dancing, prancing all the latest styles,
> 'Round the tables, up and down the aisles[?]

The invitational rhetoric then moves from description toward frank enticement, with intimations of the unending pleasures to be found there: "You will find there's some thing doing all the time, / Until the break of day. / That's the place to roam, / No one has a home, / When they reach the Cabaret." This last move, substituting mass-marketed leisure for domestic comfort and stable emotional roots, measures how much American morés had already changed before the avant-gardists of the 1910s brought those changes into the discourses of elite culture. The idea of alienation from home, which would have appalled listeners of the mid-nineteenth century perhaps above all else, is now blithely celebrated as we enter the chorus: "Take me to the Cabaret, / Take me there and let me stay." The second verse amplifies this cheerful modern rootlessness by parodying the genteel convention of the lost loved one, in the person of a man who disappears for a month before finally being tracked down by the police. Rather than go back to his frantic wife, however, he begs the police, "Please don't take me home, / Take me to the Cabaret"—now the closest thing to a home that he can imagine wanting.

Some sort of invitational structure is implicit in many of the era's most memorable songs, whether delivered by an authoritative male persona or by a newly emboldened female voice no longer content to wait upon a suitor's pleasure. Probably the best known and loved of these invitations is "Take Me Out to the Ball Game" (words by Jack Norworth, music by Albert von Tilzer), which owes much of its appeal to its narrator Katie Casey, a quintessentially modern figure of attractive female forwardness. Katie knows where she wants to spend her leisure time, chooses how to spend her own money (blowing "Ev'ry sou" at the ballpark), and relishes such unladylike snacks as "peanuts and crackerjack." When she invites her beau to "take me out with the crowd," she means it: going to the ball game for her is a fully participatory experience in an emerging public sphere sponsored by entrepreneurial mass culture, from which she wishes she might "never get back." She enjoys easily familiar relations with the players (knows them "by their first names"), rouses the crowd to sing encouragement to the home team in tight contests, and fearlessly voices her opinions and enthusiasm throughout the game: "Told the umpire he was wrong, / all along, good and strong." That the song endorses such behavior as "good and strong" depends on Katie's willingness to spend her money on forms of contemporary leisure. But if she's the perfect consumer of mass culture, she can also be read as a representation of the "new woman" asserting herself not just at ball games but in electoral politics, public health, education, social work, athletics, and every other arena of American public life.

Popular song's effort to articulate a distinctively modern paradigm of cultural value can be charted by examining songs that yearned for modern mass society while also clinging to the elevated tonalities of genteel culture, a combination capable of bizarre, even grotesque, effects. One has to marvel at the reach, if not the grasp, of songs like Charles Harris's "Hello Central, Give Me Heaven" (1901), which grafts an attitude of pious sentimentality upon a machine-age culture of pervasive

Figure 4. *Cover illustration to "Hello Central, Give Me Heaven." Words and music by Charles K. Harris, 1901. The Lester S. Levy Collection of Sheet Music, Special Collections, The Milton S. Eisenhower Library of The Johns Hopkins University.*

commodification and rapid technological change. "Hello Central, Give Me Heaven" transplants one of the heartrending scenarios of genteel poetry—a child losing a beloved mother—into an ultramodern telephonic context. The sheet music's artwork enhances this fusion by depicting a row of female operators busily plugging wires into the bank of connections, mirrored by another group of shadowy female figures representing angels inhabiting heaven.

To comfort herself and her father, who has "not smiled" once "Since dear mama's gone to heaven," the little girl concludes that she will

call her—through the telephone;

Hello Central, give me heaven,
For my mama's there
You can find her with the angels on the golden stair.

Equally adept in the metaphoric conventions of genteel sentimentalism ("golden stair") and the lingo of contemporary communications technology ("Hello Central"), this child is rewarded (if that's the right word) by connection with a sympathetic operator, whose response maintains the fantastic combination of technological and spiritual to the end of the song: "How her heart thrilled in that moment, / And the wires seemed to moan; / I will answer just to please her, / Yes, dear heart, I'll soon come home." Like the child, the operator is still capable of empathy even while performing in the mechanized and modernized world; she even perceives an empathetic charge through the wires! Adaptations of literary convention this outré (and yet not parodic) dramatize the residual lure of the genteel, but even more, the growing difficulty of maintaining familiar sentimental conventions by the turn of the century.

"Hold Fast!" (1901, words by William Jerome, music by Jean Schwartz), an evocation of big-city trolley riding, is less conflicted in its willingness to negotiate a permanent transition between genteel and modern paradigms of cultural value. Still, it too begins by nodding to the impulse to cling to escapist domesticity, complaining about the jostling, rootless textures of urban modernity: "It seemed as if nobody had a home, / I wonder why we ever care to roam." But the song's chorus veers away from fastidious piety, toward what Berman calls a "primal modern scene" (152), as the exhilarating physical pleasures offered by the trolley ride whirl away all grumbling at the psychosocial consequences of new technologies:

Hold! Fast! don't you lose your nerve!
Grab your lady by the arm we're going 'round the curve!
Keep your wits about you and you'll never get a jar,
If you listen to the man who runs a trolley car!
(Qtd. Levy 76–77)

The song cleverly redefines the virtues of being "fast" away from stability and immobility toward vertiginous motion (and, inviting its listeners to grab those next to them, toward unregulated sexuality as well). In doing so it registers the engaged urban modernism outlined by Baudelaire, who "shows how modern city life forces these new moves on everyone," but "also paradoxically enforces new modes of freedom,"

Figure 5. *Cover illustration to "Hold Fast!" Words by William Jerome; music by Jean Schwartz, 1901. The Lester S. Levy Collection of Sheet music, Special Collections, The Milton S. Eisenhower Library of The Johns Hopkins University.*

since anyone "who knows how to move in and around and through the traffic can go anywhere, down any of the endless urban corridors" (Berman 159–60). "Hold Fast!" contains just such a figure fully at home in modern urban space, "the man who runs a trolley car." Even more than the kind-hearted telephone operator of "Hello Central," this trolley driver, liberated from all genteel empathy, is defined by his impersonal competence with new technologies, rapid movement, and the modern subjects who attend him. The song validates him as the quintessential guide to modernity, redirecting the source of cultural authority away from those older sages Americans once "listened to" at home.

Berman notes that the spatial mobility of urban modernity "opens up a great wealth of new experiences and activities for the masses" (160). How surprising can it be that the American "masses," suddenly offered cultural genres validating such new experiences as trolley, subway, and amusement riding, responded with an enthusiasm that the pious edifications of genteel poetry had never provoked? The opening of the New York City subway system in October 1904 inspired a cluster of songs celebrating the physical, emotional, and social mobility promised by modern technologies of urban transport. "Come Take a Ride Underground" (words by Edward Laska, music by Thomas W. Kelley) evaluates the wealth of transportation technologies now available, from skates and bicycles to autos and steamships, ultimately announcing that "the greatest of rides has been found":

> I don't care to fly in the air,
> Looping the Loop can go back and sit down,
> Now there is but one way,
> And that is the subway,
> So come take a ride underground.

The psychic dynamics of leisure and urban transport are explored further by the speaker of "On a Good Old Trolley Ride" (words by Joseph C. Farrell, music by Pat Rooney), who describes an urban Sunday built around sampling different modes of leisure, such as "watching the spooners" in the park. But the "pleasure" that he most "treasures" is "speeding along on the trolley," which for five cents enables him to "feel like a big millionaire," an exchange he is quite happy to make. The most revealing moment of all is his punning conclusion that "Whatever you give up is fare"; here the trolley converts fairness—older values of ethical uprightness and beauty—into *fare-ness*, a condition of modernity driven by fantasies of economic aggrandizement and erotic titillation, and available at bargain prices: "The trolley's a hummer in summer, / If you've got a girl at your side, / To tease in the breeze, / While you're stealing a squeeze, / On a good five-cent trolley ride."

Such songs articulate the powerful allure of the urban landscape that the era's poetry resisted addressing. Even for the suburban married couple of "Take a Car" (1905; words and music by Rose and Snyder), who are intent upon more sedate pleasures, the elaborated transportation system of the modern metropolis offers a wealth of cheap leisure opportunity. Wondering "where shall we go, / In the summer time?" Claudie is reminded by Maudie that although they "need all we've got for a house and a lot," they can still "take a car" to traverse any metropolitan distance, at any hour, while still enjoying the summer weather ("in daylight or twilight, in starlight or skylight"). The evocative illustration to

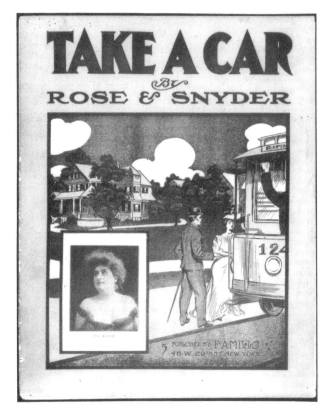

Figure 6. *Cover illustration to "Take a Car." Words and music by Rose and Snyder, 1905. The Lester S. Levy Collection of Sheet music, Special Collections, The Milton S. Eisenhower Library of The Johns Hopkins University.*

the song depicts a young couple in their summer finery boarding a trolley car in the far right of the frame.

Here the conductor, the human agent of urbanism, is almost effaced but plays a crucial role nonetheless. Though all we see is his raised arm and hand upon the bell pull, this snippet of visual information draws our attention to the bell as an invitational signifier of urbanism to the suburban subject, an emphasis reinforced by the song's final line, "All on, ding-ding, take a car, take a car." Most of the image is devoted to the spacious and lushly landscaped "house and lot" that Claudie and Maudie are shifting so diligently to keep. This palpably idealized scene is most interesting, because unlike the more jagged contrasts between urban dystopia and suburban refuge that would dominate twentieth-century American popular culture, it still endorses metropolitan pleasures, even while apotheosizing suburban comfort. This balancing act is made symbolically possible by the trolley's physical ability to bridge these two realms.[27]

Song's ability to dramatize the shift from genteel-elite to mass-market values was seen most vividly of all by the biggest hit of 1904, "Meet Me in St. Louis, Louis" (music by Kerry Mills, lyrics by Andrew B. Sterling). Created, like "On Midway Plaisance," to celebrate and advertise a world's fair, "Meet Me in St. Louis, Louis" begins by systematically neutralizing nineteenth-century ideals of gender relations, domesticity, and cultural authority.

> When Louis came home to the flat,
> He hung up his coat and his hat,
> He gazed all around, but no wifey he found,
> So he said "where can Flossie be at?"
> A note on the table he spied,
> He read it just once, then he cried,
> It ran, "Louis dear, it's too slow for me here,
> So I think I will go for a ride"—

and hence into the chorus, where Flossie promises that they will "dance the Hoochee Koochee" but only "If you will meet me in St. Louis, Louis, / Meet me at the fair!" This flouting of genteel domestic convention was no doubt made more comprehensible to bourgeois audiences by the identification of Louis and Flossie with an urban working class (through his ethnically inflected name, class-inflected speech, and housing circumstances). But the song speaks at least as much to changing gender relations as to conventional class prejudices. Offering yet another invitation to revel in the spectacle of mass consumer culture, it endorses emerging models of behavior and transportation technologies that allow women to travel alone between cities purely for their own pleasure, with little care for conjugal duty. Louis may "cry" like a deserted husband upon first reading the note, but clearly, given the promise of being Flossie's "tootsie wootsie" in the city, his next move is to check for upcoming trains.

By the song's final verse, skepticism toward the forms and authority figures of pious genteel culture has penetrated far into the middle classes, in the person of a restless churchgoer who finds the rituals of WASP gentility too slow:

> In church sat a man near the door,
> asleep, he was starting to snore,

The Minister rose, and he said,
"We will close singing, Meet on the Beautiful Shore."
The man in the back then awoke,
he caught the last words that he spoke;
He said, "Parson White, you can meet me alright,
but The Beautiful Shore is a joke."

The specific satiric target of these lines is one of the enduring classics of the popular song as hymn, "Sweet By and By" (1867; words and music by J. P. Webster), which celebrates the eventual arrival of pious souls upon the "beautiful shore" of the Christian afterlife. This reluctant modern churchgoer clearly prefers the sweet here and now on the banks of the Mississippi. The verse's last lines flirt with outright blasphemy in their rejection of genteel pieties, as he avows he will be in St. Louis "waiting at the station, for the whole darned congregation."[28] Sterling's lyrics ingeniously reenact popular song's transition during the previous decades, simultaneously evoking and rejecting earlier associations with hymns to be sung in church, eventually announcing its unabashed participation in a secular realm of mass culture. This insistence is stated with bald good humor by the chorus: "Meet me in St. Louis, Louis, meet me at the fair, / Don't tell me the lights are shining any place but there." No golden stair, no angelic light, anywhere but at the world's fair, one of whose symbolic functions can be read precisely as modern consumerism's secular substitute for heaven: a strongly iconic spatial realm, self-consciously distanced from previous dimensions of experience, promising unending fulfillment of all one's desires (until the money runs out, anyway).

By 1900, exploring new technologies and changing social dynamics, immersing its consumers in the pleasures of the present, popular song had become a potent counter-discourse to the pious timelessness of genteel poetry. On the other hand, as a form of inefficient, even frivolous play, song also challenged the gospel of utilitarian efficiency spread by the captains of the positivist culture industry like Edward Bok and H. E. Warner, who aspired to reshape all expressive forms, even language itself, on the dreary model of shorthand. Like "Meet Me in St. Louis, Louis," many mass-culture songs hit transgressive notes against sources of religious, corporate, civil, and moral authority. These transgressions almost never become revolutionary, but many do subvert inhibiting conventions and make progressive alternatives imaginable. Song's contradictory but often subversive immersion in modernity was exemplified by "Plain Little Ann" (lyrics by Juliet Wilbor Tompkins), published in

Munsey's in 1896. This song's speaker recounts a discussion of prospective brides with his male friends; all the others opt for resplendent trophy wives, who quickly take on the vices of vanity, self-absorption, and bad temper that follow from their overbred beauty. The wise speaker, however, weds "plain little freckle-faced Ann," who outshines all the others as companion ("She's a chum for a holiday journey"), lover ("A sweetheart to come to at night"), and domestic angel (who will "Nurse me herself, were I ill") (J. Tompkins 77–79). What makes the song notable in the context of the era's gender assumptions is that Ann is not limited to these domestic roles, but is also fully at home in the world of capitalist modernity as "A clear-headed, clever attorney" who, "When something comes up to set right, / [would] run my affairs and make money" (78). Despite its crass celebration of making money and the continued gender imbalance implied by "my affairs," "Plain Little Ann" still challenged its listeners to imagine a wider scope of professional identity for women.

Song's explosive popularity from the mid-1890s foreclosed any chance of broadening poetry's readership further down the economic scale, as had happened in fiction. Popular song was seldom perceived by contemporary commentators to be directly competing with poetry or diluting its cultural appeal, although in the mid-1890s *Munsey's* tried publishing sheet music on such familiar song topics as modern love ("Plain Little Ann") and sport (Tompkins's "The Winning Touchdown"), as well as more traditional verse. But many commentators drew evaluative oppositions between popular songs and elite musical forms such as the art song, which often employed genteel verse; thus Wagner scholar Henry T. Finck's remark that "I would not give one of MacDowell's or Schubert's songs for all of [Stephen] Foster's." Had Foster, like the leading American composer of the day, Edward MacDowell, "revelled in the harmonic world explored by Bach, Schubert, Chopin, Wagner, Liszt, and Grieg, no minstrel would ever have spread his songs over the country" (303). However, despite Foster's harmonies, which were "not only simple but crude," he was still worthy of "great respect" in showing "that an air need not necessarily be trashy and vulgar to be beloved of the multitude"—unlike the vast majority of popular songs, which Finck repeatedly tarred with these same two epithets (except, hilariously, for a number called "Shoo Fly," which "though vulgar, is not trashy") (303–04). Foster's songs were also notable in surviving past the moment of their initial consumption, unlike most hits, which "shoot like comets across the sky where all can see them and then vanish forever" (304).

This last remark suggests that song may have affected the status of poetry most profoundly in challenging elite culture's adherence to the values of permanence and authorial identity, and in asserting ephemerality and anonymity as central criteria of American verse production. The relatively anonymous creation of song particularly assailed the primacy of individual authorship, since, as one commentator noted, "In literature, as we know, the name upon the title page counts for a good deal; while the world will whistle an air and stop for breath, perhaps, but seldom to inquire who wrote the melody" (G. Tompkins 746). For some the genre was even inimical to artistic individualism, since, according to Brian Hooker, "most great songs have not been written by great poets nor set by great musicians, but by lesser artists, oftentimes unknown"; on the other hand, "It is hard for a creative genius to subvert his mighty personality or to compromise the native scope of his particular art" ("Songs and Song-Writing" 428). Many commentators, including Hooker, deplored the effects of mass marketing on aesthetic value. Still, the very existence of an article discussing "great songs" called into question whether clear distinctions between the individualized art object and the mass-marketed commodity could be maintained in a rapidly modernizing culture.

Watching anonymity and ephemerality emerge as important concepts in the discourse of cultural value, many predicted a quickening cycle of production, consumption, and obsolescence, as in this 1902 remark: "On the whole, hits seem to be growing shorter lived than they used to be. Floods of new melodies run out the old ones with scant ceremony" (G. Tompkins 748). The status of song as instantly consumable, endlessly reproducible, and quickly forgettable commodity was used by Gelett Burgess in *The Rubaiyat of Omar Cayenne* (1904) as a key symptom of the disarray of contemporary literary culture:

> YESTERDAY'S *This* Day's popular Song supplants;
> TO-MORROW'S will be even worse, perchance
> . . . .
>
> The Song had caught a Rag-Time girls could shout
> And Piano-Organs make a Din about;
> But syncopated Melodies at last
> Will pass away, and more shall come, no doubt. (23–24)

This accelerating cycle of "immediate forgetfulness" (Peck 98) augured the erosion of any more permanent cultural heritage. Against the endless procession of "syncopated melodies" of the moment, Burgess wondered how "the vagrant singer" (that is, poet) could possibly "compete with such a money-making Horde / Of tinsel rhymesters that infest the shops" (20). The advent of song was most threatening, then, in destabilizing the dichotomy of *popular* and *canonical* as a model for understanding the value of cultural products such as poetry. It evoked a possible future in which the very category of the canonical, valorizing individual authority and celebrating the permanence of great works, would no longer be available—an alarming prospect for the embattled cultural elite of a capitalist democracy in which money already seemed to call nearly every tune.

3

PERISHED CELEBRITIES AND SECRET DOORS

Modern Verse as Waste Paper

The pressure exerted by emerging genres and values of mass culture had complex effects on American poetry. As I'll detail in part 3, this pressure challenged some turn-of-the-century poets to productive engagement with urban-industrial modernity, a necessary step toward a vigorous modern poetics. But the spiraling mutual contempt between elite and mass culture also threatened devastating consequences for the future of verse in the United States, as most of poetry's institutional custodians refused the implications of mass culture's rise, preferring to remain safely sealed in their genteel ghetto. Between 1890 and 1910 these polarities generated pervasive anxiety over poetry's future, eluded only by those hard-hearted commentators who took its supposed obsolescence as a sign of a modernizing and maturing culture. The magazines of those decades are dotted with articles like "The Future of Poetry" (Charles L. Moore), "The Poet in an Age of Science" (C. J. Goodwin), "Poetry or Science?" (W. K. Brooks), "Have We Still Need of Poetry?" (Calvin Thomas), "The Lack of Poets," "Has Poetry Lost Its Hold on Us?" (W. D. Howells), "Current Neglect of Poetry" (H. W. Boynton), "Is Poetry Unpopular?," "The Rejection of Poetry," "Wanted: Poetry, Not Verse" (George P. Morris), "The Passing of Poetry" (Stephen Leacock), "The Need of Poets," "Is Poetry Read?"; and the most comprehensive denial of poetry's modern utility, H. E. Warner's "Will

Poetry Disappear?" In most of these, the genre's imminent end was at best imaginable, at worst expected.

Fear for poetry's future extended from aspiring young writers who found no welcoming interest in their work, to the most eminent figures of the late genteel elite such as E. C. Stedman and William Dean Howells. Most believed that the traditions of American poetry were exhausted, yet they felt powerful skepticism toward possible avenues of innovation and renewal. This impasse between tradition and innovation was not a simple contest between clearly defined partisans, but a paralytically self-conflicted discourse in which many earnestly professed a desire for experimentation in the abstract, yet wound up ferociously disparaging its actual instances. Aware of the declining influence of the Fireside canon, they doubted that any living writers could replace them, a paradox suggesting that the entire American literary tradition might be on the verge of extinction. Their complaints at the hackneyed imagery and stale technique of contemporary American poets mingled with their ridicule of newfangled and "bizarre" forms of expression being exploited by young irresponsibles who respected nothing. Their objections that American verse had become too democratized, encouraging redundant and frivolous work, collided with their bitter criticism of the literary establishment as an exclusive club uninterested in nurturing new approaches. They saw the increasing use of poetry as a fetishized prestige commodity coinciding with its almost complete loss of exchange value in nonelite cultural marketplaces. Many concluded that American poetry was becoming so much waste paper in modernity's immeasurable trash heaps.

As the century turned, only a very few commentators and poets had begun to articulate the stark choice poetry seemed to face: either open itself to the textures and problems of modern experience, or wither away in the suffocating embrace of the coterie. This chapter charts this climate of exhaustion and anxiety through a series of self-confuting formulations that revealed the conceptual poverty of those who most earnestly sought to maintain poetry's status as an elite form somehow beyond modernity's reach. By understanding this climate in which the young writers of part 3 began their careers, we can better understand their struggles and evaluate their achievements. We'll find that the introspective anguish of the period before 1910 was formative to a modern paradigm of cultural value based not on obeisance to stable universal values, but on continual self-remaking energized by the anxieties and instabilities of twentieth-century experience.

LAID ON THE TABLE

Few realized that any particular defense of poetry was necessary until its crisis of value was suddenly obvious soon after 1890, all the more startling since the Fireside writers still seemed securely canonical, their "preeminence . . . an item of national faith" that ostensibly "unified and sanctified their fellows," as Larzer Ziff puts it (15). By any comprehensible measure, their canonicity was unquestionable. Between 1884 and 1900, whenever literary publications polled their readers on the value of the nation's authors, the Fireside writers came out on top not just among poets, but across all categories.[1] In 1881 Longfellow's seventy-fourth birthday occasioned nationwide celebrations in American schools (Gioia 65), as did Whittier's eightieth in 1887 (Leary 13). In 1901 Emerson and Longfellow were inducted as original members of the Hall of Fame for Great Americans (Lowell and Whittier would be elected in their first year of eligibility in 1905, while Holmes and Bryant would join them in the third vote in 1910). The cover of a 1901 advertising brochure for Houghton Mifflin's ambitious new series of Standard Library Editions of American authors offered another clear indication of these poets' centrality, featuring an image of Longfellow at its center, ringed by Emerson, Holmes, Whittier, and Lowell (along with Hawthorne) (reproduced in Casper 179). The frontispiece of Edmund Clarence Stedman's comprehensive retrospective *An American Anthology, 1787–1900* (1900) offered busts of all the Fireside poets except Emerson, a photograph of whose grave appeared on the title page.[2]

But Stedman's curious use of modern technology to commemorate Emerson registered an increasing sense that this canon was of the past, as did the eligibility requirement for the Hall of Fame: to be dead for at least ten years. Stedman's frontispiece also included Whitman, Poe, and Sidney Lanier, indicating that the Fireside group had lost its exclusive hold on the American poetry canon. The dimming of the Fireside poets' canonical halos had been incipient as early as 1877, in Mark Twain's famously scandalous treatment of them at an *Atlantic Monthly* dinner honoring Whittier's seventieth birthday. Mark Twain's mock-Western fable about three roughs who call themselves Emerson, Longfellow, and Holmes as they abuse the hospitality of a lonely miner in the Sierras seemed calculated to affront an occasion that the *Boston Advertiser* described as having a "reverent, almost holy, air" (qtd. Fatout 110). Imbibing freely, cheating at cards, using lines of poetry to complain about the miner's food and accommodations, then to justify stealing his boots, these boorish "Fireside poets" exemplify none of the virtues the culture had invested in them. Mark Twain's most acute comment on their changing status comes when they begin to confuse their own work with that of the three absent members of the canon, "Emerson" erroneously laying claim to "Barbara Frietchie," "Longfellow" to *The Biglow Papers,* and "Holmes" to "Thanatopsis" (Clemens 113). Though he was a few years ahead of the cultural curve, Mark Twain perceived that Fireside canonicity was becoming "corporate rather than individual," as James H. Justus puts it (147), and therefore diminishing in force. Mark Twain's eventual recuperation of the men "to whom we and the world pay loving reverence and homage" by identifying the miscreants as "impostors" (Clemens 114) was also distinctly double-edged, since any suggestion of imposture to these figures, even in burlesque form, could be read as a coded insinuation that they were unworthy of reverence. Though in 1877 such disrespect could still create a "furor of indignation" that "overwhelmed Mark Twain with a sense of guilt" (Fatout 110), it augured a shift of canonical fault lines that would be fully underway by the early 1890s.

Between 1878, just after Mark Twain's transgression, when the first of the six died, and 1894, when the last of them went, the Fireside canon became one of the past. Ziff describes their last hurrah as living icons of American culture in 1887, when the surviving three presided as "the chief representatives of American literature" at a benefit for the American Copyright League (15). This was more than a purely symbolic correspondence. The long-awaited establishment of stable copyright laws culminated the construction of the individual American author as a central evaluative category; it was the Fireside poets, more than anyone, who had personified and benefited from this development. By 1887, however, the very reverence with which these figures were viewed, and their great age, evoked the ironic possibility that not only their day but the day of the individual American author was passing. This, coupled with the impending end of the century and the challenge of emerging mass culture, lent discussion of the Fireside poets in the 1890s a strongly reevaluative character and generated periodized accounts of American poetry that replaced moralistic genteel models of value with more modern aesthetic criteria.

This shift can be examined through a group of obituary commemorations published in *The Writer* in 1894. To many of the thirty-two contributors, the death of Oliver Wendell Holmes signified "the closing of an era in American literature" (Boyesen 162), the loss of "the last of our great nineteenth-century writers" (Roche 164), and the end of "the most brilliant period which American letters has known" (Bates 166). All the commentators were respectful toward Holmes and his fellows, but many used the occasion to examine the significance of this canon in notably dispassionate ways. Several took pains to distinguish between these poets' personal character and the aesthetic value of their work: "There was a richness and force of personality in these men which makes them delightful to contemplate, even apart from their achievements" (Boyesen 161). Mild as it sounds, this remark by H. H. Boyesen is quite important in showing the shift away from treating literature as a repository of ethical value and toward valuing it within a separate category of the aesthetic. Just thirteen years earlier, in "Character, and What Comes of It," Josiah Gilbert Holland had equated the value of the poets' work with their noble character as men ("value in character makes value in verse" [469]); now Boyesen and many contemporaries saw the two as quite distinct.[3] For Edward Eggleston too, Holmes's death was "The vanishing point of the old New England group of authors" (161). Eggleston clearly saw little melancholy in the waning of this New England canon. The "sobriety of purpose that gave a twilight glow of Puritan earnestness even to [their] lighter work" had been somewhat relieved by Hawthorne's "weird imagination," which "refused to draw in didactic harness," and by Holmes's "delightful vivacity and wit," "quite unknown" to the rest of them (161). The terms of this praise signal a shift away from Fireside-genteel values toward a multifarious modern conception of what makes literature valuable: originality, wit, irony, even weirdness if it refused didacticism and relieved earnestness, sobriety, humorlessness.

Even while the Fireside poets were being infused as canonical presences throughout American culture—as in their widespread presence in primary-school classrooms, which led to their other sobriquet, the Schoolroom Poets—their influence was becoming more attenuated and retrograde. After 1890 this was clear in a growing chorus of comments such as: "Our poets have been taken as read, they have been laid on the table; by a vote of the majority they are beyond discussion—they are American institutions" (Moore, "Future" 775). Thus "laid on the table," in Moore's double-edged estimation, the once-magical names of the Fireside poets were losing force as self-evident demonstrations of poetry's unique value. While their names still evoked an idealized national past, readers increasingly perceived that they had little to say about American life in the 1890s, despite all their claims to universality. Since the nation's poetry was so completely identified with this canonical configuration and its universalist understanding of value, as its writers seemed less compelling, the entire genre of poetry seemed to be in decline.

In his commemoration of Holmes, Arlo Bates went so far as to remark, "With the extinction of this group ends the continuity of literary tradition in America" (167), evoking the ironic possibility that this canonical monopoly had enfeebled the entire culture. Such remarks reveal that a central assumption about canons of literature and art—that they offer annealing continuity between past experience, present values, and future aspirations—had begun to break down. Yet despite the exhaustion of the forms, attitudes, and canons of earlier decades, these had not receded properly, but continued to inhibit poetry's contemporary power, as in this remark: "The recent publication in the *Atlantic Monthly* of a real poem by a real poet" (Lowell's "Endymion") "makes all contemporaneous magazine verse seem so worthless that the question naturally arises, why print it?" (Buckham 115). In his study of anthologies, Alan Golding demonstrates the remarkably "stable, self-perpetuating" character of American poetry evaluation between 1865 and the end of the 1880s, noting that Bryant, Whittier, and Emerson themselves produced influential anthologies between 1870 and 1875, all agreeing that "the six most important poets in America are themselves, Longfellow, Lowell, and Holmes" (18, 17). In such situations, when the canonical set the terms of (and even perform) their own evaluations, currents of restlessness and dissent often develop beneath apparently consensual surfaces and can eventually catalyze drastic shifts in the available paradigms of cultural value. Such a shift was fully mobilized by the mid-1890s.

Yet despite diminishing enthusiasm for the Fireside poets, the perceived plenitude and stability of the genteel canon continued to inhibit new accounts of poetry's value until well after 1910. H. E. Warner's 1899 argument consigning poetry to tomb and bookworm evoked this sense of canonical surfeit: "The result has been good indeed in former ages, but there is enough of it. Have we not all the treasures of the poet?" (Warner 288). Furthermore, according to Ferris Greenslet in 1899, it was now a "critical common-place" that appreciation of past traditions was inversely related to present accomplishment: those "fitted by temper and training to see visions and sing songs are too acutely conscious of all that has been beheld and sung; . . . they are awed before its extent and might, and their little creative impulse is hushed in humility and reverence" ("Propaganda" 42). I'll show in part 3 that some of the most challenging American poems of the 1890s, by Robinson, Crane, and others, grapple with exactly this anxiety: that reverence to tradition by those best trained and most desirous to enter it, might stifle rather than enrich creative energy.

In the *Dial* in 1904, the enervating effects of canonical plenitude were dramatized in an unsigned commentary called "The Rejection of Poetry," which began conventionally by noting the gap between past and present achievements: "The message of our older poets, it is true, has lost something of its timeliness with the lapse of years, and they have not found the successors that we could have wished; but we doubt greatly if a new Longfellow or a new Lowell could now become a real force in our national life" (354). The *Dial* writer pursued the implications of this gap until he or she had ruled out any appreciation whatsoever of contemporary poetry. The best present examples of the genre, overwhelmed by past canons, would no longer be able to demonstrate the value of poetry. Even "One of the noblest poems ever produced by an American writer," published just weeks earlier, faced inevitable oblivion: "We do not anticipate for it anything like popular vogue; its melody will fall upon ears deafened by the din of a material civilization, and its stately imaginings will find no general public sense attuned to their harmony" (354). The ironic decision to leave this "noble" work unnamed enforced the deafness of response predicted for it. The *Dial* thus put into play a set of impossible conditions of reception in which no contemporary work, regardless of quality, could compete with the exclusionary heft of the canon, which was itself in a state of continual weakening (presumably to end pickled in a jar like the ever-shriveling, never-dying Sibyl of *The Waste Land*).

This self-confuting view was not held just by a generation of restless, excluded young—though they did indeed hold it—but also by the most prominent bearers of the genteel torch like Stedman, whose work dramatizes a growing uneasiness with genteel accounts of poetry's value. As evidence of the constricted canons of the late genteel period, Golding notes that Stedman's *An American Anthology, 1787–1900* was the first new anthology "by a prestigious American editor" since 1875 (19). Stedman was well aware of this, and also that the end of the century demanded comprehensive retrospection. His preface outlined a periodized account of American poetry that acknowledged the central place of the Fireside poets, but asserted the present need to move away from them. Their emergence had ushered in a period of efflorescence in which "Poetry led other forms of our literature during at least forty years—say from 1835 to 1875" (AA xix). But then came a dramatic and unchecked decline in postwar American poetry and a diminution of the genre's cultural significance, so that now (echoing Warner), "Song is conceded to be the language of youth, the voice of primitive races,—whence an inference that its service in the English tongue is near an end" (AA xxxii).

Stedman blamed this decline partially on the overwhelming canonical influence of the Fireside poets, which he had complained about as early as 1885: "their very longevity, fitting and beautiful as it was, restrained the zeal and postponed the opportunities of pupils who held them in honor. Our common and becoming reverence prevented both the younger writers and the people from suspecting that these veterans were running in grooves and supplying little new; finally, when this was realized, and there was a more open field, it became evident that the public was satiated with verse and craved a change, not merely of poets, but to some new form of imaginative literature" (PA 438).

Much as he wished simply to lay them aside, however, Stedman felt compelled to protest the continuing "extension of the prerogative accorded to the 'elder poets,'" calling it "an innocent tyranny" (AA xvii). The detrimental effects of this canonical reverberation upon contemporary poetry were borne out in 1899 by another genteel eminence, William Dean Howells, who in a survey of recent verse remarked: "here, toward the end of what I have to say of the new poetry, I am tormented with an unhandsome misgiving that I have been making too much of it. . . . The names of the great poets who are gone recur to me dismayingly, almost accusingly. What are all the new Presences when confronted with such tremendous Absences . . . ? ("New Poetry" 591). Fraught with markers of accusation and confrontation, this passage suggests that Howells too felt oppressed by the tyranny of canonical obligation. He implied an evaluative imperative to the greats of the past that was demonstrable only by rejecting all "new Presences" as unworthy. His half-unwilling allegiance was not to still vital past works, but simply to "the names of the great poets," evoking the canon in its heaviest and most arbitrary sense, as a list of the sanctified few, maintained by some absent and unaccountable authority. Stedman and Howells were the two most admired and influential figures of American literary culture alive in 1900. If they felt this oppressed by the Fireside canon's lingering authority over American poetic culture, aspiring writers with no institutional authority had little hope of escaping its shadow.

PAN IS NOT DEAD!

Stedman's inclusion of Poe and Whitman in his pantheon indicates that the reevaluation of the Fireside poets was counterpointed by the growing canonicity of these two contemporaries who had been marginalized under the moralistic norms of earlier decades.[4] Poe and Whitman played central roles in the emergence of a postmoralist redefinition of poetic value after 1890. For Stedman, Poe provided a basis for understanding poetic value in terms of aesthetic achievement independent of restrictive moral frameworks, while Whitman established the value of a distinctly national poetry not limited to simplistic expressions of patriotic feeling or local description. A stronger poet than Longfellow, Poe had originated an aestheticist tradition for American poetry: he was "the eldest of the art-group," and "the first to revolt against didacticism, from the artist's point of view" (PA 56). In the 1890s Poe also served as the "role model" (Lutz 99) in Edgar Saltus's poetics of "decadence," which was undergirded by the relativist premise that "There is no criterion by which a story can be judged as moral or the reverse; there are but two classes of fiction—stories which are well-written and those which are not" (*Love and Lore* 45). Recasting the moralism of the genteel consensus not as the primary mission of literature, but as a set of practices designated by such increasingly derogatory terms as "propriety and purpose," Saltus advanced an aesthetic of defamiliarization and challenge in which "The first duty of a novelist is to irritate the reader" (78).[5] Poe was thus formative to a nascent avant-garde heritage of American writing based on the same model of aestheticist "revolt" against restrictive genteel moralism that the New Poetry would employ with such force after 1910. "Decadents" of the 1890s like Saltus and Gelett Burgess failed to have the shaping impact on American culture that later avant-gardes were assuredly to have. But they do demonstrate that a strain of literary value based on intrinsic aesthetic grounds had emerged in the United States well before 1900, and allow us to posit a greater continuity of engagement between turn-of-the-century modernity and American poetry than we have previously assumed.

If Stedman was important to Poe's late-century rise, he was also among the first to formulate a transcendentalist canon for American poetry by reorienting Emerson away from the Fireside group and toward Whitman. For him Emerson was a cultural progenitor who represented "such a union of spiritual and civic insight with dithyrambic genius as may not be seen again. His thought is now congenital throughout vast reaches, among new peoples scarcely conscious of its derivation" (AA xxiii)—very much as Whitman claimed in *Song of Myself* that he would eventually "filter and fibre" the blood of future Americans, even those unaware of his presence (93). Though not quite willing to place Whitman in this central role, Stedman valued his iconoclasm as a challenge to the complacent "art-tradition and conventionalism" of his day, which had made him an "apostle of the democracy of the future" (PA 56).

Equally important for Stedman was Whitman's assertion of the unique individual personality as the locus of poetic value: "No one more conspicuously shines by difference. Others are more widely read, but who else has been so widely talked of, and who has held even a few readers with so absolute a sway? Whatever we may think of his chantings, the time has gone by when it was possible to ignore him; whatever his ground may be, he has set his feet squarely and audaciously upon it, and is no light weight" (PA 349). Unlike less individual poets who "feel half-ashamed of their birthright" (PA 458), Whitman had maintained the courage of his convictions and established an integral linkage among individual personality, formal heterodoxy, and a distinctive national culture: unable "to work to advantage in the current mode, he concluded that the mode itself was at fault; especially, that the poet of a young, gigantic nation, the prophet of a new era, should have a new vehicle of song" (PA 376). In his treatment of Whitman, Stedman outlined a modern poetics taking originality and uniqueness as absolute values (to "shine by difference"), much as the Fireside poets and their readers had imputed absolute value to consensus-building moral universalism. In 1900 he astutely predicted that originality would be the central criterion for literary canonicity in the twentieth century:

> It is now pretty clear, notwithstanding the popularity of Longfellow in his day, that Emerson, Poe, and Whitman were those of our poets from whom the old world had most to learn; such is the worth, let the young writer note, of seeing inspiration from within, instead of copying the exquisite achievement of masters to whom we all resort for edification. . . . Our three most individual minstrels are now the most alive, resembling one another only in having each possessed the genius that originates. Years from now, it will be matter of fact that their influences were as lasting as those of any poets of this century. (AA xxiv)

A few other critics followed Stedman in embracing individual distinctiveness as a defining quality of modern poetic value. Richard Titherington's 1895 article in *Munsey's* celebrating Whitman as "The Good Gray Poet" was profusely illustrated with markers of individual canonicity: reproductions of the poet's residences, his handwriting, and likenesses at different times in his life. Titherington's most unusual canonizing strategy involved these likenesses, as he asserted that "in later life, [Whitman] bore a decided resemblance to Longfellow." Referring to an illustration of the latter published a few issues earlier, the author boldly equated the two: "Whitman's face is Longfellow's, scarred by years of toil and suffering that never fell to the peaceful lot of the New England bard" (145). This equation worked to Whitman's benefit in two ways, first establishing him as equal in stature to this pillar of national culture, then distinguishing them once again with the implication, never stated but implied throughout the article, that Whitman was the more genuine national poet, since the texture of his experience brought him closer to the lives of ordinary people than Longfellow's more privileged life could.

If a canonical halo was forming around Whitman, it was one whose very tarnish, marked by an ennobling "toil and suffering," could be taken as a source of genuine value. Such evaluations imputed to Whitman a distinctly modern ethical significance, the "courageous and self-sacrificing" patriotism of "a flannel-shirted man of the people, no respecter of dignitaries literary or civil, but honest and fearless and with the broad human sympathy of the greatest poets" (G. Morris 196; Greenslet, "Propaganda" 52–53). This persona of the dissident populist patriot implied an oppositional literature embodying "the best native ideals of America" (Greenslet, "Propaganda" 52): iconoclasm toward outworn traditions and benighted authority, empathy with social Others, and aspirations to an egalitarian society. This persona had lain nearly dormant since the abolitionist phase of Whittier's work but was beginning to emerge again in the verse of some younger poets such as Crane and Moody. By the 1910s it would become a central function of American poetry.

Still, however much the turn-of-the-century exhumation of past iconoclasts reconfirmed the inadequacy of Fireside tradition, the growing reputation of Poe and Whitman did not augur wide acceptance of innovation or originality in contemporary verse. On the contrary, those qualities provoked such distrust that they could be appreciated only in dead poets whose idiosyncrasy had been rendered comfortable by half a century of acquaintance. In effect, campaigns on behalf of these contemporaries of the Fireside poets displaced any efforts to canonize, or even appreciate, poets of succeeding generations.

Virtually all turn-of-the-century commentators perceived that the shift of the Fireside poets from contemporaries to classics, the "subjects of group portraits suitable for framing in the American home" (Ziff 17), had created a vacuum in American literary culture. Poets born between 1830 and 1860, who might have been celebrated as the living elders of American poetry, were instead enduring such dispiriting laments as this: "Where is the man among the survivors who in beauty of person and brightness of intellect can rival James Russell Lowell?" (Boyesen 162).[6] Even Stedman (born 1833), who felt an intense identification with the "cluster and train of younger celebrants" forced to walk in the starry path of the "hundred-houred" New England poets, conceded that they had failed to carry American poetry forward ("Proem" 303). The consensus was that these lost generations had produced little in the way of memorable verse and not a single poet of permanent value.

This consensual noncanonicity of the post-Fireside generations signaled not just the failure of individual reputations, but the eroding status of the whole genre. Images of decline and degeneration ran rampant through discussions of poetry between 1890 and 1910. This remark is typical: "The quality of magazine verse has grown so poor, and its substance so thin, that critics have ceased to regard it,—other than as dainty tail-pieces and convenient mechanical interludes" (Buckham 114). Surveying the publishing trends of 1893 in its annual summary, *Publisher's Weekly* remarked that in poetry and drama "the great names of the past . . . found none to take their places," and "no extensive work, either of great genius or promise, marked the year" (184). In 1901 the ominous lack of interest in poetry was demonstrated by a publisher's estimate of the average yearly sale per volume of poetry published in the United States at an abysmal 150 copies ("Confessions" 58). Poets frequently participated in this rhetoric of decline and futility, as in George Santayana's 1905 remark that "the age we live in is too cold a winter for even the best of us to do more than chirp a little" (Letter to Wallace Rice). In 1905, when President Theodore Roosevelt remarked that "the 'twilight of the poets' has been especially gray in America" (913), he made poetry's turn-of-the-century decline into an officially sanctioned article of cultural faith, one that has remained virtually unquestioned over a century of literary history.

These presumptions of decline and decay sprang up relentlessly even in commentaries trying to deny them, only to end up succumbing after all. For example, Clinton Scollard's 1903 overview of the year's poetry productions begins: "The past year of grace has seen no new planets swing into the poetic firmament; nor has it noted the advent of any clear-shining stars. This, then, it might be said, were a fitting time to give voice to the old cry—'Pan is dead!' Yet would this exclamation be no more true today than it was in decades gone" (Scollard 229). Typical of the period's self-confuting evaluative rhetoric, this attempt at affirmation was immediately enfeebled by Scollard's severely limited enthusiasm for these present-day Pans: "there are those still with us . . . not unworthy to wear the bay, albeit the number of leaves that should be apportioned for the various wreaths may be a suggestive theme for discussion" (229). A 1906 sonnet in the *Atlantic*, Torquil MacDonald's "Pan Is Not Dead," echoed this conceit with comically evasive results. After beginning with the flat statement "Pan is not dead," the poem plunges into a hermetically sealed metaphoric system willing to support the titular assertion only on the playing field of the classical pastoral. MacDonald insists that the "darkening vale," Pan's "still" flute, and "lone . . . glades where nymphs danced yesterday" are illusory, since "even as you fill / The air with lamentation, breaks the rill / Its icy fetters; lambs begin to play," until eventually "once again Pan's pipe hath found a tongue" (509). Meant to signify poetry's continued vitality, these lambs, "ethereal shapes" and "faint footfalls" are comically inadequate against the forces of modernity that darkened the vales and stilled the flutes in the first place; nor do the poem's metrical monotony and tortuously inverted diction inspire confidence. Poetry in this guise can only hearken wistfully to the songs of yesteryear as they pipe "Joyous and sweet as when the world was young" (509). That the world of 1906 was no longer "young" cannot be admitted by this self-unraveling text, but its evasions reveal the fact anyway.

Even verses with apparently impeccable genteel credentials, like Josephine Preston Peabody's "Play Up, Piper!" (1900), could turn sardonic when considering the contemporary cultural status of poetry. At first the poem seems merely a conventional encouragement to the piper to keep on playing, but it suddenly slides into puckish wonderment that he is willing to continue given the lack of purpose or reward:

> But tell us of the wage, man
> You had for this hard day;
> Play up, play up, dear Piper,
> And tell us why you play! (*Fortune* 98)

The demand "tell us why you play," implying that poetry's value must now be continually justified, became an overriding concern during these decades. In 1904 the *New Haven Register* reported that the *Atlantic Monthly*, "one of the oldest and best of the American periodicals, will print no more poetry for three years. The idea seems to be that there is little or no poetry that is worth printing, and that poetry for poetry's sake is not worth while" ("Value of Poetry" 189).[7] The *Register* writer argued that poetry's decline had been exaggerated by misguided comparisons between its readership and the new mass market for novels. Poetry might never be popular in that sense, but still it embodied "the

best thought and aspiration of the time" (190). But again, even in asserting that "In the most commercial and materialistic of ages" American
culture still had its singers, the writer could muster no enthusiasm for
actual contemporary poets, acknowledging that there were "not so many
or so great as we should like, but still some of whom we need not be
ashamed" (189–90), using the double negative tropes characteristic of the
period's commentary.

Stedman's critical style is at once the most finely calibrated and the
most obsessive instance of this rhetorical peculiarity. Persistently phrasing his affirmations in double and even quadruple negatives, Stedman
revealed his dread at poetry's future, as in this remarkable formulation:
"still, the dusk is not silent, and rest and shadow with music between the
dawns are a part of the liturgy of life, no less than passion and achievement" (AA xxviii). He responded to pervasive anxiety over poetry's supposed feminization in similar fashion, arguing that the work of American male poets was "not emasculate, and will not be while grace and
tenderness fail to make men cowards" (AA xxix). In the verse proem he
published in the *Century* to mark the appearance of *An American Anthology, 1787–1900*, Stedman took this trope to new heights (non-depths?) in
describing the poets who would carry us into "the next age":

> Others oncoming shine, nor fail to chant
> New anthems, yet not alien, for the time
> Goes not out darkling nor of music mute. ("Proem" 303)

Stedman's tortuous rhetoric struggles between the desire to maintain the
uplifting tone obligatory in genteel literary discourse and the awareness
that where poetry was concerned, there was nothing left to celebrate.
The pervasiveness of such self-undermining formulations indicates both
the exhaustion of genteel accounts of poetry's value and paralyzing
doubt that poetry could address the condition of modernity for its readers rather than just momentarily distracting them from it.

MORE SONNETS, ETC.

The turn-of-the-century profusion of double-negative affirmations was
one of the quirkier symptoms of a seemingly intractable impasse on the
issue of poetic form, in which neither traditionalism nor experimentalism could inspire appreciation. Lawrence Buell argues that the American
writer had long been expected to operate in contradictory circuits, to

develop an individual style that somehow emerged "not as bohemian-ism but, rather, as an articulation of national values" (117). Imitativeness and conventionality reminded Americans of their still colonialized cul-ture, but iconoclasm and formal innovation threatened to fragment desired "articulations of national values" into ephemeral expressions of idiosyncratic, even aberrant, sensibilities. The tension between these demands had relaxed somewhat during the genteel consensus of the previous decades, but in the belated 1890s the formal conventionality that had reigned unopposed for almost a half century became increas-ingly disabling. As commentators eyed the mounting pile of poems adhering to the old conventions, the more they doubted any one of them could command admiration. Yet apart from the problematic examples of Poe and Whitman, there were virtually no models in America for advancing a position of avant-garde individuality, and European models such as Baudelaire were familiar to few Americans and comfortable to fewer.

However, the prevailing characterization of turn-of-the-century poet-ry as simply mired in stale formal convention is incomplete.[8] In fact, the period was characterized by persistent, even urgent, demands for inno-vation, but in most cases these could only be expressed negatively in terms of a lethal formal stagnancy. To Stedman, the production of poetry in America had "for decades" been stuck in a rut of obeisance to colo-nialized traditions, and the dead weight of these past achievements had produced an urgent need for new formal directions: "Considering the accumulated wealth of English poetry, it is questionable whether more sonnets, etc., are a real addition to it, and if a place worth having can be earned by polishing the countless facets of gems dependent on the fanci-ful analysis of love and other emotions" (AA xix; PA 460). Genteel poet-ry's often rigid strictures on form also produced serious dissatisfaction in younger poets, as a fragmentary quatrain by Stephen Crane makes clear: "Tell me not in joyous numbers / We can make our lives sublime / By—well, at least, not by / Dabbling much in rhyme" (*Poems and Literary Remains* 81).[9]

In a series of verses in her 1900 volume *Idle Idyls*, another young writer, Carolyn Wells (1869–1942), who would soon give up poetry to become a prolific producer of detective and children's stories, facetious-ly decried the avalanche of poetry on the same old subjects using the same old forms. In "To a Poet. By Spring," for example, Spring pleads to a poet not to rhapsodize Her coming any further: "don't break out in paeans of glad mirth / Expressed in hackneyed rhyme," since "it grows rather stale / When I arrive, repeatedly to hear / The same old annual

'Hail!'" (24–25). The callow speaker of "An Unwritten Poem" aspires to embrace all the conventions of poetry, to inhabit a "flowery dell" because it's "the place by poets most preferred." This speaker resolves "I'll poetically tell / The sentiments of yonder little bird," but the bird rebels in terms drawn from a technology of representation more up-to-date than the poet's, complaining that "I've had my poem taken twenty-seven times this Spring." The poet's subsequent offers to celebrate apple-tree, breeze, flower, and Spring itself, are met with refusals on similar grounds of overexposure (115–17). The work ends with Spring's suggestion that the poet "Come, go a-Maying with us" and, later, "write about the song you did n't write" (117). Here Wells makes the "Unwritten Poem" the only one possible any longer to write, wittily suggesting the sense of belatedness and redundancy afflicting the young poets of the era.

In the view of many, continuing reliance on stale stylistic conventions produced an empty formalism, called by Harry T. Baker "the doctrine of form for form's sake," which he felt was the quality of poetry most "despised by the practical man" (227). This extrinsic understanding of poetic form, ironically shared by genteel poets and the philistines who despised them, was critiqued in a satiric verse by R. K. Munkittrick in the *Century* in the early 1890s. Munkittrick's "poem" consists of twenty surnames in *a-b-a-b* rhyme that add up only to the name of a fictional law firm. The structure of this text offers a metapoetic critique of empty formalism: the verse itself is a complete non sequitur, communicating nothing without its title, "The Present Style," which communicates everything.

> "The Present Style"
>
> Jones, Smith, Robinson,
> Simmons, Kent, Parr,
> Riley, Moore, Grant, Dunn,
> Little, Lillie, Carr,
>
> Marsh, Dusenbury, Bland
> Hurley, Murphy, Daw
> And Jamison, Attorneys and
> Counselors at law. (158)

More earnestly, Calvin Thomas diagnosed the decline of poetry through the telltale symptom of vacuous formalism: "It is a well-known fact of literary history that periods of magnificent production alternate more or less regularly with periods of comparative sterility, and that the sterile periods are very apt to be characterized by excessive attention to the matters of form and technic" (504). The logic of Stedman's argument that the times demanded poets with different attitudes and abilities echoed everywhere in turn-of-the-century discussions, but almost no one had a clear sense of what those new abilities might be or how to cultivate them.

Furthermore, although the view that "The day for 'retrospective refinement' in our verse is past" (G. Morris 196) had become a truism, it was almost equally truistic that such innovation had already passed the point of acceptability to become "rank excess" (Watson 178). William Watson's poem "Song's Apostasy," published in the *Atlantic* in 1904, described the contemporary situation as one in which the Muse "goes astray, / There to disown her record if she may, / Deny her lineage, turn as one ashamed / From all she was, and all that once was famed / To be her realm and birthright."[10] Watson argued that contemporary poetry's rejection of its glorious traditions, and its meretricious embrace of the "downward truth" rather than the "upward," had been "most lustily acclaimed" (178). Likewise, new formal directions such as Crane's provoked knee-jerk condemnations of the supposed formal anarchy of contemporary verse: "It seems to be believed nowadays that irregularity of form is a virtue, that the measures, the cadences which were good enough for the great poets of the past are useless for the tumultuous deliverances of true inspiration" (Review of *The Black Riders* in the *New York Daily Tribune,* June 9, 1895, in Weatherford 65). The same magazines and commentators who clamored for new forms could also be found ridiculing unusual uses of imagery and metaphor as "strange conceit[s] that never would have occurred to anyone not on the lookout for strange conceits" (Thomas 503).

In this climate of anxiety and recrimination, even such mild forms of experiment as metrical variation and imperfect rhyming were scourged by self-appointed custodians of tradition. Perceiving the distinct identity of poetry to be under threat, many responded by seizing upon the most obvious attributes distinguishing verse from prose forms, particularly rhyme, and making them the basis of their entire poetics. Richard E. Burton's 1888 article "Slovenliness in Verse-Making" opened with the dogmatic pronouncement: "Men and women who seriously take up the business of verse-writing should . . . declare to themselves that they will write nothing but perfect rhymes" (129). All other elements of their verse—meter, metaphor, style—may be "defective" "beyond their power of remedy"; "But one thing they can do, and should do always" is to make sure "that their rhymes are . . . true ear-rhymes" (129). Burton then proceeded to indict various canonical English poets, especially Barrett Browning and Tennyson, for their lapses into "defective" rhyming (130). Insisting that this plague "all comes from two causes, to wit, laziness or lack of ear" (130), he was completely unable to conceive of inexact rhyming as a form of stylistic experiment. It was not just provincial professors of English literature like Burton who tarred experimentally minded poets with accusations of "slovenliness." The unsigned review of *The Black Riders* in *Munsey's* (July 1895) called Crane "slovenly," insisting that just because "a man has genius, there is no reason for his being encouraged in making alleged poetry that is without rhyme or meter" (Review of *The Black Riders,* in Weatherford 66). William Hills, the editor of *The Writer,* voiced similar dogma concerning the "rules" of verse writing: "Even if the ambitious poet be not endowed with genius, it is at least possible for him to have metre of his lines correct and the rhymes exact." Hills cautioned that violating the formal conventions of poetry was a rare "privilege" that not even a genius such as Whitman could take for granted without risking contemptuous disparagement of his sincerity, taste, and character: "It is a question whether [Whitman's] usual habit of discarding rhyme was due so much to an honest belief that the use of rhyme hampers expression as to a constitutional laziness" (*The Writer* [1899] 68). These rather desperate efforts to shore up poetry as an aesthetic ideal rather than as a commodity could only backfire, since to define its value in terms of impersonal and rigid rules is to imply that it can be created merely by adherence to those rules—in other words, a commodity churned out by formula.

This impasse between theoretical advocacy of experimentation and disparagement of its actual instances was not merely a clear partisan line between traditionalists and innovators. Though they agreed on little else, on formal issues genteel traditionalists and mass-culture philistines presented a strange evaluative coalition against "bohemian" innovation. Experimentalists like Crane could expect to be ridiculed as "modern weaklings who affect weird forms," in the proudly philistine idiom of such captains of the mass-culture industry as Edward Bok (296). But this ridicule could come from the genteel side as well, as in this characterization in the *Atlantic* of the poetic innovator as one "anxious to deny his parentage in communal song, and to set forth his excellent differences," whose inability to resist meretricious originality would betray him: "He will daze the editor and force his way into the magazine by tricks of expression, a new adjective, a shock of strange collocations" (Gummere 827). "Absurd involutions of thought and expression" might be excusable in Browning or Swinburne, but such excess turned "positively offensive" when "minor poets affect them for the mere sake of what they consider the intricacy of art" (Buckham 115). An overweening need to experiment bespoke a poet's minority, immaturity, or primitivism, as in Howells's 1896 rejection of Crane's "near formlessness" on the grounds that it was preferable to "live in a house of the accepted structure than in a hut of logs and boughs" (Review of *The Black Riders,* in Weatherford 70).

Responses both demanding and decrying innovation often collided in the same commentaries, vitiating their coherence and argumentative efficacy. Before 1900 we find numerous attacks on forced rhymes and inverted diction that foreshadow later modern arguments—"Is it possible that there are no words in the whole English language that will rhyme with 'her fair face' or 'the wide water,' that there must be this complete upheaval [of word order]?" (Griffin 50). But these almost never produced open-minded advocacy of unrhymed, or even imperfectly rhymed, verse. Instead, such commentators merely abjured poets to produce fresher, but no less perfect, rhymes. This self-contradictory response was dramatized best in 1906 by a commentator in the *Academy* who gestured vigorously toward originality by complaining that poets today were too "tied to the conventions of their art," but who went on in the very next paragraph to object that those same poets were "running amuck among the strange and tuneless metres of their own invention" ("Great Poetry" 61). Having asserted one page earlier that "the great poet is he who is least indebted to the conventions of poetry that satisfy a shallow present-day criticism, he who is a new voice and not a mere echo," this writer completed a spectacular self-confutation by urging poets back to Palgrave's *Golden Treasury,* the ultimate symbol of canonical convention, to "learn the way of excellence" (62).

Such self-subverting advocacy of innovation extended to the most eminent critical voices of genteel culture. In 1896 Richard Watson Gilder, editor of the *Century,* objected to "the discouragement which is cast upon poets and publishers of poetry by the tone of contempt" with which new verse was generally received and urged readers to open their minds "a little more widely to these candidates and aspirants for the highest place the world can offer" ("A Plea for the Poets" 316, 317). But almost immediately this well-intentioned endorsement of innovation was overwhelmed by Gilder's need to keep poetry on its genteel pedestal: "society cannot go without what the poets can give, and must give, to save it from the slough of misconceived utility" (317). The *Century*'s commitment to the ideological position of romantic antimodernity, in which poetry must "save" society from the slough of utilitarian despond, was unquestionable. But where was its support for the exploratory modes of verse needed to meet these modern challenges? Even the perceptive Stedman unwittingly reinforced this evaluative impasse, describing a "desire for variants in creative beauty to stimulate us," an impulse to innovation quickly neutralized by his morose prediction that these variants "each, in turn, shall also pass into an academic grade" (AA xxxi), evoking the specter of a commodified culture of frantic innovation inevitably souring into orthodoxy and irrelevance. Thus, at the same time he urged tolerance of the changes in form needed to move American poetry into a new phase—"In any intermediary lyrical period its effect upon the listener is apt to be one of experiment and vacillation" (AA xxx)—Stedman undermined its actual instances as signs of weakness and uncertainty of purpose by equating experiment with vacillation.

These contradictions afflicted earnest young poets as well. The "Envoy" to Josephine Preston Peabody's 1898 volume *The Wayfarers* captures the tension between her desire to "speak a common tongue," to engage with "the voice of Everyday / With its familiar yea and nay," and her compulsion instead "To dream" of fantasy landscapes of idealized beauty ("How over walls of paradise / The darling trees lean down to shed / A petal") (83). Whereas the Fireside poets had been able to reconcile, or at least mute, this tension into a coherent worldview, younger poets found it painfully unresolvable. Peabody is more honest than most, admitting that these idealist fantasies do not refresh her work, but simply frustrate and even embarrass her: "And I wake, with eyes / Uncomforted" (83). Yet despite this admission, and her arguments in "Modern Life and Modern Poetry" that poetry ought to bridge the chasm of Real and Ideal, Peabody could never conceive this relation except through the use of conventional, "universal" diction: "I can imagine some tropic heathen newly converted to the reading of poetry, and yet barred forever from understanding a New England 'chickadee' when plain 'bird' would have dispelled his sense of alienation and heathen darkness" ("Modern Life" 61). The more nuanced modern relation of an individual style to the communal expression of a culture, such as William Carlos Williams's "universality of the local," had not yet been formulated except by Whitman, and in his work was only beginning to be appreciated.

Struggling under the burdensome weight of past canons, these self-conflicted commentators urgently desired a sense of renewal and freshness, but their nostalgia for the preindustrial culture represented by those canons rendered actual innovations in form, diction, imagery, or subject matter almost entirely unacceptable. Their persistent yearning for greater novelty, intensity, and relevance to everyday life collided with their stubborn unwillingness to put aside the halo that had made poetry "the divinest of arts," in James Buckham's phrase. In such a polarized climate, efforts to engage with the modern condition registered as attempts to "drag even poetry out of the sky, and make Pegasus eat grass" (Buckham 115). No wonder it was felt that all the great poems had been written, the canons all filled; the conditions of poetic value made exploring new territory virtually impossible.

NEXT MONTH'S SET

The era's simultaneous rejection of traditionalism and experimentalism leads to yet another defining evaluative paradox: choruses of grumbling about the overproduction of verse colliding with equally vocal complaints that new and unknown writers were being unfairly excluded. Many noted the vast amount of poetry being written and published, and some even admitted its generally high quality; but these affirmations were almost invariably qualified by conceding its extreme ephemerality: "The magazines are constantly printing verse that is better than much that is found clad in supercilious calf on the shelves of every gentleman's library. But its appeal is limited" (Greenslet, "Propaganda" 43). Often this proliferation was interpreted through a theory of overproduction assuming an inverse relationship between volume and value. In *The Lost Art of Reading,* for example, Gerald Stanley Lee characterized contemporary literature as "a mere headlong, helpless literary rush from beginning to end"(18). Blurring individual works into an undifferentiated, mechanized "sound of going" (18), Lee evoked a defining irony of modern cultural production: as more members of a society gain the economic independence, leisure, and advanced literacy prerequisite to writing books, the common knowledge base of these literate masses erodes, and culture comes to seem fragmented or atomized (not that we'd be better off without this expansion of literacy).

In an editorial in his magazine *The Writer,* William Hills revealed the disconcerting effects of this profusion of writing on people's ability to evaluate it. Noting that the editor of the *Ladies' Home Journal,* Edward Bok, had written derisively of all but a few dozen of the five thousand verses he received every year, Hills argued that the sheer volume of submissions had tempted Bok into condemning them without a fair hearing.

But Hills left unquestioned the assumption of an enormous, indistinguishable mass of American verse with no chance of a readership. Without apparent irony, he ended by estimating that "in this country of 70,000,000 people, 70,000 new poems must be produced every year and sent out hopefully for publication. . . . It's appalling, is n't it?" ("Annual Poetry Product" 221–22). Surveying the previous year's poetry in the *Atlantic* in 1905, Greenslet professed exhaustion at its undifferentiated abundance: "I have, to speak sadly and precisely, read between two and three thousand manuscript poems, and more than two hundred volumes of recently collected verse" ("Significant Poetry" 414). Comically describing "the poetry that has been written in English in the last twelve months as a kind of Purgatory"—his own—Greenslet estimated that at least 170 of these books possessed "no ponderable significance" (415). Carolyn Wells's "Of Modern Books" (1900) packaged a similar theory of overproduction in the elaborate form of the pantoum, whose repetitions of whole lines like "Each day new manuscripts are being penned," or "And then the magazines come round *again*" (145–46; italics in original), enacted graphically the sense of weary routine resulting from too many books with too little distinctiveness. A thirty-two-line pantoum employs just sixteen different lines, here playfully implying that every second "modern book" is a verbatim copy of another.[11]

As the verse produced by Americans seemed to approach an unmanageable volume, few disagreed with Gelett Burgess's conclusion that little of it would have lasting value: "You know how little Stuff is going to live, / But where it came from there is plenty More" (6). In his satiric survey of contemporary culture *The Rubaiyat of Omar Cayenne* (1904), Burgess explored this inverse relation between volume and value, sketching a cultural assembly line that churned out "next month's Set" of indistinguishable "Girls with Three Names, who know not Who from Whom!" (11). Burgess portrayed the contemporary "canon" as impossibly baggy in form and painfully self-deluded in attitude:

> So when WHO'S-WHO records your silly Name,
> You'll think that you have found the Road to Fame;
> And though ten thousand other Names are there,
> You'll fancy you're a genius, just the Same! (16)

Cultivating airy cynicism toward such solemn nineteenth-century notions as tradition and genius, "decadents" like Burgess and Wells facetiously embraced its opposite: a completely commodified notion of value, in which anyone could join the canonical record through some trifling accomplishment, even just payment to a publication willing to proclaim the equal genius of all its subscribers.

As they saw production rising and the value of particular works declining, many worried that modern cultural economics were turning poetry into an empty prestige commodity for effete, well-heeled idlers: "It would appear that poetry is no longer a power in the lives of men, but, at the best, merely the delight of refined connoisseurs,—a competitor of rare orchids and delicate china" (Thomas 503). Stedman fretted that contemporary poets had internalized that decorative function, working willingly "in the spirit of the graver and decorator," becoming "over-careful of the look of words, and not only of their little pictures, but of the frames that contain them—book-cover, margin, paper, adornment" (AA xxx). The anxiety expressed here is a further permutation of the concern over empty formalism. The congruence of external form and inner essence that undergirded analogical Fireside poetics was dissolving into a decorative understanding of the poetry book as a beautiful shell, a commodified icon of taste and class whose material splendor only pointed up the immateriality and irrelevance of its contents.

Yet at the same time such overproduction and commodification were decried, the literary press was full of indignant complaint about the lack of accessibility to print, especially from aspiring and unknown writers, and querulous dismissals of these complaints by editors.[12] Alice Dunbar-Nelson's poem "A Common Plaint," written around 1900 (but ironically not published, it would appear, until the posthumous collection of her work in 1988), articulated this sense of exclusion and its enervating effects on the writer's imaginative powers. Worrying that she should be attempting some saleable fictional potboiler, "A tale of thrilling things," the speaker upbraids herself, "And here, I scribble rhymes" (2:75). Yet despite her financial needs ("A check looms large into my sight"), she "cannot write," partially because she knows "No editor will heed my plight, / I've proved that scores of times" (2:76). The speaker chooses poetry over fiction not from a sense that only poetry can express her feelings, but from the hopeless conviction that she will be rejected no matter what she writes:

> I'd rather dream than work;
> Then what's the use, let's take to-night
> For luxury of shirk.
> Those editors would send it back,
> I cannot write, ah, well, alack. (2:76)

That even talented young poets, much less the philistines who dismissed the genre, were prone to characterize verse writing as dreaming, luxury, and shirking illuminated the evaluative corner into which poetry had been painted.

Trying to make sense of this common plaint of exclusion, some concocted irregular, even bizarre, accounts of the evaluative process. The widespread suspicion that unsolicited manuscripts were being fobbed off on bogus authorities was voiced in 1906 by Florence Finch Kelley, who, "unable to believe that the literary capacity of this country . . . could not produce something better than the current magazine verses," concluded sardonically that editors "must sift all the poetry that comes into their offices first through the discriminating hands of the typewriter and telephone girls, and afterward those 'higher up' select for publication the best of the 'pretty pieces' the young ladies have chosen" (Kelley 139). Kelley went on to complain that occasional demonstrations "that our poets are capable of better things than the editors would have us believe" go "knocking in vain at the doors of all the magazines in the country" (139–40), evoking the anxiety of other valuable work neglected and lost: "And who knows how many more there may have been, . . . that have never found even its tardy recognition and acceptance" (139–40). In her facetious account, the culprit was a lazy, timid editorial establishment deferring to an aesthetically empty mass audience, represented by the office clerical staff. In *The Writer* in 1888 an aspiring author named C. N. Hood advanced, with apparent dead seriousness, a paranoid conspiracy theory of evaluation. An unbroken pattern of rejection convinced Hood "that the first editor must mark the manuscript in some invisible way, which told to all the other editors a plain story of rejection, and warned them that the article was not worth the reading" (51). Hood described looking for the mark "many times, long, but vainly" (51). After a particularly traumatic rejection following an apparent acceptance, Hood had a sudden vision exposing the mystery: "fourteen faint, crooked, blue lines" on the last sheet of the manuscript, resulting from the mucilage of the envelopes each time it was sealed to be sent out: "Even editorial judgment was not proof against that" (51). Externalizing the trauma of rejection onto a material pattern of almost invisible coded marks, Hood indicated the extent to which writers felt excluded by a cabalistic editorial establishment ignorant or indifferent to aesthetic value.

Despite the outlandishness of some accounts of exclusion, there was considerable justice to the feelings behind them. In this era, after all, "the distinction between great literature and a publishable work" was rigidly maintained by many editors (Ziff 128), who felt comfortable acknowledging that the sheer quality, even the genius, of a submission was not enough to ensure acceptance. In fact, to some genteel sensibilities, "genius" could even militate against acceptance. In his 1912 autobiography, J. Henry Harper, head of *Harper's* magazine and publishing house, remembered a "most remarkable piece of literary workmanship" once submitted to him: "There was but one thing to do—to skim it over rapidly and get the dreadful thing out of the place. But it was literature, and great literature, too" (321).[13] Excluded authors heard such remarks as acknowledgments that they were at the mercy of extrinsic, often unstated evaluative criteria. In 1892 R. K. Munkittrick's satire "Never Despair" poked fun at this distinction between aesthetic value and publishability, offering a poet-narrator who shops a "light and airy symphony" to the magazines, receiving universal admiration from editors, but also a series of transparent excuses for rejecting it. The third editor is caught in his own devious devices when he "murmur[s], 'It's delightful, oh, delightful, but, dear me, / We printed something similar in eighteen sixty-eight,'" and the speaker realizes that the magazine had only begun in 1869 (800). This fictional editor, no doubt better-natured than his real counterparts, then chuckles "like the greatest fiend alive" as he writes "a purple checklet for a five," and the speaker leaves contented—unlike the struggling would-be contributors whose presumptions about editorial venality were being tweaked.

In this atmosphere of distrust between editors and aspiring writers, we find numerous instances of phony submissions—doctored Kipling stories, Tennyson poems, and so on—made to test the suspicion that either editorial conspiracy or incompetence would keep even unquestionably superior work from the light of day if submitted by an unknown.[14] To the editorial establishment, the "witless investigators" who perpetrated these "stupid frauds" proved nothing but their own "moral perversion" and "pitiful cowardice" and deserved to find themselves "upon more than one well-laden blacklist" ("Of Editors," 697–98). What is astonishing is this editor's assertion that "each month brings to his desk so many" meritorious manuscripts doctored in similar manner that he long ago "ceased to rebuke or invite any controversy whatsoever with the dishonest reader" (697). That such stunts occurred frequently enough to mean no more than "weary routine" (697) in editorial offices implies the breadth of this conviction among the excluded; that the blacklists were "well-laden" reveals the real contempt for the new—styles, forms, subjects—that unknown authors were faced with.

Presented in print by the same editorial elements that they were attacking, those complaining of exclusion were generally dismissed in tones of ridicule that implied they should stop whining and grow up: "The voice of 'neglected genius' is one that never grows faint in our ears. In every generation there are those who will not let us forget that Milton sold his masterpieces for a song; that [Thomas] Chatterton was goaded into suicide by an uncharitable world; and that Keats died of a broken heart. Today in America a small army of men who have evidently persuaded themselves that they are the lineal descendants of Milton and Keats are still raising the old cry, Why is genius forsaken?" ("Is Genius Neglected?" 165). The sarcasm of this comment was undergirded by an evaluative Darwinism that took a text's neglect as prima facie proof of its valuelessness, since everything of value would by definition eventually be recognized as such. This attitude was articulated most complacently by a participant in the debate "Is Genius Neglected by the Magazines?" who remarked with consummate circularity, "the man who returns your story comes pretty near knowing what he is about—he wouldn't be at the head of a responsible magazine if he didn't" (qtd. 166). Widespread complaints at the insincerity or incompetence of magazine editors, and smug dismissals of these complaints, dramatized a serious structural limitation in the American literary scene that excluded almost all unconventional literary work and afflicted poetry most severely of all. It would be left to innovative poets and editors of the 1910s to end-run these inhibiting conditions by creating alternative forms of publication not dependent on marketing a product to a large audience, above all the little magazine.

We've glimpsed the paradigm of evaluative Darwinism applied to poetry in the writings of Bryant and Lowell, but late in the century it was given greater impetus by the enormous popularity of Herbert Spencer's "Synthetic Philosophy," which, filtered through American popularizers like John Fiske, seemed "especially constructed to provide explicit and absolute reassurance" that "universal evolution naturally produced increasingly higher levels of moral good" (R. Martin 60). This line of reasoning could serve to justify "any sort of competitive or monopolistic capitalism, any measure of exploitation or imperialism, any level of social inequality" (93).[15] Darwinist accounts of value dictated there was no use in regretting the obscurity, poverty, exclusion, or other ills that poets were heir to. Instead they must simply "be silent and quietly . . . wait in the calm assurance that any word with truth and beauty in it will always find its audience, 'fit though few'" (Hornbrooke 140). This remark of 1893 echoes the chilling contempt for activism and reform held by American universe-of-force advocates like Fiske, who "urged his readers that progress occurred regardless of man's efforts and often in spite of them, and that man's appropriate reaction to social imperfections was one of patient, confident submission" (R. Martin 74). Despite the implication of hardheaded natural selection, in which the truly valuable would inevitably triumph, this Darwinist account actually mystified the concept of literary value into a nimbus of intrinsicality that unfathomably materialized around certain works and not around others.

What held true for works held true for authors, who learned courtesy of the *Atlantic* that "There is no brief maxim so incontrovertible as that *poeta nascitur, non fit*" ("Poetry In General" 702). It was a short step from the platitude that poets are born not made, to the assertion that their characters will be morally enriched by whatever difficulties they encounter. Even the benevolent Howells could remark in 1902 that "I think that a young writer's upward course should be slow and beset with obstacles, even hardships" ("Editor" 77), unable to imagine that such hardships might destroy young writers rather than strengthening them. From here, it was but one small step to the crueler conclusion that poets could not realize their full nobility *unless* they were unhappy and ignored, as Charles Moore argued: "It is happily ordained for the good of the race that poets shall be miserable" ("Future" 776). Moore hoped fervently that "there will never be a society for the prevention of cruelty to poets," since "The spectacle of a snug, self-sufficing existence can be no inspiration to him who yearns for greatness and for glory" (776). This last turn of the screw—that poverty and neglect were necessary to the growth of the true artist—was seldom applied to any other genre, as if to reassert poetry's unique claims to a transcendent ideality soaring above the mundane considerations of modernity. Such commentators fancied they were still wielding poetry in its traditional function as champion of aesthetic idealism. But given the genre's current level of debility, to claim the absence of institutional support as a virtue was simply to sacrifice poetic aspirants upon the altar of utilitarian capitalism.

WASTE PAPER

After 1890, watching the sudden disintegration of an apparently stable genre, bewildered commentators concluded that those with poetic talent must be following "other callings, forsaking the muse" so completely "that the race of poets is dying out" ("Lack of Poets" 42). A writer in the *Hartford Post* in 1900 blamed the scarcity of "high-grade poets" on adverse cultural conditions: "It is possible that as many [poets] are born as ever, but that they die young: finding the atmosphere uncongenial, they pale and perish" ("Lack of Poets" 42). These remarks participated in a distinctive rhetoric of wastage that I call the "Chatterton scenario": the worry that genius was being destroyed before it could flower by a climate of complacency, ignorance, and indifference. This topos can be connected to broader trends of the era that made "waste" into the "pejorative American byword, virtually the industrial-era devil denounced in texts of all kinds from literary criticism to advertisements," as Cecilia Tichi puts it (57). The anxiety that the most valuable poems might be utterly lost was the obverse of the theory of overproduction that feared poetry was becoming "a ceaseless tide of ink" (Wells 145) on a sea of useless and neglected papers, in its excessive profusion signifying nothing.

The coalescence of this narrative of heartbreaking tragedy out of the ambiguous episodes of Thomas Chatterton's life indicated the power of these anxieties about cultural waste. Almost immediately after his death in 1770, two interpretations of Chatterton's life began to appear: those condemning the boy-poet for his deceptions, and those defending his honor and genius against envious naysayers. Both remained available for most of the next century, but as the controversies over his literary impostures grew more distant, Chatterton came to occupy almost exclusively the role of idealized Romantic hero, the poetic genius destroyed by a harsh and uncomprehending world. Chatterton's turn-of-the-century prominence was demonstrated by the appearance of three major biographies within a decade (David Masson, 1899; C. E. Russell, 1908; and John H. Ingram, 1910). In the poetry and the commentary of those years, the Chatterton scenario emerged in several forms. Andrew Lang's satiric piece "The Poets' Trade Union" (1906) lampooned it as a commonplace of frivolous Romanticism, having his would-be organizer of a poets' union ask: "Do you remember what Alfred de Musset said, or was it Saint-Beuve?. . . . 'In each of us there is a poet who died young,'" "because he is starved out of the business, starved, no market for his madrigals" (1145). In his 1902 work "The Poet," George Cabot Lodge sketched a figure "doomed . . . / To live ever more lonely day by day / By all rejected and condemned by all" (1:159). However flat-footed and bathetic, Lodge's portrayal would have found many to agree with it.

Usually Chatterton rhetoric led to bitter but impotent denunciation of poetry's disenfranchisement. Most common, perhaps, was the ironic posthumous celebration of an artist after a life of neglect and exclusion, seen in R. W. Gilder's "A New Poet" (discussed below), and in Ellen Glasgow's "Fame" (1902): "In life he lived among them and they cast / Him stones for bread /. . . . In death, . . . / They brought a laurel wreath:

/ Honour to ashes on the coffin lid! / Fame to the skull beneath!" (*The Freeman* 20). Dunbar's "Sonnet On an Old Book with Uncut Leaves" (1899) incarnated an old, unread book analogically into the wasted body of the poet. Calling the book "impotent in age" and "unsought," Dunbar portrays it as a (de-)sexualized body in decay that still "like some old maiden, solemnly / Hugs its incongruous virginity," now capable of conveying just one meaning: the "blasted hope and lost desire" of its creator (*Complete Poems* 115). Though neither Glasgow nor Dunbar refers explicitly to Chatterton, both evoke the mythos by troping the dead or wasted body of the tragically frustrated literary aspirant. Chatterton narratives had always possessed this iconic dimension, from the publication in the *Westminster Magazine* in 1782 of an engraving of "The Distressed Poet" in his garret, an image that was made into commemorative handkerchiefs (the better to cry over his sad fate), to its Romantic apotheosis in the celebrated Pre-Raphaelite painting "The Death of Chatterton" by Henry Wallis (1856).[16] Just as Chatterton's fragile body represented wasted genius, often-repeated references to the "precious little bundle of MSS." "torn into fragments" by the despairing poet and then lost (D. Wilson 304–05) functioned as horrifying reminders that even the greatest poetry was on the verge of becoming so much waste paper.

Some tried to use the Chatterton mythos against the evaluative Darwinism that asserted genius would prevail regardless of any obstacles. Stedman, appalled at the prospect of American poetry's withdrawal into an enclave of elite culture, objected to the lack of institutional support as a shameful wastage of talent, decrying the situation in which "A collective edition of an admired poet's lifework . . . appears without being made the subject of gratulation or extended review" (AA xxxii).[17] This comment also registered fears that the category of the individual author, and the notion of a poetic career developing across decades, would be henceforth unavailable. Stedman tried to use the Chatterton scenario to deflect these disabling perceptions away from individual aspirants, proposing that even the noblest writers of the past would fail to penetrate such massive institutional indifference: "If a fair equivalent of the 'Ode to a Nightingale' were now to come into print, a reviewer of the magazine containing it doubtless might content himself with saying: 'There is also a poem by Mr.——'" (AA xxxii)—the sort of blandly deflating phrase found frequently in the reviews of the era. Relocating poetry's failure in the stolid disinterest of contemporary institutions, Stedman may have provided some psychological protection for the aspiring writer, but he offered no solution to the structural breakdown that necessitated such defensive maneuvering in the first place.

Although the Chatterton scenario spoke to those wishing to indulge a lingering attraction to Romantic agonism, as a cautionary tale it failed to challenge the utilitarian rhetoric of force and efficiency, which portrayed all poetic endeavor as wasted effort, time, and attention. Those on the other side of this rhetorical polarity, to whom poetry itself was a waste, were perfectly happy to celebrate its disappearance, and the diversion of would-be poets to other activities, as increases in the world's operational efficiency.

The usefulness of Chatterton rhetoric in energizing support for poets was further undermined by its conglomeration with a messianic "genius model" of literary value as stunting as the complacent indifference of the Darwinists. In 1901 the unsigned one-paragraph review of Josephine Preston Peabody's *Fortune and Men's Eyes* noted, "It is an understood thing that the lovers of poetry are constantly on the lookout for the coming great American poet, and if there is the slightest indication of power in any fresh aspirant for poetical fame, hope springs up that here at last is the poetical Messiah" (H. A. C. 123). In one respect, this writer was offering an astute diagnosis of the evaluative crisis of the times. But by going on to acclaim Peabody as a good candidate for *"the long-expected one"* without developing an argument that might conceivably justify such an assertion, the critic did neither the poet nor the genre any favors (123; italics in original). Richard Watson Gilder's "A New Poet" (1905) was likewise tempted away from vigorous advocacy of innovation toward a too-easy messianic resolution. At first the poem rejects the dire predictions of those who "said there were no more singers," and advances a need for "A keen, new sound" against a stale orthodoxy of "the pretty songs of schools / (Not of music made, but rules)" (748). But Gilder constructs his affirmation around the arrival of "a master voice! / A voice of the true joy-bringers," using the tone of exultant exclamation that genteel culture found so hard to put aside. Thenceforth the poem is permeated with messianic Chatterton imagery, as in the speaker's final exhortation to his pharisaical "friends": when this new master emerges, "will ye heed and rejoice, / Or pass on the other side, / And wait till the singer hath died, / Then weep o'er his voiceless clay?" However well-intentioned, Gilder cannot extricate himself from this debilitating messianism: "Know ye a poet's coming is the old world's judgment day!" Such falls into messianism were merely desperate inversions of the Chatterton scenario: if we can just recognize and nurture the coming great American poet, then the forces arrayed against poetry, no matter how formidable, will pale into insignificance. To pin all poetry's hopes on a single savior was no more constructive than to assume, like the Darwinists, that "progress" was inevitable. If the latter way of thinking would allow poetry to wither away through sheer indifference, the former threatened to suffocate it in the jealous and fickle embrace of the cult.

In any case, between 1890 and 1910 convincing messiahs were difficult to find. The aspiring poet, mired in stale tradition or contemporary irrelevance, became a shorthand emblem of cultural waste. Harriet Monroe's verse play *The Thunderstorm* (1899–1900) featured two poet characters embodying tropes of wastage: a true genius who has become an industrialist at the behest of his grasping wife and brother, and a multitalented but weak-willed writer on the verge of giving up literary endeavor for profitable hackwork.[18] The former, John Merrick, embodies Monroe's ambivalent perception that American "genius" was being diverted into commercial rather than literary endeavor, to create the astonishing edifices of modern capitalism. The latter, Felix Merivale, is a frivolous bohemian whose iconoclasm imperfectly masks a desire to submerge his individual talent in a profitable but anonymous commodity culture. Ironically given the role of Apollo in a costume masque put on by the leisure-class company of the play, Merivale outlines the poet's untenable position in a nightmarish version of modernity:

> But today it's a different role
> That the tired world bids me play;
> I who chanted of old to its soul
> Must amuse the poor world today.
> So I hint at a thousand loves
> In a delicate medley of rhymes,
> And I thrill when the spirit moves
> Over popular wars and crimes.
> But who cares what I sing to my lyre?
> It is lost in the roaring of fire,
> For in clamorous towns I dwell
> Near the steel-forged gates of hell. (*Passing Show* 29)

The poet's only choices here are to retreat into delicacy and preciosity, ignoring the urban industrial scene, or to exploit it for cheap sensation. Merivale's self-pitying conclusion articulates the fears of Monroe and her contemporaries: that neither path would allow poetry a voice in the clamorous indifference of modernity.

One of the most memorable versions of this stock character of cultural wastage would come in "Petit, the Poet," from *Spoon River Anthology*

(1915). With the aid of hindsight, Masters could precisely identify the elements that had rendered Petit and his genteel ilk symbols of cultural futility: rigid adherence to restrictive foreign forms ("Triolets, villanelles, rondels, rondeaus"), monotonous meters ("Tick, tick, tick, like mites in a quarrel"), and outworn stock images and diction ("Ballades by the score with the same old thought: / The snows and the roses of yesterday are vanished") (89). The obsolescence of these formal practices is exacerbated by Petit's deafness to vital poetic models such as Whitman and Homer, and by his disconnection from everyday American life and audience: "Life all around me here in the village . . . / All in the loom, and oh what patterns!" (89). Unlike Petit, who remained "Blind to all of it all my life long," only realizing his error in death, both Monroe (born 1860) and Masters (1868) were unwilling to accept these varieties of futility as the only choices for the poet in America. They endured the long crisis of poetic value well into their middle age, to emerge as decisive participants in the New Poetry. But as aspiring poets in the 1890s, they were well acquainted with the imputations of frivolity and belittlement implicit in names like Merivale and Petit.

Such character names, like Dunbar's trope of the uncut book as virginal old maid, evoked the turn-of-the-century poet's fierce anxieties of imaginative potency. One widespread but pernicious response to this inhospitable climate was to defend poetry by adopting philistine gender stereotypes. One of Munkittrick's verse satires in the *Century* clustered together empty signifiers of "the Poetic"—stock foreign phrases, the names of legendary poets and mythological figures, and clichés of romantic rhetoric—all portentously capitalized:

> T'is Ever Thus
>
> Ad Astra, De Profundis,
> Keats, Bacchus, Sophocles;
> Ars Longa, Euthanasia,
>
> Spring, The Eumenides. . . .

The punch line of the final stanza was:

> These are part of the contents
> Of "Violets of Song,"
> The first poetic volume
> Of Susan Mary Strong. (Qtd. John 173)

The female genteel poetaster was a conventional topos of the period. Munkittrick at least showed a light touch in proposing what others were arguing with more overt misogyny: that in the hands of versifiers such as Susan Mary Strong, poetry was undergoing euthanasia by insipid Eumenides.

In 1899 the *Dial* housed an exchange of correspondence that compactly dramatized the effects of this campaign of defensive misogyny. A writer signed "Philister" began the debate by noting that an article in the *Nation* "rightly finds" that the best recent poetry is by women. True to his(?) moniker, the writer evinced surprise that "there should now be any poetry at all . . . that is not by women," since "men (manly men, I mean) are growing more and more shy of writing poetry, or at least of letting people know they do it, because they feel that a man making verses is more or less a ridiculous object" ("Passing of the Man-Poet" 329). Reading this letter now, one concludes that the writer was seeking to twit overserious poetry lovers by mischievously parodying the arguments of philistine mass culture. (This is rather given away by Philister's over-the-top assertion that one's "gorge rises at the notion of a big, brawny, bearded he-creature like Tennyson, with the frame of a coal-heaver and the face of a buccaneer, chirping about 'Airy, fairy Lilian,' crooning cradle-songs, or caterwauling in erotic strain over love and the moon" [329]). If so, the two responses in the following issue, which take these comments with grim seriousness, suggest that Philister had exposed an anxiety too urgent to be joked about. Neither respondent could defend the virility of male poets except by denigrating females. Wallace Rice argued that the *Nation*'s finding in favor of female poets was "so unusual that it probably never happened before, and it may never happen again," and that in fact, "Women are not holding their own in poetical expression" (362). A writer signed "S. E. B." scorned the notion that two hasty and ill-considered opinions (those of the *Nation* reviewer and Philister) could mean "the passing of the man-poet." On the contrary, "In all previous literature," just two "really great women-poets have appeared: Sappho and Mrs. Browning," while "The great man-poets are almost numberless" (363). Both respondents assumed an inverse relation between the poetic accomplishments of females and males, again demonstrating the conceptual poverty of genteel defenses of poetry. In her study of American success manuals, Judy Hilkey identifies such strategies as characteristic of conceptions of male success in the Gilded Age. Many of these manuals "equated success and manhood" in ways that required "the corollary equation of failure and the feminine" (5). This model of inversion is premised upon a zero-sum Darwinian account of socioeconomic (and now literary) realms as menacing and emotionally frigid, containing only so much room for success, in which all endeavor becomes "a brutal struggle for survival" (5).

Another of Philister's assertions, that in "a hard-fact, practical age," "the impression . . . that writing verse is an effeminate pursuit . . . has to be reckoned with by men who want to keep the respect of their rugged-er fellows" (329), evoked a more specifically sexual anxiety that bedev-iled male lovers of poetry during these years. An insistent chorus of male commentators worried that contemporary poetry had become not only emotionally soft and intellectually slack, but also sexually suspect, as in this 1888 remark in *The Writer*: "There are no direct, simple voices in the choir; the trill is predominant. There are womanly voices; the falsetto is admired" (Buckham 115). However serious or whimsical, comments associating poetry writing with effeminacy could trigger antimodern homophobic rhetoric calling for poetry's return to the supposedly manly, untainted virtues of some earlier period. Lee Wilson Dodd characterized contemporary poets as "Frail Singers of Today," the title of his 1905 poem in the *Century*. Dodd did not assume that these "frail singers" were female, like Susan Mary Strong; instead, he addressed male pluck-ers of an "emasculate lute" (746). Associated with such gendered adjec-tives as *frail, sweet, comely,* and *faint,* these poetic eunuchs make a "thin yet poignant cry" that compares poorly to "yesterday" when "Men sang a manlier way, / Plucking rough chords of strength from lyres too rude / Ever to be subdued." As in Longfellow's "The Day Is Done," past canonical works function here as inaccessible and yet inhibiting sources of frustration, "Gone down forever with all those mighty hearts / Who brook no counterparts!" The difference from Longfellow is Dodd's intensely sexualized antagonism toward canonical poets, as domineer-ing male forces whose only function is to remind present aspirants of their own emasculated state, in which they would be "Far better silent" than "thus chirping on / An echo of things gone." For Dodd, this com-petition between present and past produces a stark evaluative ultima-tum in which present poets must "Awake, awake to power" or "else die": better dead than castrated.

A seldom spoken but pervasive element of this sexualized rhetoric can be described as an onanist anxiety. The transgressive sexuality hinted at in portrayals of the "effeminate" male poet was equated at some sub-terranean level with the wasteful indulgence of the literary masturbator who spends his creative powers chirping about "airy, fairy Lilian." The fact that Dodd's imagery portrayed the "manlier" poets of yore in sub-liminal terms of erection or even masturbation ("Plucking rough chords of strength from lyres too rude / Ever to be subdued") exacerbated the contrast to the emasculated singers of today. These rude lyres of the manly canon enacted the fantasy of the eternally erect, never-spent phallus; the goal of their plucking is not to waste their creative seed on unworthy ground, capitulating to venal momentary pleasure, but to maintain a virile intensity that demonstrates their unending creative power. In such a context of male performance anxiety, most poetic ejaculations on the page were bound to produce neither culmination nor procreation, but just another variety of waste paper.

Between 1890 and 1910 those few attempting to counter Darwinist, Messianist, and misogynist/homophobic accounts of value had little success advancing a less polarized relationship between poetry and the modern condition. Stedman was virtually alone in his advocacy of institutional support for poets; he had few fellow travelers in arguing for a synthesis between poetry and the defining elements of modernity. Where many simply carped at the inadequacy of will, learning, or taste in contemporary poets, Stedman astutely ascribed the ascendancy of prose over poetry to a specific failing: the poet's refusal to absorb "a new ideality conditioned by the advance of science." The novelist had done this and had also "cleverly adjusted his work to the facilities and drawbacks of modern journalism" (AA xxvii-xxviii). Stedman distanced himself from conventional genteel temperaments by refusing to judge this development as negative ("It is not strange that there should be a distaste for poetic illusion in an era when economics, no longer the dismal science, becomes a more fascinating study than letters") (AA xxviii). He claimed to hope still that the future would bring the "consensus of poetry and science foreseen by Wordsworth" (AA xxviii). A few younger critics, such as Ferris Greenslet, also saw that if the genre was to survive, those "who would keep alive a saving faith in poetry must controvert the position of invertebrate aestheticism" to which its genteel custodians clung and must show instead "that life is not a child to be smoothed and cozened, and that poetry is not an opiate but a tonic" ("Propaganda" 54). Decrying the genre's elitist drift and its proponents' unwillingness to engage with the modern condition, Greenslet posed and answered the question that most other commentators of the era could not face: "What is the mission of poetry in the life that surges around us in the street, in modern democratic society? Unless poetry in some way conforms itself in spirit and form and pressure to the spirit of democracy it is bound sooner or later to become an esoteric cult" ("Propaganda" 51). Though his was not the only answer, the question increasingly commanded the attention of the young American poets I'll examine in part 3.

Despite these isolated voices of dissent, as the turn of the century came and went there was little energetic advocacy of American poetry. One could find many repetitions of the songs of yesteryear, but these were no longer capable of enhancing—or even maintaining—the genre's status. Poetry was still in the institutional custody of the Robert Underwood Johnsons of genteel culture. Unwilling to accept the momentous social changes of the Gilded Age, much less the Progressive Era, these reactionaries embraced and confined poetry as the vehicle of their denial. For the ideologists of capitalist positivism, on the other hand, the genre was simply obsolete. It would take a response equally antithetical to the Fireside Poets and the *Saturday Evening Post* to reconstruct the value of poetry in and for American modernity. It fell to the youngest writers active during those decades to make this attempt, under the almost impossibly adverse conditions of reception I've outlined here. Part 3 traces their struggles, their limitations, and their undervalued achievement.

PART 3
Horizons

4

"TELL US WHY YOU PLAY!"

Young Poets of the 1890s

REWRITING THE TURN OF THE CENTURY

American poetry's crisis of modernity was experienced most acutely by the young writers born after 1860. Given the profusion of truncated careers and premature deaths among poets of this generation, it is not surprising that the turn of the century has been seen as "the big blank of American poetic history," in Frank Lentricchia's words (2). In alarming contrast to the six Fireside poets, whose ages averaged nearly eighty at their deaths, a remarkable number of the promising writers who began publishing verse in the 1890s, including Richard Hovey (1864–1900), Francis Brooks (1867–1898), Stephen Crane (1871–1900), Paul Laurence Dunbar (1872–1906), Guy Wetmore Carryl (1873–1904), George Cabot Lodge (1873–1909), Joseph Trumbull Stickney (1874–1904), and Arthur Upson (1877–1908), died well before their fortieth birthdays, while William Vaughn Moody (1869–1910) barely reached his. Out of financial necessity or general discouragement, numerous other aspiring and talented poets, including George Santayana, Ellen Glasgow, Carolyn Wells, Edgar Lee Masters, Charlotte Perkins Gilman, and Alice Dunbar-Nelson, gravitated to other pursuits, some never to return to verse. Those inclined to employ the Chatterton scenario to account for the decline in American poetry had models aplenty during these years. Indeed, as the best known and most ungoverned young literary celebrity of the 1890s, Stephen Crane was described in *Munsey's* as "the Chatterton of today" as early as 1895, as if his tragically premature death were merely a matter of time (Review of *The Black Riders*, in Weatherford 66). Even if we resist the notion that all these early deaths were not coincidental but somehow linked to the untenable position of the poet in turn-of-the-century America, the work of these young writers demonstrates that skepticism toward the value of poetry in America, latent but manageable in the Fireside writers, had become a serious, even fatal, stumbling block. For them, Josephine Preston Peabody's sardonic question—"But tell us of the wage, man / You had for this hard day; / . . . / And tell us why you play!" (*Fortune* 98)—was no joke. Finding reasons to continue playing, surrounded by little but indifference and contempt, became an urgent and defining concern of their work.

The critical commonplace about the generation of 1890s poets is that they possessed a melancholy temperament, a tragic sense of life, an inheritance of philosophical pessimism, or some similarly nebulous notion. Their angst-ridden pessimism becomes more meaningful when read through American poetry's crisis. Like the commentators discussed in part 2, these young writers faced a paralyzing impasse between the conviction that the traditions of American poetry were exhausted and a caustic skepticism toward actual avenues of innovation. To most, a reactionary embrace of the genre as a bastion of elite culture no longer seemed an adequate response, yet avenues of engagement with alternative or mass cultural formations were not easily accessible either. They saw few productive links left with past traditions and no particular reason to believe that the future would improve the situation.

Not surprisingly, given these Sisyphean circumstances, their work is preoccupied with images of paralysis and futility. But we have been mistaken in dismissing the period as a desolate interval in the history of American poetry between the long-settled canons of the mid-nineteenth century and the cosmopolitan formation of "high modernism." Indeed, I've found extraordinary interest in the struggles of these young writers to endure and comprehend the worst of the crisis, and for those who survived, to establish rejuvenated institutions and paradigms of cultural value after 1910. Detailed discussion of the 1910s awaits my next book, but here I want to note, as too few histories have done, that most of those crucial to the New Poetry of that decade—Edwin Arlington Robinson, Edgar Lee Masters, Harriet Monroe, Amy Lowell, Robert Frost, Carl Sandburg, Vachel Lindsay, Wallace Stevens—did not spring into middle-aged existence in 1912, but were members of this same "lost" generation born before 1880. Until 1910 its members' only recourse, and their major achievement, was to generate verse from their vexed relations to past canons, and from their anxiety over poetry's meager future prospects. Their strongest poems articulate an engagement with adversity that proved such qualities as anxiety, pessimism, and irony enabling rather than impious and morally corrosive, as genteel culture had believed. As these poets thematized the oblivion apparently awaiting them, they converted their feelings of marginalization and even despair into productive critique of obsolescent but still dominant genteel conceptions of cultural value. Their marginal position enabled them to say things about modernity that genteel verse had never uttered, and to imagine new cultural uses for American poetry. The beginning of viable "modernist" institutions in American poetry dates from 1911 or 1912. But these young poets of the 1890s and 1900s were the first to advance a modern poetics.

Part 3 describes the varied responses of these young writers to the excruciating evaluative conditions they encountered and urges reconsideration of their achievement. In this chapter I begin by sketching their increasing dissatisfaction with genteel canonical elders and their adoption of personae of youthful dissent and rebellion. I then examine the emergence, struggles, and dissolution of a group of talented poets associated with Harvard in the early 1890s who seemed the obvious heirs to the Fireside canon. The work of Santayana, Lodge, and Stickney poignantly dramatizes the breakdown of three previously crucial functions for poetry: to posit cosmic ideality, to provide emotional consolation, and to comment on sociopolitical issues. Ultimately the failures of these Harvard poets came not from their inability to create a "world elsewhere" transcending the despoliations of modernity, but from their tooeager embrace of this chimerical realm, which left them little but misanthropic revulsion toward modern American life. Their successes, particularly in the work of Moody and Robinson, came when they transmuted their alienation into clear-eyed awareness of poetry's cultural marginality and explored its possible uses.

My primary goal is to show that despite many false starts, abrupt cessations, and muted voices, a significant body of American verse between 1890 and 1910 registered the shifts in cultural value that defined the era's emergent modernity and began to rethink poetry's role in it. Foregrounding their own putative valuelessness or ephemerality, the strongest poems of this era grapple productively with the unstable evaluative dynamics of cultural modernity. This struggle was manifested through two pervasive topoi: canonical traditions portrayed as ghostly echoes of a past dead yet still oppressively present; and modern poets characterized as outcasts wandering through symbolic landscapes devoid of intelligible markers of value. These agonistic tropes both dramatize the poet's problematic cultural position and provide avenues of paradoxical enablement. The canonical ghost topos addressed the fraught relations between these poets and their literary predecessors, sometimes bogging down in despair and futility, but also (especially in the work of Robinson) generating a complex response to the threat of oppressive canonical plenitude. Through the ubiquitous figure of the wanderer, young writers evoked an urgent, sometimes aimless need to stake out territory outside the existing conventions of American poetry. The wanderer persona tempted some into escapist disengagement, but in other cases it offered liberating avenues to explore modern poetry's possibilities.

Both tropes are most productive in poems that give up the futile effort to buttress a nostalgic moral coherence, and that accept poetry's marginal position as a starting point. Such works rethink poetry's capacity to explore the phenomenology of modern perception, comment on sociopolitical conditions, and address the complex material and emotional meanings of modernization. The final chapter elaborates this thesis and challenges long-held assumptions about the escapist irrelevance of turn-of-the-century verse, by tracing a group of neglected but striking poems that directly engage the defining elements of modern mass society: the Statue of Liberty, the crowded urban thoroughfare, the World's Columbian Exposition, modern warfare and its propaganda, the daily newspaper. The young poets of these years took the first steps in American poetry's long march toward engagement with a condition of modernity driven by incorporative capitalism and articulated to most people through genres of mass culture. Their work responds to these challenges neither by rejecting modern mass culture in favor of obsolete genteel purity, nor by capitulating to its tendency to reductive utilitarianism. Their struggles were crucial in making twentieth-century poetry into a subtle and forceful vehicle for articulating the distinctive textures of modern life.

REBELLIOUS YOUTH

Even more severely than the commentators surveyed in the previous chapter, the young writers of the 1890s experienced genteel culture, and the Fireside canon that most fully embodied it, as an oppressive progenitor that excluded or inhibited them, yet allowed for no other creative realm. Though her fame would come as a novelist, Ellen Glasgow (1873–1945) harbored poetic aspirations as a young woman, and in 1902 she published her only volume of verse, *The Freeman*. In her autobiography, written decades later, Glasgow's antagonism against the turn-of-the-century genteel establishment was still palpable. She viewed "the Forty Immortals of the American Academy [of Arts and Letters]" as repressive ancestors who "had created both the literature of America and the literary renown that embalmed it" (*Woman Within* 139). In reference to these generally very old men, the metaphor of embalming was a pointed one, and Glasgow pressed the attack by describing theirs as a culture of "immature age" that "was old and tired and prudent, . . . loved ritual and rubric, and was utterly wanting in curiosity about the new and the strange" (140). Age had made these elders timid rather than wise, and they clung to premodern categories and practices, attempting to shut out a new and strange world they feared and failed to understand. Glasgow's conclusion—"at the turn of the century I owed less than nothing to these creators" (142)—would be echoed or simply taken for granted by her generation and its successors.

Expressions of youthful rebellion against tradition have long been recognized as defining elements of twentieth-century American culture. But it's less understood that such intergenerational antagonism was well established before the 1910s.[1] An emergent demographic of rebellious young artists and writers was an ironic effect of cultural developments of the later nineteenth century that entrenched age, wisdom, and experience as preconditions for meaningful participation in most arenas of American society. Glenn Wallach argues that after the Civil War there was a basic shift in the relation between younger and older generations, manifested by the precipitous decline of "age-defined organizations" such as the Young Americans, so that "By century's end, young people had few chances to participate in public" (152–53). These organizations were replaced by age-specific institutions and practices premised upon the new concept of adolescence, which "downgraded maturity and intellectuality in youth" while emphasizing instead a state of "perpetual becoming" (Kett 173). After 1890 adolescence was theorized exhaustively in psychological, educational, and familial discourses as a period of natural "storm and stress" (Wallach 153) requiring tolerance but also close adult supervision.[2] In this model, the young were expected to "practice their adult roles without direct engagement in public affairs" (Kett 211). As Kett suggests, the legitimation and indulgence of adolescent behavior may well have encouraged a youth culture of "passivity" and "insularity" (211), exemplified by the "school spirit" trend of 1890s colleges. But among some young Americans, they also made available the new subject position of rebellious bohemian youth. The more this rebellious attitude was adopted by young people alienated from adult life, the more it demonstrated to their elders youth's unreadiness to shoulder the responsibilities of adulthood—hence, more exclusion, and further rebellion.

Emerging from this youthful desire to repudiate the American literary tradition that made no place for her, the poems in Glasgow's *The Freeman* cast off restrictive social conventions by revising the domestic imagery so crucial in nineteenth-century canonical poetry. For example, in "Death-in-Life," featuring an eerie visitation by a dead lover, she recasts the fireside not as spiritually nourishing, but as insatiably consuming the speaker's attention and energies. In contrast to *Snow-Bound*, inside/outside is no longer the governing opposition, shelter no longer the ideal. The worst threat now comes from doing nothing but "Feeding the fangs of the hungry fire" (47). In the end, the speaker accepts his demonic lover ("What matter the honours that I shall miss / When I find her lying against my side?"), preferring an ecstatic death rather than unending thralldom to the hearth fire; this choice is fully justified by his dead lover's paradoxical response, "Nay, nay—ah, love, I am Life" (49). Glasgow's analysis of the cultural traditions inhibiting her youth invites us to read this poem as a rejection of genteel domesticity in favor of an avant-garde agonism she perceived as liberating in its scandalous extremity.

Like Glasgow's, many turn-of-the-century poems anticipate the familiar rebelliousness of so many twentieth-century youth, for whom a desire to shock their elders was perhaps the most precious goal, extremity of rhetoric and form the most central strategies. Lodge's "Les Bourgeois" (1902), for example, prefigures the ferocious antibourgeois lampoons produced by Pound and other avant-gardists a dozen years later. The lives of Lodge's bourgeoisie, ruled by fear, weakness, and hypocritical desire, are no more significant than those of "gaudy flies that play and perish" in a single day and are "Once vanished, like a stupid dream / That never was." Lodge ends by abjuring them to "Be something, good or bad! Be real!" (1:134), embracing modern ideals of authenticity even at the cost of virtue and respectability. Moments of violent rebellion such as these simmer right underneath the conventional formal surfaces of much turn-of-the-century poetry; beguiled by high modernism's insistence on stylistic uniqueness and disjunction, we have usually failed to see them.

Perhaps no young poet analyzed the inhibiting shadow of the genteel canon more incisively than Amy Lowell (1874–1925), for whom it was not just an imposing cultural heritage but a familial one. In middle age, released from her ambiguous birthright after long struggle, Lowell paid mischievous homage to her illustrious elder cousin and his fellows in the 1922 satire *A Critical Fable* (first published anonymously). Enumerating the leading poets of that year, the poem's narrator describes "Amy Lowell's" touchiness about her ancestry in witty terms that nonetheless make a deadly serious point: "No one likes to be bound / In a sort of perpetual family pound / Tied by *esprit de corps* to the wheels of the dead" (46).[3] Linking these feelings of familial repression to broader patterns of generational and cultural repression, Lowell's narrator explains the Fireside poets' fall by 1922:

> "At least," I said hotly, "we are not a mere sprig
> From an overseas' bush, and we don't care a fig
> For a dozen dead worthies of classic humdrum,
> And each one no bigger than Hop-o'-my-thumb
> To our eyes. Why, the curse of their damned rhetoric
> Hangs over our writers like a school-master's stick." (5)

Lowell's comic rhymes theorize the modern repudiation of the Fireside-Schoolroom poets: their ("damned"!) moralizing *rhetoric* is like a schoolmaster's *stick* repressing the American poetic imagination. Where previous generations of poets and readers had felt edified and uplifted by that rhetoric—or at least unable to rebel—Lowell's, openly resentful, felt rapped on the knuckles by it.

As the conversation continues, the narrator's companion, an old gentleman gradually revealed as the shade of James Russell Lowell, asks indignantly, "Where are Longfellow, Lowell, / With Whittier, Bryant, and Holmes? . . . / . . . are they not deserving / A tithe of your upstart, unfledged admiration?" (7). Reflecting the irritation of Amy Lowell and her contemporaries with the pious obligation ("tithe") claimed for these canonical elders, the narrator responds, "For the matter of liking, / The men he had mentioned might be each a Viking" (8)—the couplet's awkward diction and outlandish rhyme offering more sly comment on the faults of their poetry. When asked the cause of these drastic changes in American poetry over barely thirty years, her narrator wonders:

> Poor old gentleman, should I be tempted
> To tell him the fault was that he had pre-ëmpted,
> He and the others, the country's small stock
> Of imagination? The real stumbling-block
> Was the way they stood up like Blake's angels, a chorus

Of geniuses over our heads, no more porous
Than so much stretched silk; rain, sun, and the stellar
Effulgences balked by our national umbrella
Of perished celebrities. To mention a trifling
Fact, underneath them the air's somewhat stifling.
Youthful lungs need ozone and, considering the tent,
No man can be blamed if he punches a rent
With his fist in the stiff, silken web if he can. (14–15)

If Glasgow had seen the renowned Americans of nineteenth-century literature as the denizens of an embalming parlor, Lowell portrays their canonical function as an equally repressive and moribund one, in which their precious images of enclosure were no longer signs of beneficent nature, but had become umbrellas and tents, artificial and "stifling."

Lowell's old gentleman, discomfited by the unstable nature of fame, next demands to be shown "your people of parts" (12). The narrator directs him to a door marked "Skeletons Only," headed by "A notice designed to make any one lonely. / It stares over the gate in huge letters of red: / 'No person admitted until he is dead,'" a stricture conspicuously parodying the eligibility requirements for the Hall of Fame for Great Americans. Before this unprepossessing sign, a belated "shrivelled remainder" waits, eyes glued. When the door opens to admit one, "Gone over to dust and to fame," the remaining "requiem fraternal" comically emits "a chorus of 'Damns!'" (13). As she reduces the American "chorus of geniuses" to wheezing, querulous old men concerned only with their canonical reputations, Lowell plays the subversive avant-gardist to the hilt, equating fame with dust, portraying canonicity in metaphors that render ridiculous the whole notion of a sanctified national culture.

A distinction must be maintained, however, between the uninhibited hindsight of Glasgow's and Lowell's later comments and the more restricted range of rebellion against the genteel actually available to young Americans during the 1890s and 1900s. In their young adulthood, Glasgow and Lowell too struggled against the inhibiting sexist stereotype of the "girls with three names" (Burgess 11). Before 1910 even less restricted male writers found no secure cultural position from which to articulate such bracing antitraditionalism. The travails of the privileged and talented "Harvard" poets of the 1890s exemplified the urgent need of developing—and the daunting difficulty of maintaining—a sensibility of revolt against genteel canons.

PALLID CRIMSON

By the early 1840s, five of the six writers who became "Our Poets" of the American fireside had congregated in greater Boston, formed close and productive associations with each other, and begun their ascent to the canonical firmament. Apparently re-creating this pattern, between 1889 and 1895 Joseph Trumbull Stickney, George Cabot Lodge, William Vaughn Moody, Francis Brooks, and Edwin Arlington Robinson (1869–1935) all matriculated at Harvard, where George Santayana (1863–1952, class of 1886), just a few years older, was a young instructor. They had before them the social and cultural benefits of the country's most prestigious university and the intellectual enrichment of its most eminent group of thinkers—William James, C. S. Peirce, Josiah Royce. Longstanding friendships developed among these student-poets, with Moody serving as the pivotal figure equally at home with the Brahmins Lodge and Stickney, and with Robinson, much humbler in origin.[4] In an earlier time the literary world would simply have awaited the pleasure of young poets with such a pedigree. Blessed with abundant ambition, talent, and cultural capital, they seemed to have everything needed to become as dominant a canonical configuration as their Cambridge predecessors. Their inability to do so was overdetermined by the early deaths of all but Robinson. But as Cary Nelson points out, such "artistic failure" needs to be understood not as primarily about "the weaknesses and limitations of individual character," but as "culturally driven," a "complex reflection of social and historical contradictions" (*Repression* 69)—in this case, as a structural failure revealing the untenable position of even the most advantageously situated young poets during these years.[5]

To a significant extent, the failures of these poets were those of Harvard itself, whose intellectual atmosphere in the 1890s hampered their efforts to develop a poetics adequate to turn-of-the-century American modernity. In a 1936 letter quoted often by historians (most influentially by Van Wyck Brooks in *New England: Indian Summer* [447]), Santayana expressed this failure rather melodramatically by remarking: "all those friends of mine, Stickney especially, . . . were visibly killed by the lack of air to breathe. People individually were kind and appreciative to them, . . . but the system was deadly" (*Letters* 306).[6] Santayana's metaphors imply cultural suffocation; at the other extreme, Larzer Ziff portrays Harvard in the 1890s as a desert of too much freedom, arguing that the revolutionary elective curriculum of President Charles William Eliot constituted an admission that the university "could no longer define education, and threw the burden on the individual," resulting in the displacement of true intellectual community by exaggerated emphasis on social distinctions and the "artificial community" of school spirit (308). While this may ascribe too much importance to the elective system, it is clear that the insular atmosphere of 1890s college life, which to most young Americans meant fraternal organizations, athletics, and extracurricular activities, generated among these seriously literary Harvard undergraduates a quasi-monastic, agoraphobic idealism that strongly inflected American poetry by the turn of the century.

Despite the dynamic engagement with modernity in the work of James and Peirce, the dominant intellectual force at Harvard during these years, as Bernard Duffey has shown, was the recently rediscovered Arthur Schopenhauer, as interpreted by Royce and Santayana, the young poet-philosopher who straddled the faculty-student divide (143–47). The embrace of Schopenhauer, dead since 1860, indicated literary Harvard's fascination with a spiritual idealism defined by its contrast to the despoiling materialism of modernity. This idealism derived its identity—and some of its debilitating insularity—from Royce's emphasis on "the spiritual body" of a community, which, as Lentricchia points out, tends to mean that genuine community "can have nothing but *spiritual* body, that the values he associates with community can keep their integrity only in the inner life's realms of nostalgia and hope, memory and imagination" (37). This vision of the elite college as quasi-monastic ideal, disdainfully repudiating modern materialism, was captured in an untitled verse fragment by Philip Henry Savage. Describing a "sunset in the college close," falling "like a benediction softly down," Savage then evokes the forces of urban modernity that the *closeness* of the college (in all its senses) must keep at bay:

> . . . but on the sky
> The city in the distance casts a light
> Brilliant and false, electric, publishing
> Confusion and false day, nature betrayed,
> And all the dark disguises of the town.
> ("Fragment IV" 84–85)

The city is doubly damned here: associated with an electrified modernity that blazons a false and disorienting brilliance, it is also condemned for its dark patches and tendency to self-concealment. Savage's use of "publishing" is particularly intriguing, implicating the act of writing for an audience into the false and despoiling realm of commercialized modernity.

We can be forgiven for doubting that Harvard in the 1890s was still relying on sunlight and candles, as Savage seems to imply. His anachronistic imagery suggests that despite its devotion to spiritual idealism in the abstract, literary Harvard during these years was motivated even more strongly by disdain for materialist modernity. Its dominant pose was a cynical indifference to just about everything, even the idealism of its own organizations. This whimsical but ultimately self-defeating pose was taken to its extreme in 1892 by the "Laodicean Club," named in tribute to the church cursed by God thus: "So then because thou art lukewarm, and neither cold nor hot, I will spue thee out of my mouth" (Revelation 3:16; qtd. Whittle 45–46). Electing Santayana as "Pope," this organization faithfully embodied the paradoxes of its intellectual environment: having adopted the rule that "if at any meeting a quorum should be present the club should *ipso facto* cease to exist," the very interest of its members doomed it after two meetings (Lovett 46). Savage's sonnet "To G. S." presents to Santayana an apologia for the same fastidious passivity that the Laodicean Club embodied; it begins "PRAY God to give me power to keep / Life's cureless evils out of sight; / Nor wander o'er the world and weep / The things I cannot do aright," and ends "I scorn / To add one weight to weakness more" (159). "To G. S." functions as an antimanifesto, a rationale for not writing—no surprise given Savage's treatment of the act of publishing in "Fragment IV." It bespeaks a sensibility so radically alienated that it cannot even freely proclaim its alienation and must instead remain cloistered within a small circle of like-minded peers and mentors, never acting at all except to reiterate its disdain for despoiling publicity.

Santayana's aesthetic influence on a brace of Harvard-educated poets, not just those of the early 1890s but also Stevens, Eliot, and Conrad Aiken between 1897 and 1911, has been well documented, but seldom has the role of his own verse been thoroughly considered. His 1894 volume of "Schopenhauerian sonnets," as Duffey calls them (145), offers perhaps the purest articulation of literary Harvard's tendency to binarize experience as either worldly or spiritual and to embrace a radically subjective "spiritual" consciousness. This inclination is enacted in the first two lines of the sonnet that begins: "There may be chaos still around the world, / This little world that in my thinking lies" (*Sonnets* 16). Initially the reference to the "chaos" of "the world" seems to suggest that even if the poem does nothing but decry a state of chaos, it will at least acknowledge some awareness of a contemporary social realm. But the second line reduces the poem's scope to the "little world" of the speaker's own thought, the only world that turns out to matter, as "Within my nature's shell I slumber curled, / Unmindful of the changing outer skies" (16). These lines evoke the sheltering natural images through which the Fireside poets dramatized the workings of a benevolent deity. Here, however, "nature," like "the world," analogizes no category of larger spiritual understanding, but remains the solipsistic subjectivity of "my nature." The next sonnet in the volume uses another image of enclosure to describe the spiritual self-isolation the poet hankers for: "A wall, a wall around my garden rear, / And hedge me in from the disconsolate hills" (17). Here the distance from Fireside analogical communitarianism is even greater; this enclosure is purely a signifier of economic elitism, erected to keep out both the natural world and the human one ("Come no profane insatiate mortal near / With the contagion of his passionate ills"). The hills are disconsolate for the same reason the profane mortal is insatiate: because poetry's powers of consolation and satisfaction, which once offered access to spiritual experience, no longer function. All that remains of value is silent, pure consciousness, an "ancient quiet" that "broods from pole to pole" in this walled shrine (17).[7]

Such self-quarantine against the contagious strife of modern materialism became all but obligatory in the verse of the Harvard poets, as in Santayana's lines "My heart rebels against my generation, / That talks of freedom and is slave to riches" (*Sonnets* 69), and in Francis Brooks's condemnation of a "Cursèd inebriate nation" wallowing in gold, "Drunk with the dollar's damnation" (*Margins* 78).[8] This antipathy to modernity was often dramatized by fetishizing cultures and literatures of the distant past, as in Hugh McCulloch's celebration of "The golden age of medieval France" as a time "when powers of Light were fain / Against the powers of Darkness to advance" ("Praeteria," *Quest* 74).[9] Robinson remained in the grip of neomedievalism throughout his life, as his voluminous Arthurian narratives attest; his satiric self-portrait "Miniver Cheevy" shows he also maintained a healthy skepticism toward these potentially disabling obsessions. Most of his Harvard contemporaries, not as sensitive to self-irony, were less fortunate. Whether the past they aspired to inhabit was Biblical, classical, or medieval, it was invariably distant.[10] Moody, Stickney, and Lodge followed a remarkably similar pattern in the latter years of their brief careers, gravitating toward long blank verse dramas that mined ancient myths for symbols of disaffection and rebellion. Both Stickney in "Prometheus Pyrphoros" and Moody in *The Fire Bringer* essayed the personage of Prometheus, magnetically attractive to the ambitious and frustrated young poet, while Lodge's

Herakles and *Cain* are "built around the struggle of the central characters to attain Promethean stature" (Riggs 417).[11] Thomas Riggs Jr. argues plausibly that Henry Adams, a friend of Lodge and Stickney, was the main philosophical influence on their Promethean works (though not on Moody's), encouraging them to transform a narrative of human illumination into an Adamsian recognition of the futility of progress, in which "the emotional weight" is entirely "on the side of the laws of dissipation and decay" (409). The autobiographical resonance of this agonistic nostalgia was comprehensively evoked by Stickney's fragmentary drama on the Roman emperor Julian the Apostate, a belated classical idealist who struggled against the tides of irrationality and chaos that overwhelmed his time, before dying tragically young, his work unfinished and virtually forgotten.[12]

This common turn toward archaic forms of poetic drama that self-consciously intervened into the high literary tradition, but had little or no chance of being performed in a contemporary theater, again suggests the escapist tendency of Harvard's idealism.[13] They dreamed of creating work in the great tradition that would free them from the despoliations of modernity. McCulloch's sonnet "Refuge" constructs the high canon in exactly this escapist role. The octave establishes the need for escape from "these barren lands / Where I was born," then embarks on a fantasy journey to "the magic isles / Of tropic seas" where the speaker might "wander on the golden sands." The sestet analogizes that notion of escapist "refuge" to another type of magic isle, the great works of distant times and cultures: "Then Homer to the Old World carries me / In hollow ships across the crested main," while Spenser "gives enchanted sea, / His summer woods and purple pageantry" (*Quest* 57). In a sonnet beginning "I HATE the vast array of 'modern' things," Savage took this agoraphobic trope a step further to suggest that in philistine modernity, even the escapist function of the high canon might be losing its potency. The speaker notes with distaste that "Every season brings" a new set of "Dull imitations and a thousand light / And weightless books of verse and copyings," and further, that "fashion" "Proclaims them beautiful," besieging him "till I take flight / And turn me to the masters and the kings." But the degrading force of commodity fetishism has infected even the elite realm of the masters, and he gains no satisfaction there either:

> I find my Walton in a showy dress;
> Find all the bright, old-age simplicity
> Bedecked and botched; the years of good Queen Bess

Are made the dull philistine's property;
And Burns is 'popularly' sent to press. (73)

As Savage's bitter elitism suggests, the Harvard poets' agoraphobic pronouncements, and their ransacking of the past for inklings of an idealism Santayana called "Some greater waking" (7), did not often afford them access to enriching spiritual experience. On the contrary, their rejection of modernity was usually accompanied by disabling skepticism toward the attainability of any spiritual value. For example, in "L'Enfant du Siècle," Lodge incarnated twentieth-century modernity as a "dim dying child" in whom "Faith has died" and to whom "no new God appears" (1:94). They favored metaphoric constructions that linked an absent, ineffectual, or capricious deity to the futility of poetic utterance itself. In another of his many sonnets, Santayana connected such skepticism to the acutely despiritualized character of modernity and to poetry's enfeebled position within it:

> I would I had been born in nature's day,
> When man was in the world a wide-eyed boy,
> And clouds of sorrow crossed his sky of joy
> To scatter dewdrops on the buds of May.
> Then could he work and love and fight and pray,
> Nor heartsick grow in fortune's long employ.
> Mighty to build and ruthless to destroy
> He lived, while maskèd death unquestioned lay. (*Sonnets* 6)

The desires expressed here would have been easily recognized by the Fireside writers. Santayana's representative human is "a wide-eyed boy," where Whittier's had been barefoot, but his nostalgic wish is for the same unreflective analogical coherence that the Fireside poets had sought. The difference in the two formulations is one of attainability. In "The Barefoot Boy," *Snow-Bound,* and other works, Whittier had used idealized memories of his childhood to buttress the emotional and spiritual coherence his age urgently desired. For Santayana, in a belated age of debilitating uncertainty, where poets "Now ponder . . . the ruins of the years, / And groan beneath the weight of boasted gain," any transparency poetry had once enabled between worldly and spiritual realms is long gone:

> No unsung bacchanal can charm our ears
> And lead our dances to the woodland fane,

> No hope of heaven sweeten our few tears
> And hush the importunity of pain. (*Sonnets* 6)

Santayana's syntactic parallelism ("No unsung bacchanal," "No hope of heaven") evokes poetry's contemporary inability to image spiritual experience and suggests that this loss has resulted from its very profusion in a bloated world of "boasted gain," in which the phrase "no unsung bacchanal" also implies that all bacchanals have been sung, all poems already written.

The "hope of heaven" that might "hush the importunity of pain" evokes another once viable way of understanding the value of poetry: as a source of emotional consolation. More or less an afterthought in Santayana's sonnet, the rejection of the consolatory genteel poetics that had drawn reassuring analogical relationships between human, natural, and cosmic realms was made devastatingly explicit in other turn-of-the-century works. In Lodge's "L'Enfant du Siècle," "The soul's sweet choristers that once did toll / Thro' God's immensity are fallen dumb," and the new century's child is doomed to "come / Thro' life a mourner" (1:94). But the quality of this mourning is so debased that the child of modernity has utterly "lost the power of natural tears" and will thus remain "mute and pitiful." Less ponderously, Brooks's "For Such" employs a rhetoric of analogical consolation for the apparent purpose of comforting one who "sits with breaking heart and filling eyes alone," hearing "fond laughter on the passing breeze" and "slow footsteps . . . pacing twain" (*Margins* 12). Such a grief-stricken figure was a familiar one from innumerable genteel elegies, but Brooks uses it instead to lampoon poetry's consolatory tradition as little more than specious sentimentalism. The poem ends by reiterating, "For such the consolation will remain," but it will come only in the unhappy one's knowledge that despite the "fond laughter" of those who are now happy, eventually *"Death will strangle each alone"* (13; italics in original). Brooks thus cuts the rug out from under the consolatory tradition, endorsing instead an appallingly bitter view of life defined by the ultimate desolation of every human soul instead of just some of them. Replacing the empathetic Fireside deity cognizant of human suffering with an indifferent, equal-opportunity annihilator, this poem exemplifies the corrosive agnosticism of fin de siècle Harvard.

In "The Dead Village" (1897) Robinson extended this critique of consolatory verse, imagining a world utterly devoid of poetry. The genre's spiritual function had once enabled humans to discern a precious connection between material and ideal realms ("small soft hands . . . once did keep in tune / The strings that stretch from heaven"). But "too soon / The change came, and the music passed away" (*Children of the Night* 50); poetry had now lost the ability to ascribe spiritual significance to the material realm, and thus (in one of the many turn-of-the-century echoes of the last lines of "Dover Beach"), "Now there is nothing but the ghosts of things,—/ No life, no love, no children, and no men." The implacable sequence of clauses that ends the poem—"The music failed, and then / God frowned, and shut the village from His sight" (50)—reinforces Robinson's fear that the end of poetry's efficacy means the loss of the entire spiritual dimension of existence.

The skepticism these writers felt about modern poetry's ability to evoke spiritual experience led them to frequent expressions of cosmic emptiness, memorably captured by Stickney's phrase "the big night of time," which Duffey used to entitle his fine chapter on this period in American poetry. Stickney's spiritual anguish deepens when we understand it as a response to poetry's crisis of modernity:

> Who is this God our prayer pursues?
> Down the big night of time,
> On wings of ancient wind
> The gray smoke from a thousand altars rolls,
> And anthems cried by choired souls
> Immeasurably combined
> Crowd in the sky sublime.—
> Who is he? where? and may he be divined?
> ("Fragment of an Ode for Greek Liberty" 292)

Without doubt, the devoted classicist Stickney conceived this work in response to the oppression of contemporary Greece, but its more potent function is to evoke the futility of poetic expression in the modern world. The imagery of the passage emphasizes failing methods of poetic divination: "prayer" hopelessly pursuing the notion of God, and choirs of "anthems" attempting to celebrate it. Despite his restiveness with old prayers and anthems, Stickney is diverted from a position of revolt or iconoclasm by an alienating human clutter that evokes turn-of-the-century anxieties of cultural overproduction and fragmentation. These anthems "crowd in the sky," and the crowds of souls who choir them, so "combined" as to be immeasurable, signal the erosion of the individually conceived canon of value, and by extension, the surrender of elite culture to the commodified anonymity of mass culture. For Stickney, the question posed by God's absence is now answerable in only one way:

through a cry of sheer misery signifying the replacement of human speech with frenzied animalistic utterance:

> . . . must their piteous wrong
> Of slaughtered men, women befouled
> And nurslings trampled in the mire,
> Hurl its terrific song,
> The crying measure of a last desire? (292–93)

The poetry still to come will be only a "crying measure" (in two senses) of the "last desire" of human aspiration. The final fragment begins, "He shall not rise. Let hope in veils of pall / This widely crimson morning close" (293), acknowledging the anguished sense of pointlessness that pervades the whole work. Given this recognition of its own futility, we can hardly be surprised that the poem remained incomplete. Like the drama on Julian, its fragmentary state was not due to Stickney's untimely death. The editors who posthumously collected his work dated it 1897, the year of the Greco-Turkish War in Crete. We can only surmise that in working on this topic, Stickney found poetry unviable as a vehicle for social commentary and simply stopped.

GHOSTLY CANONS

The many false starts, blind alleys, and abrupt endings in the work of the Harvard poets vividly demonstrate that Romantic-genteel accounts of poetry's value had broken down. Poetry was still just potent enough to motivate a young writer to begin, say, an ode commemorating a war or a friend's death, but often not potent enough to allow its satisfactory completion or reception. Like the commentators I examined in the previous chapter, younger poets of the 1890s were grappling with two contradictory convictions: (1) that American poetic traditions were exhausted and useless, and (2) that no viable avenues of innovation and renewal existed. Not surprisingly, their verse frequently depicts both empty desolate space and exasperating clutter, exuding enormous tension between oppressive stasis and restless movement. These clashing impulses manifested themselves in two interdependent tropes pervading verse of these decades: (1) the portrayal of canons as ghostly echoes of now inert and useless traditions that refuse to recede into the past, and (2) the figuring of the modern poet as a vagabond wanderer in landscapes that lack comprehensible markers of value or ethics.

The topos of the "ghostly canon" articulated young poets' vexed relations of present and past poetry. Its most important practitioner was a lonely man haunted his whole life by family tragedies and alcohol-driven demons, who lacked the personal brilliance of his glossier Harvard contemporaries. Yet Edwin Arlington Robinson was the only Harvard poet who evaded creative impasse and early death to become an important force in American verse after 1910. The canonical ghost motif allowed him (and sometimes others) to articulate their troubled relationships with canonical predecessors and to question, if not reject outright, the subject position of pitiable aspirant that poetry's crisis threatened to mire them in. Robinson's approach to tradition certainly generated more productive resistance than the abject antiquarianism of Santayana, Savage, McCulloch, and Stickney, who diffused their rebellious energies by immersing themselves in the distant past, never learning how to use these enthusiasms to challenge the modern world's spiritual vacuity. In contrast, most poems that trope canonical ghosts, particularly Robinson's, clung stubbornly to that modern world even as they agonized over it. As efforts to comprehend the oppressive reverberation of the past upon the present, they were less glamorous than plunges into lost golden antiquity, but much healthier to the spirits of their creators and more conducive to American poetry's rejuvenation.

We can measure the anxious, ingenious, and paradoxically energizing responses to the ghostly canon by first understanding how being haunted could inhibit and disable. In "Visitation" (1891) Richard Hovey's attitude toward his canonical fathers is one of abjection that tries but fails to mask feelings of oppression and hostility. The speaker's annoyingly obsequious phrasings ("I would that I could deem / That I were worthy"; "I would that I could think that my poor song / Had reached thee") culminate in a wish that his verse, paltry as it is, "pleased thee but so much as thou shouldst turn / And yield one sigh for those who still must mourn / On this harsh earth" (*Along the Trail* 100–01). In describing the dead poet's presence as "like a flower / That sends a heavy odor through the air" (101), Hovey comes close to conceding the unnatural and unwelcome power of the canonical ghost over the living aspirant. Yet he seems not to realize that his verse, itself wallowing in the conventional diction and imagery of genteel homily, evokes the "hothouse" gentility of contemporary poetry that he reviled in other contexts. Hovey never gains control of this contradiction, and the poem comes across as passive-aggressive groveling.

This experience of canonical haunting was the same one articulated by Howells in his survey of contemporary poetry in 1899: what can poets of the present do that will measure up to those "tremendous Absences" left by departed greats? ("New Poetry" 591). But if this was a challenge young poets had to confront, it was also an opportunity to rethink the possible functions of poetry in a time that exhibited little reverence for canons. In "Visitation" Hovey was not up to the task, but in another poem, "The Shadows" (1898), he gained some purchase on his angst-ridden relationship with his predecessors. "The Shadows" reads like a fragment from a Gothic horror story, in which the speaker apprehends a nightmarish procession of shadows he describes as "dull red, like embers in a grate" (*Along the Trail* 98), marking them as the denizens of the Fireside canon, gone yet still unnaturally present. Ironically, "the grisliest horror" of the experience is that the speaker cannot make the shadows acknowledge his presence, as they stride on "with a stony stare, / Nor heed me where I lie." Conversely, no matter how much he attempts to "strain my eyes as I freeze and cringe / Till the sockets sizzle dry," he cannot actually see them clearly ("they will never impinge mine eye"). The touch of canonical inspiration that the poet dreads but desperately wants will never be forthcoming. The poem ends with the shadows playing "about the feet of Fate / Their awful game of tag," a strained but intriguing metaphor portraying the canon as a closed circle whose members interact only with another. In this work Hovey has at least shed the paralyzing pretense that this relation was based on benevolent mentoring rather than deadly intergenerational competition.[14]

In "Prometheus" (1899) Dunbar gets further than Hovey in confronting this tension between present-day poets and canonical ancestors, represented here by Shelley and Prometheus himself. Here the Promethean myth of poetry's origins, created "To lift men's souls above their low estate," becomes a sardonic commentary on the genre's modern obsolescence:

> But judge you now, when poets wield the pen,
> Think you not well the wrong has been repaired?
> 'T was all in vain that ill Prometheus fared:
> The fire has been returned to Heaven again!
> (*Complete Poems* 117)

Though Dunbar's response to this perception of canonical plenitude is clearly pessimistic ("We have no singers like the ones whose note / Gave challenge to the noblest warbler's song"), it is an honest, self-respecting pessimism, unlike the obsequious flattery of "Visitation." And it catalyzes a bracing transformation in the poem's diction, from the more indirect and highfalutin language of the first stanzas, to the crisp, minimal affect of the final lines:

> The measure of our songs is our desires;
> We tinkle where old poets used to storm.
> We lack their substance tho' we keep their form:
> We strum our banjo-strings and call them lyres. (117)

Even if Dunbar intended the spareness of these lines to concede his lack of an adequate language to stand up to the canon, it represents an impressive cleansing of genteel poeticisms, a significant step toward the minimal styles that flourished after 1910, and a sign of Dunbar's importance not just as an pioneer of African American writing but as a stylist of modern verse.

The sense of being haunted by lingering canonical presences was an obsessive subject in Robinson's early work. Never inclined to launch onto an open road as Crane was, Robinson's restlessness manifested itself instead as complex dissatisfaction with his predecessors. In his 1897 volume *The Children of the Night*, this impulse catalyzed an impressive series of poems that thematize common notions of canonicity, including "The Wilderness," "Ballade by the Fire," "The Clerks," "The House on the Hill," "The Pity of the Leaves," "Sonnet," "The Dead Village," and "Ballade of Broken Flutes." While Robinson's pessimistic survey of poetry's status may be a litany of futility, it is far from an exercise in futility. By problematizing the oppressive reverberation of past canons in conceptually ingenious and linguistically rich forms, these poems wind up reasserting (even while they doubt) the genre's continued imaginative value.

Robinson articulates his stalemate with the domestic conventions of the American poetic tradition in his volume's title, which evokes Longfellow's breakthrough book of 1839, *Voices of the Night*. Robinson clearly identifies himself with the progeny of the Fireside, but this is hardly an unambiguous homage, since to be "children of the night" implies deprivation as much as enrichment and evokes a group forced forever to "wait for the light," as he put it in "Richard Cory" (*Children of the Night* 35). This ambivalence toward his Fireside predecessors is theorized in "The Wilderness," whose wandering speaker hears a nebulous voice offering solace in the Fireside style, "an old song calling us to come" home and "roam no more" (88). The speaker urges his listener to "Come away" out of the wilderness since "a window gleams to greet us, / And a warm hearth waits for us within" (89). But Robinson can neither repudiate nor embrace this fear-gripped traditionalism. All he can do is forcefully register his ambivalent awareness of it and its diametric opposite: "dead men all around us—/ Frozen men, that mock us with a wild, hard laugh" (90). If these rebels who rejected the canonical hearth for the wilderness ultimately failed, the ghostly echoes of their struggle toward liberation still fill the speaker with shame and envy. Robinson thus implies that adherence to tradition reveals only fear and weakness; yet still he cannot see its rejection as anything more than a quick way to a cold grave.

But a superficially similar poem, "Ballade by the Fire," demonstrates that this impasse could be converted into self-affirmation almost in spite of the poet's apparent intentions. The speaker here begins in the familiar fireside setting but immediately announces his distance from genteel domestic conventions by his isolation and bachelor habits: "Slowly I smoke and hug my knee" (*Children of the Night* 20). This speaker's only communion is with the dim visions in "The falling embers," which he terms "a witless masquerade" that "Floats in a mist of light and shade." The spiritual ameliorations of remembering one's childhood by the fireside, so dear to his canonical predecessors, are reduced to the "weak, remindful glow" of a nicotine haze (20). In the next stanza, these rather complacent musings on past canons and his own poetic aspirations suddenly coalesce into a visionary moment:

> Then, with a melancholy glee
> To think where once my fancy strayed,
> I muse on what the years may be
> Whose coming tales are all unsaid,
> Till tongs and shovel, snugly laid
> Within their shadowed niches, grow
> By grim degrees to pick and spade
> As one by one the phantoms go. (20)

The speaker is startled to find that his fireside (Fireside) tools, which had seemed "snugly" ensconced "within their shadowed niches," have metamorphosed into reminders of inevitable and all-encroaching oblivion, preempting the "unsaid" tales he had aspired to tell.

Vincent Bertolini has shown that the antebellum scene of "the solitary lounging bachelor dreaming before the glowing embers" was "a widely diffused cultural topos" (707) of peculiar liminal significance, hosting "the active and passive, the transgressive and normalizing, sides of bachelor identity contending against one another" (716), and often including a strongly sexual component: "the bachelor has left properly constituted boyhood, in which the young man's sexuality is monitored, chastened, and directed towards proper objects by the mother, but not yet entered properly constituted manhood, in which the wife extends the maternal regime within the bounds of a limited, procreative conjugal sexuality" (710). The posture of Robinson's speaker—hugging his knee, enjoying his cigar, mesmerized by the "visions" he imagines in the fire— strongly resembles this ambiguously sexualized bachelor scene. In this context, the fireplace tools evoke repressive parental-canonical figures who throw ashes over the speaker's powers of transgressive fantasy. Bertolini suggests that by the turn of the century, a more modern con- tented bachelor, "unbound by either the constraints on excessive sexual subjectivity or the injunction to procreative norms," had emerged (730).[15] Robinson's speaker strives to become that more modern bachelor, jaunti- ly resolving to resume his bachelor existence, to "live and laugh, nor be dismayed / As one by one the phantoms go" (*Children of the Night* 21). But the old inhibitions, sexual and canonical alike, are not so easily dis- carded, and his affirmation of bachelor pleasures pales compared to the hallucinatory shape-shifting of those Fireside tools. This poem is typical of the 1890s verse at its most paradoxically interesting: at a literal level it despairs of poetry's continued value, but in the very framework of its failure it creates a rich, edgy demonstration of what poetry can do.

At the turn of the century, the supposedly overwhelming profusion of new poetic work was often portrayed as an avalanche of waste paper—an enormously discouraging image to the aspiring poet. In "The Pity of the Leaves," Robinson uses canonical-ghost imagery to challenge this waste-paper trope, revivifying the well-worn pun on "leaves" as from both trees and books. Here an old man hears a "bleak, sad wind that shrieked" "Loud with ancestral shame" (*Children of the Night* 45). Surely one possible source of this "ancestral shame" is the oppressive reverberation of a tradition upon its contemporary aspirants. Robinson likens "words of the past" from "lips that were no more to speak" to "brown, thin leaves that on the stones outside / Skipped with a freezing whisper." These leaves are not just frozen but "freezing," chilling the speaker's own aspirations. The final lines powerfully evoke an impasse, neither fully past nor present:

> . . . Now and then
> They stopped, and stayed there—just to let him know
> How dead they were; but if the old man cried,
> They fluttered off like withered souls of men. (45)

In decisive contrast to the "withered words" of Lowell's "A Winter-Evening Hymn to My Fire," which were given incandescent life by the domestic inspiration of the fireside, the only function of these withered canonical writings is to remind the speaker of their complete lack of vitality to him. They disintegrate the moment he tries to use them for expressive purposes. In the face of this bleakness, a faint but important affirmative resonance emerges through the poem's double-edged title. Usually the image of waste paper was applied to new, unwanted verse; by using it to portray canonical poetry, by pitying the tradition rather than simply allowing it to pity him, Robinson deflects some of the image's disabling force away from the aspirant.

One of Robinson's key strategies for challenging the canon's oppressive force was to lampoon its conventional portrayal as a sacred space—academy, pantheon, museum, mausoleum—by instead linking it to the rundown and obsolete physical structures of deteriorating New England market towns. In "The House on the Hill," an abandoned dwelling houses an ingenious ghost story on the impotence of the canonical edifice the poet has inherited. Here is the poem in full:

> They are all gone away,
> The House is shut and still,
> There is nothing more to say.
>
> Through broken walls and gray
> The winds blow bleak and shrill:
> They are all gone away.
>
> Nor is there one to-day
> To speak them good or ill:
> There is nothing more to say.
>
> Why is it then we stray
> Around that sunken sill?
> They are all gone away,
>
> And our poor fancy-play
> For them is wasted skill:
> There is nothing more to say.
>
> There is ruin and decay
> In the House on the Hill:

> They are all gone away,
> There is nothing more to say. (*Children of the Night* 34)

Despite acknowledging three times that the inhabitants "are all gone away," this speaker and his peers "still stray / Around that sunken sill," unable to give up the notion of a canonical house on the hill. Since the tradition is in "ruin and decay," their efforts to communicate with the dead are met with utter indifference ("our poor fancy-play / For them is wasted skill"), but the aspirants continue to try, their aimless obsessiveness echoed by the stubborn *a-b-a* rhymes of the villanelle form. They have prematurely adopted the role of ghosts, attempting to inhabit a scene of past vitality, unable to understand their status in limbo. Robinson puts the other distinctive formal feature of the villanelle, the two-line refrain, to good use as well, the repeated phrases embodying the two sides of contemporary poetry's dilemma: the decrepitude of its canonical inheritance is clear to see ("They are all gone away"), but this clarity makes no new directions possible ("There is nothing more to say"). It is hard to imagine a starker or more precise articulation of the impasse that Robinson and his contemporaries were faced with.

In "The Clerks" Robinson ingeniously uses the theme of the reverberant canon to ponder poetry's role in commodified turn-of-the-century culture. Here past poets are figured as "a shop-worn brotherhood" hanging on "with an ancient air" ("I did not think I should find them there / When I came back again; but there they stood"), who offer the speaker and his fellow aspirants a painful lesson in the futility of their own canonical hopes:

> And you that ache so much to be sublime,
> And you that feed yourselves with your descent,
> What comes of all your visions and your fears?
> Poets and kings are but the clerks of Time. (*Children of the Night* 54)

The shabby figures still "standing" in the same spot evoke not just the clerks in a dusty small-town shop, but their shopworn wares as well, books or other goods on neglected shelves, a display of cultural decay waiting helplessly for a customer-reader who may never come. This metaphoric equation of creator with both seller and object for sale tropes the period's anxiety that the individual creative spirit was being submerged in a headlong rush toward commodity culture. What these clerk-poets unsuccessfully peddle is not just the material forms of poetry, but also an obsolete account of its value, whose emphasis on sublimity and transcendence is thoroughly unsuited for the markets of modern culture. Having little hope of "selling," they persist in weaving intricate, ephemeral arabesques signifying only their own redundancy ("Tiering the same dull webs of discontent," "Clipping the same sad alnage of the years" [54]).

With "alnage," an old word designating a quantity of material measured by the ell, Robinson again considers the threat of commodification, but also implies poetry's need to develop a productive relationship with commodified modernity. The terms *alnage* and *ell* (etymologically related to *ulna* and *elbow*) derive from the length of the forearm, ingeniously troping both the act of writing and the skeletal character of the decrepit clerk-poets. The finicking precision of these figures pokes fun at poetic traditionalists obsessed with precisely measuring out their lines, whom Robinson satirized more directly in another poem as "little sonnet-men" "Who fashion, in a shrewd mechanic way, / Songs without souls, that flicker for a day, / To vanish in irrevocable night" (*Children of the Night* 63). But since the clerks' irrelevance comes from their reliance upon obsolete units of measure, as the flagrant archaism of "alnage" suggests, it follows that the mechanical use of traditional poetic forms, no matter how shrewdly executed, is equally suspect. Thus Robinson questions whether commodified modernity per se has rendered poetry irrelevant, and proposes instead that poetry, having stood still as the world has changed, must now generate new "measures."

Robinson's little sonnet-clerks ingeniously embody the period's central anxieties about poetry: overproduction, ephemerality, the empty ("mechanic") repetition of conventional forms and images, the cliquish careerism implied by their shrewdness. The poem in which he most directly lampoons them, also contained in *The Children of the Night*, ends by affirming both the continued need for poetry and the undiminished existence of *materia poetica*:

> What does it mean, this barren age of ours?
> Here are the men, the women, and the flowers,
> The seasons, and the sunset, as before.
> What does it mean? (*Children of the Night* 63)

In this poem Robinson proposes that poetry might still be valuable in two crucial ways: to articulate the meaning of the age, even of its barrenness, and to maintain a place for the individual consciousness in a world defined by ephemerality and anonymity: "Shall there not one arise / To wrench one banner from the western skies, / And mark it with his name forevermore?" (63). It is impossible not to notice, however, that here as in "The Clerks," Robinson embeds his critique of mechanical formalism in flawlessly traditional sonnet form; that the line uttering his fondest desire—"To put these little sonnet-men to flight"—is in note-perfect iambic pentameter; and above all, that this poem castigating the little sonnet-men is itself entitled "Sonnet"! This paradox is reminiscent of the self-contradictory calls of the 1890s for American poets to achieve individual expression by burying themselves in the *Golden Treasury*. But Robinson has full control of the contradiction: we know, and we know he knows we know, that he didn't set out to make a poem lampooning sonneteers, write it in sonnet form, and name it "Sonnet" by accident. The clash he creates between acquiescent construction and iconoclastic declaration is so knowing and witty that it becomes not a sign of creative disarray, but a sardonic metacommentary on the difficulties of poetry writing in a belated period, in its very negation of originality affirming the value of traditional poetic forms to nurture a quirky and ironic sensibility that might challenge the era's paralyzing evaluative binaries.

FALLEN BY THE WAYSIDE

The turn-of-the-century verses best demonstrating poetry's continued value are those that give up a nostalgia for moral coherence and explore the unstable evaluative dynamics of modernity through isolated figures wandering through desert, wilderness, or other symbolic spaces emptied of ethical or cultural value. The strongest of these works reimagine the key conceptual relationship of center and margin in American poetry, exploring the phenomenology of perception, commenting upon sociopolitical conditions, and giving voice to a modern consciousness that, finding itself dispossessed of traditional verities, seeks to live self-possessed in the contemporary world.

A paradigmatic expression of the wanderer topos can be found in the opening and title poem of Ellen Glasgow's collection *The Freeman* (1902), which scripts the poet as an avant-garde "vagabond between the East and West" who has rent the "clankless chains that bound" and now flings "defiance" to the elements and obstacles that would block his wandering way (13). Similarly, the vagabond speaker of Glasgow's "The Traveller" careens through a wintry nocturnal landscape (past "hamlets draped in frozen white") evoking the pastoral premodern America of *Snow-Bound* and innumerable Fireside poems. But this speaker can experience that world only from the outside, glimpsing the fires through "the frames of ruddy windows," since "The homely hearths are lit in vain / For one who rides across the plain" (*Freeman* 16). In situation and imagery the poem closely parallels Longfellow's well-known "Excelsior" (1841), whose young traveler excludes himself on an icy night from "happy homes," in which "he saw the light / Of household fires . . . warm and bright" (*Complete Poetical Works* 19). But the divergences are ultimately more telling: Longfellow's figure of aspiration, striving "toward the heights" (the meaning of his title), and perishing in the attempt, is effortlessly apotheosized into a mythic immortal "Lifeless, but beautiful," whose "voice fell, like a falling star" "from the sky, serene and far" (19). In contrast to the Olympian third-person narrator of "Excelsior," Glasgow's aspirant speaks in urgent first person, inviting the reader to perceive these feelings of disconnection from the domestic realm as the poet's own. There is little closure, and certainly no apotheosis, to her poem. It simply stops with an expression of ongoing wanderlust and alienation that looks not backward so much as sideways, to an emerging genre of popular modern narrative, the Western: "Death waits to woo me to her will. / I press my spurs, I ride alone, / I laugh and journey to my own" (17). That we now hear these final images as cowboy clichés is a measure of how widely early-twentieth-century Americans embraced this vocabulary of agonistic rebellion to articulate their cultural situation. Indeed, during these decades the figure of wayfarer, wanderer, or vagabond became a virtual synonym for "young person with creative aspirations," as in Herbert S. Stone's invitation to Harriet Monroe to join "a Bohemian sort of club" in Chicago, which became the famous Little Room group: "It is altogether informal but we are filled with great ideas about making the life of Chicago tolerable and furnishing inspiration for artistic vagabonds" (Letter of January 2, 1895).

Glasgow's self-conscious rewriting of genteel convention suggests that the turn-of-the-century poetic vagabond was above all a figure uprooted from the poet's own cultural past. In his study of fin de siècle France, Matt K. Matsuda establishes an important link between the vagabond topos and the dislocating effects of modernization. The disruption of long-stable social and economic patterns by the emerging industrial, bureaucratic, and military institutions of modern France had drawn vast numbers of people away from their rural and village origins, while improved roads and transportation technologies had made the traversal of large distances more possible. These converging forces produced a large rootless population whose nomadic presence was interpreted by poets and criminologists alike as "the sign of an unsettled modernity" (126–27). In American verses seeking to articulate the sensibility of the fin de siècle, the alienated wanderer is a nearly ubiquitous convention. George Cabot Lodge's "The Poet" offers just such a figure, defined by his resistance to comfort and convention, motivated by an overriding compulsion to noble vagabondage: although "Bright lips beseech him,—yet he cannot stay" but must venture alone "in the large night his outward way" (1:159). Lizette Woodworth Reese characterizes her speaker-poet as "*A wayfarer blown to and fro*" ("The Wayfarer" 44; italics in original), while the speaker of Hugh McCulloch's "Search" "has the untiring passion of the sea" and urges his listener "Let us go seek the sun" somewhere far away from "this quickly-aging North" (*Written in Florence* 13). Guy Wetmore Carryl's "Whom the World Calls Idle" describes the poet as one "brother-born to the wind of morn," who "must share its endless quest" in search of "The stretch of the open road, the challenge of heights unmounted" (*Garden of Years* 76). In "Pioneers" Charlotte Perkins Stetson (Gilman) gives the metaphor a more social dimension by celebrating the "thought-seekers of the printed page" who must "lead the world down its untrodden way," braving "drear wastes" and "lonely deaths" to do so (74).

Matsuda argues that the vagabond's deterritorialization implies estrangement from a moral conscience that had typically been maintained through memory, and notes that some fin de siècle psychologists accounted for vagabondage as a form of quasi-clinical amnesia (126, 129). In the case of American poets, the "amnesia" of vagabondage was self-induced and strategic, warranting their antinostalgic repudiation of the oppressive conscience of genteel moralism. The vocabulary of vagabondage enabled them to convert disaffection toward settled social structures into forms of resistance and offered enticing prospects of self-liberation and renewal, as in Dunbar's "Morning": "With staff in hand and careless-free, / The wanderer fares right jauntily, / For towns and houses are, thinks he, / For scorning, for scorning" (*Lyrics of Sunshine* 51). From its title through its final poem, Josephine Preston Peabody's 1898 volume *The Wayfarers* plays one variation after another upon the wanderer-poet. "A Road Tune" announces, "And I must up and wander / Away against the rain" (72). "The Piper" is proffered "hearth and home, / And neighbors at thy side," even audiences ("flocks"), but refuses them all for the comforts of the open road: a single companionate bird, a "friendly star at night, / And a brook to follow" (72). The long title poem of Peabody's volume depicts a group of intrepid figures on a quest for a female cosmic principle variously identified as Life, Song, Death, Love, and so on; these identifications are so vague and all-encompassing that the wayfaring quest, rather than any specific result, becomes its own end. Like the endings of Glasgow's vagabond poems, the final stanza of "The Wayfarers" is sheerly gestural, but the point of the gesture is clear enough. The world of genteel culture holds nothing more for the poet and her peers.

The exhilaration of lighting out for the territories is generally sustainable only if one does not have to portray one's arrival there. When the young poets of the era attempted to deal with that next step—if we leave here for somewhere else, what will that somewhere be like?—they all struggled, though some were more able than others to acknowledge it. The thoughtful "Envoy" that concludes Peabody's *The Wayfarers* presents a speaker, seemingly identical to the poet, who prays she can overcome the need to "eat my bread with furtive tears / Of home-longing," and can learn instead to "go where lights and highways call, / To hear the soothsay of them all, / And rest by any door" (83). Though Peabody claims to believe that the highways and lights of modernity have prophetic powers, her soothsaying aspiration remains only a hope that she "some day with better grace / May take the bounty of the place" that she cannot presently perceive or accept (83). As her ambivalence suggests, the poet-as-wanderer's skepticism toward communitarian tradition did not always open viable avenues of experimentation. Moody's "Road-Hymn for the Start" confronts this dilemma, beginning with a seemingly unequivocal repudiation of American genteel poetry's domestic traditions: "Leave the early bells at chime, / Leave the kindled hearth to blaze" (*Poems* 9). This vagabond speaker sees the domestic aspects of poetry as just "a part" of existence and resolves to "strive to see the whole" (9). But in a characteristically skeptical turn, the poet then cuts his wandering pilgrims adrift with no clear object for their peregrinations: "We have heard a voice cry 'Wander!' That was all we heard it say" (10). Moody puts a good face on this aimless wanderlust, referring to "the boon of endless quest," but he remains acutely conscious of inhabiting a world whose deity "maketh nothing manifest" (11).

Another couplet from Moody's "Road-Hymn," "Careless where our face is set, / Let us take the open way" (10), articulates the frequent objectlessness of these young poets' desire to take to an open road. Such moments remind us that the wanderer is an ambiguous persona, offering not just liberating rebellion from convention, but also the possibility of spiraling disengagement from all social structures. In writers less self-aware than Moody, the urgent impulse to wander led to some notably misguided uses of the wayfarer-poet that produced only solipsistic anti-modernity no more constructive than the genteel quietism they sought to reject. In particular, George Cabot Lodge's use of Whitman's vision of the wanderer on the open road ended in misanthropic disarray.

In "To W. W.," which opened his second volume, *Poems 1899–1902*, Lodge announced this allegiance by weaving Whitmanesque phrasings ("backward glance," "vistas," "leaves of love") into his portrayal of the earlier poet as a Christlike progenitor: "I toss this sheaf of song, these scattered leaves of love! / For thee, Thy Soul and Body spent for me, /— And now still living, now in love, transmitting still Thy Soul, Thy Flesh to me, to all!" (1:117).[16] But from his early writings, Lodge had also been drawn to poems recoiling from the social realm, in the manner of another W. W., and following hard upon the tribute to Whitman was "The World's Too Long about Us," which melded Wordsworthian antiurbanism with the "Outward" mode to repudiate materialist modernity: "Let us go / Far from . . . / The trivial loveless women and the low / Abortive men, the fashions stale and slow, / The greed of riches and the crime of want!" (1:131).

By the time of his ambitious late work "The City," Lodge's devotion to Whitman had collided disastrously with his revulsion toward "the world" and his compelling need to imagine a better one elsewhere. "The City" still contains vestiges of allegiance to Whitman, such as the opening sentence, which offers fifty-five lines of elaborate grammatical parallelisms in the manner of "Crossing Brooklyn Ferry." But the verse now has rhyme and, worse, a monotonous iambic meter. The poem's schizophrenic ambivalence combines Whitmanesque rhapsodism with a nightmarish interpretation of the modern city. The payoff that ends the fifty-five-line sentence is this resoundingly vacuous (not to mention rhyme-led) assertion: "There, interlocked inseparably, / Diverse yet single near and far, / There is the City!—where the ways / And byways of the City are" (11. 52–55). The next section bogs down right away in equally empty phrases: "There is the City!" (1. 56); "The self-same City, all in all, / Is here and there, first and last!" (11. 59–60); "There is the City—there and then! / And there and thence the City is" (11. 70–71). It is as if Lodge wants to explore and even celebrate the city as Whitman had done, but having mustered the necessary rhapsodic rhetoric, he cannot think of a single meaningful thing to say about it. This rhetorical bluster eventually gives way to a fixation on an ideal realm defined by its distance from the "mean, familiar street" (1. 99). The ellipses are the original poem's:

> Here is the City!—here are we! . . .
> Here is the City—Here! . . . But there,
> There where the brave are gone before,
> There where the lamps of Truth and Love

Shine steadfast at the Secret Door,
Is not the City! (11. 103–08)

The remainder of the work celebrates the celestiality of this ideal noncity in terms uncomfortably prescient of the contrast between the cities of the workers and managers in Fritz Lang's *Metropolis:* "Not in these purlieus of the City where / The sunless hovels of man's indigence / Crowd meanly on the sordid thoroughfare, / But there where thought's immeasurable dome / Kindles and clears and is fulfilled with light!" (11. 160–64). At this point Lodge's idealizing impulse has turned entirely inward, and he damns the actual cities of modernity, equated to "hovels of man's indigence," as roundly as in any Fireside poem. Evoking all the elitist revulsion toward the urban social Other that T. S. Eliot would, with little of Eliot's exhilarating formal brilliance or conceptual sophistication, Lodge's wandering poet ends up the very embodiment of misanthropic disengagement.

Given the weight of Lodge's elite pedigree, the antimodern destination of his verse is perhaps less surprising than his lingering fascination with Whitman. Poets less heavily invested in and by the Eastern social elite, such as the Illinois native and self-proclaimed socialist Richard Hovey, had perhaps a better chance to use the wanderer persona to rethink the modern value of poetry. Hovey's poems of "Vagabondia," coauthored with the Canadian native Bliss Carman (1861–1929), were the most successful American verse of the 1890s in attaining a readership and some critical following. The popularity of the Vagabondians testified to readers' incipient yearning for a poetry embracing a life of vigor rather than shrinking from the world. The untitled envoi printed on the front and back endpapers to Carman and Hovey's *More Songs from Vagabondia* (1896), illustrated by Tom B. Meteyard, begins by evoking the domestic ideology of Fireside poetry in order to reject it. Here even the most single-minded seeker of domesticity ("Whose furthest footstep never strayed / Beyond the village of his birth") can be "but a lodger for the night / In this old wayside inn of earth." Longfellow had used his wayside inn to dramatize the formation of an impromptu community, in the manner of the Canterbury pilgrims and the storytellers of the Decameron. As in those works, the setting of *Tales of a Wayside Inn* determines its structure as a series of communitarian narratives, exemplified by the most famous section, "Paul Revere's Ride." But for Hovey and Carman, the American poet is now "an alien and a vagabond" ("Envoy"), and the rejection of the village for the transience and impersonality of the wayside inn is not a choice but a condition of existence.

Hovey and Carman's modernized wayside inn, more like an anonymous motor court, provides no access to a community revealing the benevolent workings of God, as Longfellow's homier hostelry does. The only path in this world of isolation was to embrace one's companionate vagabondage, as they did with a vengeance. But to what purpose? The canonicity that might result from such an embrace ("If any record of our names / Be blown about the hills of time") was uncertain and likely ephemeral. Its sole value ("Of all our good, of all our bad, / This one thing only is of worth") was their understanding that true comradeship, "the league of heart to heart," was "The only purpose of earth." Like Arnold's alienated speaker in "Dover Beach," wistfully proposing to his lover that their fidelity to one another might compensate for the lack of any larger social commitment, the Vagabondians insisted that they had redefined spiritual value into a tiny coterie of three ("the man of paint, the men of rhyme"). But Arnold knew that this effort was doomed to fail, and out of that knowledge created a defining (though not complete) articulation of modern sensibility. The Vagabondians admitted no such illuminating disenchantment, opting for the less psychologically burdensome mask of blithe immaturity (one recent critic calls it "sophomore exuberance" [Meyer 219]), which would date so severely that to many avant-garde poets of the 1910s Hovey and Carman became objects of ridicule, despite being in some ways their most immediate predecessors.

As the American 1890s ended in a spasm of imperialist expansionism, Hovey's ideological position degenerated into a peculiar but not implausible amalgamation of two iconoclastic rebels, Whitman and Henry George, with Theodore Roosevelt, whose version of wandering the open road involved iconoclasm of a more literal and violent nature. Hovey's socialism slid into unguarded antimaterialism, contemptuous of the American populace as dupes of capital. Although he died suddenly in 1900 while the occupation of the Philippines was still a subject of fierce debate, his notoriously jingoistic poems about the war left little doubt of his enthusiasm for an American imperial destiny.[17] "Unmanifest Destiny," inscribed "July 1898," acknowledges that the destiny of American culture is not clear ("I do not know beneath what sky / Nor on what seas shall be thy fate; / I only know that it shall be high, / I only know it shall be great" [*Along the Trail* 17]). But its unironic use of the central catchphrase of American expansionism, coupled with its characterization of God as "The Admiral of Nations" who "guides / Thy blind obedient keels to reach / The harbor" (16) where America's future resides, made clear that this destiny properly involved expansion into other nations, absorption of other peoples. Hovey's fetishization of the vagabond thus curdled into imperialist apologetics that demonstrated his own ample capacity to play the dupe of capital.[18]

WANDERING THE MARGINS OF MODERNITY

The fatal flaw in Hovey's exploration of the wanderer persona was his stubborn unwillingness to accept the ramifications of marginality. In fact, the antitraditional posturing of the Vagabondians masked a deep nostalgia for a time when poetry housed the yearnings and energies of privileged Romantic youth. Hovey's embrace of the Rooseveltian man of action—whose "wandering" takes place at the head of an imperial expeditionary force—betrayed the need to cling to some model of cultural centrality in his poetry, at whatever intellectual or ethical cost. I trust that the previous pages have traced the pitfalls that some of these young wanderer-poets encountered. But others, accepting poetry's cultural marginality as a starting point, used the trope productively to reimagine the genre's uses for urban-industrial modernity. Both Stephen Crane and Edwin Arlington Robinson continually generated images of wanderers who make their way through a world of nothing but margin, stripped bare of familiar spiritual landmarks. The ambivalence habitually evoked in their wanderer-poems represents a significant departure from the insistent verities of genteel verse and marks the beginnings of American poetry's deep oppositional engagement with modern experience. Robinson's sonnet "The Altar" (1897) offers a speaker wandering "Alone, remote, nor witting where I went," who encounters in a dream "A fiery place," clearly having to do with poetry, that offers "a gleam / So swift, so searching, and so eloquent / Of upward promise" that the speaker is struck by a bracing flash of oppositional understanding: "Alas! I said,— the world is in the wrong" (*Children of the Night* 61). This visionary moment crystallizes his wanderlust into a "quenchless fever of unrest," and he feels the thrill "of that martyred throng" who rebelled against convention. But it still does not show him a clear purpose in the waking world, and he awakens to realize that he is "the same / Bewildered insect plunging for the flame / That burns, and must burn somehow for the best" (61). This turn does not negate his impulse to rebellion, but the shift from eloquent "upward promise" to "bewildered insect" radically problematizes its efficacy and the fate of those who try to live by it. Despite—or more precisely, because of—this uncertainty, Robinson is able to imagine a constructive role for poetry in an unstable modern condition in which ambivalence, not surety, is the only appropriate response: plunging into heterogeneity and uncertainty, he hopes for the best.

Robinson's "Ballade of Broken Flutes" (1897) uses the wanderer topos to imagine a desolate world devoid of poetry, beginning, "In dreams I crossed a barren land, / A land of ruin, far away" (*Children of the Night* 22). Unlike most of Crane's wanderers, Robinson's encounters no cosmic being, not even an indifferent or contemptuous one, just a decayed, silent space of trees, where once "pipes and tabors had their sway," now become leafless "skeletons in cold array" (22). Despite the desolation, the speaker still harbors vestigial dreams "to command / New life into the shrunken clay." But these aspirations merely foreground the futility of continued poetic endeavor, which emerges in a startling passage of self-reflection near the end:

> I tried it. Yes, you scan to-day,
> With uncommiserating glee,
> The songs of one who strove to play
> The broken flutes of Arcady. (23)

The ironic "Envoy" to the poem then announces miserably that the speaker plans to "join the common fray, / To fight where Mammon may decree; / And leave, to crumble as they may, / The broken flutes of Arcady" (23). This ending indicts the contemporary reader as Mammon's coconspirator, taking unempathetic pleasure from the poet's discomfiture. "Ballade of Broken Flutes" links the wanderer topos with the ghostly canon, as the wandering speaker in effect proclaims himself the end of the ghostly line. Unable to breathe new life into the canon's shrunken clay, he becomes ironically canonical in his very futility (if the canon itself is a failure, one's own failure is prerequisite for canonization). His departure for another kind of wandering, the "common fray" of alienated capitalist modernity, signifies the final giving up of the canonical ghost.

If Robinson's is the voice that most vividly captured the ambivalence of young turn-of-the-century writers toward poetry's changing cultural status, Crane's is the richest and most heartbreaking expression of its persistent impulse to rebellion and innovation. The wanderer is certainly Crane's central poetic persona, occurring again and again across his oeuvre. Pursuing its implications, Crane develops a position of radical skepticism toward all cultural orthodoxies. The six-line poem beginning "If I should cast off this tattered coat" (1894) moves toward an oppositional position equally skeptical of timid convention and its facile alternatives.

The poem's speaker yearns to be free from the burdens of tradition, but is utterly unable to imagine what that freedom would be like:

> If I should cast off this tattered coat,
> And go free into the mighty sky;
> If I should find nothing there
> But a vast blue,
> Echoless, ignorant—
> What then? (*Black Riders* 73)

End of poem. Here Crane evokes the double anxiety that comes from chafing against oppressive tradition and from discovering that its disappearance offers only vertiginous disorientation. The articulation of "what then?" is one of poetry's most urgent functions, and Crane is rigorously honest in acknowledging that he has no answer to it. Yet this very admission is a crucial departure from the too easily generated, no longer adequate answers offered by genteel poetry. The answer that comes only in giving up on answers: this paradox thematizes the value of poetry in the modern condition as a discourse that, by embracing its very marginality, might take on unsuspected power.

Crane often considers poetry's crisis and its changing potentials by synthesizing the canonical-ghost and poet-wanderer topoi. The many wanderers in his poems are not just symbols of spiritual aimlessness and cosmic isolation, as they've often been taken.[19] His articulation of the crisis of poetry would have been less fraught with anxiety, and less rich, if such wanderers were truly alone. Many of his wanderer poems, perhaps most, depend upon encounters with ghosts: indifferent, arbitrary, or malevolent figures of evaluative authority. Some of these represent debilitated but still oppressive past traditions, while others signify an alienated and commodified present, but all lack the necessary judgment or ethical force to legitimate their authority in the poet's eyes. The paradigm for this sort of encounter takes place in the poem beginning "A youth in apparel that glittered" (1894), which Crane might have been aiming at the Harvard poets and their medieval obsessions. A youth wandering in "a grim wood" encounters a figure of repressive and unreasoning past canonicity, "an assassin / Attired all in garb of old days" who inexplicably accosts and stabs the youth (*Black Riders* 28). David Halliburton aptly describes this youth's "apparel" as "radiant in a shallow way" (290), as if its glitter were his specious attempt to recapture some radiance he imagines to be characteristic of the distant past. But the past he actually encounters is represented by the much less glamorous "garb" of the assassin. Crane notes bitterly that what is assassinated, youth's proper role as defier of stale convention, is unwanted anyway, as this one is "'enchanted, believe me, / To die thus, / In this medieval fashion, / According to the best legends; / Ah, what joy!'" (28). Self-deluded to the end, the youth dies "smiling" and "content," though Crane's satiric intelligence is clearly discontent that American youth should feel so.

In contrast to this acquiescent youth, Crane liked to portray himself as a defiant blasphemer wandering the cultural margins, alienated from all authority. Even when his poems do not announce any literal wandering, they often employ an avant-garde conceptual structure, thematizing the poet as a figure of marginal opposition who confronts a body of received opinion unchallenged by anyone else. Here is a highly schematized version of this structure:

> There were many who went in huddled procession:
> They knew not whither;
> But, at any rate, success or calamity
> Would attend all in equality.
> There was one who sought a new road.
> He went into direful thickets,
> And ultimately he died thus, alone;
> But they said he had courage. (*Black Riders* 18)

This single-minded little poem announces the rebellious sensibility that would explode upon American poetry soon after 1910. In an 1896 note to an admirer of his work, Crane revealed how fully he had internalized this persona of alienated opposition: "You delight me with your appreciation and yet too it makes me afraid. I did not bend under the three hills of ridicule which were once upon my shoulders but I don't know that I am strong enough to withstand the kind things that are now sometimes said about me" (*Correspondence* 195). In using this alienated persona to thematize the value of his poetry, and to live out his own vagabond existence, Crane modeled the oppositional profile that would define the modern American avant-garde.

Virtually the only epigraph to any of Crane's poems places this rebellious persona against an oppressive canonical legacy: "And the sins of the fathers shall be visited upon the heads of the children, even unto the third and fourth generation of them that hate me" (Exodus 20:5) (*Black Riders* 13). Crane was temperamentally unable to imagine himself in the role of the father; throughout his poetry he is the son who discovers he will be oppressed by his ancestors' actions regardless of his own and therefore decides he may as well explore the exhilarations of scandal and blasphemy. He replies to the epigraph:

> Well, then, I hate Thee, unrighteous picture;
> Wicked image, I hate Thee;
> So, strike with Thy vengeance
> The heads of those little men
> Who come blindly.
> It will be a brave thing. (13)

The imagery here suggests that Crane's rejection of Christianity was closely linked to his resistance to the oppressive iconography of genteel culture. Versions of these "unrighteous pictures" and "wicked images" recur with notable frequency in his work, as in "There was a great cathedral," where a solemn "white procession" appears at first to be the target of Crane's satiric energy. But the poem develops unexpected empathy for the Stedman-like "chief man there" who leads the procession: "some could see him cringe, / As in a place of danger, / Throwing frightened glances into the air, / A-start at threatening faces of the past" (*Black Riders* 70). These "threatening faces of the past" can no doubt be linked to Crane's evangelical Methodist upbringing, as in Daniel Hoffman's fine reading of the religious writings of his father and uncles as influences on his poetry (48–62). A reading of the poem's thematics of value, on the other hand, might fancifully recall the most righteous pictures of American culture, the Fireside portraits on hundreds of thousands of middle-class parlor walls, perhaps now with something less than benevolent detectable around their eyes. The fact that only "some could see" the chief man cringe supports this reading, implying that to most, he seems the most loyal and estimable keeper of tradition; but to the perceptive, skeptical reader he is haunted, like Stedman and Howells, by these icons of oppressive canonicity.

To Crane's rebellious temperament, religious orthodoxies and cultural canons are often barely distinguishable, both signifying equally the oppressiveness of obsolete, arbitrary, or cynical authority. The weight of such authoritative writing inspires him to one of his most gnomic and sardonic condemnations of canonicity:

> You tell me this is God?
> I tell you this is a printed list,
> A burning candle, and an ass. (1897; *War Is Kind* 35)

This time Crane achieves the desired effect of blasphemy by tossing off a definition of God in a three-line poem. Refusing to allow anyone else to tell him what God is, he shoots back his own tripartite definition that reduces the conventional symbolic pomp surrounding God to a single "burning candle." The "printed list," the first of the three parts, is yet another image of religious and cultural authority imposed with no genuine ethical warrant. That the list is printed adds a further intriguing irony, evoking a "God" who is propped up by techniques of modern mass production. God's third element, the "ass," is both more and less cryptic, presumably having reference to some Biblical beast, but also serving, especially in close conjunction with the candle, a scatological function. Responding to oppressive orthodoxy with rude physical gestures of defiance, Crane advances a subversive sensibility that prefigures such 1910s texts as Pound's "The Temperaments" and Millay's "First Fig," which use similarly scatological implications to flout conventional gentility and assert their avant-garde allegiances.

But Crane is well aware that such guerrilla assaults on oppressive canonicity, no matter how ferocious, don't in themselves establish a viable account of modern poetic value. As he tries to articulate what he would put in place of traditional notions of value, we find his iconoclasm inflected by ambivalence and anxiety. In "Once I saw mountains angry" (1894), for example, Crane offers a picture of canonical ancestry reminiscent of Robinson's congenital ambivalence. A wandering "little man" "no bigger than my finger" is pitted against "mountains angry, / And ranged in battle-front" (*Black Riders* 23). The little man's size tropes the writer's creative capacity (and phallically expressed anxieties about it). His ability to "prevail" against an angry cosmos derives from "His grandfathers," who "beat them many times," suggesting the continued potency of canonical ancestry. But the speaker's final remark on the issue is, if I may, clearly ambiguous: "Then did I see much virtue in grandfathers,—/ At least, for the little man / Who stood against the mountains" (23). "At least" seems to qualify this virtue, yet the "little man" and his dependence on his grandfathers are not ironized and ridiculed as such figures often are in Crane's work. A similarly bracing ambivalence tinges "Tradition, thou art for suckling children" (1894), whose first line efficiently rejects canon and tradition, going on to allow that they might offer "enlivening milk for babes," "but no meat for men" (*Black Riders* 48). But the end of the poem calls that rejection into radical doubt: "Then—/ But alas, we are all babes." The pause functions as an ingenious graphic signifier of the paralytic ambivalence toward past canons felt by the young poets of the 1890s. Having confidently asserted his repudiation of them, the speaker looks forward to a new direction ("Then") but quickly perceives the lack of viable alternative avenues ("—"), a realization that ignominiously reinfantilizes him.

The opacity and ambivalence that sometimes seem to dilute Crane's rebellious positions should be read not as signs of his incomplete liberation from convention, but of his unwillingness to sacrifice the complexity of these issues for more direct but reductive statement. Indeed, Crane's awareness of the abyssal character of meaning—the meaning of experience, the meaning of writing—is one of the centrally modern qualities of his writing. Michael Fried's brilliant book makes clear that this unfathomability characterizes much of Crane's prose. But there it emerges within socially embedded narratives that can be refamiliarized into the critical traditions of realist fiction. In his verse, on the other hand, Crane is free to use this metalinguistic level of signification to valorize a modern poetics of complexity and irreducibility. A number of his poems explore the infinite regress of meaning through a distinctive trope of uncontrolled dissemination, in which something representing poetic material suddenly bursts its containing bounds and is diffused throughout an environment. Akin to the impulse to wander, this dispersive gesture constitutes a forceful repudiation of the virtues of enclosure, coherence, and security so dear to American genteel verse. Perhaps his fullest use of this trope to theorize modern poetic value comes in this poem:

> Once, I knew a fine song
> —It is true, believe me—
> It was all of birds,
> And I held them in a basket;
> When I opened the wicket,
> Heavens! They all flew away.
> I cried, "Come back, little thoughts!"
> But they only laughed.
> They flew on
> Until they were as sand
> Thrown between me and the sky. (*Black Riders* 72)[20]

As he often does, Crane here uses a twisted version of Fireside analogical method. We can measure his distance from that earlier poetics by contrasting this text to a Fireside classic using a similar trope, Longfellow's "The Arrow and the Song" (1845), whose poet-speaker sends an arrow into the air, then a song, to ostensibly unknown results (both "fell to earth / I knew not where"). Ultimately, of course, Longfellow's method of analogical homily requires tidy denouement, and in the final stanza the arrow is found "unbroke," embedded in an oak, while the song, "from beginning to end," resides "in the heart of a friend" (*Complete Poetical Works* 68). Fireside poetics presumes that arrow and song, no matter how far or indirectly they might have traveled, will always remain whole, their essence unchanged from the moment of their creation and launching, and that they can be found in some coherent place (oak tree, friend's heart) that reaffirms a coherent world. In Crane's diffusive trope, on the other hand, the little birds, identified as both songs and thoughts, burst forth from their container, and despite the creator's wistful desire to retain them for himself (or at least to know whither they fly), they endlessly recede from view. Far from offering reassurance of the integral character of meaning, the little bird-poems become hindrances to vision, microscopic grains of "sand" that obscure his view of the sky, images of the infinite regress of meaning. Using the analogical method to exorcise the shades of the genteel canon, Crane advances a modern account of poetry that revels in multiplying the loose ends of imagination and meaning that genteel poetics could no longer keep tied up.

AT HOME ON THE ROAD

Crane's subversive play with images of infinite regress was matched, perhaps even outdone, by one of his forgotten contemporaries. Francis Brooks, dead by 1898 after publishing just one book, was the era's closest forerunner of the phenomenological strain of modern American verse epitomized by Wallace Stevens and William Carlos Williams.[21] I have made glancing reference to Brooks as a participant in the agoraphobic idealist ethos of 1890s Harvard. But unlike Lodge and Stickney, who were inhibited and ultimately stifled by their idealism, Brooks used his to explore how poetry's meanings might elude the reductive stenographic models of modern language authorized by capitalist enforcers like Edward Bok and H. E. Warner. Brooks's finest work, "Titular," appears early in his 1896 volume *Margins*. His cross-referencing play of titles suggests that the poem is premised on its own marginality, which eventually becomes explicit in these self-evaluating lines: "So, mayhap, just on the marge / Of superior and truer, / Lovelier things, these verses cling" (6). Since the poem is titular as well as marginal, that makes the entire project of the book marginal, and the whole genre of poetry as well. This frank acknowledgment frees Brooks to explore marginality as a condition of possibility rather than defeat. The first half of "Titular" weaves an imagistic mosaic of visual pictures, spatial relationships, and emotional impressions that construct marginality as a threshold to "dream what lies beyond":

> Margins of the mere and moor,
> Margins of the sea by shell
> Convoluted, many-hued,
> Mosses manifold, defined;
> Margins of the furrowed fields,
> Daisy-decked, and aster-starred;
> Margins of the woods when Spring,
> Joyous from the shadowed depths,
> Smiles in every violet;
> Margins of the day and night,
> Dimness of the dusk and dawn;
> Margins of the sky and earth,
> Faint horizons, mystic, far;
> Margins of the city streets,
> Endless, tense humanity;
> Margins of life, pure infancy
> And serene old age—to know
> These and dream what lies beyond,
> Children of men! untraveled worlds. (*Margins* 5–6)[22]

The poem's extraordinary first line offers two words, "mere" and "moor," that capture the multiple virtues of marginality both for apprehending the phenomenal world and for the act of poetic inscription. Literally, the "margins of the mere" refer to the edges of a lake, pond, or sea, but this also means they refer to a state of unrestricted otherness (whatever borders water but is not itself water, since if it were water it would be the mere and not its margin). This state is "mere" in being only marginal; but the rich etymology of *mere* also offers "pure," "unmixed" (Latin, *merus*). Thus the marginal's mere-ness is countered and compensated by the purity of its otherness, in which its identity comes from its very unidentifiability. Yet another signification of *mere* expresses not merely a thing or its other, but the liminal pivot between the two, a boundary or boundary marker (from Latin *mūrus*, wall). Not only do we have a margin that is (a) mere, but a mere that is a margin. Thus the "mere" is simultaneously the object itself (the body of water), the absence of that same object (merely its margin), and the liminal boundary between the two. These Möbius-like convolutions recur in the image of margins of a "moor." They are the edges of a heath or bog, but the moor is itself a liminal space between (solid) ground and (liquid) bog, between one terrain and its other. And while the signifier "moor" might imply the action of securing (mooring) such an image to a single determinate meaning, as with "mere" that supplementary signified is itself evidence of the multiple potentialities scintillating in the linguistic sign, belying the possibility of any easy reduction.

To generate such abyssal significations from this poem should not be seen as an arbitrary activity, since "Titular" contains two symbols of itself offering patterns of infinite regress, the "shell / Convoluted, many-hued," and the "mosses manifold, defined." The shell is unlimited both in the intricate coils that constitute its form and in the imperceptible merging of its unquantifiable colors. Similarly, like the ambiguity of the signifier "grass" that Whitman exploited so ingeniously, "moss" refers both to the patch of moss as a whole and to each tiny individual leaf. In a further convolution, this symbol of infinitude is "defined" by its manifold multiplicity of forms. To be defined by marginality and indistinctness is thus transmuted by etymological play into a richer and more varied identity than to be one definite thing or another. In the many forms the poem articulates them—convolutions, horizons, hems, borders, tangents, "shadowed depths," and "dimness of the dusk and dawn"—margins function not as delimiting boundaries but as thresholds offering liberating access to more multiple and profound meanings ("untraveled worlds") than do centers. This self-reflexive play is developed further in the poem's second half, where "these verses," marginal as they are, "cling—/ Like the curling tender vine, / Creeping 'long the vast cliff's brow, / Void below, a world above" (*Margins* 6). This poetic vine signifies the margin of all margins, that between earth and sky, material and ideal. But in an intriguing reversal utterly in character with the poem, the clinging vine's cliffside setting, and its ability to defy gravity, invert conventional relations of earth and space: the world is "above," the "void below"—another instance of Brooks's fascination with abyssal images. Thus by accepting and exploring poetry's marginality, Brooks posits its value as a liminal form of expression, a window to new dimensions of perception, and in doing so, initiates modern American poetry's powerful engagement with the phenomenology of imagination.

In his study of turn-of-the-century neurasthenia, *American Nervousness, 1903*, Tom Lutz demonstrates how an ostensibly marginalizing condition actually enabled many sufferers to explore alternative subjectivities that inhibiting social conventions had rendered otherwise unavailable. Lutz draws upon Arnold Van Gennep's formulation of "liminal rites" that "suspend normal social expectations and create an unstructured space in which individuals slough off old social positions in preparation for new ones awarded in postliminal rites," though he suggests that such spaces are not so much unstructured as mirror structures (21). If neurasthenia could function as such a mirror structure that enabled psychosocial transformation, Brooks's contemporaneous poem proposes, in its linguistic and phenomenological play of mirroring opposites, that a poetry of marginality might offer a similar liminal and transformative function. Lutz concludes that his neurasthenic subjects (including Theodore Roosevelt, Theodore Dreiser, Edgar Saltus, and William James) "each refashioned, however unconsciously or unintentionally, their own life styles and subjectivities" through their self-marginalization as neurasthenics (22). Similarly, verse of the 1890s such as "Titular," even as it appears to languish under the weight of self-doubt and dispossession, begins to refashion the value and meanings of poetry for twentieth-century modernity.

"Titular" is the key poem of *Margins* not just in its wit and intricacy but in its assertion of the margin as a dominant conceptual element. The material form of Brooks's book, which was published in 1896 by the obscure Chicago firm Searle & Gorton, contributes to this reimagining of the value of poetry as well. In its thick paper, elegant typeface, clean cover design, and overall level of visual refinement, *Margins* participates in the decade's aestheticist impulse, seen also in *The Chap-Book,* in the work of Stone & Kimball and other small publishing houses, and abroad in *The Yellow Book* and the spectacular later productions of William Morris's Kelmscott Press. In *The Black Riders,* Jerome McGann argues that the stupefyingly elaborate designs of Morris's last books initiate a modern understanding of the poem as object, both material and aesthetic, whose "subject is poetry itself—or more particularly, poetry as it may be carried out in an age of capitalist mechanical reproduction" (46). Such texts as the 1896–1897 Kelmscott edition of *The Earthly Paradise,* which McGann calls "the culminant work of Morris' life" (71), "foreground textuality as such, turning words from means to ends-in-themselves" in opposition to a dominant culture that uses print merely as "a vehicle for linguistic meaning" (74). McGann thus adapts to his materialist analysis the classic formulation of modernist style as an act of resistance to modern forces of commodification and mass consumption: "The text here is hard to read, is too thick with its own materialities. It resists any processing that would simply treat it as a set of referential signs pointing beyond themselves to a semantic content" (74).

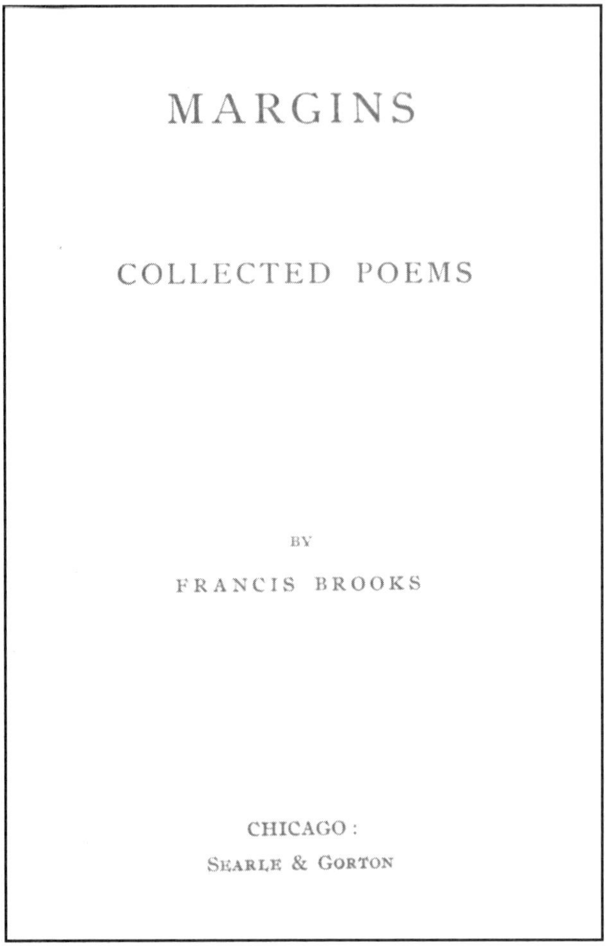

MARGINS

COLLECTED POEMS

BY

FRANCIS BROOKS

CHICAGO:
SEARLE & GORTON

Figure 7. *Title page of* Margins, *by Francis Brooks (Chicago: Searle & Gorton, 1896). Courtesy of the University of Illinois Urbana-Champaign Library.*

The slim and minimal elegance of *Margins*, which is certainly not difficult to read, could scarcely contrast more strongly to the intentionally cluttered and murky affect of *The Chap-Book* and Kelmscott books. But in the very modesty of its minimalist aesthetic, *Margins* offers an alternative to the familiar resistance-of-consumption model of modernism, challenging the commodification of poetic value in arguably more affirmative fashion than does Morris. Unlike the aggressive escapism of *The Earthly Paradise* (whose first lines urge us in screaming capitals to "FORGET SIX COUNTIES OVERHUNG WITH SMOKE, / FORGET THE SNORTING

STEAM & PISTON STROKE, / FORGET THE SPREADING OF THE HIDEOUS TOWN"), *Margins* strips down to a bare minimum every aspect of book production that might lend it a commodified aspect. The book has no table of contents; the title page gives no date of publication, while the copyright page contains just five words—"Copyright, 1896, by the author"—that reassert the individual creator against impersonal economic forces. All pages on which a poem begins are left unnumbered, so only about half of the book's pages have numbers. Rather than fill the margins with intricate patterns as Morris does, Brooks's book leaves them empty; on most pages they are much wider than the text. Given the centrality of margins in Brooks's poetics, the empty space in these pages functions as a tangible reminder of poetry's liminal power to convey us into "what lies beyond." In Van Gennep's model of "liminal social rites," the stage described as liminal (the transition proper) will be followed by "postliminal rites" that consolidate and situate the new subjectivity produced by the transition (Lutz 21). If in "Titular" the conceptual force of margins makes such liminality imaginable, the physical margins of the book provide a space for this postliminal reconstitution of the individual reader's consciousness. The margins of *Margins* remain empty but prominent, as if to signify that the re-creative process is still in a nascent—but now imagined—state.

In her study of the early modern book as a material object, Evelyn Tribble establishes a vital connection between the margins of the printed book, often filled with glosses both printed and handwritten, and the period's contested and fluid conceptions of authorship and authority (6). Tribble's analysis ends with Ben Jonson's consolidation of his collected works into a "corpus" imposing a "uniform typographical order upon a diverse career" (9), an event signaling the emergence of modern-individualist literary authority. This individualist model of the author was brought under attack by the advent of mass commodity culture in the late nineteenth century. Both Morris and Brooks can be seen as responding to this threat of commodification, in effect acknowledging the cultural marginality of their projects. Morris's strategy for recuperating the author as individual is to construct the materiality of the book in the most idiosyncratic style possible, defensively cramming every inch of the page with signifiers of his distinctive vision, assuming a restive reader who must be subdued through sheer perceptual overload. In its minimal but still indisputable aestheticism, Brooks's book offers a more hopeful anticipation of the postliminal space in which an individual consciousness adequate to modernity may be constituted in and through poetry's cultural marginality. Ultimately it is the understated elegance of *Margins*, not the flamboyance of *The Earthly Paradise,* that best anticipates the modern understanding of fine printing as "invisible typography," theorized by Beatrice Warde in 1932 as the effort "to *reveal* rather than to hide the beautiful thing which it was meant to *contain*" (11; italics in original).

The last two poems in *Margins,* "Still" and "Thus," adopt a tone of quiet expectancy, as if awaiting that postliminal re-creation of consciousness. The former, beginning "Still midst the prose a poem we weave, / Pallid with doubt yet dare to believe," confronts the period's conventional anxieties about the value of poetic activity and insists that poetry still "Touches the dross and turns it to gold" (*Margins* 79–80). The poem's title is its most efficient conveyor of its theme: though the era's poets may appear to be stilled, they are in fact still capable of evoking the benefits of imaginative liminality, here portrayed as alchemy.[23] The title of the final poem, "Thus," implies an action or process that follows from what has gone before and will continue past the end of the book. "Thus" imagines in its minimal eight lines a modern conception of poetic value based on an individual authorial consciousness striving to discover new forms and subjects:

> Some unworn thought,
> > Some unused word,
> Some tone untaught,
> > Some rhyme unheard;
> Some nobler aim,
> > Some further lore,
> Shall add a name,
> > A poet, more. (80)

This coalescence would bring to life the individual vision of "a poet," but also "more": the distinctive subjectivity of a modern reader, who, the book's design implies, can be relied upon not to consume poetry heedlessly as just another commodity, but to use it wisely. The book's abundant marginal space invites all manner of material glosses through which such readers might articulate their own emerging subjectivities. Thus without sacrificing conceptual complexity, Brooks's modern poetics of value rewarrants the authority of the individual creator not by alienating but by involving the Other-reader.

Margins was the only volume Brooks published before his health was seriously undermined, and he drowned in Lake Geneva in 1898, an apparent suicide, at the age of 31. Yet another truncated and unrealized turn-of-the-century life, it seems, but this one contains some striking elements that foreshadowed the vigorous cultural roles available to American poets after 1910. Like Robinson and Moody, Brooks was sufficiently detached from the ethos of Harvard to escape its most inhibiting aspects. In the fall of 1890 Brooks matriculated (not graduated as Carlin T. Kindilien states), but he stayed just two years before departing for successful legal training in Chicago, followed by a brief interval of practice, then by medical studies and a degree, and finally by an extended period of strenuous wandering across North America and Europe, where he died. Kindilien calls his peripatetic existence "a quest for a purpose in life that he failed to find" (131), but its more precise significance derives from the conscious self-marginalization Brooks undertook.[24] Despite a sympathetic family, Brooks found himself unable to commit to their milieu of upper-middle-class professional comfort, and like Crane, he eventually embarked upon an intellectual and financial vagabondage that his friend Rice attributes to empathy with "the great majority of his fellow men and women who grasped the thorns of the rose that he might enjoy its fragrance" ("Francis Brooks" xiv). Brooks had always felt "sympathy for their struggles," but after his experience of wandering, "he was now to incarnate this sympathy in his own person" (xiv).

Thus the exploration of marginality seen in "Titular," which predated most of Brooks's wanderings, was no passing whim in his poetics but was central to his vision of the modern poet as one empathetic toward the socially marginalized. In the late work "Night: A Fragment," Brooks describes this commitment in terms that would be echoed a half century later by Allen Ginsberg in "A Supermarket in California": on a summer evening the wandering speaker sees the lights of homes and hears voices

> . . . borne to me, a stranger, full of care
> And lonely, shuffling down the darkened street
> My life the focus where all shadows meet. (*Poems* 72)

If the poet of modernity is "driven still to wander and to yearn" (72) through the night, Brooks's use of the role was more thoughtful of its social implications than the self-dramatizing of Glasgow, Peabody, Lodge, and the Vagabondians. Sadly, Brooks's personal awakening coincided with declining health. But several of his late works, such as "Cities' Streets" and "The Age of Steel," muse upon the contradictions of modernity with greater ethical complexity than most poems of the era were able to summon. Like Crane's more famous vagabond existence, Brooks's life reveals the personal hazards—and some of the benefits—of becoming a poet-wanderer on the margins of modern culture.

5

THE BUSINESS
OF MODERN VERSE

Investigating the resistant force of the wanderer persona in its
many guises, we discover an array of American verses written
between 1890 and 1910, most now virtually unknown, that respond productively to poetry's marginality. Like Brooks's "Titular," such poems
comprehend the margin not just as static spatial metaphor but as a
source of temporal energy. They seek to convert marginality into *horizon-
tality,* in a strong sense: not just something low and wide, but something
on the horizon, an incipient element capable of growing in significance.
Younger poets of these years made the first productive attempts since
Whitman to imagine American poetry's horizons in a modern condition
driven by incorporative capitalism and articulated to most people
through commercialized forms of mass culture. Given that they struggled toward this renewed relevance during the worst years of poetry's
institutional crisis, it's not surprising that their work is sometimes
unsure of its footing, self-contradictory, even despairing of its objec-
tives—above all it is, to borrow Paula Bennett's term, "heavily negotiated" ("Not Just Filler" 204). But exactly in being so, in leaving behind the
closed-minded verities of genteel verse to negotiate the drastically
uncertain terrain of the twentieth century, these works took crucial steps
toward a modern American poetics.

My final chapter focuses on a significant subset of this turn-of-the-
century modern verse that directly addresses defining phenomena of

urban-industrial modernity. In these decades, to choose modern subject matter, when the entire ideological force of late genteel culture asserted that poetry was poetry only when it stayed out of the modern world, became an important statement of discontent with existing traditions and a willingness to explore new possibilities. I group these modern subjects into three related categories—material, political, and discursive— that collectively highlight the breadth of turn-of-the-century poetry's address to modernity. The first of these deals with poems addressing iconic urban objects and places in which physical space intersects with social landscape. The second examines poets' evolving responses to media-manipulated military action in the Caribbean and the Philippines between 1898 and 1902, which challenged them to reconsider national identity in the face of an emerging imperialist modernity. In the strongest of these modern war poems, the marginal character of poetry becomes a politically aware counterdiscourse based not on certitude and conviction but on skeptical detachment toward official stories. The book's final section elaborates what I call the "poetry-writes-the-news-paper" topos: a small but impressive group of poems that use the newspaper to explore the impact of mass culture on changing models of social and cultural value in America. Two major poems in this category, Alice Dunbar-Nelson's "Legend of the Newspaper" and Crane's "A newspaper is a collection of half-injustices," ingeniously explore poetry's capacity to resist more thoroughly hegemonized discourses of capitalist media. The writers examined here span an ideological spectrum from nostalgic conservative to anarchist radical; their work spans a stylistic range from traditional metrical form to experimental free verse. This variety is important because it shows that the desire to make poetry relevant to modern experience did not emerge from within any single style or politics, but across the entire range of American verse writing.

COLUMBIA MODERNIZED: THE STATUE, THE STREET, THE FAIR

The appearance in the 1890s of poems thoughtfully, even critically, exploring the meanings of modernized public space (rather than simply commemorative celebrations of their openings, of which there were many) indicated that American verse was moving fitfully toward engagement with modernity.[1] Perhaps the best-known poem in this category was "The New Colossus" (1883), written by Emma Lazarus (1849–1887) at a moment when the Statue of Liberty's supporters were struggling without much success to raise the funds necessary for its pedestal.[2] No one doubted that Frédéric-Auguste Bartholdi's statue, if built, would be an American icon, but there was much question what it might signify. Officially, as stated in an 1884 article by William Howe Downes, it was meant to symbolize "the historic friendship of the two great republics" and "the idea of freedom and fraternity which underlies the republican form of government" (153). Downes referred to "The New Colossus" and to the question of "American hospitality to the European emigrant" (153) as a secondary meaning, suggesting that the poem had already begun to influence, but not to dominate, interpretations of the statue even before construction was complete. Lazarus's poem was recited at the unveiling ceremony in 1886, indicating its growing importance, but it would be another seventeen years before this interpretation was officially authorized by being inscribed on a plaque inside the pedestal.

The poem's highly rhetorical final section, which features the statue's self-defining statement ("Give me your tired, your poor, / Your huddled masses") is better known, but the lines that precede it are more impressive poetically and politically:

> Not like the brazen giant of Greek fame,
> With conquering limbs astride from land to land;
> Here at our sea-washed, sunset gates shall stand
> A mighty woman with a torch, whose flame
> Is the imprisoned lightning, and her name
> Mother of Exiles. From her beacon-hand
> Glows world-wide welcome; her mild eyes command
> The air-bridged harbor that twin cities frame.
> "Keep, ancient lands, your storied pomp!" cries she
> With silent lips. (1:202–03)

Lazarus defines the statue first and foremost as a symbol of modernity: it will be a *new* colossus, repudiating the old world's history of expansionist conquest, its monumental iconic gestures signifying "world-wide welcome" to other peoples, its electrified torch lighting the way to a world of peaceful, permeable borders among nations. The poem has never been understood as a stylistic harbinger of modernism, and yet its syntax and diction—particularly the declarative constructions "here . . . shall stand / A mighty woman with a torch," and "her mild eyes command / The . . . harbor"—are notably plainspoken for the year, especially in such a self-consciously public poem. If the poet slightly overindulges her liking for compound adjectives, each of these is fresh and effective in its own terms; with "beacon-hand" and "air-bridged," she generates compact metaphors that anticipate twentieth-century preferences for efficiency and clarity over euphuistic indirection. The statue's rejection of the "storied pomp" of older cultures both celebrates a national skepticism toward outworn social hierarchies and predicts the emergence of more direct modes of expression in the stories told by modern Americans and their icons.

After 1890 the big-city thoroughfare, the quintessentially modernized space that Bryant had thoroughly repudiated for Fireside poetry in "The Crowded Street," gradually reappeared as a site of poetic engagement. Lazarus's "City Visions" (1880s) proposes that the city-dwelling poet is not bereft of "Fancy" but can "soar cloud-high," no less than the consciousness taking imaginative sustenance from the natural world (1:219). Yet in this poem Lazarus avoids actually looking at the street, still inhibited by the binary model employed by antiurban poetic traditions, which scripts the city as a "restricted sphere" of the "dismal now and here" in contrast to another realm, "free as the winds are free," defined by its separation from the actual textures of modern life (1:219). But other poets during these years reentered the urban street and looked around more openly. The sonnet "Broadway at Midnight" (before 1910), by Frank Dempster Sherman (1860–1916), contrasts the artificially lit "motley show" of the theater district's streets at night to "serene" stars that look down "From their blue balconies forevermore" (274). But the knee-jerk repudiation of the urban that conventionally followed from such binary oppositions never comes. Instead the speaker destabilizes the old binaries by emphasizing the modern city street as a place where opposites freely mingle ("Here Wealth and Poverty together stray; / Here Virtue walks with Vice, and does not know"). This post-theater crush of Broadway, a "motley show" whose participants are "The tireless actors of an endless play," contains the "busy whirl of life," and Sherman ultimately prefers it to the cool silence of the stars, "mute spectators of our mortal strife." As they "look down" from their balconies like passive spectators of a play, Sherman reminds us that despite their resonance as symbols of immutable beauty, they can only hover above, indifferent and remote, while "the human comedy" takes place on the street, not above it.

Like Bryant's "The Crowded Street," Francis Brooks's "Cities' Streets," written in the later 1890s, portrays the street as an ambiguous site where all aspects of human activity are concentrated. But Brooks declines to seek refuge in pastoral nostalgia or consolatory Christianity, instead remaining in the city even as he notes its chaotic impersonality. Here is the poem in full:

> Upon the pave, the ceaseless lave
> Of life and trade; the cities rave
> And jostle—egotism's own grave
> Upon the pave.
>
> And here compassion's well is digged
> Or charity's felucca rigged;
> And eyes made wise observe how chance
> Doth mix with varied circumstance.
>
> Even the will is shaped to fill
> The needs that time and place distil—
> The fateful flow of weal and ill
> Upon the pave. (*Poems* 221)

In this realist rewriting of Bryant, markers of individual consciousness central to the Enlightenment worldview—ego, wisdom, will—are subordinated to such motive forces of modernity as blind chance and environmental circumstance. Yet these forces are not dismally deterministic but generate a complex mixture of "weal and ill" found on the urban street. While acknowledging the jarring textures of metropolitan life that Georg Simmel was theorizing during this same decade, Brooks doesn't, as some naturalists might, dismiss the weal produced by the modern city as illusory, but acknowledges that this challenging urban environment can generate compassion as well as rapacity. Perhaps most importantly, Brooks asserts his modernity of outlook by admitting no world elsewhere into this urban milieu: he makes "life and trade" apposite rather than opposite terms and conceives the city's continual destruction and reconstruction as a renewal of experience, laving rather than sullying.

The underrated Edith M. Thomas (1854–1925) carried American verse closer yet to finding itself in and through the modern urban street. Like much of her work, "Broadway," published in *Scribner's* in 1889 and then in the 1893 volume *Fair Shadow Land*, mounts a bracing synthesis of sentimental, transcendentalist, and modern sensibilities. "Broadway" draws upon the same metaphor of city as river that Bryant had used, but rather than fleeing the urban for pastoral refuge, Thomas uses it to consider the new spatial perspectives and patterns of movement created by the skyscraper city:

Between these frowning granite steeps
The human river onward sweeps;
And here it moves with torrent force,
And there it slacks its heady course.
(*Fair Shadow Land* 44)

Bryant's flight from the urban led him eventually to call upon the deity "who heeds, who holds them all, / In His large love and boundless thought" (*Poetical Works* 320), proposing that only God can make sense of the incoherence of the modern city. Thomas rewrites this portentous evocation of divinity as a good-natured agnostic admission of the city's incomprehensibility ("what controls its variant flow / A keener wit than mine must show" [*Fair Shadow Land* 44]). But this incoherence is paradoxically enriching, allowing her to "cast myself upon the tide, / And merging with its current glide," become a Whitmanesque "drop, an atom, of the whole / Of its great bulk and wandering soul" (44). Thomas's wholehearted willingness to mingle in the experiential textures of urban modernity is a crucial step toward the New Poetry of the 1910s, in which dozens of American poets as different as Carl Sandburg, T. S. Eliot, and Edna St. Vincent Millay took the city as the venue and inspiration for their modern poetics.

The playful second section of "Broadway" further pursues the street-as-river image to destabilize the conventional genteel opposition of rural and urban:

O curbless river, savage stream,
Thou art my wilderness extreme,
Where I may move as free, as lone
As in the waste with wood o'ergrown,
And broodings of as brave a strain
May here unchallenged entertain,
Whether meridian light display
The swift routine of current day,
Or jet electric, diamond-clear,
Convoke a world of glamour here. (*Fair Shadow Land* 44–45)

Bryant's image had exploited a convenient metaphoric relation (masses of people streaming through streets, water flowing through riverbed), but had never faced up to the subversive implications of confusing natural and artificial. Once you make the city into a river or other natural object, even to demonize it, you allow someone else to assert the city as natural, or as an affirmative synthesis of natural and constructed. Thomas takes this step here, playing the modern urbanite so accustomed to constant noise that she now needs it to sleep. For her, electric light evokes not garish falsity but the exhilaration of the twenty-four-hour city, and the rural world seems "a waste" of meaningless, random overgrowth.

Thomas was perhaps the first American poet (at least since Whitman) to mount a comprehensive challenge to the genteel convention in which urban space was necessarily defined as dirty, noisy, dangerous, immoral, emotionally jarring, and spiritually alienating. For her, indeed, the city is not the disease of modernity but the cure, offering safety, comfort, companionship, and spiritual balm. To rural vacancy and loneliness she prefers the city's perceptual kaleidoscope, not always beautiful but continually surprising and various. She experiences urban space not as confinement but as liberation, where she "may move as free, as lone" (44) as she likes, brooding about anything she wants to, unhindered by the intrusive arbiters of taste or morality that a middle-class woman of her generation would have encountered in small-town America. Put another way, the modern city allows an Edith Thomas, born on a farm in Ohio before the Civil War, to reinvent herself in her thirty-third year and to live thereafter in New York as an independent woman in charge of her own life (Gray 235). The city's very impersonality makes this freedom possible, affording "solitude" when she desires it, but unlike the desperation that attends remote rural solitude, also offering instant "comradeship" through renewing encounters with others, "Where all to all are firm allied, / And each hath countenance from the rest" (*Fair Shadow Land* 45). The noun "countenance" carries both neutral connotations (the appearance of a human face) and positive ones (an expression of approval or support). Thomas draws upon both senses here, asserting that the modern city's continual procession of human countenances, no matter how "unconfessed" the bond may be, still implies and enables recognition, alliance, mutual support.

Having established this theme of a transcendent bond among city dwellers, Thomas reimagines the city of modernity not as the random collisions of fragmented monads, but as a cohesive collective entity:

> I muse upon this river's brink;
> I listen long; I strive to think
> What cry goes forth, of many blent,
> And by that cry what thing is meant. (*Fair Shadow Land* 45)

In musing upon the city, making it her muse, the poet seeks a visionary liminal realm ("Sometimes I move as in a dream" into a space of "wondrous quiet") where she may experience frenetic city life no longer as random and entropic, but as a collective journey that "seems in summoned haste to urge, / Half prescient, towards a destined verge!" (45). This section emphasizes images of marginality—the river's brink, the barely heard human voice, and particularly the "destined verge." They all imply that the city's "swift, phantasmal stream," the inexorability and haste of its movements, the impossibility of comprehending it in the puny terms of individual ego—the very same qualities that caused the genteel poet to repudiate it—might carry a powerful liminal prescience, as yet "inarticulate," but heralding humanity's eventual destiny.

Despite her tendency to "poetic" diction, at a conceptual level Thomas fully inhabits the machine-age paradigm of cultural value celebrating efficiency and decrying waste (superbly described by Cecilia Tichi, 63–75). "Waste" is a key word in the poem, and Thomas returns to it in the poem's final lines.

> The river flows,—unwasting flows;
> Nor less nor more its volume grows,
> From source to sea still onward rolled,
> As days are shed and years are told;
> And yet, so mutable its wave,
> That no man twice therein may lave,
> But, ere he can return again,
> Himself shall subtle change sustain;
> Since more and more each life must be
> Tide-troubled by the drawing sea. (*Fair Shadow Land* 45–46)

In contrast to the overgrown "waste" of rural wood, the "unwasting" city achieves material efficiency and stability even while taking its identity from constant change—much as a river maintains its course and form despite its individual molecules of water being in constant flux. Thomas thus rounds out her central metaphor with a ringing affirmation of the city's organic identity. In critiquing the genteel-Romantic poetics that insisted on opposing city to river, modernity to nature, "Broadway" establishes several premises that would underwrite the urban American verse of the 1910s: that the city minimizes waste and maximizes resources; that its electrification puts an end to the squandering of time by making the night available for human uses; that its profusion of people allows both comfortable anonymity and convenient companionship as one prefers; that its density of materials intensifies energies and compounds material wealth; that its innumerable voices might articulate a collective consciousness.[3]

I've ordered these poems to indicate that by the 1890s American poets were starting to treat the urban street not as an abstraction or convention whose meanings were fixed and prior to any particular experience of it, but as a concrete material reality, whose character varied from one circumstance to another. Lazarus, still largely within the binary paradigm of Romantic antiurbanism in "City Visions," can barely look out her city window unless she looks up at clouds and sky; Sherman still treats the street as metaphor rather than as material site, but affirms the city's motley mixture as the genuine emblem of modern experience. Brooks rejects the binary opposition of two worlds in favor of a wholly urban milieu, and Thomas adds an ardent emotional investment in the life of the city, as well as the conviction that its physical textures carry emotional and even spiritual meaning. This process of concretization culminates in "The Road Builders," by the radical anarchist writer Voltairine de Cleyre (1866–1912). Here, perhaps for the first time since Whitman, an American poet describes a specific event that happens on an American city street. The poet earns the right to abstract a broader social meaning from this event by focusing intently on the physical materials that comprise the modern street—earth, macadam, sweat, blood. Here is the poem in full:

The Road Builders

("Who built the beautiful roads?" queried a friend of the present order, as we walked one day along the macadamized driveway of Fairmount Park.)

I saw them toiling in the blistering sun,
Their dull, dark faces leaning toward the stone,
Their knotted fingers grasping the rude tools.
Their rounded shoulders narrowing in their chest,
The sweat drops dripping in great painful beads.
I saw one fall, his forehead on the rock,
The helpless hand still clutching at the spade,
The slack mouth full of earth.

And he was dead.
His comrades gently turned his face, until

The fierce sun glittered hard upon his eyes,
Wide open, staring at the cruel sky.
The blood yet ran upon the jagged stone;
But it was ended. He was quite, quite dead:
Driven to death beneath the burning sun,
Driven to death upon the road he built.

He was no "hero," he; a poor, black man,
Taking "the will of God" and asking naught;
Think of him thus, when next your horse's feet
Strike out the flint spark from the gleaming road;
Think that for this, this common thing, The Road,
A human creature died; 'tis a blood gift,
To an o'erreaching world that does not thank.
Ignorant, mean, and soulless was he? Well,—
Still human; and you drive upon his corpse. (68)

Philadelphia, July 24, 1900.

The epigraph identifies the poem as a response to a real question asked by a particular person, strengthening its immediacy as an intervention into a specific set of social circumstances. So too does the attachment of an exact date and place to the text; even if July 24 marks the poem's completion rather than the events narrated, both the man's death and the act of composition are situated firmly in 1900 Philadelphia. The poem's structural apparatus thus contributes to its political force in somewhat the same way that Jacob Riis's and Lewis Hine's contemporaneous photographs of slum life documented the actuality of the conditions decried by urban reformers and denied by some supporters of the existing order. The poem's authenticity is further asserted by the opening phrase "I saw," in which de Cleyre takes on the responsibility of witness. Judiciously she repeats this phrase just once, but at a crucial moment, when the man collapses (1. 6). Rhythmically, the phrase "I saw one fall" requires us to accent each of its four syllables, slowing down the iambic pentameter into an emphatic, ominous trudge (an effect re-created two lines later in the phrase "The slack mouth full of earth," which offers four heavy stresses in six long syllables). These strategies allow de Cleyre to avoid any evocation of the inevitable cosmic suffering of the generic poor and help her describe an actuality that can be comprehensively located in geographic, temporal, and political dimensions.

Like its rhythmic effects, the poem's imagery and diction are more complex than they might first appear. De Cleyre's contrast between light and darkness challenges the notion of a natural social hierarchy. In the workmen's "dull, dark faces"; in the association of the dying man with the dark soil that he consumes as he falls, and will then consume him; and finally in the eventual revelation of his actual racial difference, darkness appears to carry conventional Euro-American connotations of deprivation, ignorance, and exclusion. But ironically, the imagery that opposes darkness does not signify enlightenment, refinement, innocence, or any other conventional meaning. Instead light signifies onerous pressure: the "blistering," "fierce," and "burning" sunlight, the "cruel sky," and the spark thrown by the horse hooves on the "gleaming road." All trope the forces that confine the dead man and his "comrades" in darkness (as the sun glitters "hard upon his eyes"). This imagery supports de Cleyre's primary political goal in the poem: to implicate people who enjoy the luxury of thinking theirs is an enlightened, beautiful society, into the structural inequities that darken the lives of so many of its inhabitants. For the poet, as for the dying workman, the capitalist world's light is inextricably part of its darkness.

De Cleyre effectively uses the poem's particularized setting—a modernized road in one of the nation's greatest public parks—to intensify her commentary on the structural injustices of turn-of-the-century America. Unlike New York's Central Park, Fairmount had been developed in stages, and its elongated dimensions—more than thirteen miles from one edge to the other—required the maintenance of elaborate, lengthy roads (Weigley 427, 517).[4] Despite the difficulty of getting there from Center City, and the vast distances between some of its highlights, the park was Philadelphia's major leisure attraction, an urban pleasure ground unique for its size, variety of terrain, and removal from noise and smoke, described by Lafcadio Hearn in 1889 as "the most beautiful place of the whole civilized world on any sunny, tepid summer day," in which "100,000 people make scarcely any more sound than a swarm of bees" (Bisland 470). De Cleyre uses "beautiful" as well, to describe the conventional view of the park's new roads, a usage that becomes bitterly ironic as the poem continues. The word here may remind us of the ideological functions of the "City Beautiful" movement, which by the turn of the century had begun to shape the development of public spaces across the nation. Between 1895 and 1925, City Beautiful rhetoric drove one of the nation's most grandiose (and protracted) civic works projects, which sited the new Philadelphia Museum of Art on high ground at the edge of Fairmount Park and built a grand parkway (later named the Benjamin

Franklin) to link the park and museum to city hall and the business district (D. Brownlee 15). During these same years, in sprawling areas to the northeast and southwest of the park, tracts of cheap row housing and often substandard infrastructure were developed to house the city's laboring class, much of it immigrant or African American. As she identifies the worker's body with the road itself, de Cleyre reminds her readers of the connection between these two types of urban space and proposes that human labor is the truest resource of a society. This workman, one among many, is "driven to death" upon "this common thing, The Road," so that others may "drive upon his corpse." The road is "common" in being both something an ordinary laborer ("ignorant, mean, and soulless" to his ungrateful social betters) would live and die upon, but also something public, owned in common and freely traversed by all members of the metropolis, at least in theory. But for those not fully enfranchised, denied opportunity and freedom of movement, the road's commonality as an ideological construct becomes a bitter joke. De Cleyre conveys this irony through the shift of the verb "drive" from its primary older meaning, of pushing something forcibly forward, to its more typical twentieth-century usage, of moving in a vehicle under one's own control. Those who promenade themselves comfortably through this beautiful civic space are heedlessly driving upon one whom an unjust society has driven to death, in the grim older sense. Through these multiply signifying common words, de Cleyre links the nation's slave-driving heritage, obviously still not eradicated, to its modern leisure-seeking character. In doing so, she puts an implacable political critique into effective rhetorical and aesthetic form that anticipates the radical modern verse of the 1910s sponsored in *The Masses, The Liberator,* and elsewhere.

In the United States between 1890 and 1910, the material and ideological significations of modern public space were instantiated most comprehensively by the World's Columbian Exposition, held in Chicago in the summer of 1893. The Exposition's class-stratified design, frankly segregating the spheres of White City and Midway, elite and mass culture (as seen in Figure 3, chapter 2), embodied a dominant but increasingly embattled binary paradigm in American architecture and city planning that corresponded to the polarized evaluative model of late genteel poetry. The greatest congruence between these two disciplinary formations was precisely their resistance to the chaotic heterogeneity of the immigrant metropolis, of which Chicago was exemplary. The custodians of genteel verse, like the architects of the White City, knew that a literary Midway Plaisance existed and perhaps even needed to exist. But that didn't mean they had to admit it into the Arcadian realms of poetry: let it remain across the cultural tracks, in the doggerel of popular song lyrics and the prose of "city fiction." Poetry should remain enclosed within its own sanitized white city of the soul, strictly regulating its visitors' perceptions, ennobling them whether they liked it or not. But in the 1893 Exposition, this segregated model of cultural value threatened to come apart at the seams; despite the elegant proportions and gleaming surfaces of the White City, the magnetic midway stole the fair from its organizers. As this book has suggested, something similar would need to happen before the status of poetry in America would be rejuvenated.

For several American poets, the Columbian Exposition provided an occasion to explore the meanings of the modernized nation and verse within it.[5] Their works offer us most when they remain rooted in the Exposition space itself—its layout, its attractions, its social dynamics— rather than departing on windy generic journeys through American history. The "Chicago Exposition Ode" (1897) of Mary Weston Fordham (1862–19—?) begins promisingly by merging Exposition imagery with the immigrant iconography of the Statue of Liberty: "Columbia, to thee / From every clime we come, / To lay our trophies at thy feet—/ Our sunbright, glorious home" (30).[6] But the poem soon metamorphoses into a severely sentimentalized account of the arrival of European Christians in the western hemisphere, as "'Pale Faces' on their knees!" bringing "the Holy Cross" to the natives of the place thereby named "San Salvador, the blest!" For Fordham, receiving "God's benison" is alone sufficient to make the New World "Home of the free, the brave!" to whom "Nations beyond the seas / Shall worship at thy shrine" (31–32).[7]

The "Columbian Ode" of Harriet Monroe was first read (and partially performed in choral settings composed by George W. Chadwick) on October 21, 1892, at a grand ceremony dedicating the Exposition and also commemorating the ostensible four-hundredth anniversary of Columbus's "discovery." The poem does not much engage the Exposition as a material reality either, since it was composed months before opening day. Suffering from the typical faults of nineteenth-century romantic-epic verse—ornate imagery, strained allegory, lumbering gait, overemphatic tone—the work is a far cry from Monroe's mature verse written after 1905, which is vividly engaged with the defining technological, material, and emotional textures of modernity.[8] Still, the "Columbian Ode" was a crucial American poem, a formative experience for the person most instrumental to the institutional emergence of modern poetry in the United States. Monroe knew many of the fair's organizers well. In fact, her sister was married to John Wellborn Root, the first supervising architect of the Exposition, whose sudden death in January 1891 deprived it of an architectural vision more attuned to American vernacular styles. Even before 1890 Monroe was working to integrate poetry with the cultural life of Chicago: her "Cantata" rhapsodizing the city had been delivered at the dedication of an early landmark of American civic modernism, Louis Sullivan's Auditorium Building, on December 9, 1889.[9] A few months later she began pursuing a role for poetry in the Exposition planned for 1893. Though her main success was being invited to write the ode rather than achieving a more integral place for verse throughout the fair, her efforts did establish the notion of civic support for poetry among Chicago's business and cultural leadership, which would bear fruit two decades later. She achieved this precedent in part by having the astonishing nerve to spring a bill for one thousand dollars on the Committee on Ceremonies late in the planning, even though everyone knew that she had suggested the ode to the committee rather than the other way around (*Poet's Life* 124). These monetary demands engendered initial opposition, but when they were finally accepted, Monroe had achieved an "entrepreneurial triumph": the "resilient, inventive promotion of the poet and her poem" (Massa 58), which in the audacious context of Chicago capitalism must have impressed the businessmen in spite of the extra minus sign on the Exposition's ledger. In 1911 she would again use that audacity to find guarantors for *Poetry: A Magazine of Verse* among the same group who had supported and subsidized the Exposition and other institutions of civic culture: the Art Institute, the Symphony, and the Chicago Opera.

Though the ode had only a brief public vogue, Monroe's participation in the Exposition reverberated long afterward. She sued Pulitzer's *New York World* for its unauthorized publication of excerpts from her poem and in 1895 was awarded the impressive sum of five thousand dollars. As an early test case of the copyright laws passed in the 1880s, this suit was appealed unsuccessfully by the newspaper all the way to the U.S. Supreme Court. The experience fired Monroe's zeal for defending the rights of individual cultural entrepreneurs—poets and editors—against an impersonal and careless publishing establishment. As she later put it proudly, "my little lawsuit, being without precedent, established its own precedence and became a textbook case, defining the rights of authors to control their unpublished works" (*Poet's Life* 139). Her commitment to authorial rights would echo forcefully through the editorial rhetoric and policies of *Poetry* from 1912 into the 1930s and had a shaping impact on the economics of modern poetry. When Monroe brought her suit, such mass-media ideologists as Pulitzer and Edward

Bok were proceeding as if the individual author—and especially the poet—had passed into obsolescence. The *World*'s brazen and sloppy publication of the ode, as an anonymous bit of news rather than as someone's intellectual property, was vivid evidence of this disregard. In contrast, Monroe's tenacious conviction that authors of verse should retain economic control of their work asserted poetry as a full-fledged participant, not a charity case, within modern culture. This would be the sort of forceful advocacy American poetry needed, and fortunately would receive, in its stunning shift from crisis into renaissance in the 1910s.

Two other substantial poems used the specific design and arrangement of the Columbian Exposition to examine the models of cultural value available in 1890s America. Edgar Lee Masters's "The White City" (published 1898) begins by situating itself into the material textures of the fair:

> The autumnal sky is blue like June's,
> > The wooded isle is sere below
> Reflected in the still lagoons
> > Beneath the full noon's brilliant glow.
> Around the wondrous buildings show
> > Their sculptured roofs and domes and towers.
> (*A Book of Verses* 120)

The early autumn setting imparts a belatedness that tempers the awestruck speaker's enthusiasm with a wistful sense that the fair's splendor is ephemeral.[10] The "wooded isle" was a parklike preserve in the middle of the White City, designed to allow people to depart the bustling avenues for a more meditative, bucolic experience. It affords the poet a metaphor of preindustrial America from which he can begin to describe the emergence of modernity. The island's reflection in the surrounding lagoons also establishes the presence of visual echoing, confusion, and perhaps illusion, in the apparently shadowless scene of sunlit noon.

From this point Masters turns toward the allegorical entities still obligatory in poems about great public events, but he maintains an engagement with the Exposition's material textures by describing them as they appear on actual buildings and statuary: "triumphal columns crowned / By Neptunes"; Augustus Saint-Gaudens's Diana on the roof of the Agriculture Building, her "tense bow ready to rebound"; the figures of winged Victory and "Liberty within her chair," both seen on F. W. MacMonnies's Columbian Fountain; and of course, the eye-catching

Figure 8. *The Columbian Fountain of F. W. MacMonnies. World's Columbian Exposition, Chicago, 1893. Author's collection.*

Statue of the Republic by Daniel Chester French, a structure made of gold leaf over plaster, which rose 105 feet from the lagoon of the Court of Honor:

> And over all the Republic stands,
>   With countenance serene and fair,
> The staff and eagle in her hands,
>   Whom we adore, because she loosed our bands. (121)

Just behind the Republic is the dramatically sited columnar structure called the Peristyle, which "Protects the land against the sea" (121) (by forming a barrier between the Court of Honor and the open water of Lake Michigan) and contains various iconic statuary, including an orator, a young fisherman, a Native American, and Columbus (de Wit 87). These allegorical presences inspire renewed idealism and even "reverence" in the poet, who concludes that an appropriate response would be "the head / . . . bowed for truths we have inherited" (122).

Figure 9. *The Court of Honor. World's Columbian Exposition, Chicago, 1893. Author's collection.*

Yet despite Masters's sincerely felt idealism toward America as purveyor of Liberty to the world, hints of unease creep in, first through the sudden proliferation of conditional verb forms ("A solemn splendor which may be / The presence of the majestic dead, / Reigns in the air until the knee / Would bend in reverence"). The next section begins with renewed idealistic energy, but this is almost immediately deflected by another realization of the fair's impermanence:

> Aye, truths and beauty and the power
> > Which makes this vision all our own,
> Though for a brief and passing hour. . . . (122)

"This vision" is both the faith that a better world is possible, which created and maintains American democratic ideals, and also the splendid visual illusion of the fair itself. For the poet, the ephemerality of the latter troubles the power, beauty, even perhaps the truth of the former. These two notes—celebration of the republic's best social ideals, and anxiety that America's exemplary status might be no more permanent than the plaster structures of the fair—challenge each other throughout the poem and create its distinctive tone, wistful yet cynical, already nostalgic for a resonating, magical moment that is not yet past but may not be fully present at all.

Masters next turns to a conventional but concise and rhetorically effective narrative of the coming of modernity, beginning with Bacon's turn away from superstition toward empiricism, leading eventually to industrial technologies—steam engine, railroad, telegraph. The unveiling of the earth's mysteries, the creation of a world dominated not by miracle but by "enterprise," brings a desire for political enlightenment and the emergence of "Justice" and "Liberty" as motive forces in the world. Yet despite all these causes for celebration, surrounded by emblems of eternal truth, Masters still cannot shake an obscure sense of mutability and deprivation:

> And thus where art and science hoard
>   The trophies of the fruitful years,
> The mighty spirits which out-soared
>   The shadows of their trials and tears,
> Dante's and Homer's and Shakespeare's
>   Seem hovering in the sun-lit air,
> Now when the attentive spirit hears
>   The first sighs of the year's despair,
> While sorrow dyes the earth in hues most fair. (124–25)

The trophies of modernity's art and science, accumulated in the great buildings of the Exposition, evoke those great poetic spirits who sustained humane ideals through darker times. Yet hints of autumn mute this evocation as well. If the earth is at its "most fair" exactly because of the year's coming "despair," what does that imply about the Exposition? Is its hoarding of beauty, its presentation of human accomplishments in all their fairest forms, somehow a harbinger of coming loss or decline?

There seems no obvious or necessary reason why this should be so, yet as Masters ends the poem with a description of the Exposition's spectacular display of nighttime fountains ("Ten thousand lamps blaze in the jet / Of water, shadowed nook, and tree"), he is continually conscious of the experience as a "heavenly fantasy—/ Ah, that this dream should ever cease to be." The final lines maintain this paradoxical blend of plenitude and loss:

> And lo! How white, how glorious
>   These fanes and temples now appear;

How pure a mood is now o'er us,
> The evening bell is sweet and clear.
And there by Dian's brow, how near
> A star shines singly and alone;
Right o'er the dome's symmetric sphere!
> The flags against the sky are blown—
And all we cherished once is quickly gone. (125–26)

This time the consciousness of loss is not countered by any further affirmation: we are left wondering if what's ending is not simply a happy day at the fair, but somehow the ideals that the fair has so strikingly evoked. Again, such melancholy and loss seem unmotivated in a poem of evidently celebratory intent. Perhaps their persistence only makes sense as the poet's obscure intuition that the experience of modernity exists in the gap between our yearnings and even the most beguiling material objects we surround ourselves with. By maintaining a focus on the physical textures of the fair, Masters has approached an unsought and perturbing understanding of the insufficiency of commodity fetishism to satisfy our spirits. The Columbian Exposition has proven American expertise in material realms, but has not finally reached the modern spirit.

Perhaps the most politically acute American poem about the Exposition is "The Captive of the White City" by Ina Coolbrith (1841–1928), which challenges supremacist racial ideologies by pondering the presence on the Chicago Midway of the Sioux chieftain called Rain-in-the-Face, the reputed killer of General George Armstrong Custer in 1876. The Columbian Exposition has been critiqued by Robert Rydell, Curtis Hinsley, and others for both its racial exclusions and inclusions: for the exclusion of Native Americans, African Americans, and women from equal participation in the official spaces of the White City; and for the Midway's "ethnological" attractions—people of foreign extraction, the more exotic the better, who were brought to Chicago and exhibited as emblems of "primitive" cultures, in contexts that inevitably claimed this nation's material, moral, and genetic superiority (Rydell 143–70). Here, constructing a distinctive version of chauvinistic cultural value, Midway and White City worked not in opposition but in concert. Visitors drawn to the heterogeneity and vitality of the former could gawk at the dark skin, strange dress, lamentable living conditions, and absurd rituals of the outlanders. Meanwhile, the mere presence of the White City shimmering in the background offered comforting reassurance that they lived in a civilized place of rationality, beauty, and homogeneous whiteness (even if, like the persona of the song "On Midway Plaisance," they might be bored silly by the White City's attempts to edify them).

Clearly the midway's ethnology reflected the era's predominant racist and imperialist sensibilities. As Rydell notes, however, "the motives and reactions of the people put on display are less clear"; not just "passive victims" of commercial exploitation, some may have been complicit, others resistant, toward representations of their ethnicity (158). The exhibition of the notorious Rain-in-the-Face, killer of Custer, is an especially problematic case. Described in an 1876 biography of Custer as a "great warrior," "considered brave beyond precedent" by his nation, Rain-in-the-Face had been imprisoned for several months under Custer's command in 1875 before escaping to rejoin Sitting Bull and the Sioux some months before the Little Big Horn, where he took his revenge (Whittaker 518–19). On the midway, the warrior was perceivable simultaneously as exotic and native, distant yet powerfully present, silent and assertive, beyond history and torn from the headlines. Was he, as Rydell surmises, among those Native Americans who petitioned the government for control over their own representations at the fair, urging the organizers to "Give us . . . some reason to be glad with you that [America] was so discovered" (qtd. Rydell 160)? Or was he there, as Coolbrith claims in a footnote, "by permission of the United States Government (so read the record), under guard in the log cabin" in which his associate Sitting Bull died (57)? Or could he somehow have been both petitioner and prisoner at once?

Despite the seventeen years since the Little Big Horn, the destruction of Custer's company was still fresh in American minds, the most resounding defeats of the nation's military by an enemy force. In the decade before the Exposition, Custer's widow, Elizabeth, had built a public career as a writer and speaker from her husband's famous demise. In 1886 Libbie Custer had been "a familiar figure backstage" when Buffalo Bill Cody had first taken his Wild West Show (of which the climax was a depiction of the Little Big Horn) to Madison Square Garden (Frost 261). In January 1892 the *Century* published a major article by Captain Edward S. Godfrey, who had been at the battle under another commanding general. Godfrey's article and its reception reopened the controversial possibility that Custer precipitated the disaster by disobeying orders or exceeding his authority (Frost 268). In Chicago in May 1892, a year before the Exposition began, Libbie Custer initiated a nationwide tour of public appearances, giving addresses on such topics as "Garrison Life" and "Buffalo Hunting" (Frost 275). Meanwhile, upon being refused permission to locate his enterprise within the midway, Cody planned to set up just outside its borders during the summer of 1893, threatening formidable competition to the officially sanctioned attractions (Rydell 160) and intensifying their need to offer an authentic element of this momentous event. What could be more authentic than the living presence of Rain-in-the-Face?[11]

The persistent publicity hovering around "Custer's Last Stand," which mingled the most serious aspects of the "Indian question" with Wild-West commodification, is the context into which Coolbrith's poem intervenes. She begins with a lyrical evocation of the White City as the "Flower of the foam of the waves / Of the beautiful inland sea," the exemplary modern metropolis that houses "Children of every zone / The light of the sun has known" (57). In this "Marvel of human hands," "the banners of all the lands / Are free on the western breeze, / Free as the West is free." The double-edged impact of this last phrase is the first indication of Coolbrith's thoughtful critique of the ideologies of officialdom, since the American West is clearly not free of strife; nor, as we soon discover, are its native peoples free. In the midst of the midway's "surging crowd," Rain-in-the-Face sits "silent, and stern, and proud." Coolbrith asks, as we might upon first learning of this unnerving juxtaposition, "Why is the captive here?" This interrogative resonates from the specific, doubting the redeeming social value of such a display, to the general, questioning the necessity or justice of turning the continent's natives into outlaws, victims, and prisoners: "For the beautiful City stands / On the Red Man's wrested lands," and "There is blood on the broken door" and on the "bronzed hands" of Rain-in-the-Face. This blood conveys meaning at several levels: the blood of Custer and the soldiers killed by the Sioux; the blood of Sitting Bull, killed in his own cabin, whose walls now display "relics of the fight"; and the blood of his and other tribes, displaced and killed by whites.

Coolbrith next appears to make a conventional turn toward the magnetic figure of Custer, "Like a sun-god overthrown." But instead of evoking his spirit as heroic or eternal, she merely establishes a parallel between soldier and brave, by noting that they are both "Shut from the sunlit air" and by referring to Custer as "chief." Concluding that he is now "Dust and a name alone," the poet then makes a surprising shift to his living widow and envisions an encounter that in 1893 was entirely possible, if difficult to imagine: "What if she walked today / In the City's pleasant way," and "there to her sudden gaze" after all the "terrible years, / Stood Rain-in-the-Face" (58–59)?[12] What would they say to one another? This question, like the earlier "Why is the captive here?" is one to which the poet has no plausible answer. Instead she offers elaborate metaphors of irreconcilability: one might as well try to "Quench with a drop of dew / . . . / The prairies' burning plains" as to "tame / The hate in the Red Man's veins." But Coolbrith refuses to locate this implacable hatred in the Sioux's natural savagery, as the fair's ideologists might have done. Instead it is the inevitable result of "the wrongs of the White Man's rule," from which "Blood only may wash the trace" (59).

The poem concludes by reiterating the unnerving incongruity of this juxtaposition. Jests and glad songs "Ring through the sunlit space" of the bustling modern city, built for the desires and enjoyment of its inhabitants. Yet in the midst of this "wild, free breeze," like a visage from another time or world, "The captive sits apart, / Silent, and makes no sign," answering none of the poet's final questions: "But what is the word in your heart, / O man of a dying race? / What tale on your lips for mine, / O Rain-in-the-Face?" (60). Rain-in-the Face can assert himself only through maintaining both his public presence and his silent dissent from Euro-American modernity. He cannot speak to the well-meaning white poet except by refusing to speak; she cannot speak of or for him without falsehood, except to reiterate his silence. Coolbrith thus discovers another way in which poetry's marginality might become productive. In its indirection, its resonating obscurity, in all the qualities that provoked ideologists of mass culture to declare it useless, poetry speaks of what modernity cannot say about itself. It can approach the saying of the unsayable, as Coolbrith does with her title. Literally, Rain-in-the-Face is the captive of the midway and its voracious demand for living displays that could make its promoters money. But in describing him instead as "The Captive of the White City," Coolbrith foregrounds the relationship between the midway's ethnological ghetto and the shining city on the lagoon, built on usurped land. Evoking the various levels at which the city can be understood as "white," the poem asserts racial difference not as something that can be ghettoized and forgotten, but as a shaping and wounding principle of American society, and does so with a subtlety and thoughtfulness that few discussions of race in the period were capable of sustaining.

YOU PROVIDE THE PROSE POEMS, WE'LL PROVIDE THE WAR

It's remarkable how little attention has been paid to the Spanish-American War in American cultural studies. Featuring simultaneous military operations across two hemispheres, this complex event signaled the entry of the United States into a modern arena of global politics, and combined moral idealism, paranoid isolationism, and naked imperialism into a self-contradictory ideological brew. It also set the pattern for many of the armed conflicts of the twentieth century, as indigenous guerrilla forces were pitted against an occupying army more powerful but less able to adapt to quickly changing circumstances. In an interval of only two years the United States acted from both sides of this axis. The war and its aftermath dramatized the fraught relations between the United States and peoples of color around the world, which continue today in terms of foreign aid and economic colonization. Finally, as my section title lifted from *Citizen Kane* implies, the Spanish-American War demonstrated the powerful and troubling links between the modern nation's foreign policy and the mass-media sources by which information is distributed to its populace. The role of the American news media in fomenting the conflict has long been acknowledged.[13] It is less well known that the nation's poets not only responded to the fact of the war, but also commented powerfully upon "the War" as an ideological formation. As euphoria over victory in the Caribbean turned to confusion and outrage over events in the Philippines, American poetry was challenged to become a force of resistance to political rhetoric and inflammatory journalism driven by blatant ideological and economic expediency.

Despite all the forces inhibiting their engagement with contemporary subject matter, many turn-of-the-century poets treated the events of 1898–1902 as crucial to determining the political and ethical character of American modernity. Aaron Kramer has helpfully traced the broad trajectory of American verse pertaining to the war, beginning with poets' widespread enthusiasm for the notion of the United States as liberator of the oppressed Cuban people and moral policeman of the western hemisphere, which produced an outpouring of conventional pieties and slogans in verse from early 1898 into the following year (276–87). This pro-interventionist verse can be surveyed in several anthologies hurried out in 1898: the largely jingoistic *War-Time Echoes: Patriotic Poems, Heroic and Pathetic, Humorous and Dialectic, of the Spanish-American War*, edited by James Brownlee; the slightly more balanced *War Poems, 1898;* and the most comprehensive, *Spanish-American War Songs: A Complete Collection of Newspaper Verse during the Recent War with Spain*, edited by Sidney J. Wetherbee.[14]

Not all the verse collected in these anthologies expressed blind, pious patriotism. Some offered more thoughtful consideration of the war's consequences and meanings, such as "The Negro Soldier" by R. M. Channing, which argued that "we've got to reconstruct our views on color, more or less, / Now we know about the Tenth at La Quasina" (a unit of African American soldiers who distinguished themselves by their valor in a June 1898 battle) (105–06). This poem also included the hopeful notion, which echoes through much 1898 verse, that the Cuban volunteer force, drawn from all over the country and trained in Florida and Tennessee, had helped to heal the scars of the Civil War (now "the feud is done forever, of the blue-coat and the gray") (106). Other anthology verses ventured outright critique of American behavior and policies. To note one example, James Barton Adams's "The Jingo's Soliloquy," written as a parody of Hamlet's ("To go or not to go—that is the question"), ridicules the jingoist who howls for war until his voice "Ran up a hefty bill for overtime," yet soon reconsiders, deciding to play "the old rheumatic dodge, / Or vermiform appendicitis, or—/ Well, any old disease I think will stick," because he doesn't want to risk turning up, "name misspelled, perchance, upon / The telegraphic list of hero dead" (41–42). While not quite calling into question the courage of those who did go, this last cynical phrase certainly deromanticizes ideologies of military heroism. All in all, the poem presents home-front jingoism as a vicious form of compensation for the inadequacies of those Americans "somewhat streaked with yellow up the back" (41).

Despite poets' widespread enthusiasm for the intervention of 1898, the euphoric notion of a "splendid little war" fought for all the right reasons did not outlast the century. The Treaty of Paris ending hostilities between the United States and Spain, ratified by Congress in February 1899, alarmed liberals and anti-imperialists in specifying that control of the Philippines would be ceded to the United States. In that same month, the first skirmishes between American and Philippine forces occurred in the outskirts of Manila. Over the next year the situation grew steadily worse as the Filipino willingness to continue armed resistance to achieve self-government became clear. By the beginning of 1900 the nation's policy makers had committed the U.S. military to a campaign of outright imperialist repression, and most of the poets who had been enthusiastic about the liberation of Cuba were plunged into silence, shame, or indignation (Kramer 293–308).

Many poets who did continue to write about these events after 1899 distinguished between liberation and aggressive annexation, realizing that the geopolitical dynamics of modernity were too complex and dark to sustain the nation-as-liberator ideal without self-delusion. Kramer's study emphasizes, and values most highly, poetic utterances that admit the least uncertainty of their own position and can be placed into clearcut categories (such as "prophetic" and "anti-prophetic"). Instead of traversing that same territory, I'll offer something lacking from literary histories of the period: sympathetic attention to the responses of poets distressed over the fall of idealistic hopes into imperialist venality, who struggle to articulate both their disillusion and their continuing political engagement, however chastened. I find that the most enduring poems of the war tend to be those least certain of their ethical footing, most aware of their own implication in the ideologies they struggle to challenge. Through this ambivalent self-awareness, these works begin to rethink the relation of poetic utterance to sociopolitical actuality. At their strongest they propose a skeptical idealism that resists the discourses of official certainty, not by countering with their own set of certitudes, but by embracing modern strategies of obliquity, uncertainty, and irony.

Some poems in this category don't mention the Spanish-American and Philippine-American conflicts at all, yet still powerfully evoke their effects and meanings. Many employ images of ruined empire to express anxiety at the prospect of an imperial American future. "The Statue of Liberty (New York Harbour, A.D. 2900)," a sonnet written by Arthur Upson (1877–1908) probably in 1900, measures how harshly the idealism of American poets had been assailed in the few years since Emma Lazarus had celebrated the statue's creation:

> Here once, the records show, a land whose pride
> Abode in Freedom's watchword! And once here
> The port of traffic for a hemisphere,
> With great gold-piling cities at her side!
> Tradition says, superbly once did bide
> Their sculptured goddess on an island near,
> With hospitable smile and torch kept clear
> For all wild hordes that sought her o'er the tide.
>
> 'Twas centuries ago. But this is true:
> Late the fond tyrant who misrules our land,
> Bidding his serfs dig deep in marshes old,
> Trembled, not knowing wherefore, as they drew
> From out this swampy bed of ancient mould
> A shattered torch held in a mighty hand. (254)

Though Upson does not directly link the shattering of American liberties to imperialist practices in the Caribbean and the Philippines, he challenges readers to ask difficult questions: Would the American future be an imperial one? And what consequences would follow from that? Upson envisions a grim regression into the tyranny and serfdom that

Americans associated with reactionary European nations, most of all Spain, whose imperialist scepter the United States had seized ostensibly to smash, but perhaps, it seemed by 1900, to keep for its own. We don't know whether the misruling tyrant of 2900 is a native or a foreign conqueror, but in an interesting sense this doesn't matter: either the nation's fortunes eventually turned, and foreign tyrants now treat Americans as conquered colonists, as we had once treated others; or the American impulse to accumulation and control, our very success as imperialists, has destroyed our own liberty. Only dusty "records" and rumored "tradition" still preserve an earlier energy and idealism that promised, if never fully realized, a strong hospitable nation, inviting others into itself as guests, trading partners and citizens: in short, the antithesis of an imperialist power, as the United States had presented itself during the Cuban insurrection. Upson shows admirable restraint at the end, allowing just the merest hint, in the intact "mighty hand" and the tyrant's unexplained trembling, that those earlier energies could still be revived. In managing this so subtly, he achieves the balance of disillusioned critique and persistent idealism that characterizes the most effective verse responses to the nation's turn-of-the-century imperialist engagements.

Joseph Trumbull Stickney's "Mnemosyne" (1902), perhaps the most mesmerizingly beautiful poem written in the United States between 1890 and 1910, is even further from direct reference to Spain, Cuba, or the Philippines, but it too imagines a wasted landscape of the future, a culture self-destroyed. As Kramer notes, "Mnemosyne" is but one of Stickney's many verses "saturated with images of doomed empire" (301). Here Stickney, like Robinson in "The Dead Village," transcends the conventional antimodernity of literary Harvard to achieve great elegiac intensity.

> It's autumn in the country I remember.
>
> How warm a wind blew here about the ways!
> And shadows on the hillside lay to slumber
> During the long sun-sweetened summer-days.
>
> It's cold abroad the country I remember.
>
> The swallows veering skimmed the golden grain
> At midday with a wing aslant and limber;
> And yellow cattle browsed upon the plain.

It's empty down the country I remember.

I had a sister lovely in my sight:
Her hair was dark, her eyes were very sombre;
We sang together in the woods at night.

It's lonely in the country I remember.

The babble of our children fills my ears,
And on our hearth I stare the perished ember
To flames that show all starry thro' my tears.

It's dark about the country I remember.

There are the mountains where I lived. The path
Is slushed with cattle-tracks and fallen timber,
The stumps are twisted by the tempests' wrath.

But that I knew these places are my own,
I'd ask how came such wretchedness to cumber
The earth, and I to people it alone.

It rains across the country I remember.
(*Poems of Trumbull Stickney* 29–30)

A hymn in admirably direct language to the loss of life's treasures, "Mnemosyne" is certainly nostalgic, but it eschews the simplistic polarity of bad modern present and golden mythic past. These disappearances are never attributed directly to the consequences of imperialism. Yet the wrathful "tempests" that have felled trees and twisted stumps, and the totality of loss (warmth, birds, companion, children, and home), suggest no simple change of seasons, or single disastrous act of God, but the cataclysmic self-immolation of an entire society. The final three-line group completes this enigmatic nightmare future. The speaker "would ask" how such "wretchedness" could have come to his world and why he must now "people it alone"; but he doesn't really need to ask, because "these places are my own." The title ironically invokes the goddess of memory; the single lines all end "I remember": clearly the speaker remembers everything, including why his world is devastated. It would be a mistake to assume that Stickney must have had the Philippines in mind. And yet, viewed in the specific context of its composition—the final months of this protracted, venal, and remarkably destructive national misadventure—the poem certainly registers American poets' growing "hesitation," in Moody's terms, their unwillingness to accede to the consoling official pronouncements put forward to rationalize foreign conquest.

Another group of verses makes more direct reference to the Caribbean and Pacific conflicts, urging clear-eyed scrutiny of the values driving American policy. Edith M. Thomas's "One Woman's Voice against War" (published 1903) is among the most forceful of these, responding to American women who in print and in their personal relationships urged men to join the fight. The poem exploits the chasm between the imagery of war's glory and the actualities of modern combat, a gap that would become a rhetorical and ethical staple of twentieth-century war poetry. Here there is no need for any governmental propaganda machine, since belligerent women have taken into their own hands the idealistic modeling of war, deceiving their loved ones into accepting the nobility of the fight. But Thomas also portrays the "valor" of the young men as a form of self-delusion that will eventually corrupt the American social stock, spilling "the blood of the brave," while sparing the "sons of the craven" who will sire successive generations with "blood too pale to be shed" (*Dancers* 56, 57). In the poem's most telling moment, she asserts, "One is the life of each mortal—and that is not theirs, which they yield!" (57): in other words, nobody has the right to yield up the life of anybody else. This negative assertion anticipates the postnational ethics of individualism embraced by disillusioned artists and intellectuals after the Great War, which admits no other person's or institution's right to determine the fate of the free, though necessary alienated, individual subject of modernity.

On the other edge of the tonal spectrum, the light verse "Humbler Heroes" (1903) by Edmund Vance Cooke (1866–1932) also critiques official wartime stories by redefining heroism away from the ideology promulgated by national war policy, toward a radically different set of values:

> It might not be so difficult to lead the light brigade,
> While the army cheered behind you, and the fifes and bugles
>   played;
> It might be rather easy, with the war-shriek in your ears,
> To forget the bite of bullets and the taste of blood and
>   tears.
> But to be a scrubwoman, with four

> Babies, or more,
> Every day, every day setting your back
>> On the rack,
> And all your reward forever not quite
> A full bite
> Of bread for your babies. Say!
>> In the heat of the day
> You might be a hero to head a brigade.
> But a hero like her? (*Impertinent Poems* 45)

The second stanza offers a similar contrast, between a political "reformer" tempted away from his ideals by the acclaim of the public, and the greater courage of one who "alone and unknown," stays "true / To his view" (45). To the cynical Cooke, modern wartime heroism smacks of a peculiar sort of conformity and weakness: easier to do what one is bid than to follow one's conscience. This poem, coming not from rarefied intellectual circles but from a writer routinely publishing in mass magazines like the *Saturday Evening Post,* furnishes striking evidence that the pressure to fall in behind official policies of national unity was far from uniformly effective, and that alternative political formulations were available to and through American popular verse.

In "Spain in America," a long poem composed in early 1901, read in excerpts in June and published later that year in the volume *A Hermit of Carmel,* George Santayana looked critically at imperialism, particularly American expansion into the Caribbean.[15] The main body of this poem offers an interpretation of Spanish culture, which is eventually degraded by the hideous mistake of attempting to control a distant empire:

> What mounting miseries! What dwindling gain!
> To till those solitudes, soon swept of gold,
> And bear that ardent sun, across the main
> Slaves must come writhing in the festering hold
> Of galleys.—Poison works, though men be brave and bold.
> (228)

Centuries of colonial exploitation had corrupted not just Spain's American holdings, but the mother country's ethical and practical efficacy as well: "By sloth and lust and mindlessness and pelf / Spain sank in sadness and dishonor down, / Each in her service serving but himself" (228). Now forcibly "withdrawn" from the western hemisphere, Spain enters another phase, which the poet hopes will be "healing." It leaves its former colonies to "watch the skies from Cuba to the Horn," pondering their future, warily noting the United States, a "dove or eagle" hovering to the north. In the poem's final pages, these former colonies address the United States, warning it against the same temptations that had undone Spain. Urging their powerful neighbor to "fear the southward flight," they ask it to wait, to "Haunt still thy storm-swept islands, and endure / The shimmering forest where thy visions live," until they are ready to intermingle with it on terms of equality. Till then, they plead, "Thrust not thy prophets upon us, nor believe / Thy sorry riches in our eyes are fair" (230). What the United States can do now is to "inspire" them as an example of austerity, industriousness, idealism, and hope: "Hang paler clouds of reverence about / Our garish skies," and "leave in our skies, strange Spirit passing there, / No less of vision but of courage more" (231). The end of the poem thus struggles to wrest the definition of *courage* in the United States away from those urging military aggression as a form of valorous adventure, toward an anti-imperialist restraint that would help these societies groping toward identity and self-determination without trying to control them.

Divergent as they are in tone, the poems I've just discussed all register dissatisfaction with American official policy and public opinion. They demonstrate that turn-of-the-century American poets persisted in the belief that verse might possess political force. Two major figures of the era, Moody and Crane, moved beyond occasional critique into a more thoroughgoing oppositionalism. Sadly, neither man lived to participate in the great upwelling of socially engaged modern verse beginning around 1911. If they had done so, the continuity between turn-of-the-century verse and modern American poetry would be much clearer.

Perhaps the most widely discussed poem commenting on the war and its aftermath was Moody's "An Ode in Time of Hesitation," first published in the *Atlantic Monthly* in May 1900. The poem was a response to months of grim revelations detailing "the barbarity of American soldiers, and complaints of news correspondents about censorship of their reports" (M. Brown 104).[16] By early 1900 Moody understood that the U.S. government had committed itself to an overseas military campaign of dubious morality, indefinite duration, and appalling ferocity. He sets the poem on a "bright March morn" (593), producing an ironic contrast between the anticipated approach of spring, which ought to be rejuvenating, and the benighted state of American policy and public opinion. Like many contemporaries, but more intensely than most, Moody was struggling with a fall of disillusionment, from initial pride at the nation's willingness to sacrifice on behalf of Cuban freedom fighters, to the realization that continued involvement in the Philippines could not be justified on similar grounds, but was instead "pure conquest put to hire" (20)—which threatened to taint claims that earlier actions in the Caribbean had been righteous.[17] The emotional jaggedness of the poet's transition from enthusiast to dissenter is evident everywhere in the poem and becomes one source of its considerable power.

Moody's intervention into the Philippine debate is the first in a great series of artistic commentaries upon Augustus Saint-Gaudens's bronze bas-relief overlooking the Boston Common, which honors the Massachusetts 54th regiment, the first African American combat troops in the American military, and their young abolitionist commander, Colonel Robert Gould Shaw, who were decimated attacking Fort Wagner in 1863.[18] The statue had been unveiled on Memorial Day 1897 while Moody was in Europe, but according to his first biographer, the poet was immediately struck by its significance, and by the speech made by his former teacher William James at the opening ceremonies (Henry 51–52).[19] In early 1900, living just a few blocks from the Common, Moody saw the statue for himself. Deploring the drift of national policy into rank imperialism, he drew upon the statue as a symbol of American idealism challenged by continuing racial injustice. Martin Halpern notes that Moody was likely evoking James Russell Lowell's 1865 celebration of the Union dead, "Ode Recited at the Harvard Commemoration," while his use of Shaw and the Massachusetts 54th as symbols of American ideals follows upon Lowell's little-known 1863 elegy to Shaw, "Memoriae Positum" (73). Despite Lowell's occasional evocations of America's failures, however, his odes remain "firm patriotic affirmations" (Halpern 78), while Moody's veers into oppositionalism halfway through and never returns.

Sixty years later in "For the Union Dead," Robert Lowell would emphasize the struggle of black Americans for full citizenship by linking the volunteer soldiers of the 54th, yearning to demonstrate their honor in combat, to African American schoolchildren braving jeers and threats to desegregate southern schools. Moody uses the statue instead to evoke foreign peoples of color who had welcomed American military intervention in the (now-endangered) hope that it would convey them toward self-determination, not colonial status. Yet Moody and Lowell sound many similar notes, particularly about the "heedless" culture of their own times, which they fear no longer comprehends Shaw's moral example. And as Lowell would, Moody includes a penetrating exploration of his own role as a comfortably situated white American in the events of the moment. This self-examination is the quality that makes the ode most important to the emergence of a modern sensibility in American poetry. Not immune to the moral lassitude of his era, Moody's speaker has "striven, striven to evade" his duty to create what the soldiers' example demands: a "swift and angry stave" indicting deeds that should outrage American ideals, but are instead by "careless lips in street and shop [averred] / As common tidings" (18). Moody knows his mission: to denaturalize imperialist ideology by refusing to accept it as common tidings, as simply the way things are. The pressing question is whether he feels adequate to accept it. In acknowledging his impulses to evasion, the poet marks himself as the ethical and intellectual wanderer of modernity, alienated not just from social convention but from his own felt responsibility to express that alienation through swift and angry verses.

Moody foregrounds this self-examination through a striking appropriation of the canonical ghost topos I described in the previous chapter. In the first section, as he looks upon the "stern" faces of Shaw and the soldiers, and imagines that he hears their "fatal" tread, the statues become the sort of weighty predecessors by whom poets of this era felt oppressed yet often ironically inspired as well. The section's final line makes this comparison explicit, as by the "pangs" of approaching spring "these resolute ghosts are stirred" (594). The ghosts are at once the figures of the dead on the statue, the vestiges of American idealism that they represent, and the poet's own moral conscience, which he dreads yet still hopes may be stirred into useful action. Later, in the fourth section, oppressed by "Sounds of ignoble battle," the speaker shrinks from the soldiers' legacy ("Too sorely heavy is the debt they lay / On me and the companions of my day"), and yearns to retreat into remembrance of "My country's goodliness," to use his poetic gift to "make sweet her name." But at this pivotal moment, implacable ghosts again appear to haunt his escapist desires: "Alas! what shade art thou / Of sorrow or blame" that "Liftest the lyric leafage from [America's] brow, / And pointest a slow finger at her shame?" (595). This "shade" is again the shostly soldier, whose bravery disturbs the poet's restless conscience and measures the nation's shame (the pointing finger prefigures Lowell's comparison of Shaw to the needle of a compass). As we discover in the sixth section, this ghost also evokes Moody's canonical predecessors. His self-doubt is intensified by the weight of past political poets who spoke out against their times:

> Surely some elder singer would arise,
> Whose harp hath leave to threaten and to mourn
> Above this people when they go astray.

> Is Whitman, the strong spirit, overworn?
> Has Whittier put his yearning wrath away?
> I will not and I dare not yet believe! (597)

The "intolerable self-disdain" that will eventually turn Americans against their cupidinous leaders is also Moody's nagging sense of inadequacy at the role thrust upon him. The time of hesitation is not just the nation's, but the poet's as well.

The ode's last section recapitulates the stages of the conflict, from the creation of "Beautiful armies" willing to fight for Cuban freedom, through the blood spilled on San Juan Hill by "eager boys / Who might have tasted girls' love and been stung / With the old mystic joys / And starry griefs" (lines that echo through Wallace Stevens's works). Moody urges Americans not to allow these sacrifices to be stained by lust for economic gain, using a further enrichment of the ghost motif:

> For save we let the island men go free,
> Those baffled and dislaureled ghosts
> Will curse us from the lamentable coasts
> Where walk the frustrate dead. (598)

The ghosts now are the newly dead soldiers of Cuba and the Philippines, who believed that by dying for a noble cause they might take honored places beside Shaw, but whose sacrifice is now "dislaureled" by corruption and shame. However, the ghosts of the Massachusetts 54th, men of color whose going free was the central moral issue of the earlier war, hover around this passage as well. The freedom or enslavement of a racial other is still America's crucible in 1900, no less than in 1861. Not to free these "island men," to sell out the nation's best ideals in "the market place of war," will turn America into an accursed place.

Moody's ode marks an important shift away from poetry's traditional role celebrating the deeds of "our side," to its usual twentieth-century function as antiwar commentary using negative gestures of alienation and repudiation to critique war's immorality. Rather than developing a specific political critique of American policy in the Philippines, the poem's primary achievement consists in honestly admitting the difficulty of this effort, while still persisting in it. And this was an achievement, since by 1900 the crumbling of their Caribbean idealism had thrown most American poets into confusion or silence. The distance Moody feels from his predecessors suggests that the crusading poet of Whittier's type, absolutely convinced of the righteousness of his position, is not a model that twentieth-century poets would generally follow. But the ode offers another model of the modern poet as dissident patriot: deprived of an authoritative position from which to speak, challenged by self-doubt, yet still aspiring to resist official stories and to maintain the best ideals of the nation's heritage. In accepting limitation and uncertainty as preconditions to achievement rather than fatal impediments, Moody imbued "hesitation" with a complex affirmative charge. After all, in the moment of 1900, hesitation to pursue the Philippines—rather than the headlong conviction of the Hoveys and Roosevelts—was the moral position. By hesitating in a rhetorically forceful and institutionally prominent poem, which despite its self-questioning can't possibly be read as endorsing the nation's Philippine policy, Moody made a major contribution to the oppositional discourse against turn-of-the-century imperialism and helped to reinvigorate American poetry's political relevance.[20]

Moody's "On a Soldier Fallen in the Philippines," written in late 1900 and published in the *Atlantic* in February 1901, draws upon the memorializing imagery of the ode, but moves further into oppositional political statement. Here is the poem in full:

> Streets of the roaring town,
> Hush for him, hush, be still!
> He comes, who was stricken down
> Doing the word of our will.
> Hush! Let him have his state,
> Give him his soldier's crown.
> The grists of trade can wait
> Their grinding at the mill,
> But he cannot wait for his honor, now the trumpet has been blown;
> Wreathe pride now for his granite brow, lay love on his breast of
> stone.
>
> Toll! Let the great bells toll
> Till the clashing air is dim.
> Did we wrong this parted soul?
> We will make up it to him.
> Toll! Let him never guess
> What work we set him to.
> Laurel, laurel, yes;
> He did what we bade him do.
> Praise, and never a whispered hint but the fight he fought was
> good;

Never a word that the blood on his sword was his country's own
   heart's-blood.

A flag for the soldier's bier
Who dies that his land may live;
O, banners, banners here,
That he doubt not nor misgive!
That he heed not from the tomb
The evil days draw near
When the nation, robed in gloom,
With its faithless past shall strive.
Let him never dream that his bullet's scream went wide of its island
   mark,
Home to the heart of his darling land where she stumbled and
   sinned in the dark. (288)

This poem initially presents itself as a dignified eulogy to the loss of American lives and ideals, but underneath this tonal reserve bitter opposition to the nation's dominant values emerges. The dead soldier, brought back to his native town, is another ghostly moral compass, whose posthumous treatment will measure his country's worth. Moody portrays the town as barely willing to pause from the roar of trade to acknowledge the arrival of its dead son. The signs of honor the town grudgingly supplies—tolling bells, laurel wreath, flag on his bier—purport to commemorate one who lost his life believing in a righteous cause, but instead merely expose the dishonor of the nation that does not live by its professed ideals. The nation told him this was a good fight; this deception must now outlast even death, as we will continue to feed him "Praise, and never a whispered hint but the fight he fought was good." Moody here arrives at a forcefully modern awareness of the soldier as someone who fights simply because he's following orders. Propaganda has replaced ethical volition or political understanding as the driving force in the relationship of soldier to nation. Even death brings no illumination, merely the same delusion maintained forever, a grotesque inversion of the eternal flame of remembrance. The soldier has become part of the "grists of trade," the key phrase of the first stanza. *Grist* is something ground, but also anything that can be used to advantage, a double meaning that opens up a disturbing avenue of analogy. The "falling" of the soldier evokes the grinding up of material in the mills of trade, while his return, clothed in the trappings of honor, implies the packaging of this processed material to best advantage. The honoring of dead soldiers thus becomes further grist for the propaganda mills of the new century, trading in human bodies and illusions. As for this dead soldier, the least—and the most—we can do is to prevent him seeing that, as he carried out the nation's will, he succeeded only in spilling "his country's own heart's-blood." But the poet now seems to believe that nothing will stop the approach of "evil days" when "the nation, robed in gloom," will rue its past misdeeds.

These two works of Moody's exemplify the modern poem whose power emerges through awareness of its own marginal position. Several of Stephen Crane's late poems use war scenarios to develop this sort of oppositional function for poetry. The difficulty of dating Crane's verse clouds the question of whether his "war poems" refer to the events of 1898–1900.[21] But whether or not we see these poems responding to the Spanish-American War, they do speak to the conflicts Crane had seen in Mexico, Greece, and elsewhere over the previous decade. Some of them are eerily prescient of the problems that American involvement in Cuba and the Philippines would create.[22] In such poems Crane works toward a mature politics that would maintain his precious skepticism toward conventional pieties, while also advocating positive action according to humane ideals.

The poem beginning "When a people reach the top of a hill," sometimes known as "Blue Battalions," exemplifies this uncertainty over the directness of reference to contemporary events. Its composition is dated by Hoffman as April 1896 (162) and by Bowers as sometime in 1897 (*Poems and Literary Remains* 232), but it wasn't published until May 1898 in *The Philistine.* It reached a broader audience later that year by appearing in Witherbee's *Spanish-American War Songs,* a venue that claimed it as a war poem regardless of the poet's initial intentions. Here, pondering the United States' emerging status as a world power, Crane portrays modernity as a hallucinatory panoply of chaotic change. It begins:

> When a people reach the top of a hill
> Then does God lean toward them,
> Shortens tongues, lengthens arms.
> A vision of their dead comes to the weak.
> The moon shall not be too old
> Before the new battalions rise
> —Blue battalions—
> The moon shall not be too old
> When the children of change shall fall
> Before the new battalions

— The blue battalions—
("Blue Battalions" 182).

Ever sensitive to modernity's dynamics, Crane notes that arriving at "the top of a hill," the global centrality that the United States was about to achieve (as Spain had done long before), would not end the convulsive processes of change that had produced this shift in the first place. As Marshall Berman's reading of Marx proposes, perhaps the greatest irony of bourgeois society is that its ideological apparatus seeks the very condition of stasis and equilibrium that if ever achieved would spell the end of the bourgeoisie's power.[23] The United States, the quintessential nation of bourgeois modernity, populated by "the children of change," thrives only in the state of continual disruption and instability that brought its ascendancy; but that same logic of change must fell its children before the next set of modern conquerors. Whether or not these "new battalions" will wear blue like the U.S. Army, they too will ask God to "lead them high," "lead them far," as they trample "mistakes and virtues" together.

The verse beginning "There exists the eternal fact of conflict," if written in 1897 as Bowers proposes (*Poems and Literary Remains* 232), suggests that a "Spanish-American War" was going on in American minds and media well before the destruction of the *Maine* in February 1898.[24] Crane begins by redefining war not as concerted moral crusade but as absurdist blur, retrospectively interpreted and justified according to ideological expediency. The first lines propose that in a world of conflict so continuous as to be virtually a cosmic principle, war erupts mostly out of trivial ("mere") local circumstances, not out of any coherent goal or vision. Only "Afterward," once the conflict has flared, do people scramble for interpretive prisms, "patriotism" above all, to justify their actions (*Poems and Literary Remains* 84). But in one of Crane's more direct verse utterances, patriotism is condemned as a "godly vice" that "makes us slaves." The poem's shifting voice speaks both as a craven American "patriot" seeking easy answers and, more ironically, as a harsh critic of these venal desires:

And—let us surrender to this falsity
Let us be patriots
Then welcome us the practical men
Thrumming on a thousand drums
The practical men, God help us.

> They cry aloud to be led to war
> Ah—
> They have been poltroons on a thousand fields
> And the sad sacked city of New York is their record
> Furious to face the Spaniard, these people, and
>   crawling worms before their task
> They name serfs and send charity in bulk to better men
> They play at being free, these people of New York
> Who are too well-dressed to protest against infamy. (84)

Even if interventionists know at some level that their reasons for war are specious, they feel the urge to "surrender," to cede political responsibility to the "practical men" eager to receive it. These practical types evoke the planners and implementers of realpolitik whose inhumane pragmatism would disfigure the next century of American history (William McKinley, Henry Cabot Lodge, Herbert Hoover, Robert Moses, Allen Dulles, Dean Rusk, Henry Kissinger, Donald Rumsfeld). In a disorienting pronominal shift, "they" also become those clamoring for war, particularly the small-minded jingo who insists on his own hardheaded pragmatism and loudly demands "to be led to war," in this case "furious to face the Spaniard." But true jingoes again and again have proved themselves "poltroons," even "crawling worms" who are pathetically inadequate to the task, and so they find the naive and powerless ("serfs") to fight instead and keep themselves "well-dressed," imagining they are "free."

Crane offers as the jingo's "record" an unnerving image, "the sacked sad city of New York." In what sense has New York been sacked? Not literally, since its preening inhabitants still go about well-dressed, but probably because their capacity for critical thought and free debate has been expropriated by a jingoist press, led by still more practical men whose politics are driven by their circulations and profit margins. Here Crane, like Upson, Stickney, and Moody, glimpses a vision of a nightmare American future, a culture incapable of protest, sacked by its own imperial pragmatists and ethical indifference. Yet if the nation's moral lassitude comes in its inability to "protest against infamy," then Crane is not arguing for isolationism at any cost but for principled humanitarian intervention against Spanish oppression in the Caribbean, which could demonstrate America's ethical mettle. This position was ethically tenable in 1897 in contemplation of Cuba, whereas four years later about the Philippines it would have been mere imperialist apologetics. We can only regret once again that this most prominent poetic iconoclast of the age was not around to dramatize in his distinctive idiom the transition from Cuba to the Philippines, from idealism to oppositionalism.

Crane's exploration of American imperialist modernity gains in power as he pushes his own subject position furthest in the direction of marginality. "On the brown trail," which Bowers estimates as being from late 1897, Katz from late 1898, critiques American imperial munificence by using the marginalized voice of an oppressed, now ostensibly freed peasantry. Eschewing the pitfalls of attempting unfamiliar dialect, Crane constructs a collective persona of plainspoken dignity. Here is the poem in full:

> On the brown trail
> We hear the grind of your carts
> To our villages,
> Laden with food
> Laden with food
> We know you are come to our help
> But—
> Why do you impress upon us
> Your foreign happiness?
> We know it not.
> (Hark!
> Carts laden with food
> Laden with food)
> We weep because we don't understand
> But your gifts form into a yoke
> The food turns into a yoke
> (Hark!
> Carts laden with food
> Laden with food)
> It is our mission to vanish
> Grateful because of full mouths
> Destiny—Darkness
> Time understands
> And ye—ye bigoted men of a moment—
> —Wait—
> Await your turn. (*Poems and Literary Remains* 85)

Rather than portraying a social and racial Other from the outside, emphasizing its conventional quaintness, exoticism, backwardness, or abjection, Crane earnestly tries to imagine the perceptions people in such a position might have toward their "liberators." The insistent refrain "(Hark! / Carts laden with food / Laden with food)" acknowledges their real need for the sustenance the outsiders bring. But the poem makes a sharp distinction between this material openhandedness and the effort to control the lives of its recipients often implicit in American foreign relations. As they hear carts of food lumbering into their midst, the villagers are already aware that the generosity of a powerful neighbor is a mixed blessing: "But your gifts turn into a yoke / The food turns into a yoke." Challenging the notion of imperialism as the benevolent enlightenment of benighted cultures, Crane embraces instead the oppositional position that it's the powerless "Other" who best grasps the ambiguous political and emotional logic of charity and the self-aggrandizing psychology of the liberator: "It is our mission to vanish / Grateful because of full mouths."

The final lines denaturalize America's role as the world's liberator, portraying it instead as merely a temporary king-of-the-hill. In seeing through the attempt to co-opt them into the "mission" of imperial adventure, these liberated assert their refusal to vanish from the relationship—just as Crane's open-hearted attempt to subvert longstanding ideological hierarchies of self and other, haves and have-nots, American and foreign, light-skinned and dark, reasserts poetry's value for oppositional political statement. Long into the twentieth century, many white American poets found it difficult to identify with people of other races and nationalities without condescension or parody. Crane achieved this empathetic position before 1900 because he was so willing to wander in the social and cultural margins of his era and so unwilling to segregate this experience of marginality from contemporary political events.

POETRY WRITES THE NEWSPAPER

Poems that consider the media's role in the conduct of the war challenge conventional accounts of modern poetry's emergence by demonstrating urgent engagement with turn-of-the-century modernity. So too do several turn-of-the-century poems on the daily newspaper, which explore the gap between literary poetry and commercialized mass culture. The strongest of these works demonstrate how poetry's response to mass culture, by avoiding the twin pitfalls of uncritical naiveté and knee-jerk elitism, could address central contradictions of capitalist modernity. Verses juxtaposing poem and newspaper foreground the problematic status of individual experience in a culture of information packaged for the millions. Significantly, none of the works I examine below dismisses the latter to embrace the former. They all take seriously the need for sources of information and opinion capable of reaching the vast literate populace of modernity, and refuse to treat poetry as a vehicle of rearguard individualism that warrants ignoring that population.

Like her verses of the urban street, Edith M. Thomas's "Cries of the Newsboy" (1893) explores the modern city's capacity to voice collective human experience. The newspaper is a key symbolic arena for this theme, since those who package and disseminate papers seek to shape the nebulous yet powerful force of "public opinion," which exists somewhere in the space between individual and collective consciousness. Here Thomas develops these themes in surprising and whimsical fashion, through the disembodied cries of newsboys hawking papers, heard from afar:

> Cruel the roar of the city ways,
>> Where life on a myriad errands whirled;
> But suddenly up from the jarring maze,
>> Like a rocket thrown high, went a ringing cry:
> "New-Sunny-World! New-Sunny World!" (*In Sunshine Land* 103)

As the poem's epigraph indicates, the boy is selling the *News, Sun,* and *World.* In the lines that follow, aware that her misprision could become mere sentimentality, Thomas addresses its implications directly: "There wasn't a glimpse of the sun anywhere" in an urban landscape of "grim" light and "leaden" air. It's not a new sunny world most of all, one may imagine, for the newsboys themselves, at the bottom of the economic ladder, beset by media corporations that seek not just to exploit their labor, but also to mold them into docile citizens who will go where newspapers take them and no further. But Thomas is unwilling to reduce them to passive victims of economic injustice. Instead she wants to explore what the newsboys' presence means to the consciousness of the modern city. If the boys lack agency over most aspects of their lives, Thomas still assigns them an active role in the city that allows physical mobility, an outlet for their energies, and a sense of purpose. Who's to say that starting as newsboys, immigrants who arrived with nothing could not have chased and found some American dream, as Thomas had found her dream of an independent life in the city? In the second section the poet hears another sales cry as "*morning piapers,*" inflected by the "old-world accent" of immigrants, and converts it into "morning pipers, piping blithe and clear / From some imagined sward or thicket near" (104–5). Their cries signify "wonderful news" to her, but not because of anything in the papers they sell. She knows that the "new sunny world" that these morning pipers offer is imaginary or even false, that there are no "sweet country sights and sounds" near. They are good news to her instead because of the ebullience of their sellers, who embody the inextinguishable high spirits of youth and the stimulating energies of the city. Shaping their surroundings with penetrating "rocket cry" and "shrill alarm" that cut through the sodden air and "murky streets," clarifying the "maze" of city life, they evoke future prospects of a better world.

In the 1895 volume *Violets and Other Poems,* the twenty-year-old Alice Ruth Moore (1875–1935), who would later write under the compound surnames of two of her husbands as Alice Dunbar-Nelson, published a major poem of the era, "Legend of the Newspaper." The poet approaches her subject in a mock-legendary tone and trochaic tetrameter line that gently parody the central mythic epic of the American genteel canon, Longfellow's *The Song of Hiawatha* (1856), whose first lines are "Should you ask me, whence these stories? / Whence these legends and traditions . . . ?" (3). Here is the full text of "Legend of the Newspaper":

> Poets sing and fables tell us,
> Or old folk lore whispers low,
> Of the origin of all things,
> Of the spring from whence they came,
> Kalevala, old and hoary,
> Aeneid, Iliad, Aesop, too,
> All are filled with strange quaint legends,
> All replete with ancient tales,—
> How love came, and how old earth,
> Freed from chaos, grew for us,
> To a green and wondrous spheroid,
> To a home for things alive;
> How fierce fire and iron cold,
> How the snow and how the frost,—
> All these things the old rhymes tell,
> Yet they ne'er sang of the beginning,
> Of that great unbreathing angel,
> That soul without a haven,
> Of that gracious Lady Bountiful,
> Yet they ne'er told how it came here;

Nc'er said why we read it daily,
Nor did they even let us guess why
We were left to tell the tale.
Came one day into the wood-land,
Muckintosh, the great and mighty,
Muckintosh, the famous thinker,
He whose brain was all his weapons,
As against his rival's soarings,
High unto the vaulted heavens,
Low adown the swarded earth,
Rolled he round his gaze all steely,
And his voice like music prayed:
"Oh Creator, wondrous Spirit,
Thou who has for us descended
In the guise of knowledge mighty,
And our brains with truth o'er-flooded;
In the greatness of thy wisdom,
Knowest not our limitations?
Wondrous thoughts have we, thy servants,
Wondrous things we see each day,
Yet we cannot tell our brethren,
Yet we cannot let them know,
Of our doings and our happenings,
Should they be parted from us?
Help us, oh, Thou Wise Creator,
From the fulness of thy wisdom
Show us how to spread our knowledge,
And disseminate our actions,
Such as we find worthy, truly.["]
Quick the answer came from heaven;
Muckintosh, the famous thinker
Muckintosh, the great and mighty,
Felt a trembling, felt a quaking,
Saw the earth about him open,
Saw the iron from the mountains
Form a quaint and queer machine,
Saw the lead from out the lead mines
Roll into small lettered forms,
Saw the fibres from the flax-plant,
Spread into great sheets of paper,
Saw the ink galls from the green trees,

> Crushed upon the leaden forms;
> Muckintosh, the famous thinker
> Muckintosh, the great and mighty,
> Felt a trembling, felt a quaking,
> Saw the earth about him open,
> Saw the flame and sulphur smoking,
> Came the printer's little devil,
> Far from distant lands the printer,
> Man of unions, man of cuss-words,
> From the depths of sooty blackness,
> Came the towel of the printer;
> Many things that Muckintosh saw,—
> Galleys, type, and leads and rules,
> Presses, press-men, quoins and spaces,
> Quads and caps and lower cases.
> But to Muckintosh bewildered,
> All this passed in a dream,
> Till within his nervous hand,
> Hand with joy and fear a-quaking,
> Muckintosh, the great and mighty,
> Muckintosh, the famous thinker,
> Held the first of our newspapers. (72–75)

In Dunbar-Nelson's satiric conceit, epics of ancient cultures—Iliad, Aeneid, Kalevala—are ludicrously, anachronistically faulted because they don't account for the newspaper, characterized as the "Lady Bountiful," the source of modern endeavor and record of modern experience, in need of its own myth of origin. This farcical celebration lampoons the antihistorical attitude encouraged by the newspaper's relentless ephemerality—a new issue coming each day, drowning us in ink, swamping our ability to make structural links between present events and past causes.[25] Yet, declaring that poets must "sing . . . / Of the origin of all things," the work also challenges the generic conventions that have ruled such defining features of modernity as the newspaper out of poetry's purview. So although the poet does not actually blame ancient mythic texts for neglecting the newspaper's origins, the parodic echoes of *Hiawatha,* which does indeed substitute "strange quaint legends, / All replete with ancient tales" for serious understanding of Native American civilization, suggest her unwillingness to let more recent poetry off the hook as easily. Hence her attempt to create a modern "legend" that balances facetious mythical spectacle against serious exploration of

emerging mass-market systems of information. This balance is embodied in the poem through the profoundly ambiguous figure of Muckintosh, who is both a Promethean disseminator of the "flame" of human
knowledge and a venal paper baron raking through the muck and "sul-
phur" of modern experience to aggrandize himself into "Muckintosh,
the famous thinker," "the great and mighty." (One thinks of Hearst and
Pulitzer in the poem's time, of Charles Foster Kane, and in our own day,
of Ted Turner.) Though Dunbar-Nelson gives us good reason to suspect
the motives of Muckintosh's "prayer," she also suggests that the needs it
evokes are very real: to organize the proliferating information that
threatens to "o'er-flood our brains," and to share it with others who are
otherwise "parted from us" through the fragmentation of modern
knowledge.[26]

The poem's deep engagement with modernity emerges in its willingness to consider that despite all shortcomings, the newspaper may have
value in addressing those real needs. The narration's preposterous mythic claims of iron and lead leaping from their mines straight into the elaborate shapes of printing equipment again lampoon the self-importance
of the press, but at the same time, the technological detail in which the
industry is rendered refuses to dismiss the newspaper as merely the vul-
garian target of an elitist critique. The poet is clearly interested in the
material processes of newspaper production and assumes that her readers ought to be as well.

The infernal epos surrounding these technologies of modernity,
which playfully evokes the palace of Hell in *Paradise Lost*, also takes a
more contemporary social turn, as from this pit of sulfurous earth leaps
not some satanic figure but the young "printer's devil," joined by the
immigrant printer. They signal the emergence of a heterogeneous working class of many ethnicities, identified with a vigorous labor movement that provides a collectivist counterforce to the oligarchic capitalism that Muckintosh signifies. Thus Muckintosh might well feel
"bewildered" and "nervous," obscurely aware that the forces he has
unleashed might not be fully controllable after all, might include "men
of unions," "men of cuss-words," whose ability to master the technological and organizational demands of modernity will eventually convey them "From the depths" of subsistence labor toward full agency
within a culture of information. The poem leaves us with two crucial
questions about the value of modern cultural forms: might newspapers
play a role in challenging capitalist oligarchy in spite of the Muckin-
toshes who own them? And if poetry can take account of the newspaper, might it also have a role?

Like Dunbar-Nelson, Stephen Crane spent much of his brief adult life as a newspaper journalist, working for both Hearst and Pulitzer in the same month in 1898 (Wertheim and Sorrentino 265). Some very fine recent scholarship, culminating in Bill Brown's fascinating study *The Material Unconscious,* has shown that Crane's prose engages in continuous and intricate dialogue with contemporary mass culture. In a historicist project seeking to interrogate long-unexamined assumptions about cultural value, Crane's centrality is not surprising, since more than any other canonical American author, he challenges traditional distinctions "between the decent art of high culture and the vulgar art of the dime novel and the slums," as Keith Gandal puts it (74). Still, none of this historicist work has dealt in a serious way with Crane's poetry, which clings precariously to the margins of his canon.[27] Yet his verse is not dead to historicist approaches. In fact, it is studded with tantalizing evocations of contemporary mass culture: newspapers and journalism, public "opinion," sports, and "strange pedlers" transacting business in a recognizably modern world defined by heavily mediated and commodified forms of experience. Though sometimes responding to commercialized mass culture with skepticism or suspicion, Crane's verses refuse to pretend lofty ignorance of its significance as the era's genteel strictures dictated poetry ought to do. Collectively his poems assert that American verse writing has a key role in comprehending modern cultural conditions that sustain discourses as diverse as the lyric poem and the daily newspaper.

To suggest how Crane's poems can be seen not as gnomic existential platitudes but as vivid responses to contemporary mass culture, we can look again at some of the many poems using the wanderer topos. Earlier I proposed that Crane's wanderers are seldom truly alone but usually undergo some sort of socially resonant encounter. Several such poems feature cryptic economic encounters between wandering figures pitching some commodity to one another. In the verse that begins "There was one I met upon the road, / Who looked at me with kind eyes" (1894), the speaker is a wandering peddler, asked by the one with kind eyes, "'Show me your wares.'" In the ensuing exchange, a nightmarish one for the aspiring purveyor of cultural wares, the wanderer-peddler-poet becomes an object of pity and moral condemnation:

> And this I did,
> Holding forth one.
> He said, 'It is a sin.'
> Then held I forth another;

> He said, 'It is a sin.'
> Then held I forth another;
> He said, 'It is a sin.'
> And so to the end;
> Always he said, 'It is a sin.'
> And, finally, I cried out,
> 'But I have none other.'
> Then did he look at me
> With kinder eyes.
> 'Poor soul,' he said. (*Black Riders* 34)

The fourfold repetition of the condemnatory refrain "'It is a sin'" pointedly exceeds the conventional narrative structure of parables and jokes in which the third element brings a moral or punch line. This structural excess marks the figure as capable only of reflexive condemnation, and for Crane, delegitimizes his moral or cultural authority. His "kind eyes" get even kinder as more moral condemnation issues from them, suggesting his kinship with those repressively benevolent icons (righteous pictures) of moralistic genteel culture whose influence still dominated American poetry.[28] We have seen Crane make this sort of critique of genteel culture before, but here he has thematized it as a primal scene of modern artistic creation: the individual "on the road," with no ready audience or intrinsic authority, forlornly hoping to interest whoever comes along in his or her wares.

In "I stood upon a highway" (1894), Crane takes this primal scene of cultural modernity a step further, blurring sellers with customers. Here the wandering speaker on the highway is approached by equally itinerant salesmen ("Many strange pedlers") hawking versions of God, each making his own curious "gestures" and holding forth "little images," saying, "'This is my pattern of God. / Now this is the God I prefer'":

> I said, "Hence!
> Leave me with mine own,
> And take you yours away;
> I can't buy of your patterns of God,
> The little gods you may rightly prefer." (*Black Riders* 35)

The speaker's refusal of commerce implies the poet's rejection of the hairsplitting sectarianism of organized religion. But by conceding that the peddlers "may rightly prefer" their own patterns to anyone else's, Crane elevates a simple critique of religion into an ironic affirmation of the unalienable right of individuals—not only the speaker, but the peddlers—to choose their own "patterns," "gestures," and "images." One thing this refusal of commerce does not imply, however, is that cultural and religious commodities, "patterns of God," cannot be bought and sold. In fact, the only stated reason he "can't buy" their patterns is because he already has his "own"—a satiric gambit that foreshadows the reply of the demoniac French knight to King Arthur's invitation to join the quest for Monty Python's holy grail ("We've already got one!"). Noting the rhetorical symmetry of this poem's speaker with the peddlers, we may suspect him of being a strange peddler himself, only temporarily off duty. We may also recall that "images" is the term that Crane paired with "pictures" to evoke the repressive icons of established culture in *The Black Riders*.[29] Then as now, the selling of images and pictures typifies the cultural commerce of modernity. Given how much of Crane's own life was devoted to producing fungible journalistic "pictures," we can hardly doubt that he intends to satirize a futile genteel elite that clings to a dusty and shrinking corner of the marketplace, still refusing to acknowledge its own commodified character.

In other poems, Crane uses scenes of mass commercial culture to reimagine poetry as a vehicle of oppositional social commentary—though his conclusions are not always optimistic. "There was a crimson clash of war" (1894), although written years before the Spanish-American War, presciently imagines its effect on American public discourse: "One who understood not" the reasons for going to war asks "Why is this?"—evoking poetry's capacity to question authoritative versions of the political world (*Black Riders* 15). This questioner is met not by a cosmic void of silence, or even by a single hegemonic official story, both comprehensible answers of sorts, but by "a million," all striving to answer him simultaneously, producing "such an intricate clamor of tongues / That still the reason was not" (15). Crane here dramatizes the same primal paradox of modernity that Dunbar-Nelson sketches in her legend. Distanced from direct access to the world's crimson clashes, we receive instead a fragmented overload of information that can destroy our ability to evaluate or oppose them, because no one can even understand what anyone else means to say. Dunbar-Nelson's poem is more sanguine about the role of mass print media in this process, positing that the newspaper might have a role in reintegrating this informational babel, whereas Crane here seems doubtful that the mass media will do anything but exacerbate it.

As this poem suggests, Crane is finally less interested in cosmic isolation or existential loneliness than in dramatizing the experience of living in a frantic commodity culture. In the six-line verse "There came whisperings in the winds" (1894), unidentifiable and uncountable "Little voices called in the darkness" without end; but exasperatingly, all the voices ever say is "Good-bye! Good-bye!" (*Black Riders* 46). In the two middle lines, this speaker, like Robinson's in "The Pity of the Leaves," seeks communion with these voices but fails utterly: "Then I stretched forth my arms. / 'No—no—.'" The poem's last four lines merely repeat the first four verbatim, reiterating the mechanical and inaccessible character of all these good-byes. In "A slant of sun on dull brown walls" (1895), the world sends "Toward God a mighty hymn" that appears initially to evoke a Whitmanesque all-inclusiveness of experience ("A song of collisions and cries, / Rumbling wheels, hoof-beats, bells, / Welcomes, farewells, love-calls, final moans, / Voices of joy, idiocy, warning, despair"). But this soon degenerates into a giddy cacophony in which every utterance becomes the same futile existential lamentation, which Crane lampoons with fierce brio:

> The unknown appeals of brutes,
> The chanting of flowers,
> The screams of cut trees,
> The senseless babble of hens and wise men—
> A cluttered incoherency that says at the stars:
> "O God, save us!" (*War Is Kind* 42)

For Crane, this futility is not an inevitable consequence of the activity of writing, as occasional more affirmative poems such as "There was a man with tongue of wood" (1894) suggest. This poem anticipates a twentieth-century thematics of audience in which if even a single listener can perceive a distinct artistic truth ("But there was one who heard / The clip-clapper of this tongue of wood, / And knew what the man / Wished to sing"), then even a "lamentable" song could be judged valuable ("And with that the singer was content") (*War Is Kind* 44). But another poem counters by proposing that in a society so large, literate, and heterogeneous that even elite forms such as poetry were produced in overwhelming profusion, genuine communication had become next to impossible:

> Yes, I have a thousand tongues,
> And nine and ninety-nine lie.
> Though I strive to use the one,

> It will make no melody at my will,
> But is dead in my mouth. (*Black Riders* 4)

Even if the poet finds his one true tongue out of the thousand, the resulting writing will remain at the level of neglected commodity, lying indistinguishably among its infinite likenesses, as in the 1897 poem that begins:

> A little ink more or less!
> It surely can't matter?
> Even the sky and the opulent sea,
> The plains and the hills, aloof,
> Hear the uproar of all these books.
> But it is only a little ink more or less. (*War Is Kind* 21)

The uncontrollable proliferation of "all these books" of modernity produces a condition of uproar and fragmentation in which any one book can hardly command value. Thus even for the poet most intensely engaged with turn-of-the-century modernity, the very concept of "mass culture" threatens to become a contradiction in terms, since the unlimited reproducibility of cultural activity seem to vitiate the coherence and communicability that its ideologists claim for it.

But this anxious frustration, while important, is only part of Crane's response to the mass-market culture of modernity. Just after arriving at these morose insights, "A little ink more or less" makes an intriguing turn in which immersion in the incoherent "uproar" of modern culture creates a space for energetic opposition. The turn begins, as if responding to an offstage voice of unwelcome authority, "What? / You define me God with these trinkets?" (*War Is Kind* 22). Again we see Crane's refusal to accept dictation that triggered the violent blasphemy of "You tell me this is God?" As soon as anyone—even his more defeatist alter ego of the poem's first part—tries to define him reductively against some heavy figure of authority, Crane responds with sardonic fury:

> Can my misery meal on an ordered walking
> Of surpliced numskulls?
> And a fanfare of lights?
> Or even upon the measured pulpiting
> Of the familiar false and true?
> Is this God?

Where, then, is hell?
Show me some bastard mushroom
Sprung from a pollution of blood.
It is better.

Where is God? (22)

Echoing Huck Finn's willingness to go to hell if staying with God means accepting the godliness of social institutions, Crane stands his ground and finally achieves a blasphemous self-affirmation, defiantly asking "Where is God?"—as if by staring down the godly and accepting hell instead, he has rid himself of God's oppressive presence. The phrase "fanfare of lights" can refer equally to the showier rituals of organized religion and to the spectacular imagery of new mass amusements with which Crane was intimately familiar. This ambiguity suggests that the poet is still not confident of mass culture's role in his struggle toward self-definition. Still, his avant-garde energy is catalyzed by realizing that "uproar" and incoherence are defining qualities of modern experience. After all, the surpliced numskulls are the ones defined and limited by their "ordered walking"; it follows that only by accepting and plunging into the very disorder that the text initially decries can the modern poet survive as an individual personality. In the face of "all these books" that threaten to submerge creative identity in a wash of generic sameness, the only kind of self-definition that Crane can accept involves total commitment to differentiation, and so he finds even a hellish recipe of "some bastard mushroom / Sprung from a pollution of blood" to be "better" than God's measured pulpiting. The efflorescences of Crane's avant-garde poet of modernity may well be off-color, unwholesome, even polluted, but they are without doubt his own bastards, expressing and nourishing his own misery.

Crane achieves this avant-garde sensibility not by constructing the "world elsewhere" of classic high modernism, but by consistently engaging the messy world of modernity. His enactment of primal modern encounters is pressed furthest in two poems that develop a direct (if never transparent) commentary on mass culture's quintessential symbolic form, the newspaper. The briefer of these reads:

In a lonely place,
I encountered a sage
Who sat, all still,
Regarding a newspaper.

> He accosted me:
> 'Sir, what is this?'
> Then I saw that I was greater,
> Ay, greater than this sage.
> I answered him at once,
> 'Old, old man, it is the wisdom of the age.'
> The sage looked upon me with admiration. (*Black Riders* 12)

This verse aims its barbs equally at the head-in-the-sand mentality of genteel culture, exemplified by the unworldly "sage" who has no understanding of the newspaper's significance, and at the philistine speaker whose smug confidence ("I answered him at once") reveals a ludicrously uncritical acceptance of the newspaper as the "wisdom of the age." Of course Crane is also playfully critiquing his own deep involvement in the world of newspapers, but like Dunbar-Nelson, he knows that the vexed question of the newspaper's meanings cannot be adequately answered by simplistic disdain.

The poem beginning "A newspaper is a collection of half-injustices" (c. 1894) is Crane's nimblest elaboration on the ambiguous significance of modern mass culture and the newspaper as its emblem ("a newspaper is a symbol," he eventually announces). Here is the text in full:

> A newspaper is a collection of half-injustices
> Which, bawled by boys from mile to mile,
> Spreads its curious opinion
> To a million merciful and sneering men,
> Where families cuddle the joys of the fireside
> When spurred by tale of dire lone agony.
> A newspaper is a court
> Where every one is kindly and unfairly tried
> By a squalor of honest men.
> A newspaper is a market
> Where wisdom sells its freedom
> And melons are crowned by the crowd.
> A newspaper is a game
> Where his error scores the player victory
> While another's skill wins death.
> A newspaper is a symbol;
> It is feckless life's chronicle,
> A collection of loud tales
> Concentrating eternal stupidities,

That in remote ages lived unhaltered,
Roaming through a fenceless world.
(*Poems and Literary Remains* 52)

The poem presents a series of nouns laden with paradoxical adjectives and adverbs: the million men are both merciful and sneering; the jury of readers, at once squalid and honest, judge everyone kindly but unfairly; in the economy ("market") of the newspaper, wisdom "sells its freedom" so that it may be disseminated more widely. Crane makes an acute analysis of modern cultural value in which families now use the newspaper to "cuddle the joys of the fireside / When spurred by tale of dire lone agony." Genteel poetry was designed to enhance familial joy by offering idealized models of behavior and experience that readers might aspire to re-create around their own fires. Nearly a century before Don DeLillo's *White Noise* explores the theme with great wit, Crane demonstrates that in mass-culture discourses, the relationship between reader and subject matter has already been inverted into a spectatorial hunger for vicarious experience so extreme that few could possibly want to emulate it. Thus the newspaper, like radio and television after it, contributes to a suburbanization of information reinforcing what Berman calls the "modernized pastoral" of twentieth-century American life (168), in which domestic joy is measured by one's distance from what one reads, hears, or watches.

However, Crane cannot fairly advance this critique (and it is a critique) of the newspaper's modeling and valuing of modern experience without acknowledging that as a daredevil journalist sending back these same tales of agony, he himself was inextricably implicated in the emergence of a spectatorial mass culture. The poem makes this acknowledgment in two ways that demonstrate poetry's embeddedness in modern culture and its capacity for incisive commentary on that culture. Crane signals this self-critique by strategically adopting the accelerated urgency of the newspaper's linguistic conventions. The only plausible syntactic models for the oddly clipped phrase "tale of dire lone agony" are either the telegraph by which journalists relayed their information, or the newspaper headline itself.[30] Indeed, the poem's entire structure is drawn from the newspaper's distinctive sectional form: first there is the sensational front-page headline; then the more sober section of court reporting "where everyone is kindly and unfairly tried" by a million readers; a business ("market") section; a feature section where "melons"—the frivolous celebrities of the moment?—are "crowned by the crowd"; and, as we will see below, there is a sports section. Crane's willingness to structure his poem after the object of its critique provides another instance of his interest in multiple levels of irony, and signals that the critique, while necessary, is not a sufficient account of the newspaper's relation to modernity, or of poetry's relation to the newspaper.

The irreducible heterogeneity and ambiguity Crane associates with the newspaper are theorized by the poem's first line. The phrase "a collection of half-injustices" does not mean that half the newspaper's items are true and half false, but that every item functions as half injustice, therefore half justice. Crane here anticipates the poststructuralist premise that the character of knowledge, justice, truth, or what you will, is structurally transformed by its medium of transmission into a textuality whose relation to truth-value is murky at best (but not necessarily invalid, since all textuality must be similarly compromised). This exploration of ambivalence intensifies in the superbly calibrated final lines, where the newspaper becomes "feckless life's chronicle"—hardly a complimentary description, yet if life is indeed feckless, the newspaper can be seen as its accurate chronicle.[31] Likewise, the "stupidities" reproduced by the newspaper are indeed stupid, but to a sensibility as dark and skeptical as Crane's, they may well represent the "eternal" elements of human nature. When he wrote this poem Crane still had ahead of him the corrosively disillusioning experience of seeing the United States in a Hearst-kindled war against a pathetically unequal opponent. But its last lines reveal his already acute awareness of the power of modern mass culture to "concentrate" human stupidities, once diffused and largely unknown outside local circles, into a critical mass capable of incendiary results. And yet, this critique is not the whole story either. The muckraking journalism of the 1890s had produced some serious social benefits, as Crane also knew from personal experience. In gathering the record of human stupidities into one place and exposing them as relentlessly as possible, the newspaper might "halter" them from roaming freely through the world.

Perhaps the most interesting of the poem's many paradoxes is the oblique metaphor of newspaper as "game," which evokes Crane's personal investment in athletics as college baseball player and then as sports reporter, as well as the newspaper's role in the construction of sports as central to modern spectatorial culture.[32] Yet this is by no means an unambiguous site of hegemonic oppression either. In a February 1896 letter, Crane remarked, "I see also that they are beginning to charge me with having played base ball. I am rather more proud of my base ball ability than of some other things" (Wertheim and Sorrentino 169). Since those "charging" him of having played baseball were undoubtedly the same critics deploring his sordid fiction and formless verse, Crane here defiantly embraces sports as a locus of opposition to codes of normative behavior.

The newspaper is an important form of spectatorial culture, because, as Trachtenberg points out, it provides and valorizes "surrogate experience" that can increase the separations it purports to overcome (125). If the newspaper is game, it is game as box score. At some points in his fine analysis, however, Trachtenberg reifies the contrast between experience and information, between "active" participation and "passive" spectatorship (122), into a binary that does inadequate justice to the variety and fluidity of spectatorial experience. Spectators at theatrical productions and sporting events do engage in forms of participation, if not in the show or game, then in the spectacle itself. Usually they do not interact directly with the players, but they do interact with other spectators, generating a variety of emotional, imaginative, and social meanings (as William Carlos Williams's 1923 masterpiece "At the Ball Game" will explore).

Furthermore, the disjunction between undergoing an "actual" experience and perusing a discursive account of that experience in a newspaper may not be such a clear-cut opposition of activity and passivity. In fact, as diehard baseball fans know, the box score is a fascinating discursive statement because it can be used to generate infinitely many imaginative versions of the game.[33] To substitute a discursive account of a game for physical participation may not inevitably close off recreative experience. It may even constitute a space of play, of possible resistance to the forces of hegemonic closure. Describing the newspaper as a specifically paradoxical "game," in which error can produce victory and skill defeat, in which unpredictable bounces can determine hero and goat and then invert them during the next inning or play, this poem, like Dunbar-Nelson's, posits an unsealable gap between the intentions of the captains of capital who would impose iron laws of modernity upon a passive spectatorial populace, and the unanticipated outcomes that might result from these interactions.[34]

In his book on Crane, Bill Brown describes a problematic that is central to accounts of the political significance of mass, popular, and recreational cultures, one typically articulated through theories of play: "though play has a history of exceeding theoretical structure in (or as) the margin of unpredictability, the dynamics of capital have a history of converting any such excess into surplus value. Still, if we recognize capital itself as an incomplete (permanently developing) system, then we can understand its recreational pleasures as strongly marking, while masking, the paradoxes of capitalist life" (11–12). The newspaper is an undoubted component of a capitalist economics of culture. Must it (like forms of organized sport and, for that matter, all of mass culture) therefore function only as an instrument of hegemonic oppression? Or in its voracious, one might say excessive, drive to collect and disseminate all kinds of information, might the newspaper possess enough unpredictability, enough play, to function as a site of creative resistance to the hegemonic? If, as Brown concludes, "the question whether the transformative potential of play lingers in the field of commercial pleasure remains a question" (13), these works of Crane and Dunbar-Nelson richly demonstrate that turn-of-the-century poets made it their business to play with such questions.

Both "Legend of the Newspaper" and "A newspaper is a collection of half-injustices" value the newspaper's ability to gather information from the world into new forms that can then be deployed to influence that world. I see this refractive trope as mirroring these texts' own achievement in thematizing the value of poetry in the modern scene. They demonstrate that poetry can gather the multifarious elements of the newspaper's significance into a structurally intensified meditation that is more complex and insightful than the newspaper is capable of producing about itself. These texts respond to poetry's turn-of-the-century crisis neither by capitulating to the reductive instrumentalism of mass culture, nor by fleeing into the phantom purity of genteel culture's drafty house on the hill. They invite us to reread the era's apparent expressions of futility, such as Crane's "A little ink more or less—/ It surely can't matter," as articulating productive incoherencies of American modernity. True, poetry is so submerged in the seas of ink generated by newspapers, novels, and other forms of mass culture that its presence is often barely detectable. Yet, these verses posit, modernity may be sufficiently heterogeneous and self-contradictory that poetry's "little ink more" might continue to perform valuable social functions that confound the captains of capital. In arguing that various cultural forms constitute a society's "material unconscious," Brown proposes that literature, "in its conscious and unconscious relation to other recreational forms, discloses their liberating and restricting contradictions" (13)— and I would add, its own as well. If we accept this characterization even provisionally, it follows that the poetic ink of the 1890s and 1900s, invisible for so long, deserves to be reread as articulating the seismic shifts of cultural value that shaped modern American experience.

NOTES

Notes to Introduction

1. In my argument "high modernism" refers to the specific intellectual formation that descends from the polemical arguments of Pound, Yeats, Eliot, and Lewis, through the evaluative premises of the Fugitives and Agrarian New Critics, into the mid-century literary academy, where its dominance "largely silenced the century's complex and contentious social context," as Walter Kalaidjian puts it (2). As I use it, high modernism does not encompass any poet's corpus of verse, even Eliot's or Pound's. Their poetry was central to that formation, but at least some of it was (and is) capable of functioning in other intellectual and ideological frameworks. I reject broader uses of the term to refer to any American poet who wrote complex verse and eventually became canonical; it makes little sense, in my view, to refer to such poets as Williams, Stevens, Moore, or Hart Crane as "high modernist."

2. Rachel Blau DuPlessis's fine recent study demonstrates the lingering influence of these stylistic priorities upon the chronological outlines of modern poetry. Describing "'new' social subjectivities" produced by changing racial, ethnic, and gender dynamics—New Black, New Jew, New Woman—DuPlessis hints at a revised modernist chronology by locating their "'incipit' dates" firmly in the 1890s (or earlier in the latter case) (2–4). Yet despite her clear sense of the 1890s as a pivotal decade for American modernity, virtually all the verse DuPlessis examines falls firmly within a traditional high-modernist time frame between 1910 and 1935—a disjunction explained by her frank attachment to "writers who tend to stylistic innovation" (26).

3. Among these stimulating works combining formalist interpretive sensitivity with historicist particularity are Miles Orvell's *The Real Thing*, Martha Banta's *Taylored Lives*, Cecilia Tichi's *Shifting Gears*, Bill Brown's *The Material Unconscious*, and Michael Brooks's *Subway City*.

4. Note, for example, the complete absence of verse from a project consciously conceived as the "inaugural event for an emergent field of new American studies" (Pease vii): the group of essays first published in *Boundary 2* in the spring of 1990 and then issued as the volume *Revisionary Interventions into the Americanist Canon* by Duke University Press in 1994. Except for a single fleeting mention of Emily

Dickinson, this volume contains no reference to any of the significant poets of nine-teenth-century America, not even Whitman. Harrington's *Poetry and the Public* offers an excellent account of the disappearing-verse phenomenon in the contemporary academy (160–69).

5. See Bennett's articles, "Not Just Filler," "'The Descent of the Angel,'" and "Late-Nineteenth-Century American Women's Nature Poetry," and her forthcoming volume *Poets in the Public Sphere: The Emancipatory Project of American Women's Poetry, 1800–1900;* Dobson, "Reclaiming Sentimental Literature" and "Sex, Wit, and Sentiment: Frances Osgood and the Poetry of Love"; Baym, *American Women Writers and the Work of History;* Walker, *The Nightingale's Burden and Masks Outrageous and Austere;* Clark, *Sentimental Modernism.*

6. For major contributions to the study of socially engaged verse after 1910, see Nelson, *Revolutionary Memory;* Kalaidjian, *American Culture between the Wars;* DuPlessis, *Genders, Races and Religious Cultures in Modern American Poetry;* Harrington, *Poetry and the Public;* Michael Thurston, *Making Something Happen;* Robert Shulman, *The Power of Political Art;* Mark Van Wienen, *Partisans and Poets;* Rita Barnard, *The Great Depression and the Culture of Abundance;* Alan Wald, *The Revolutionary Imagination* and *Exiles from a Future Time;* and Nancy Berke, *Women Poets on the Left.*

7. A few of the studies cited here do not ignore the turn of the century, but Nelson's *Repression and Recovery* (50–51, 235–36) and *Revolutionary Memory* (12–26) are so far the only ones to propose that this period might be integral to a historical revision of modern American poetry.

8. I'm aware that current disciplinary usage of "modernity" extends as far back as the sixteenth century. However, I have no intention of claiming five hundred years of verse as a unitary discourse of "modern poetry." If desired, the reader may imagine the words "urban-industrial" as sounding before every appearance of "modernity" in this book, and will no doubt understand if I don't actually include them every time.

9. "The New Poetry" was the term most commonly used in the 1910s to describe the dramatic rejuvenation of creative energy and institutional prominence in American verse that can be dated from 1911–1912. I have adopted it in this book as an alternative to "poetic modernism," because in practice the latter commonly degenerates into a prescriptive label designating a narrow set of poets who employ radical stylistic innovations and (it is claimed) seek aestheticist disengagement from an alienating modern scene. The term "New Poetry" implies inclusion rather than exclusion, incorporating the vast range of styles, politics, and attitudes manifested across the landscape of American verse after 1910.

10. As Harrington notes, Bourdieu's analytical divisions such as "legitimate" and "popular" are suggestive for the evaluative history of American poetry (*Poetry and the Public* 22). See also Beach, *Poetic Culture*, 45–47.

11. I advance this position more fully in the article "The Footprint of the Twentieth Century: American Skyscrapers and Modernist Poems."

Notes to Chapter 1

1. Nina Baym has traced a "nationalistic narrative" institutionalized by acade-mics writing histories of American literature in the half century after the Civil War,

which located "American history in New England" and proclaimed "the carefully edited New England Puritan," exemplified by the Fireside poets, as "the national type" (*Feminism* 81–82).

2. By grouping the Fireside poets together in this analysis, I'm not implying that they were alike in every important respect. No doubt most generalizations about the group are contradicted by at least one of the six. Bryant was almost ten years older than all the others, Lowell ten years younger. Bryant was never closely associated with the *Atlantic Monthly* as the other five were. Early on, Emerson was more inclined to literary nationalism and to an "Orphic mode of revelation and transcendence" (Beach, *Politics* 53) than the others. Lowell and Holmes, "Tempted by demons of irreverence," as Lawrence Buell puts it, were accused of "using a more vigorous language than the traditionally polite" in some of their most popular works (45); so was Whittier in his antislavery verse, for different reasons. But such exceptions notwithstanding, these six figures comprised a coherent canonical formation central to the "hegemonic poetic discourse" (Beach, *Politics* 53) of the century's latter decades. As they grew more entrenched as American classics, their differences on such questions as abolition and nationalism became less important and their cultural force became thoroughly collective, as Mark Twain's notorious speech at the Whittier birthday dinner of 1877, discussed in the third chapter, dramatizes.

3. In 1900 E. C. Stedman summarized their canonicity using similar domestic imagery: "the works of our 'elder American poets' lay on the centre-tables of our households and were read with zest by young and old alike" (*American Anthology* xxii).

4. Charvat estimates that original poems published in *Graham's* magazine in the early 1840s "were instantly reprinted, without payment, by half the magazines in the country" (109).

5. Charvat's *The Profession of Authorship in America, 1800–1870* offers a good summary of the amateur model of authorship that dominated American literary activity until around 1840 (6–7). *Harper's* began to identify most of its contributors in the early 1860s, while the *Atlantic Monthly* included authors' names only in its yearly index from 1862, not attaching them to the articles until 1870. But as Paula Bennett notes, most periodicals had dropped the policy of anonymity by around 1860 ("Not Just Filler" 203).

6. Due to his precocious early publications, Bryant had been well known in literary circles since 1820. By the early 1840s he had arrived at "the center of the nation's culture": as editor-publisher of the *New York Evening Post,* he had become a prominent champion of abolition and reform; as president of the fledgling American Art Union (1844–1846), he helped its membership grow by more than 120 percent (Shapiro 85). During these years Whittier was making a precarious living as an editor of various antislavery periodicals and also publishing verse prolifically, with seven volumes between 1836 and 1846. His partisan prominence in the abolition movement meant that he was less consensually accepted than Bryant and Longfellow; nor did he make much money from his work, since most of it went gratis to impecunious antislavery publications. But his public profile grew throughout the 1830s and 1840s as he became the national poet of abolition. Though Emerson enjoyed enormous renown as an essayist from the late 1830s, his transcendentalist and nationalist associations placed him somewhat outside the Fireside circle until the 1850s, when he began to adopt notably more conservative positions. Christopher Beach suggests that Emerson's famous turn away from Whitman after

an enthusiastic first reaction to *Leaves of Grass* may have been precipitated by his ongoing "*rapprochement* with the fireside poets and other members of the Boston literati" (*Politics* 192, n. 38), whose reaction to Whitman ranged from indifferent to scandalized. Holmes, pursuing his medical career, would achieve national notoriety as a poet much later than these three. But he had published "Old Ironsides" in 1831 while still a student, and by 1841 was ensconced within the cultural ambit of the Cambridge circle. Lowell, a decade younger than the other Fireside poets, first came to prominence in 1848 with the initial installment of *The Biglow Papers* and cemented his national reputation over the next decade.

7. For an example of this interlocking economy, note Ticknor and Fields's publication of Longfellow's volume *Tales of a Wayside Inn* on November 25, 1863, which was preceded by five days by a feature-length article on the poet in the *Atlantic* by G. W. Curtis. Observing this, Whittier wrote to Fields on Christmas Day to ask, "Is there no use to do for me . . . what Curtis has done for Longfellow . . . ?" (Austin 89–90). Fields then arranged a similar package upon the publication of Whittier's volume *In War Time* the following March (the collection's title poem already having appeared in the magazine).

8. Paula Bennett notes that "even highly trained readers" of the nineteenth century "ranked poetry's music and its power to elicit high-minded sentiment as or more important than its ability to encourage thought" ("Introduction" xxxi).

9. Whitman and Emily Dickinson, not Poe, are now the fully canonical poets of nineteenth-century America. But Dickinson as a classic American author is a construction of the twentieth century. Before she became available, it was Poe who functioned as the "other" poetic rebel of nineteenth-century America, no less iconoclastic than Whitman but upholding a distinct set of alternative values.

10. Concerning *Leaves of Grass*, Griswold expressed amazement that anyone "could have conceived such a mass of stupid filth, unless he were possessed of the soul of a sentimental donkey" ("Review" [*Criterion*] 8–9), while to the *New York Daily Times*, Whitman "roots like a pig among a rotten garbage of licentious thoughts" and appears as a "Centaur," "half man, half beast, neighing defiance to the world" ("Review" 40). A London reviewer judged Whitman "as unacquainted with art, as a hog is with mathematics. His poems . . . resemble nothing so much as the war-cry of the Red Indians" ("Review" [*Critic* (London)] 32). Even more viciously, the London *Critic* reviewer insisted that "the man who wrote page 79 . . . deserves nothing so richly as the public executioner's whip" ("Review" 32), while a Boston reviewer also mentioned "the lash," and despite calling Whitman "some escaped lunatic, raving in pitiable delirium," showed no pity, urging that he "be kicked from all decent society as below the level of a brute" ("Review" [Boston *Intelligencer*] 37).

11. Edward Wagenknecht supplies further evidence of the Quaker poet's lifelong antipathy, noting that decades later he resisted contributing to a fund for a horse and carriage for the infirm Whitman in fear that this would be misconstrued as approbation of Whitman's work (116).

12. In her analysis of the postwar "nationalistic narrative" of American literary value, Baym notes that the "disruptive" Whitman and Poe were "cast as pretenders—writers who were not 'really' American—and thus as foils to the central authors" (*Feminism* 81–82, 93). In effect, this process sophisticated the more heavy-handed moralistic distinctions of "character" predominant in evaluations of Poe and Whitman in the 1850s.

13. In *Kavanagh* Longfellow asserted that American literature "is growing slowly but surely, striking its roots downward, and its branches upward, as is natural," and that it must strive to be "worthy of our forefathers" (85, 84). These metaphors of graduated organic development implied that literary value was defined by stability and continuity, even in a world of rupture and heterogeneity. Responding to a buffoonish nationalist who demands "a national literature altogether shaggy and unshorn, that shall shake the earth, like a herd of buffaloes thundering over the prairies" (85), Longfellow's spokesman, Churchill, insists, "All that is best in the great poets of all countries is not what is national in them, but what is universal" (86).

14. For another, earlier example of this nationalist rhetoric, note Sarah Josepha Hale's 1830 assertion that the "greatest obstacle to the production of works of originality among us is this—our writers copy European models" (qtd. Okker 87).

15. Lowell had already assaulted cultural nationalism in his 1848 satire of the literary scene, *A Fable for Critics,* where some of his harshest barbs were aimed at thinly disguised versions of nationalists Margaret Fuller, Rufus Griswold, and the "Young American" leaders Evert Duyckinck and Cornelius Mathews (36–42, 72–76).

16. The nationalist rhetoric Lowell and Longfellow were parodying can be sampled in this passage from Fuller's "American Literature": "What suits Great Britain . . . does not suit a mixed race, continually enriched with new blood from other stocks the most unlike that of our first descent, with ample field and verge enough to range in and leave every impulse free, and abundant opportunity to develope [*sic*] a genius, wide and full as our rivers, flowery, luxuriant and impassioned as our vast great prairies, rooted in strength as the rocks on which the Puritan fathers landed" (299–300).

17. In her *Poetry* editorials after 1912, Monroe would redefine the work of genius as thoroughly a product of its environment: "A masterpiece of art is not a miracle of individual genius so much as the expression of a reciprocal relation between the artist and his public" ("The Poet's Bread and Butter" 197). For further discussion of her challenge to prevailing elitist models of literary value, see my forthcoming article "*Poetry*'s Opening Door: Harriet Monroe and American Modernism."

18. From their earliest writings, the Fireside poets asserted the harmlessness, even the benefits, of the poet's worldly penury. Note these comments from Bryant's 1825 lecture series at the New York Aetheneum: "Who would think of fattening a race-horse? Complaints of the poverty of poets are as old as their art, but I never heard they wrote the worse verses for it" (*Prose Writings* 33).

19. In "Woodnotes II" (1841), Emerson theorized the analogical function of formally conventional verse, proposing that couplet rhyme corresponded to "the natural order of things" (Buell 111) and urging the reader to

Come lift thine eyes to lofty rhymes,
Of things with things, of times with times,
Primal chimes of sun and shade,
Of sound and echo, man and maid,
The land reflected in the flood,
Body with shadow still pursued,
For Nature beats in perfect tune,
And rounds with rhymes her every rune. (*Collected Poems and Translations* 45)

Thirty-five years later, in the late essay "Poetry and Imagination" (1876), Emerson returned to these same images to reassert the universality of rhyme and meter on analogical grounds (41). Beginning from powerfully analogical premises ("Nature itself is a vast trope"; "all thinking is analogizing" [13–14]), Emerson insisted on the value of formal regularity in verse, using the term *rhymes* to refer to formative "correspondences of parts in nature" such as "acid and alkali, body and mind, man and maid" (43). Given these commitments to convention, which led Emerson to approve Ben Jonson's condemnation of Donne ("Donne, for not keeping of accent, deserved hanging" [qtd. 47]), we can't be too surprised that he rejected Whitman's work for the less jarring tones of the Cambridge circle.

20. For another evocation of the Fireside poets in their last years as ageless saints, see the 1888 remembrance in *The Writer* called "Whittier's Advice to a Boy," by Fred Lawrence Knowles, later a popular anthologist (*Golden Treasury of American Songs and Lyrics* [1901]). Though less ideologically resonant than Bok's vivid narrative, it indicates that such reminiscences form an identifiable genre and suggests their role in the maintenance of a national genteel canon.

21. Bok's autobiography is written in the third person.

22. Further evidence of the abundance of these gender stereotypes is supplied by Alicia Suskin Ostriker (30–32). This rhetoric of gender separation had both ideological and mundanely economic functions: Griswold's sharp eye for the main chance meant that after he put together the 1854 volume *The Female Poets of America* (largely from material he had generated in assembling the 1842 *Poetry and Poets of America*), he left woman poets out of subsequent editions of the latter, creating two separate and unequal canons, one of "American Poets" (all male) and one of "American Female Poets."

23. Beginning in the 1960s, feminist history and literary criticism took up the separate-spheres model with renewed vigor, reigniting interest in texts by nineteenth-century women: in Linda K. Kerber's words, it "enabled historians to move the history of women out of the realm of the trivial and anecdotal into the realm of analytic social history" (37). But in recent years most of its basic assumptions have been challenged. In the issue of *American Literature* she edited in 1998, Cathy N. Davidson's preface proclaims "No More Separate Spheres!" and argues that the separatist model perpetuates essentialist gender binaries "too rigid and totalizing . . . for understanding the different, complicated ways that nineteenth-century American society or literary production functioned" (445). In the same volume, Amy Kaplan's essay "Manifest Domesticity" works to "shift the cognitive geography of nineteenth-century separate spheres" (582) by describing how the ideology of familial domesticity, supposedly elevated above the amoral fray of politics, instead helped to create "an American empire by imagining the nation as a home at a time when its geopolitical borders were expanding rapidly through violent confrontations" (583).

24. As early as 1832 we find Longfellow responding to conventional notions that literature, particularly poetry, begat "an effeminate and craven spirit" ("Defence of Poetry" 62) and "disqualified" its practitioners from "'active life'" in a democracy (Haralson 333–35). Longfellow's "Defence of Poetry" attempts an elaborate anti-instrumentalist definition of poetry's use value, but even as he denies charges of effeminacy he fears their truth, remarking, in an unguarded moment a few pages later, "Another circumstance which tends to give an effeminate and unmanly character to our literature, is the precocity of our writers" ("Defence" 77). Longfellow has

insisted that poetry does not have to beget an effeminate and craven character, but "our literature" apparently has one nonetheless.

25. A growing interest in gender studies has yielded excellent discussions of the gender dynamics of Longfellow's work by Eric Haralson and Matthew Gartner. Much as I propose here, Haralson argues that a "key source of Longfellow's appeal" was "his advocacy of a cross-gendered sensibility—and, crucially, of a 'sentimental' masculinity—that answered to the experiential trials and affective needs of his audience" (329). Along slightly different lines, Gartner argues that Longfellow constructed in his work a "gentle male paternalism" that offered "safe places for women and men seeking shelter" (67). These arguments cannot be applied equally to all the Fireside writers, since Longfellow was in his day (and presumably is now) perceived as a more "sentimental" poet than, say, Emerson or Holmes. But I do propose that a similar combination of patriarchal authority and emotional sensitivity undergirded their canonicity in the century's second half.

26. Bryant was the editor, publisher, and part owner of a major daily newspaper, the *New York Evening Post,* taking positions on almost every issue of public importance, for nearly forty years. When he died in 1878, he was "New York's first citizen," without whose presence "no large public affair was considered complete" (C. Brown 1). Despite lifelong ill health, Whittier served as an antislavery editor, lobbyist, and state legislator, and became one of the most prominent figures in the abolitionist movement. Emerson left the Unitarian ministry to become a prominent essayist and commentator, making a good living by giving public lectures (Buell 57). Holmes lectured on poetry and medicine, contributed important papers on medical research in the 1840s, coined the term *anaesthesia,* and from 1847 was Professor of Anatomy and Dean of the Harvard Medical School (Small 13–15, 50–55, 64–65). Longfellow was Smith Professor of Modern Languages and Literatures at Harvard before leaving to make a lucrative living by his verse. Lowell, also an intermittently active abolitionist, edited various publications, succeeded Longfellow as Smith Professor at Harvard, and served as a convention delegate and Presidential elector for the reform wing of the Republican party (Duberman 277–81); he eventually became U.S. Minister to Spain and then to England, as well as the first president of the Modern Language Association.

27. Patricia Okker argues convincingly that Lydia H. Sigourney should "share the credit now often reserved for Longfellow" for improving the economic conditions of American writers during the 1840s (95).

28. For discussion of this and a few other city poems of the Fireside writers, see Beach, *Politics* 118–22.

29. Along similar lines, Nancy F. Cott asserts that nineteenth-century canons of domesticity did not "challenge the modern organization of work and pursuit of wealth," but rather "accommodated and promised to temper them" (69).

30. Female poets used images of the fireside as well. Mary Hewitt's well-known verse "The Hearth of Home" (1854), for example, offered a textbook opposition of domestic and worldly: "My humble hearth though all disdain, / Here may I cast aside the chain, / The cold world-fetters that restrain" (137). However, Cheryl Walker usefully distinguishes between the psychological functions of the "sanctuary poem" in the work of male and female writers. For female writers, she argues, such poems usually reflect "a longing for isolation" (54) from the demands of domestic society and an ambivalent but powerful desire for the self-reliance that female consciousness

was conventionally denied. In contrast, male poets found in these poems a soothing space of domestic comfort and community, psychic respite from the alienating daylight world. This divergence can be linked to asymmetrical changes in the patterns of work done by men and women in nineteenth-century homes. Ruth Schwartz Cowan argues that "in almost every aspect of household work, industrialization serves to eliminate" tasks traditionally assigned to men (*More Work for Mother* 63–64). In particular, the replacement of the hearth by the coal-fired stove as the method of cooking and heating made it both more feasible and "more necessary that a man be employed outside the home" in wage labor, since unlike wood, coal required cash, but once procured, demanded less time and labor to maintain (Cowan, *Social History* 194–95). Exempted from such time-consuming and strenuous chores as wood chopping and pounding meal, men came to perceive the home as "a place of leisure," whereas for most women "it retained its character as a place of labor" (Kerber 32–33). Cowan agrees, arguing that technological advances such as the enclosed stove "meant more work rather than less" for women (*Social History* 195). Imagery of enclosure remained a productive and prevalent trope throughout twentieth-century American women's verse, as Lesley Wheeler's recent study *The Poetics of Enclosure* demonstrates.

31. Cook describes these "vulgar and babyish" fake fireplaces as the "funniest of all the fashionable humbugs of our time" (112, 111). But he doesn't appear to be smiling.

Notes to Chapter 2

1. There are no intensive critical studies of these alternative verse venues of the 1890s and 1900s. They are still part of what Cary Nelson calls the "yet unwriteable" history of modern poetry, unwriteable because we lack intellectual grasp of—and often, physical access to—the "full range of modern poetic texts" dealing with sociopolitical issues (*Revolutionary Memory* 12). This history becomes a bit more writeable with each attempt to address these long-invisible writings, especially ones as painstaking as Mark W. Van Wienen's exhaustive archival analysis of American verse about the Great War.

2. One of the most revealing defensive dynamics of turn-of-the-century genteel culture was its busy, even obsessive, generation of new venues of institutional authority, such as the Modern Language Association (1884); the exclusive National Institute of Arts and Letters (1899); its even more exalted inner circle, the American Academy of Arts and Letters (1904); and the Hall of Fame for Great Americans (1900).

3. The *Oxford English Dictionary* dates the use of "jingle" to refer specifically to advertising from 1930, but the disparaging connotations of the word to refer to trifling, repetitive, or singsong sound go back centuries.

4. For an excellent discussion of the turn-of-the-century "Demise of the Gentle Reader" (though it makes no reference to poetry), see Christopher P. Wilson's "The Rhetoric of Consumption" (41–43).

5. This view of modernity as impending cataclysm was exacerbated by the turn of the century itself, an event characterized, as Hillel Schwartz notes, by a "runaway inflation of rhetoric . . . due to a feeling that the times were racing ahead faster than ever before" (167).

6. The number of magazines published in the United States jumped from about

700 in 1865 to around 3,300 by 1885 and 5,100 by 1895 (Tebbel and Zuckerman 57, 68). Jay Martin details the increasingly energetic and aggressive marketing methods used by magazine publishers after the Civil War (17). Theodore Greene describes the improvements in magazine distribution made possible by the growing railroad system and, after 1879, by "increasingly indulgent treatment of magazines in the Post Office" (61).

7. The largest circulation of the quality group was achieved by the *Century*, which peaked at 222,000 in 1887, but after 1890 declined to around 150,000 and to 125,000 after 1900. In 1930, with a circulation of 20,000, it was merged with the *Forum* (John 233, 271).

8. Greene points out that mass-magazine publishers and editors came not from "the world of books," as most genteel magazine editors had, but from "the worlds of business and of newspapers" (66).

9. Though he is referring to the daily newspapers of these years rather than to magazines, Trachtenberg's description of an emergent "language of mass intelligibility" (124) also emphasizes the necessity of seeing beneath the strategic claims of stylelessness made by ideologists of mass culture.

10. The items in "Etchings" had never been indexed individually, but the sections had always appeared in the volume indices. After 1903, however, "Etchings" and its successor "Light Verse" floated weightlessly through the volumes, entirely indexless.

11. See Saltus, "The Colossal City" and "New York from the Flatiron." In the May 1905 issue, offering his editorial impressions from the eighteenth floor, Frank Munsey concluded that he "couldn't tell in a hundred magazines all there is to be seen from this aerial floor" ("Impressions by the Way" [1905] 188).

12. We can measure this poem's deficient identification with its urban subjects by comparing it to a poem of similar situation, William Blake's "London." Blake's speaker is aware of a certain distance from his subjects–the hapless soldier, the forlorn chimney sweep, the horrifying young harlot and blasted baby—a distance that comes from his ability to observe, synthesize, and articulate their pain rather than being consumed by it. But he admits no essential difference between himself and them, saying that "I wander" through every "charter'd street" just as they must, and "mark in every face I meet" their "marks of weakness, marks of woe" (65). Blake's speaker, genuinely empathetic, does not exclude himself from the scarring experiences of city life: as he marks the faces of these others, they mark him.

13. See such celebrations of manly struggle as "A Man-Song" by William R. Lighton and "The Love of the Day's Work" by S. H. Kemper; Susan Buell Hale's patriotic "The Alamo—March 6, 1836"; Cy Warman's "Will the Lights Be White?" and Arthur Stringer's "In the Open," both evocations of the thrills of railroad life; and Warman's "The Search for Gold," a surprisingly ambivalent meditation on prospecting in the West. Through his Associated Literary Press, which sold material to a syndicate of newspapers, McClure had been largely responsible for introducing the young Rudyard Kipling to American audiences in 1890 (H. Wilson 53). When he began his own magazine, he drew upon Kipling early and often. The first volume featured "The Merchant-Man," and several other verses, including the notorious "The White Man's Burden," appeared within the first ten years.

14. See also Henry Newbolt's "Admiral Death" (July 1898) and Mary Stewart Cutting's "On the Field" (July 1899).

15. More interesting examples of this martial verse can occasionally be found, such as the series "Songs of the Ships of Steel" (June 1898) by the naval historian James Barnes. These verses are composed in balladlike forms evoking traditional nautical chanteys (which Barnes was engaged in compiling and editing); yet they explore various aspects of contemporary nautical experience and technology, including the ferocious incendiary capabilities of modern warships, the careerism of ambitious young officers, and the endurance of the brave fire-room "gang" who maintain the ship's mechanical operations.

16. *McClure's* continued to feature Markham's politically charged verse through 1899, including "Dreyfus" in September and "The Song of the Muse of Labor" in December. The latter, an optimistic counterpart to "The Man with the Hoe," suffers from the sense of anticlimax that afflicts many sequels; however, its celebration of "Unselfish Service" reinforces the moral authority of the earlier poem, making clear that it is not labor per se that Markham protests against, but the soul-killing toil of a "world gone wrong." Of course "Labor" refers not just to physical toil, but also to organized labor movements, which "bring the hope of Nations" and the promise of a "Fraternal State" (123).

17. Yearly advertising revenues for the *Post*, which totaled $6,933 in 1897 when Curtis bought it, reached $1,266,937 in 1907 and topped $16 million by 1917 (Tebbel and Zuckerman 141).

18. Others in this series of parodic nursery rhymes, which Carryl took to calling "Grimm Tales Made Gay," were "Little Red Riding Hood," "The Bottled Giant," "Jack and the Beanstalk," and "Pearls and Toads." "Little Red Riding Hood" exemplified the magazine's campaign against both genteel poetry and Progressive do-gooding, describing an insufferably perfect little girl: "at six she was so notably smart / That they gave her a check for reciting The Wreck / Of the Hesperus wholly by heart" (but of course she gave this money to the poor). By the age of eleven she was teaching Sunday school, and the following year she "wrote a volume of verse." She is eventually eaten by the wolf masquerading as her grandmother, mercifully so in the facetious speaker's view, since it saves her from the hideous fate of being a "woman of awful renown / Who carried on fights for her feminine rights," a creature who would no doubt "come to write verse for the Big Magazines!" Carryl's moral fell comfortably into line with the *Post*'s distrust of the exceptional achiever in artistic and intellectual pursuits: "There's nothing much glummer / Than children whose talents appal. / One much prefers those that are dumber."

19. Braxton's introduction to Dunbar's *Collected Poems* surveys the cultural debates that Dunbar's African American dialect poems triggered (x, xxiii-xxviii) and describes the limiting effects of white advocates like Howells, who tended to emphasize Dunbar's verse in black dialects while ignoring his work in traditional literary forms and voices (xvi-xvii).

20. For examples contemporaneous to the poem, see the ads for Knox's in the issues of January 5, 1901 (14), and March 2 (16); for Cream of Wheat on February 23 (inside front cover); and on April 20, for a "Rubber Brownie," a strange toy figurine manufactured by B. F. Goodrich depicting a strutting and goggle-eyed black male in tuxedo and tails (which the ad makes a point of describing as "lifelike") (18).

21. Joan Morris's booklet notes to *After the Ball* (Elektra/Nonesuch 9 79148-2) put the song's sales at five million, while Nicholas Tawa estimates its sales at "over 2 million" (44); this is a large discrepancy, but there is no disagreement over its posi-

tion as the genre's first true mass seller. Morris notes that until "After the Ball," a sale of 100,000 copies had been considered "a miracle."

22. On the nineteenth-century hymn book, see Ann Douglas, *Feminization* 216–20.

23. Sandy Petrey suggests the curious tonal influence of Dresser's sentimental popular songs on his brother's *Sister Carrie* (108–9).

24. Note also Fred J. Barnes's lyrics to "The Girl I Loved 'Way Out in Indiana" (1906): "Years have passed since I left dear old Indiana, / And perhaps I'll never see its soil again." Perhaps because the songwriters could count on their audiences' familiarity with the sentimental "Hoosier Poet" James Whitcomb Riley, Indiana became the geographical epicenter of the nostalgic song—rather in the same way that the major political parties routinely chose Ohioans for their presidential candidates between 1865 and 1920.

25. David Nasaw notes that even in the 1870s and 1880s, "'nightlife' was still the preserve of the wealthy few" (2). His book *Going Out* details the startling emergence after 1890 of new sites of urban leisure geared to mass audiences: nickelodeons, amusement parks, professional baseball and other sports, vaudeville and melodrama theatres, and dance halls.

26. Figure 2, a scene of Cairo Street on the Midway, suggests exactly the sort of mingling evoked in the song. The group posed in the center of the picture consists of male and female tourists in their finery, posing with two dark-skinned men, presumably Arab, wearing white headgear.

27. In contrast, the cover illustration of the 1922 song "You Can Have Ev'ry Light on Broadway (Give Me That One Little Light at Home)" (words by Benny Davis, music by Seymour Simons) captures the growing segregation of urban and suburban realms even two decades later. The cover of "Take a Car" affirms continuity between these two realms through the presence of the trolley and conductor in the suburban pastoral. On the later song's cover, this continuity is replaced by two separate and irreconcilable spaces, in which the innumerable lights of the Great White Way are confined to an inset, while the main image is a lone cottage silhouetted against a night sky, surrounded by foliage. This binarized conceptual model is also evoked by the parenthetical syntax of the song's title. All these signifiers reiterate that the earlier synthesis of urban and suburban is giving way to a rigidly framed choice of either/or.

28. The intervening verses have airily celebrated horse racing, prostitution in the "tenderloin," and even embezzlement (in the person of a cashier who absconds with the entire contents of the company's safe, leaving "not a cent inside, just a card that was all, and it read: / Meet me in St. Louis, Louis").

Notes to Chapter 3

1. Many of these polls were related to recurrent debates concerning an official institution of American culture, eventually realized in the National Institute of Arts and Letters. The 1884 poll in *The Critic* asked its readers to choose "Our Forty Immortals," just from persons living at that time: the three living Fireside poets, Holmes, Lowell, and Whittier, were the top three vote-getters ("Our Forty Immortals" 169). In *The Critic*'s 1893 poll on "The Best Ten American Books," the collected verse of Longfellow, Holmes, Lowell, and Whittier placed between third and

eighth, matched only by Emerson's *Essays* and three works of fiction (*The Scarlet Letter, Uncle Tom's Cabin,* and Irving's *Sketch Book*).

2. Stedman's many contributions to poetry of this era included *An American Anthology, 1787–1900* (hereinafter cited as AA), the detailed critical commentary *Poets of America* (1885) (hereinafter cited as PA), and an edition of the complete poems of Poe, coedited with George Edward Woodberry (1895).

3. Many commemorations echoed this distinction between Holmes's personal worth and the aesthetic value of his work: "As a writer of verse, he is scarcely entitled to a place among the immortals" (Boyesen 162); he "may not have been great, in the sense of genius, nor immortal, as the world writes its narrowing record of fame" (E. Brooks 164); "Nothing he did in verse will entitle him to be called great" (Fawcett 166); "As a poet, his work . . . has not the highest imaginative quality" (Burton 166); "the essayist rises higher than the poet" (Garland 167). Oscar Fay Adams devoted his remarks to describing the damaging results of too freely using the adjective "great" in reference to poets; for him Holmes was "A delightful author . . . but hardly more" (162).

4. Even in 1885, Stedman had noted of his "collection of sketches, articles, debates" on American poets that "the Whitman and Poe packages, before the deaths of Emerson and Longfellow [in 1882], were each much larger than all the rest combined" (PA 350). In the same year, a volume on Poe by George E. Woodberry was issued in Houghton Mifflin's prestigious American Men of Letters series (Casper 199). The publishers pushed for Whitman's inclusion in this project, citing "a continuous and permanent interest in him" (qtd. Casper 190), but this was blocked by series editor Charles Dudley Warner's distaste for the poet. After Warner's death, the publishers brought out their Whitman volume by Bliss Perry in 1906.

5. Though Saltus (1855–1921) was older than the poets I discuss in part 3, he anticipated their skepticism toward genteel traditions and their anxiety over the apparent futility of literary endeavor. His 1884 poem "History" deconstructs the notion of history as a discipline of human enlightenment. Instead, from the pages of history books "streams / The incoherent story of the years, / The aimlessness of all we undertake" (*Poppies* 5). Much as George Santayana's sonnets would do a few years later, the poem's final lines reject genteel assumptions about community, society, and materiality for an alienated, "spiritual" individualism: "I think our lives are surely but the dreams / Of spirits, dwelling in the distant spheres, / Who as we die, do one by one awake" (5). The value of poetry for Saltus, as for Santayana, was to enact that rejection and to evoke that otherworldly ideality.

6. Holmes "leaves neither successors nor imitators" (N. Brooks 163); New Englanders "are not watching as eagerly to-day for the words of our singers as their fathers did for the poems of Lowell, Whittier, and Holmes, which were so splendidly prophetic as well as truly poetic" (G. Morris 195).

7. This rumor about the *Atlantic*'s waning commitment to poetry was not wholly inaccurate. By 1904 the number of poems in the magazine had been declining for several years. In 1900 (volumes 85 and 86), 75 poems had appeared in its pages, but in 1901 this dropped to 51, followed by 46 in 1902, 40 and 41 in 1903 and 1904; in 1905 the magazine's support for poetry reached a nadir, when just 24 poems appeared there. The numbers began to rise a bit again in 1906, but only to 33.

8. The notion that turn-of-the-century poets were defined by imitativeness and conventionality has dominated American literary history from its beginnings as an

academic field, at least since 1930, when Fred Lewis Pattee described them as "The Transition Poets" and concluded that the "twenty years following 1890 produced little of distinctive verse" (194). See also Larzer Ziff's influential assertion that with few exceptions, the poets of the 1890s "wrote sonnets, odes, and dramatic monologues which they believed to be American extensions of English Victorian poetry. Their lines were sounded with the flatness of a tone-deaf singer" (307).

9. In this quatrain "rhyme" can refer to *the genre of poetry,* as it often does. But this is virtually the only extant Crane verse employing a systematic rhyme scheme. Its uniqueness suggests that he also had the specific meaning of a formal technique now seen as obsolete and artificial, as does his parodic echo of Longfellow's "A Psalm of Life," the quintessential homiletic text of American poetry, which begins, "Tell me not, in mournful numbers, / Life is but an empty dream!—/ For the soul is dead that slumbers, / And things are not what they seem" (*Complete Poetical Works* 5).

10. The *Atlantic*'s implicit endorsement of Watson's reactionary position came just one year before it published the advocacy of messianic innovation made by R. W. Gilder's poem "A New Poet" (discussed below). This incongruity cannot be attributed merely to the happenstance of an eclectic, wide-ranging publication. The *Atlantic* was not eclectic; it had formulated, and had come to embody, the well-defined ideology of American genteel culture. Its internal contradictions reflected the growing incoherence of that culture.

11. Even the aged Oliver Wendell Holmes shared the anxiety of late-century writers that their creations would be lost amid an endless swarm of writing, the more anonymous and ineffectual as it expanded in volume. In "Cacoëthes Scribendi" (1890), Holmes imagines a world in which

> . . . all the trees in all the woods were men;
> And each and every blade of grass a pen;
> . . . . every sea
> Were changed to ink, and all earth's living tribes
> Had nothing else to do but act as scribes,
> And for ten thousand ages, day and night,
> The human race should write, and write, and write. . . .

Yet even after all this writing, Holmes concludes whimsically, "Still would the scribblers" "Call for more pens, more paper, and more ink" (300–1).

12. To some degree this constricting writer's market can be viewed as a consequence of the rise of mass magazines. By commissioning many articles, soliciting pieces by well-known writers, and maintaining a cadre of staff writers, these new magazines had "an often-drastic effect" on unsolicited acceptances from little-known writers (C. Wilson, *Labor* 53). For discussion of these perceptions of exclusion, see Howells, "The Editor's Relations with the Young Contributor"; "Of Editors and Their Critics"; "Is Genius Neglected by the Magazines?" and "Why Are Manuscripts Rejected?: A Symposium."

13. In his classic account *The American 1890s* (1966), Ziff saw this kind of censoriousness as so central to the quality magazines that he entitled his chapter on them "The Tinkle of the Little Bell"—a metaphor used by Howells as *Atlantic* editor to describe the editorial alarm at anything that might be considered offensive: "I tried to catch the tinkle of the little bell when it was not actually sounded" (qtd. Ziff 126).

14. On the other hand, there were also schemes to profit from this sense of exclusion by throwing open the doors of publication to anyone willing to pay for an overpriced anthology volume, such as *Local and National Poets of America* (1890), whose epigraph read "Great oaks from little acorns grow" (Herringshaw i); and the unrealized project for a periodical called *Columbia Poetica,* which, as *Munsey's* put it derisively in 1899, aspired "to embalm in type the metrical effusions of the great army of the perpetually 'rejected'" ("A Poets' Pantheon" 472).

15. As Ronald Martin details, the Spencerian notion of the "universe of force" had a much greater impact in the United States than in Europe: "not only did it become a factor to be reckoned with in American science, philosophy, and religion, but it penetrated to levels of the American population never before reached by any formal philosophy save Christianity" (9). Martin's study traces "a motley school" of American pseudo-philosophers who used "the broadest, vaguest ideas of force, God, evolution, progress, providence, and ideality" to present "visions of a force-reconciled universe" (79). For a discussion of poetry's future that partakes of exactly this cluster of ideas, complete with adulatory references to Spencer and Fiske, see Charles J. Goodwin's 1895 essay "The Poet in an Age of Science" (131–34).

16. The Chatterton handkerchief is reproduced and briefly described by E. H. W. Meyerstein (475–76).

17. If well-established writers of the era contended with entrenched institutional indifference, younger poets had to count themselves lucky even to be mentioned, and if mentioned, to have their names printed correctly. Among the less fortunate was Robinson, whose reviewers, while mildly favorable overall, turned him with comical frequency into "Edward" Arlington Robinson. Richard Cary estimates that almost one-fifth of Robinson's notices before 1910 made this error, including, ironically, "his glittering impresario Theodore Roosevelt" (15). Even when the reviewer got it right, things could still go awry, as in Clinton Scollard's article of 1903, which included an elegant photograph of the poet, captioned "Edward" (Scollard 234). Perhaps Robinson's most enthusiastic early notice, William Morton Payne's review of *The Children of the Night* (1897) in the *Dial,* was just a single paragraph in length and identified the author as "E. H. Robinson" (Payne, "Recent Poetry" 92).

18. The date of the play's composition is taken from Monroe, *A Poet's Life* 179.

Notes to Chapter 4

1. After 1880, apprenticeship in skilled trades declined precipitously, as a growing middle class, financially able to delay the entry of its children into the workforce, sought more education to secure rewarding white-collar careers (Kett 144–50). The result was a phenomenal increase in enrollment in high schools, colleges, and professional and technical schools between 1875 and 1900, which suddenly prolonged the period of education far beyond the norms of just a few years earlier (Kett 154–55, 178–79).

2. The classic elaboration of the concept is G. Stanley Hall's *Adolescence: Its Psychology and Its Relations to Physiology, Anthropology, Sociology, Sex, Crime, Religion, and Education* (1904).

3. Cheryl Walker's helpful analysis of Amy Lowell employs the Bloomian notion of the "covering Cherub" to describe James Russell's inhibiting effect on her early creative development (*Masks* 34).

4. Not all of these young men were from privileged backgrounds. But Stickney,

the son of a classical scholar, was descended from a colonial governor of Connecticut and spent most of his childhood in the European emigré circles Henry James wrote about. Lodge, son of the powerful Senator Henry Cabot Lodge, possessed so much social and cultural capital that the preface to his posthumous collected works was written by Theodore Roosevelt and his biography by Henry Adams! Lodge and Stickney were intimate friends for many years, entering the Sorbonne together in 1895 after their graduation from Harvard. Though they became close only after their college years, Robinson and Moody remained literary confidantes to the end of the latter's life. In 1902 Moody worked hard to get Houghton Mifflin to publish Robinson's *Captain Craig*, which was the volume that garnered him national (and presidential) attention and, thanks to Roosevelt, a sinecure in the United States Customs House in New York City (*Letters to Harriet* 27–28). Moody and Lodge (along with John Ellerton Lodge) served as Stickney's literary executors and coedited the posthumous edition of his works.

5. In later decades Santayana would commemorate several other luckless poetic aspirants, all in residence at Harvard during these same years, who died before they could develop any reputation at all, such as Thomas Parker Sanborn (1864–1889), Philip Henry Savage (1868–1899), and Hugh McCulloch (1869–1902) (Santayana, "Thomas Parker Sanborn" 46–47; Santayana, *Letters* 306; for a brief discussion of these poets, see Whittle 47–49).

6. Santayana makes virtually the same argument in his *Dial* review of the 1922 volume *Civilization in the United States* ("Marginal Notes" 563–64).

7. In suggestive readings of the philosophical treatises *The Sense of Beauty* and *Interpretations of Poetry and Religion*, which were published in the five years after these poems appeared, Lentricchia offers a different Santayana, a pioneer of modern engagement grounded in "the immediacy and inviolable integrity of perception," who seeks to move "from isolate sensibility to community, from poems as aids to perception to poems as aids to connection" (6). These illuminations are not borne out in Santayana's verses of the 1890s. While some may evoke the pleasures of perception, they almost never escape, and are often built upon, a fin de siècle sense of being "imprisoned in an isolated subject" (5) that Lentricchia's more modern Santayana reacts against. In effect, the sonnets dramatize the impasse that the philosophical works move beyond.

8. In "Arion" Brooks sardonically elaborated on this convention by describing a contemporary poet who "with surpassing minstrelsy" creates "such ravishing delights" as have never been heard before. But the fate of even this unmatched poet is grim: "But what can break the links of lucre's chain: / The sailors scowled, the bard plunged in the main" (*Margins* 34). Brooks's metaphors flatly equate modernity with the enslaving force of money.

9. This equation of medieval culture with spiritual integration was also seen in the philosophical underpinnings of *The Chap-Book*, whose founder Herbert S. Stone arrived as a freshman at Harvard in 1890. Stone began issuing *The Chap-Book* there as an undergraduate periodical, and with his classmate H. I. Kimball started their publishing firm at the university before moving to Chicago in 1894, at which point Stone undertook the magazine's production on a lavish and ambitious scale (Schlereth 9). Also notable is the presence at Harvard during this same period of Herbert Copeland and Fred Holland Day, who stayed in Boston to set up their own publishing company (Schlereth 32). Both Stone & Kimball and Copeland & Day

exemplified the American aestheticist approach to the book not as a commodity of modern mass production, but as a unique object of beauty.

10. This generalization applies not only to Harvard poets but to some of their Ivy League contemporaries. The Dartmouth graduate Hovey hatched a monumental cycle of nine verse dramas on Arthurian mythography, managing before his death to complete three of them (*The Marriage of Guinevere, The Birth of Galahad,* and *Taliesin*).

11. Though he has garnered almost no attention from historians, Hugh McCulloch traced exactly the same path as his better-known classmates; the only volume he published during his lifetime took its title from the longest poem, *The Quest of Heracles* (1894).

12. This work, begun in 1901 well before Stickney's death but never completed, was published posthumously as "Fragments of a Drama on the Life of the Emperor Julian" (*Poems* 133–60).

13. Of the Harvard poets, Moody was the most capable of engaging with modern themes, and his "western" play *The Great Divide* actually enjoyed significant success on Broadway in 1906 and on the London stage the following year. But this play was not written in verse, thus preserving the era's conventional divide of subject matter between prose and poetry.

14. The theme, imagery, and tone of "The Shadows" are strikingly reproduced in Hugh McCulloch's "Obsession" (1902), suggesting their centrality to aspiring turn-of-the-century poets. The speaker of "Obsession" describes a "vivid dream of hidden might" in which his "incantations" evoke the spirits of the canonical dead, whom he commands to "tell / Their wisdom, glory, ignorance, and fright." But his feelings of might are illusory, and the experience quickly turns alienating ("The outlines of their forms I could not see, / I could not understand the words they said"). He finds that these spirits, once evoked, are impossible to control or escape and ends up confined by them in a prison of his own learning: "The spells which called them could not make them flee. / And still surrounding me with shapes of dread, / They who obeyed me once now master me, / And life is like a vigil with the dead" (*Lines Written in Florence* 16).

15. For an example of the more contented erotics of the turn-of-the-century bachelor, see Archibald Douglas's verse "To My Cigar," published in *Munsey's* in 1896. Eulogizing his diminishing cigar in terms that would be grotesque if they were not so preposterous, this speaker has no need of an actual fireside, since "The warmth, the fire / That in you lies, / I've valued with / A lover's eyes"; and no need of an actual lover, since "I've touched your lips / In fond caress, / I've smoothed the wrinkles / Of your dress" (152).

16. The poems that immediately follow—"Outward," "The Voyage," "A Song for Waking," and "The Greek Galley"—insistently reiterate the impulse to "Sail ever on thy mystic voyages, / Cut loose, up anchor from the shores of thought" (1:120) that Lodge identifies with Whitman. These intensifying rhetorical gestures culminate in perhaps Lodge's most Whitmanesque poem of all, "A Song for Revolution." But this poem's impassioned rhetoric never quite makes it clear what the poet is revolting against and eventually substitutes classical reference for contemporary specificity, asserting that "the fire of rebellion we cherish is Promethean" (1:138).

17. This is not to say that Hovey's response to expansionism was not rife with

unexamined self-contradiction, a problem perpetuated by this remark from the only critical book on the poet: "If Hovey had any doubts about the righteousness of America's cause, all he needed to do was watch the stock market go down with every news release about the war; for anything that hurt Wall Street had to be good" (Linneman 44). Such an attitude testifies to the intensity of Hovey's convictions, but in its assumption that "America's cause" in Cuba was inversely related to the fortunes of "Wall Street," to their extreme political naiveté as well.

18. For more of Hovey's intemperate responses to the war, see "The Word of the Lord from Havana," "The Call of the Bugles," and "America," grouped together in the 1898 volume *Along the Trail*.

19. The classic articulation of cosmic isolation in Crane's verse is Daniel Hoffman's view of the poet as the "literary figure as isolato" (6; see also 6–8). While I certainly agree that Crane's wandering personae are isolated, this isolation emerges most vividly when they are placed into jostling proximity with a contrasting Other.

20. The poem beginning "Many red devils ran from my heart / And out upon the page" (*Black Riders* 49) is another well-known example of this topos. Other variations can be found in "Many workmen" (*Black Riders* 32); "'I have heard the sunset song of the birches'" (*War Is Kind* 27); "The trees in the garden rained flowers" (*War Is Kind* 65); and the fragment beginning "intermingled" (*Poems and Literary Remains* 77).

21. Stevens and Williams are apposite references here for another reason: Brooks is likely unique in American poetry in receiving extensive training in both law and medicine. The only informative scholarly reference to Brooks is Carlin Kindilien's brief commentary, which draws heavily upon the memoir by Wallace Rice introducing Brooks's posthumously published poems. Kindilien does accurately note that Brooks "broke cleanly with the sentimental and humorous tradition" of the day's popular poetry to engage in intriguing formal experimentation (131, 203–04).

22. The verse form of "Titular," a loose trochaic tetrameter without rhyme, conveys to today's reader a modernity surprising for its date of origin. Here and elsewhere, Brooks found quietly effective ways of passing beyond the slavish reproduction of traditional forms. According to his close friend Wallace Rice, by the time *Margins* was published, Brooks had been powerfully influenced by Whitman, as suggested by the invocatory poem "To Him" (x-xi). That this influence is not obvious in Brooks's verse, in contrast to the painfully unassimilated imitation of Whitmanesque diction and imagery seen in Hovey and Lodge, suggests Brooks's promise as an original creative figure and makes his demise all the more poignant.

23. In "Autumn Refrain" (1931) Wallace Stevens would use this ambiguity of "still" for very similar purposes, again suggesting Brooks's sensitivity to strategies of the New Poetry he did not live to see: "And yet beneath / The stillness of everything gone, and being still, / Being and sitting still, something resides, / Some skreaking and skrittering residuum. . . . / And the stillness is in the key, all of it is, / The stillness is all in the key of that desolate sound" (*Collected Poems* 160).

24. Brooks's fascination with marginality might have been catalyzed by personal misfortune: a laboratory accident at Harvard that "sadly marked" his face with acid burns, "not to a degree which would cause repulsion or even criticism, but internally, . . . setting him apart from his fellows, and leaving a scar upon an ambitious and sensitive nature" (Rice, "Francis Brooks" viii).

Notes to Chapter 5

1. In the 1910s, this intense interest in the meanings of modern structures would become a defining manifestation of the New Poetry's power to address the everyday experience of twentieth-century life. See my article "The Footprint of the Twentieth Century: American Skyscrapers and Modernist Poems."

2. The $250,000 needed to build the statue had been raised in France during the later 1870s, and construction was almost complete by early 1883. In the United States, however, the comparable amount needed for the foundation and pedestal was not easily forthcoming, and in March 1883 Congress rejected another appropriations request, requiring the statue's supporters to redouble their private fund-raising efforts. Lazarus wrote "The New Colossus" for an auction of manuscripts and artworks held on December 3, 1883, an event that included contributions by Longfellow, Whitman, Mark Twain, and Bret Harte (Vogel 159). Over the next two years the cause was led by Joseph Pulitzer of the *New York World,* who hoped the issue would establish him as the nation's most important publisher. Finally, on August 11, 1885, Pulitzer ran the headline "Triumphant Completion of the World's Fund for the Liberty Pedestal"—along with a cartoon depicting the statue on a pedestal prominently blazoning the name of his paper! The real pedestal (without this feature) was completed in April 1886 and the statue unveiled on October 28 (Bell and Abrams 35–50).

3. The title of another of Thomas's important urban poems, "Anima Urbis," echoes Whitman's assertion of a modern materialistic poetics in "Crossing Brooklyn Ferry": that the material things of the city furnish "parts toward the soul" (188). "Anima Urbis" is a highly personal appreciation of New York City, which the poet frankly admits adoring as a "lover," for "many years" the very circumference and center of her world. She has no love for "Great Nature," whose "vacant heavens" and "lonely wind-tides" seem "sad to me as Sophoclean seas." In contrast, she tells the city raptly, "Your casual glimpses of the stars suffice, / Your chary sunsets are of precious sard; / Your yearning towers bloom agate as they rise, / Where men enskied do work—and Heaven keep guard!" (378). Thomas's city allows people to achieve the sky, yet still do productive work in this world. As in "Broadway," Thomas here evokes an important liminal function for urban verse: to explore yet unrealized but newly imaginable horizons of modern experience.

4. Decades before the Civil War, land bordering the Schuylkill River west of the city had been set aside as a preserve for the metropolitan water supply. The buildings of the Fairmount waterworks, opened in 1822, became one of the central tourist attractions in the eastern United States for the next half century, far outstripping Philadelphia's historical sites in popularity (Stevick 72; cf. 72–86). Designated a city park in 1867, Fairmount was greatly enlarged over the next few years and housed the 1876 Centennial Exhibition. By 1900 it was the second largest city park in the world (Rhoades 348), containing an extensive boating culture, colonial mansions and other historic buildings, a Horticultural Hall and zoo, and the faded but still famous elegance of the reservoir.

5. Of course, there were plenty of verses toeing the designers' party line, such as Richard Watson Gilder's "The 'White City'" (1893), which portrays the Neoclassical Court of Honor as modern embodiment of the "undying seed" of originary Euroamerican ideals: "Ah! happy West—/ Greece flowers anew, and all her temples

soar!" (602). Interestingly, Gilder does acknowledge one of the tricky ironies of the Columbian Exposition: the ephemerality of the White City as a physical structure, at odds with its ostensible significance as a symbol of eternal human ideals ("One bright hour, then no more / Shall to the skies / These columns rise"). But genteel idealism demands that Gilder immediately neutralize this disquieting insight, and he flees flawed materiality for weightless metaphor: "But though art's flower shall fade, again the seed / Onward shall speed / Quickening the land from lake to ocean's roar" (602).

6. Fordham was an African American writer of whom little is known other than her 1897 volume *Magnolia Leaves,* printed in South Carolina with a preface by Booker T. Washington.

7. Fordham's "Atlanta Exposition Ode" portrayed the 1895 fair in Atlanta as bridging the "chasm" of North and South, unionist and rebel, black and white. Quoting the famous catchphrase of Booker T. Washington's Atlanta speech, "Cast down your buckets where you are" (32), her poem strikes a strongly conciliatory note, as did the whole Exposition (which included buildings "devoted to women and to African-Americans, the latter portraying blacks as an economic asset" to soothe the concerns of prospective investors that the South had a continuing "'race problem'" [Gray 323]).

8. Occasionally the ode strikes an arresting image that points toward modern directness, as in the portrayal of Columbia-America as a lithe young female athlete: "what would she / With all the out-worn pageantry / Of purple robes and heavy mace and crown? / Smiling she casts them down, / Unfit her young austerity / Of hair unbound and strong limbs bare and brown" (*Valeria* 225).

9. Monroe recounts this experience in *A Poet's Life* (98–100). The text of the cantata is reproduced in her 1892 volume *Valeria* (213–19).

10. Most structures in the White City were made of staff, a plaster and fiber material designed, as Miles Orvell notes, for ease of demolition (35). In the event, many of the Exposition's buildings proved rather too easy to demolish, outlasting the fair by just a few months before being devastated by fire in January 1894. Neil Harris notes in nicely deadpan fashion that "The White City vanished more quickly than it had appeared" (9).

11. According to L. G. Moses, Buffalo Bill's Wild West Show made almost a million dollars profit in Chicago in 1893 (218). Moses's article "Indians on the Midway" is the most thorough recent study of the contesting representations of Native Americans on the midway, which included a model Indian School sponsored by the Bureau of Indian Affairs, a more "primitive" Indian village constructed by the fair's Department of Ethnology and Archaeology, various unregulated commercial concerns, and Cody's show just outside the gates (210–19). But it does not clarify the position of Rain-in-the-Face as captive or showman.

12. Given Libbie Custer's friendships with Chicagoans, her tendency to showmanship ("There was a bit of the ham in her," her biographer Lawrence Frost remarks [275]), and her longtime association with Cody and other Wild West spectacles, it is surprising that she apparently did not visit the Columbian Exposition. Possibly the actual presence of Rain-in-the-Face took all the savor away.

13. This relationship has been a convention of historical accounts of the war at least since the 1930s; see studies by Wilkerson (1932) and Wisan (1934).

14. The anti-imperialist anthology *Liberty Poems,* published two years later after

the war had turned sour, is briefly discussed by Cary Nelson as part of an "oppositional intertext" within turn-of-the-century American poetry (*Revolutionary Memory* 23).

15. This chronology is drawn from the editor's notes in Santayana's *Complete Poems* (671–72).

16. Beginning in the second half of 1899, anti-imperialist editors around the country had reprinted a series of sensational personal letters written by American soldiers to their families, describing atrocities against Filipino soldiers and civilians. By the time of the poem's composition, the issue was a subject of inflamed public debate, exacerbated by the military administration's extreme reluctance to pursue any corrective action. The knowledge and tacit acceptance of American atrocities has been traced all the way up to Elwell S. Otis, the self-proclaimed "Military Governor" of the Philippines (S. Miller 52, 64, 88–89).

17. In a July 1902 letter to his future wife, Harriet Brainard, Moody articulated this complex combination of pride in American idealism, shame over its corruption, and anxiety over its future course: "Poor blundering, grudging, generous land! To free Cuba with one hand, and with the other quietly remove all possible chance for her to live decently—or indeed to live at all. . . . As for the recent disclosures in the Philippines, . . . they are too sickening to talk or think about. Shall we ever be able to hold up our heads again? The little flag you sent me on the Fourth of July seemed striped and stained with that innocent blood. I wonder how we shall wash it out" (*Letters to Harriet* 136–37).

18. Other evocations of Saint-Gaudens's relief include Charles Ives's tone poem *Three Places in New England* (1903–1914), John Berryman's "Boston Common" (1940s), Robert Lowell's "For the Union Dead" (1960), and the 1989 film *Glory*, directed by Edward Zwick.

19. Garth Wilkinson James, William's brother, was an officer in the Massachusetts 54th who was wounded at Fort Wagner. The section of William's dedication speech perhaps most resonant for Moody was his redefinition of true courage away from bravery in battle with an external enemy, toward the struggle against the structural injustices of one's own society, a form of courage that Shaw and his soldiers exemplified: "of five hundred of us who could storm a battery side by side with others, perhaps not one could be found ready all alone to risk his worldly fortunes in resisting an enthroned abuse. The deadliest enemies of nations are not their foreign foes; they always dwell within their borders" (qtd. "Memorable Words" 635).

20. The ode was received as a significant intervention in the Philippine debate, generating nationwide acclaim in anti-imperialist circles. *Atlantic Monthly* editor Bliss Perry felt it was "the finest American political poem in thirty years"; *Nation* editor Oswald Garrison Villard remembered "the sensation it created in newspaper offices around the country"; and Massachusetts Senator George F. Hoar, a leader of the anti-imperialist faction in Congress, cited lines from it in his speeches and writings (M. Brown 107).

21. The textual evidence amassed by Fredson Bowers in the Virginia edition of Crane's works leads him to conclude that almost all these poems were written before Crane went to Cuba in 1898 (*Poems and Literary Remains* 232–33). In his 1966 critical edition *The Poems of Stephen Crane*, however, Joseph Katz places several of them later than Bowers, during the war itself. In the discussion that follows, where it seems important to do so, I will indicate both scholars' dating.

22. Crane reported on the Greco-Turkish War between April 1897 and its armistice in May. However, David Halliburton and others have noted Crane's ability, famously in *The Red Badge of Courage* but also in his verse, to capture the bitter and chaotic experience of battle before he actually witnessed it. Halliburton concludes aptly, "the poet was disillusioned before the correspondent" (301).

23. "The one specter that really haunts the modern ruling class, and that really endangers the world it has created in its image, is the one thing that traditional elites (and, for that matter, traditional masses) have always yearned for: prolonged, solid stability" (Berman 95). In modernity, "stability can only mean entropy, slow death, while our sense of progress and growth is our only way of knowing for sure that we are alive." For Marx, of course, the perpetual development of modernity augurs the bourgeoisie's fall to a revolution generated by "the active and activistic energies that the bourgeoisie itself has set free" (94).

24. Katz dates the poem as late 1898 or early 1899 (223). Many American newspapers, especially the New York dailies pioneering "the journalism that does things" (qtd. Wilkerson 83), which they called "New Journalism" (and we're now inclined to call "Yellow") had lobbied for American intervention in Cuba as early as 1895, aggressively seeking out sensational incidents designed to increase circulation. By then stories and pictures generated by these major dailies were being syndicated nationwide, drastically increasing the impact of their interventionist rhetoric (Wisan 33). In February 1897 a correspondent for the *New York World,* one of Crane's close friends (Crane, *War Dispatches* 274), was arrested by Spanish authorities while attempting to gain access to the rebel forces. The monthlong detainment of Sylvester Scovel, decried from Congress and state legislatures to small-town churches and newspapers, dramatically inflamed American attitudes toward Spain (Wilkerson 10–12). The bitter rivalry between Pulitzer's *World* and the *Morning Journal,* which Hearst had taken over in 1895, drove both papers to escalating interventionist fireworks that garnered phenomenal increases in daily circulation (both topped eight hundred thousand by early 1898, and the *Journal's* morning run spiked to over one million in the days after the *Maine* disaster [Wilkerson 8, 118; Wisan 26]). See Marcus Wilkerson and Joseph Wisan for exhaustive accounts of the intertwining of the Cuban insurrection with the developing ideologies and economics of American newspaper journalism.

25. This critique of the daily newspaper's influence upon its readers' sense of history has been well expressed by Alan Trachtenberg: "Unlike the printed page of a novel, the newspaper page declares itself without mistake as good only for a day, for this reading only: as if today's history of the world has nothing in common with yesterday's or tomorrow's, except the repetition of the typographical form" (125).

26. For many years Dunbar-Nelson worked as a journalist, and all her life she contributed articles of political commentary to periodicals, clearly maintaining a belief in journalism's progressive potential.

27. For other stimulating recent studies of Crane's prose, see Michael Fried, *Realism, Writing, Disfiguration;* Mary Esteve, "A 'Gorgeous Neutrality'"; Christopher P. Wilson, "Stephen Crane and the Police"; and Keith Gandal, *The Virtues of the Vicious.* The most substantial recent work on Crane's verse is the chapter in David Halliburton's *The Color of the Sky* (1989), which does note the protean qualities of Crane's writings but leaves the critical tradition largely intact by identifying his verse as primarily "philosophical"—that is, "Poetry about life in general" (269–70).

The standard Virginia edition of Crane's complete writings pairs his verse with his fragmentary and miscellaneous prose in a volume entitled "Poems and Literary Remains." Though no doubt based on sound organizational exigencies, this arrangement offers ironically appropriate comment on the odd relation of Crane's verse to his canonicity within American letters.

28. This "one" whose kindness exasperates and inhibits the aspiring creator also evokes Crane's minister father, a "loving, unworldly soul" (Hoffman 48) who died before Stephen's eleventh birthday, his kind, admonishing eyes remaining only in family pictures and in the memory of his son, who was thus deprived of a flesh-and-blood object for his rebellion against genteel piety.

29.   Well, then, I hate Thee, unrighteous picture;
          Wicked image, I hate Thee;
          So, strike with Thy vengeance
          The heads of those little men
          Who come blindly.
          It will be a brave thing. (*Black Riders* 13)

30. Christopher Benfey makes a related point in discussing the striking typography of Crane's first volume of verse, *The Black Riders* (Copeland & Day, 1894) which is printed entirely in bold capitals that "suggest scare headlines" (127). However, Benfey undermines the force of this observation when he refers to "In a Lonely Place" as "one of the few poems in *The Black Riders* that address contemporary reality" (127), implying that the dominant mode of Crane's verse is philosophical abstraction.

31. The manuscript has "fetless," presumably a misspelling of "feckless," which most editions have substituted.

32. Linda Davis provides a helpful account of Crane's college years (26–34). It's fair to call baseball the most wholesome of his majors.

33. The difficulty of maintaining clear-cut divisions between experience and information is also illustrated by the practices of very early sports broadcasting, in which a studio announcer with just a schematic telegraphic or telephonic account of the action would invent details that enlivened the game for radio audiences who had no other access to it. In this scenario we can posit at least four categories, including "active participation" (the players), "active spectatorship" (those physically present at the stadium), "passive participation" (the announcer who constructs its events though he was not there), and the "passive spectatorship" of the radio audience (even here, it can be argued that this last group must "re-create" the game imaginatively).

34. Christopher Wilson's painstaking account of the wildly varying newspaper accounts concerning Crane's run-in with the New York Police Department in the "Dora Clark Affair" provides a related demonstration that discourses of mass culture, in the "journalistic carnival" of turn-of-the-century metropolitan newspapers, resist a single "detached, Panoptical vantage point" ("Stephen Crane and the Police" 279).

WORKS CITED

Adams, Henry. *The Life of George Cabot Lodge.* 1911. Delmar, N.Y.: Scholars' Facsimiles and Reprints, 1978.

Adams, James Barton. "The Jingo's Soliloquy." 1898. In Witherbee, *Spanish-American War Songs.* 41–42.

Adams, Oscar Fay. "Personal Tributes to Dr. Holmes." *The Writer* 7 (1894): 162.

Aldrich, Thomas Bailey. "Longfellow." *Atlantic Monthly* 99 (1907): 289.

Andrews, Annulet. "Narcissus the Near-Poet." *Saturday Evening Post* 180 (July 20, 1907): 3–5, 22–23; 180 (July 27, 1907): 15–17, 28; 180 (August 3, 1907): 13–15, 21–23; 180 (August 10, 1907): 16–17, 27–28.

Austin, James C. *Fields of the* Atlantic Monthly: *Letters to an Editor, 1861–1870.* San Marino, Calif.: Huntington Library, 1953.

"S. E. B." "Is the 'Man-Poet' Passing?" *Dial* 26 (1899): 362–63.

Baker, Harry T. "Poetry and the Practical Man." *Forum* 42 (1909): 227–36.

"The Banker-Poet." *Saturday Evening Post* 180 (August 10, 1907): 12.

Banta, Martha. *Taylored Lives: Narrative Productions in the Age of Taylor, Veblen, and Ford.* Chicago: University of Chicago Press, 1993.

Barnard, Rita. *The Great Depression and the Culture of Abundance: Kenneth Fearing, Nathanael West, and Mass Culture in the 1930s.* Cambridge: Cambridge University Press, 1995.

Barnes, Charles Williams. "Fin de Siècle." *Munsey's* 15 (1896): 761.

Barnes, Fred J. "The Girl I Loved 'Way Out in Indiana." 1906.

Barnes, James. "Songs of the Ships of Steel." *McClure's* 11 (1898): 115–19.

Bates, Arlo. "Personal Tributes to Dr. Holmes." *The Writer* 7 (1894): 166–67.

Baudelaire, Charles. *Paris Spleen.* Trans. Louise Varèse. New York: New Directions, 1970.

Baym, Nina. *American Women Writers and the Work of History, 1790–1860.* New Brunswick, N.J.: Rutgers University Press, 1995.

———. *Feminism and American Literary History.* New Brunswick, N.J.: Rutgers University Press, 1992.

Beach, Christopher. *Poetic Culture: Contemporary American Poetry between Community and Institution.* Evanston, Ill.: Northwestern University Press, 1999.

———. *The Politics of Distinction: Whitman and the Discourses of Nineteenth-Century America.* Athens: University of Georgia Press, 1996.

Beatty, Richmond Croom. *James Russell Lowell.* Nashville, Tenn.: Vanderbilt University Press, 1942.

Bell, James B., and Richard I. Abrams. *In Search of Liberty: The Story of the Statue of Liberty and Ellis Island.* Garden City, N.J.: Doubleday, 1984.

Benfey, Christopher. *The Double Life of Stephen Crane.* New York: Knopf, 1992.

Bennett, Paula. "'The Descent of the Angel': Interrogating Domestic Ideology in American Women's Poetry, 1858–1890." *American Literary History* 7 (1995): 591–610.

———. "Introduction." *Palace-Burner: The Selected Poetry of Sarah Piatt.* Urbana: University of Illinois Press, 2001.

———. "Late-Nineteenth-Century American Women's Nature Poetry and the Evolution of the Imagist Poem." *Legacy* 9.2 (1992): 89–103.

———. "Not Just Filler, Not Just Sentimental: Women's Poetry in American Victorian Periodicals, 1860–1900." *Periodical Literature in Nineteenth-Century America.* Ed. Kenneth M. Price and Susan Belasco Smith. Charlottesville: University of Virginia Press, 1995. 202–79.

———. *Poets in the Public Sphere: The Emancipatory Project of American Women's Poetry, 1800–1900.* Princeton, N.J.: Princeton University Press, 2003.

Berke, Nancy. *Women Poets on the Left: Lola Ridge, Genevieve Taggard, Margaret Walker.* Gainesville: University of Florida Press, 2001.

Berman, Marshall. *All That Is Solid Melts into Air: The Experience of Modernity.* 1982. New York: Penguin, 1988.

Bertolini, Vincent J. "Fireside Chastity: The Erotics of Sentimental Bachelorhood in the 1850s." *American Literature* 68 (1996): 707–38.

"The Best Poems in the World." *Saturday Evening Post* 171 (January 7, 1899): 445.

"The Best Ten American Books." *The Critic* 589 (May 27, 1893): 3.

Bigelow, Walter S. "The Poet's Morn." Music by Charles F. Webber. Boston: White/Smith Music Publishing Co., 1893.

Bingham, G. Clifton. "Love's Old Sweet Song." Music by James J. Molloy. New York: Hitchcock, 1884.

Bisland, Elizabeth. *The Life and Letters of Lafcadio Hearn.* Vol. 1. Boston: Houghton Mifflin, 1906.

Blake, William. *Songs of Innocence and Experience.* London: Basil Montagu Pickering, 1866.

Bok, Edward. *The Americanization of Edward Bok.* New York: Scribner's, 1920.

Boutelle, Grace Hodsdon. "A City Window." *Munsey's* 33 (1905): 407.

Bouvé, Thomas Tracy. "The Last Charge." *McClure's* 15 (1900): 416.

Boyesen, Hjalmar Hjorth. "Personal Tributes to Dr. Holmes." *The Writer* 7 (1894): 161–62.

Boynton, H. W. "Current Neglect of Poetry." *Dial* 33 (1902): 385–86.

Braxton, Joanne M. "Introduction: The Poetry of Paul Laurence Dunbar." *The Collected Poetry of Paul Laurence Dunbar.* Ed. Joanne M. Braxton. Charlottesville: University of Virginia Press, 1993. ix–xxxvi.

Briscoe, Frank. "On Midway Plaisance." Chicago: National Music Co., 1893.

Brodhead, Richard H. *Cultures of Letters: Scenes of Reading and Writing in Nineteenth-Century America.* Chicago: University of Chicago Press, 1993.

————. "Literature and Culture." *Columbia Literary History of the United States*. Ed. Emory Elliott. New York: Columbia University Press, 1988. 467–81.

Brooks, Elbridge S. "Personal Tributes to Dr. Holmes." *The Writer* 7 (1894): 164.

Brooks, Francis. *Margins: Collected Poems*. Chicago: Searle & Gorton, 1896.

————. *Poems*. Ed. Wallace Rice. Chicago: R. R. Donnelley, 1898.

Brooks, Michael W. *Subway City: Riding the Trains, Reading New York*. New Brunswick, N.J.: Rutgers University Press, 1997.

Brooks, Noah. "Personal Tributes to Dr. Holmes." *The Writer* 7 (1894): 163.

Brooks, Van Wyck. *New England: Indian Summer, 1865–1915*. Cleveland: World Publishing Co., 1946.

Brooks, W. K. "Poetry or Science?" *Science* n.s. 2 (1895): 437.

Brown, Bill. *The Material Unconscious: American Amusement, Stephen Crane, and the Economies of Play*. Cambridge, Mass.: Harvard University Press, 1997.

Brown, Charles H. *William Cullen Bryant*. New York: Charles Scribner's Sons, 1971.

Brown, Maurice F. *Estranging Dawn: The Life and Works of William Vaughn Moody*. Carbondale: Southern Illinois University Press, 1973.

Brownlee, David B. *Building the City Beautiful: The Benjamin Franklin Parkway and the Philadelphia Museum of Art*. Philadelphia: Philadelphia Museum of Art, 1989.

Brownlee, James Henry, ed. *War-Time Echoes: Patriotic Poems, Heroic and Pathetic, Humorous and Dialectic, of the Spanish-American War*. Akron, Ohio: Werner [1898].

Bryant, William Cullen. *Poetical Works*. Ed. Parke Godwin. New York: D. Appleton, 1883.

————. *Prose Writings*. Ed. Parke Godwin. Vol. 1. New York: D. Appleton, 1901.

Buckham, James. "Some Needs of the Versifiers." *The Writer* 2 (1888): 114–15.

Buell, Lawrence. *New England Literary Culture from Revolution through Renaissance*. New York: Cambridge University Press, 1986.

Burgess, Gelett. *The Rubaiyat of Omar Cayenne*. New York: Frederick Stokes, 1904.

Burton, Richard E. "Personal Tributes to Dr. Holmes." *The Writer* 7 (1894): 166.

————. "Slovenliness in Verse-Making." *The Writer* 2 (1888): 129–31.

"H. A. C." "American Poetry of the Past Year." *Poet-Lore* 13 (1901): 123–40.

Cameron, Kenneth Walter, ed. *Longfellow among His Contemporaries: A Harvest of Estimates, Insights, and Anecdotes from the Victorian Literary World*. Hartford, Conn.: Transcendental Books,1978.

Cameron, Susan E. "The Passing of Poetry: A Reply to Professor Leacock." *Canadian Magazine* 27 (1906): 505–07.

Carman, Bliss, and Richard Hovey. *More Songs from Vagabondia*. Boston: Copeland & Day, 1896.

Carryl, Guy Wetmore. "The Babes in the Wood." *Saturday Evening Post* 173 (January 5, 1901): 9.

————. "The Bottled Giant." *Saturday Evening Post* 174 (July 13, 1901): 7.

————. *The Garden of Years and Other Poems*. New York: G. P. Putnam's Sons, 1904.

————. "Jack and the Beanstalk." *Saturday Evening Post* 174 (August 3, 1901): 5.

————. "Little Red Riding Hood." *Saturday Evening Post* 173 (April 13, 1901): 3.

————. "Pearls and Toads." *Saturday Evening Post* 174 (November 9, 1901): 11.

Cary, Richard. *Early Reception of Edwin Arlington Robinson: The First Twenty Years*. Waterville, Maine: Colby College Press, 1974.

Casper, Scott E. "Defining the National Pantheon: The Making of Houghton Mifflin's Biographical Series, 1880–1900." *Reading Books: Essays on the Material Text and*

Literature in America. Ed. Michele Moylan and Lane Stiles. Amherst: University of Massachusetts Press, 1996. 179–222.

Channing, R. M. "The Negro Soldier." Compiled by the California Club. *War Poems, 1898.* San Francisco: Murdock Press, 1898. 105–06.

Charvat, William. *The Profession of Authorship in America, 1800–1870.* Ed. Matthew J. Bruccoli. Columbus: Ohio State University Press, 1968.

Clark, Clifford Edward, Jr. *The American Family Home, 1800–1960.* Chapel Hill: University of North Carolina Press, 1986.

Clark, Suzanne. *Sentimental Modernism: Women Writers and the Revolution of the Word.* Bloomington: University of Indiana Press, 1991.

Clark, T. J. *Farewell to an Idea: Episodes from a History of Modernism.* New Haven, Conn.: Yale University Press, 1999.

Clarke, Graham, ed. *Edgar Allan Poe: Critical Assessments.* Mountfield, East Sussex: Helm Information, 1991.

———. *Walt Whitman: Critical Assessments.* Robertsbridge, East Sussex: Helm Information, n.d.

Clarke, Walter Irving. *The Writer* 2 (1888): 32.

Clemens, Samuel. "Dinner Speech ('The Whittier Birthday Dinner Speech')." *Mark Twain Speaking.* Ed. Paul Fatout. Iowa City: University of Iowa Press, 1976. 110–15.

Coates, Henry T., ed. *The Fireside Encyclopaedia of Poetry.* Philadelphia: Porter & Coates, 1878.

Cohn, Jan. *Creating America: George Horace Lorimer and the* Saturday Evening Post. Pittsburgh: University of Pittsburgh Press, 1989.

"Confessions of an American Publisher." *Boston Transcript. The Writer* 14 (1901): 57–58.

Cook, Clarence. *The House Beautiful.* New York: Scribner's, 1881.

Cooke, Edmund Vance. *Impertinent Poems.* 1903. New York: Dodge, 1907.

———. "In Nineteen Hundred and Now." Saturday Evening Post 179 (January 5, 1907): 23.

Coolbrith, Ina. *Songs from the Golden Gate.* Boston: Houghton Mifflin, 1895.

Cott, Nancy F. *The Bonds of Womanhood: "Women's Sphere" in New England, 1780–1835.* New Haven, Conn.: Yale University Press, 1977.

Cowan, Ruth Schwartz. *More Work for Mother: The Ironies of Household Technology from the Open Hearth to the Microwave.* New York: Basic Books, 1983.

———. *A Social History of American Technology.* New York: Oxford University Press, 1997.

Crane, Stephen. *The Black Riders and Other Lines.* Boston: Copeland & Day, 1896.

———. "The Blue Battalions." 1898. In Witherbee, *Spanish-American War Songs.* 182.

———. *The Correspondence of Stephen Crane.* Ed. Stanley Wertheim and Paul Sorrentino. Vol. 1. New York: Columbia University Press, 1988.

———. *Poems and Literary Remains.* Ed. Fredson Bowers. Charlottesville: University of Virginia Press, 1975. Vol. 10 of *The University of Virginia Edition of the Works of Stephen Crane.* Ed. Fredson Bowers. 10 vols., 1969–1976.

———. *The Poems of Stephen Crane.* Ed. Joseph Katz. New York: Cooper Square Publishers, 1966.

———. *The War Dispatches of Stephen Crane.* Ed. R. W. Stallman and E. R. Hagemann. New York: New York University Press, 1964.

————. *War Is Kind*. New York: Frederick Stokes, 1899.

"Cupid Out of Practice." *Munsey's* 11 (1894): 541.

Cutting, Mary Stewart. "On the Field." *McClure's* 13 (1899): 219.

Dana, Charles. "Review." *New York Daily Tribune*, July 23, 1855. In G. Clarke, *Walt Whitman: Critical Assessments*. Vol. 2. 3–4.

Davidson, Cathy N. "Preface: No More Separate Spheres!" *American Literature* 70 (1998): 443–63.

Davis, Benny. "You Can Have Ev'ry Light on Broadway (Give Me That One Little Light at Home)." Music by Seymour Simons. New York: Irving Berlin Inc., 1922.

Davis, Fred. *Yearning for Yesterday: A Sociology of Nostalgia*. New York: Free Press, 1979.

Davis, Linda H. *Badge of Courage: The Life of Stephen Crane*. New York: Houghton Mifflin, 1998.

De Cleyre, Voltairine. *Selected Works of Voltairine de Cleyre*. Ed. Alexander Berkman. New York: Mother Earth Publishing Association, 1914.

DeJong, Mary G. "Her Fair Fame: The Reputation of Frances Sargent Osgood, Woman Poet." *Studies in the American Renaissance, 1987*. Ed. Joel Myerson. Charlottesville: University of Virginia Press, 1987. 265–83.

Diepeveen, Leonard. "The Difficult Pleasures of Modernism." Modernist Studies Association Conference. Philadelphia, Penn. October 11, 2000.

Dillon, Will. "Take Me to the Cabaret." New York: Leo Feist, Inc., 1912.

Dobson, Joanne. "Reclaiming Sentimental Literature." *American Literature* 69 (1997): 263–88.

————. "Sex, Wit, and Sentiment: Frances Osgood and the Poetry of Love." *American Literature* 65 (1993): 631–50.

Dodd, Lee Wilson. "Frail Singers of Today." *Century* 70 (1905): 746.

Douglas, Ann. *The Feminization of American Culture*. New York: Knopf, 1977.

Douglas, Archibald. "To My Cigar." *Munsey's* 16 (1896): 152.

Downes, William Howe. "The Bartholdi Colossus." *Bay State Monthly* 2 (1884): 153–59.

Dreiser, Theodore. "Birth and Growth of a Popular Song." *Selected Magazine Articles of Theodore Dreiser: Life and Art in the American 1890s*. Ed. Yoshinobu Hakutani. Vol. 2. Rutherford, N.J.: Fairleigh Dickinson University Press, 1985. 19–22.

————. "The Home of William Cullen Bryant." In *Selected Magazine Articles of Theodore Dreiser*. Vol. 1. 92–99.

————. "Whence the Song." In *Selected Magazine Articles of Theodore Dreiser*. Vol. 2. 50–61.

Dresser, Paul. "On the Banks of the Wabash, Far Away." New York: Hawley, Haviland, 1897.

Duberman, Martin. *James Russell Lowell*. Boston: Houghton Mifflin, 1966.

Duffey, Bernard. *Poetry in America: Expression and Its Values in the Times of Bryant, Whitman, and Pound*. Durham, N.C.: Duke University Press, 1978.

Dunbar, Paul Laurence. *The Complete Poems of Paul Laurence Dunbar*. New York: Dodd, Mead and Company, 1913.

————. *Lyrics of Sunshine and Shadow*. New York: Dodd, Mead, 1905.

————. "'W'en the Colo'ed Ban' Comes Ma'chin' Down de Street.'" *Saturday Evening Post* 173 (February 16, 1901): 9.

Dunbar-Nelson, Alice. *The Works of Alice Dunbar-Nelson*. Ed. Gloria T. Hull. Vol. 1. New York: Oxford University Press, 1988.

DuPlessis, Rachel Blau. *Genders, Races, and Religious Cultures in Modern American Poetry, 1908–1934.* Cambridge: Cambridge University Press, 2001.

Duyckinck, Evert. Review in the *Literary World.* 1850. In G. Clarke, *Edgar Allan Poe: Critical Assessments.* Vol. 2. 252–54.

Eggleston, Edward. "Personal Tributes to Dr. Holmes." *The Writer* 7 (1894): 161.

Eliot, T. S. *Prufrock and Other Observations.* London: Egoist House, 1917.

———. "Tradition and the Individual Talent." *The Sacred Wood: Essays on Poetry and Criticism.* 1920. London: Methuen, 1950. 47–59.

Emerson, Ralph W. "The American Scholar." *Complete Works.* Boston: Houghton Mifflin, 1895. Vol. 1. 81–116.

———. *Complete Poetical Works.* Boston: Houghton Mifflin, 1888.

———. "Poetry and Imagination." *Letters and Social Aims.* Boston: James R. Osgood, 1876. 1–67.

Esteve, Mary. "A 'Gorgeous Neutrality': Stephen Crane's Documentary Anaesthetics." *ELH* 62 (1995): 663–89.

"Evangeline." 1865. In K. Cameron, *Longfellow among His Contemporaries.* 77–78.

Farrell, Joseph C. "On a Good Old Trolley Ride." Music by Pat Rooney. New York: Howley Dresser, 1904.

Fatout, Paul, ed. *Mark Twain Speaking.* Iowa City: University of Iowa Press, 1976.

Fawcett, Edgar. "Personal Tributes to Dr. Holmes." *The Writer* 7 (1894): 166.

Ferlazzo, Paul J. "Edwin Markham." *Encyclopedia of American Poetry: The Nineteenth Century.* Ed. Eric L. Haralson. Chicago: Fitzroy Dearborn, 1998. 281–83.

"Filosofy of Beans." *Saturday Evening Post* 180 (September 21, 1907): 31.

Finck, Henry T. "What Gives a Popular Song Its Vogue?" *Lippincott's* 65 (1900): 298–305.

Firkins, Oscar W. "Poetry and Prose in Life and Art." *Poet Lore* 15 (1904): 77–87.

Fordham, Mary Weston. *Magnolia Leaves.* Charleston, S.C.: Walker, Evans & Cogswell, 1897.

Fried, Michael. *Realism, Writing, Disfiguration: On Thomas Eakins and Stephen Crane.* Chicago: University of Chicago Press, 1987.

Frost, Lawrence A. *General Custer's Libbie.* Seattle: Superior Publishing Co., 1976.

Fuller [Ossoli], Margaret. "American Literature." *Art, Literature, and the Drama.* Ed. Arthur B. Fuller. Boston: Roberts Brothers, 1874. 298–335.

Gandal, Keith. *The Virtues of the Vicious: Jacob Riis, Stephen Crane, and the Spectacle of the Slum.* New York: Oxford University Press, 1997.

Garland, Hamlin. "Personal Tributes to Dr. Holmes." *The Writer* 7 (1894): 167.

———. *The Trail of the Goldseekers: A Record of Travel in Prose and Verse.* New York: Macmillan, 1899.

———. "The Trail to the Golden North." *McClure's* 12 (1899): 505–07; 13 (1899): 65–68.

Gartner, Matthew. "Becoming Longfellow: Work, Manhood, and Poetry." *American Literature* 72 (2000): 59–86.

Gates, Henry Louis. *The Signifying Monkey: A Theory of Afro-American Literary Criticism.* New York: Oxford University Press, 1988.

"A Gem from Shakspere." *Munsey's* 11 (1894): 94.

Gilder, Richard Watson. *Letters of Richard Watson Gilder.* Ed. Rosamond Gilder. Boston: Houghton Mifflin, 1916.

———. "A New Poet." *Atlantic Monthly* 95 (1905): 748.

———. "On the Reading of Poetry." *Century* 59 (1900): 960–61.

———. "A Plea for the Poets." *Century* 52 (1896): 316–17.

———. "The 'White City.'" *Poems of American History*. Ed. Burton E. Stevenson. Boston: Houghton Mifflin, 1905. 602.

Gilfillan, George. "Henry Wadsworth Longfellow." 1852. In K. Cameron, *Longfellow among His Contemporaries*. 43–46.

Gilmore, Michael T. *American Romanticism and the Marketplace*. Chicago: University of Chicago Press, 1985.

Gioia, Dana. "Longfellow in the Aftermath of Modernism." *The Columbia History of American Poetry*. Ed. Jay Parini. New York: Columbia University Press, 1993. 64–96.

Glasgow, Ellen. *The Freeman and Other Poems*. New York: Doubleday, Page, 1902.

———. *The Woman Within*. New York: Harcourt, Brace, 1954.

Godfrey, Edward S. "Custer's Last Battle." *Century* 43 (1892): 358–84.

Golding, Alan C. *From Outlaw to Classic: Canons in American Poetry*. Madison: University of Wisconsin Press, 1995.

Goodwin, Charles J. "The Poet in an Age of Science." *The New World* 4 (1895): 121–37.

Gray, Janet, ed. *She Wields a Pen: American Women Poets of the Nineteenth Century*. Iowa City: Iowa University Press, 1997.

"Great Poetry." *The Academy*. *The Writer* 18 (1906): 60–62.

Green, Harvey. *The Light of the Home: An Intimate View of the Lives of Women in Victorian America*. New York: Pantheon, 1983.

Greene, Theodore P. *America's Heroes: The Changing Models of Success in American Magazines*. New York: Oxford University Press, 1970.

Greenslet, Ferris. "A Propaganda for Poetry." *Poet-Lore* 11 (1899): 41–54.

———. "Significant Poetry." *Atlantic Monthly* 96 (1905): 414–23.

Griffin, M. Lane. "A Word to Our Lesser Poets." *The Writer* 11 (1898): 50–51.

Griswold, Rufus W. "Frances Sargent Osgood." *The Memorial Written by the Friends of the Late Mrs. Osgood*. Ed. Mary E. Hewitt. New York: Putnam, 1851. 13–30.

———, ed. *The Poets and Poetry of America*. 1842. 9th ed. Philadelphia: Carey & Hart, 1848.

———. Review of *Leaves of Grass* by Walt Whitman. New York *Criterion*, November 10, 1855. In G. Clarke, *Walt Whitman: Critical Assessments*. Vol. 2. 8–10.

Gummere, Francis B. "The Old Case of Poetry in a New Court." *Atlantic* 89 (1902): 824–28.

Hale, Susan Buell. "The Alamo–March 6, 1836." *McClure's* 14 (1900): 469–71.

Hall, G. Stanley. *Adolescence: Its Psychology and Its Relations to Physiology, Anthropology, Sociology, Sex, Crime, Religion, and Education*. New York: D. Appleton, 1904.

Halliburton, David. *The Color of the Sky: A Study of Stephen Crane*. Cambridge: Cambridge University Press, 1989.

Halpern, Martin. *William Vaughn Moody*. New York: Twayne, 1964.

Haralson, Eric L. "Mars in Petticoats: Longfellow and Sentimental Masculinity." *Nineteenth-Century Literature* 51 (1996): 327–55.

Harper, J. Henry. *The House of Harper: A Century of Publishing in Franklin Square*. New York: Harper & Bros., 1912.

"Harriman's Favorite Poet." *Saturday Evening Post* 180 (August 10, 1907): 12.

Harrington, Joseph. *Poetry and the Public: The Social Form of Modern U.S. Poetics*. Middletown, Conn.: Wesleyan University Press, 2002.

———. "Why American Poetry is Not American Literature." *American Literary History* 8 (1996): 496–515.

Harris, Charles K. "After the Ball." Milwaukee: Charles K. Harris, 1892.

———. "Hello Central, Give Me Heaven." Milwaukee: Charles K. Harris, 1901.

Harris, Neil. "Memory and the White City." *Grand Illusions: Chicago's World's Fair of 1893.* Chicago: Chicago Historical Society, 1993. 1–40.

Hart, Loring E. "The Beginnings of Longfellow's Fame." *New England Quarterly* 36 (1963): 63–76.

Henry, David D. *William Vaughn Moody: A Study.* Boston: Bruce Humphries, 1934.

"Henry Wadsworth Longfellow." 1843. In K. Cameron, *Longfellow among His Contemporaries.* 6–9.

Herringshaw, Thomas W., ed. *Local and National Poets of America.* Chicago: American Publishers' Association, 1890.

Hewitt, Mary E. *Poems: Sacred, Passionate, and Legendary.* New York: Lamport, Blakeman & Law, 1854.

Hilkey, Judy. *Character Is Capital: Success Manuals and Manhood in Gilded Age America.* Chapel Hill: University of North Carolina Press, 1997.

Hills, William H. "The Annual Poetry Product." *The Writer* 6 (1892): 221–22.

———. *The Writer* 12 (1899): 68.

Hinsley, Curtis M. "The World as Marketplace: Commodification of the Exotic at the World's Columbian Exposition, Chicago, 1893." *Exhibiting Cultures: The Poetics and Politics of Museum Display.* Ed. Ivan Karp and Steven D. Lavine. Washington, D.C.: Smithsonian Institution, 1991. 344–65.

Hoffman, Daniel G. *The Poetry of Stephen Crane.* New York: Columbia University Press, 1956.

Holland, Josiah Gilbert. "Character, and What Comes Of It." *Scribner's* 21 (1881): 469–70.

———. "The Old Cabinet." *Scribner's* 13 (1877): 867.

Holmes, Oliver Wendell. *Complete Poetical Works.* Boston: Houghton Mifflin, 1895.

"Holmes Redivivus." *Munsey's* 30 (1903): 153.

Hood, C. N. "Rejected Manuscript." *The Writer* 2 (1888): 51–52.

Hooker, Brian. "Songs and Song-Writing." *Forum* 39 (1907): 417–29.

Hornbrooke, Francis B. "What Should Be the Poet's Attitude toward His Critics." *Poet-Lore* 5 (1893): 135–43.

Hovey, Richard. *Along the Trail: A Book of Lyrics.* Boston: Small & Maynard, 1898.

———. *To the End of the Trail.* Ed. Mrs. Richard Hovey. New York: Duffield, 1908.

Howe, M. A. DeWolfe. *The Atlantic Monthly and Its Makers.* Boston: Atlantic Monthly Press, 1919.

Howells, William Dean. "The Editor's Relations with the Young Contributor." *Literature and Life.* New York: Harper & Bros., 1902. 63–77.

———. "Has Poetry Lost Its Hold on Us?" *Harper's* 104 (March 1902): 671–74.

———. "The New Poetry." *North American Review* 168 (1899): 581–92.

———. Review of *The Black Riders* by Stephen Crane. In Weatherford 70–72.

Huyssen, Andreas. *After the Great Divide: Modernism, Mass Culture, Postmodernism.* Bloomington: Indiana University Press, 1986.

Ingram, John H. *The True Chatterton: A New Study from Original Documents.* London: T. Fisher Unwin, 1910.

"Is Genius Neglected by the Magazines?" *Current Literature* 42 (1907): 165–66.

"Is Poetry Read?" *Harper's* 115 (June 1907): 147–50.

"Is Poetry Unpopular?" *Living Age* 240 (1904): 820–23.

Jackson, Richard. "Angels' Visits and Other Vocal Gems of Victorian America." *Angels' Visits and Other Vocal Gems of Victorian America.* New World Records, 1977.

Jameson, Fredric. "Reification and Utopia in Mass Culture." *Signatures of the Visible.* New York: Routledge, 1992. 9–34.

Jarrold, Ernest. "The Makers of Our Popular Songs." *Munsey's* 13 (1895): 289–95.

Jenks, Tudor. "Immortality." *Munsey's* 22 (1899): 360.

———. "King and Minstrel." *Munsey's* 22 (1899): 72.

Jerome, William. "Hold Fast!" Music by Jean Schwartz. New York: Shapiro, Bernstein, and Von Tilzer, 1901.

John, Arthur. *The Best Years of the Century: Richard Watson Gilder,* Scribner's Monthly, *and the* Century Magazine, 1870–1909. Urbana: University of Illinois Press, 1981.

Johnson, Robert Underwood. *Remembered Yesterdays.* Boston: Little, Brown, 1923.

Justus, James H. "The Fireside Poets: Hearthside Values and the Language of Care." *Nineteenth-Century American Poetry.* Ed. A. Robert Lee. London: Vision/Barnes & Noble, 1985. 146–65.

Kalaidjian, Walter. *American Culture between the Wars: Revisionary Modernism and Postmodern Critique.* New York: Columbia University Press, 1993.

Kaplan, Amy. "Manifest Domesticity." *American Literature* 70 (1998): 581–606.

Kelley, Florence Finch. "Magazine Editors and the Poets." *The Writer* 18 (1906): 139–40.

Kemper, S. H. "The Love of the Day's Work." *McClure's* 21 (1903): 290.

Kerber, Linda K. "Separate Spheres, Female Worlds, Woman's Place: The Rhetoric of Women's History." *Journal of American History* 75 (1988): 9–39.

Kett, Joseph F. *Rites of Passage: Adolescence in America, 1790 to the Present.* New York: Basic Books, 1977.

Kindilien, Carlin T. *American Poetry in the Eighteen Nineties: A Study of American Verse, 1890–1899.* Providence, R.I.: Brown University Press, 1956.

King, Charles. "West Point As It Was and Is." *Saturday Evening Post* 173 (February 16, 1901): 8.

Knowles, Fred Lawrence. "Whittier's Advice to a Boy." *The Writer* 2 (1888): 247.

Knowles, Frederic Lawrence, ed. *The Golden Treasury of American Songs and Lyrics.* Boston: L. C. Page & Company, 1901.

Kramer, Aaron. *The Prophetic Tradition in American Poetry, 1835–1900.* Rutherford, N.J.: Fairleigh Dickinson University Press, 1968.

"The Lack of Poets." *The Writer* 13 (1900): 42.

Lang, Andrew. "The Poets' Trade Union." *Independent* 60 (1906): 1144–45.

Larkin, Jack. *The Reshaping of Everyday Life, 1790–1840.* New York: Harper & Row, 1988.

Laska, Edward. "Come Take a Ride Underground." Music by Thomas W. Kelley. New York: Shapiro & Remick, 1904.

Lazarus, Emma. *Poems of Emma Lazarus.* Vol. 1. Boston: Houghton Mifflin, 1889.

Leacock, Stephen. "The Passing of Poetry." *Canadian Magazine* 27 (1906): 71–73.

Leary, Lewis. *John Greenleaf Whittier.* New York: Twayne, 1961.

Lee, Gerald Stanley. *The Lost Art of Reading.* New York: G. P. Putnam's Sons, 1902.

Lentricchia, Frank. *Modernist Quartet.* Cambridge, UK: Cambridge University Press, 1994.

Levy, Lester S. *Give Me Yesterday: American History in Song, 1890–1920.* Norman: University of Oklahoma Press, 1975.

Liberty Poems Inspired by the Crisis of 1898–1900. Boston: James H. West Co., 1900.

Lighton, William R. "A Man-Song." *McClure's* 14 (1900): 580.

Linneman, William R. *Richard Hovey.* New York: Twayne, 1976.

Lodge, George Cabot. *Poems and Dramas of George Cabot Lodge.* Boston: Houghton Mifflin, 1911. 2 vols.

Longfellow, Henry Wadsworth. *Complete Poetical Works in Six Volumes.* Ed. Horace E. Scudder. Boston: Houghton Mifflin, 1886.

———. "Defence of Poetry." *North American Review* 34 (1832): 57–78.

———. *Kavanagh: A Tale.* 1849. Ed. Jean Downey. The Masterworks of Literature Series. New Haven, Conn.: College & University Press Services, 1965.

———. *Outre-Mer and Driftwood.* Boston: Houghton Mifflin, 1886.

———. *The Song of Hiawatha.* Boston: Ticknor & Fields, 1856.

"Longfellow's 'Song of Hiawatha.'" 1855. In K. Cameron, *Longfellow among His Contemporaries.* 52–57.

Loomis, Charles Battell. "Explanatory Lines to a Hen." *Saturday Evening Post* 174 (August 24, 1901): 7.

Lovett, Robert Morss. *All Our Years: The Autobiography of Robert Morss Lovett.* New York: Viking, 1948.

Lowell, Amy. *A Critical Fable.* Boston: Houghton Mifflin, 1922.

Lowell, James Russell. *A Fable for Critics.* 1848. Boston: Houghton Mifflin, 1891.

———. "Letter Extracts." In G. Clarke, *Walt Whitman: Critical Assessments.* Vol. 2. 7.

———. *Poetical Works of James Russell Lowell.* Boston: Houghton Mifflin, 1978.

———. Review of *Kavanagh: A Tale* by Henry Wadsworth Longfellow. *North American Review* 69 (1849): 196–215.

Lowell, Robert. "For the Union Dead." *For the Union Dead.* New York: Farrar Straus, 1964. 70–72.

"Lowell's Poems." *North American Review* 58 (1844): 283–99.

Lutz, Tom. *American Nervousness, 1903.* Ithaca, N.Y.: Cornell University Press, 1991.

MacDonald, Torquil. "Pan Is Not Dead." *Atlantic* 97 (1906): 509.

Markham, Edwin. "Dreyfus." *McClure's* 13 (1899): 387–88.

———. "The Man with the Hoe." *McClure's* 13 (1899): 15–16.

———. "The Song of the Muse of Labor." *McClure's* 14 (1899): 123.

Martin, Jay. *Harvests of Change: American Literature, 1865–1914.* Englewood Cliffs, N.J.: Prentice-Hall, 1967.

Martin, Ronald. *American Literature and the Universe of Force.* Durham, N.C.: Duke University Press, 1981.

Marx, Leo. *The Machine in the Garden: Technology and the Pastoral Ideal in America.* New York: Oxford University Press, 1964.

Massa, Ann. "'The Columbian Ode' and *Poetry, A Magazine of Verse:* Harriet Monroe's Entrepreneurial Triumphs." *Journal of American Studies* 20 (1986): 51–69.

Masson, David. *Chatterton: A Biography.* 1856. London: Hodder & Stoughton, 1899.

Masters, Edgar Lee. "Apollo at the Plow." *Munsey's* 12 (1894): 158.

———. *A Book of Verses.* Chicago: Way & Williams, 1898.

———. *Spoon River Anthology.* 1915. New York: Macmillan, 1944.

Matsuda, Matt K. *The Memory of the Modern.* New York: Oxford University Press, 1996.

May, Caroline, ed. *The American Female Poets.* Philadelphia: Lindsay & Blakiston, 1848.

McClure, S. S. *My Autobiography.* New York: Frederick Stokes, 1914.

———. "The Third Anniversary of the Founding of *McClure's* Magazine." *McClure's* 7 (1896): 97.

McCulloch, Hugh. *The Quest of Heracles and Other Poems.* Cambridge, Mass.: Stone & Kimball, 1894.

———. *Written in Florence: The Last Verses of Hugh McCulloch.* London: J. M. Dent, 1902.

McCullough, Joseph B. "Hamlin Garland." *Encyclopedia of American Poetry: The Nineteenth Century.* Ed. Eric L. Haralson. Chicago: Fitzroy Dearborn, 1998. 169–71.

McGann, Jerome J. *The Beauty of Inflections: Literary Investigations in Historical Method and Theory.* New York: Oxford University Press, 1985.

———. *Black Riders: The Visible Language of Modernism.* Princeton, N.J.: Princeton University Press, 1993.

McKible, Adam. *The Space and Place of Modernism: The Russian Revolution, Little Magazines, and New York.* New York: Routledge, 2002.

McLean, Albert F. *William Cullen Bryant.* New York: Twayne, 1964.

McMartin, Gaines. "Patterns of Enclosure: Unity in the Poems of William Cullen Bryant." *William Cullen Bryant and His America.* Ed. Stanley Brodwin and Michael D'Innocenzo. New York: AMS Press, 1983. 97–111.

"Memorable Words." *Century* 54 (1897): 634–36.

Meredith, George. *Poetical Works.* New York: Charles Scribner's Sons, 1912.

Meyer, Bruce. "Richard Hovey." *Encyclopedia of American Poetry: The Nineteenth Century.* Ed. Eric L. Haralson. Chicago: Fitzroy Dearborn, 1998. 217–19.

Meyerstein, E. H. W. *A Life of Thomas Chatterton.* New York: Charles Scribner's Sons, 1930.

Miller, Stuart Creighton. *"Benevolent Assimilation": The American Conquest of the Philippines, 1899–1903.* New Haven, Conn.: Yale University Press, 1982.

Monroe, Harriet. *The Passing Show: Five Modern Plays in Verse.* Boston: Houghton, Mifflin, 1903.

———. "The Poet's Bread and Butter." *Poetry* 4 (1914): 197–98.

———. *A Poet's Life: Seventy Years in a Changing World.* New York: Macmillan, 1938.

———. *Valeria and Other Poems.* Chicago: A. C. McClurg, 1892.

Moody, William Vaughn. *Letters to Harriet.* Ed. Percy MacKaye. Boston: Houghton Mifflin, 1935.

———. "An Ode in Time of Hesitation." *Atlantic Monthly* 85 (1900): 593–98.

———. "On a Soldier Fallen in the Philippines." *Atlantic Monthly* 87 (1901): 288.

———. *Poems.* Boston: Houghton Mifflin, 1901.

Moore, Charles Leonard. "The Future of Poetry." *Forum* 14 (1893): 768–77.

———. "In Regard to Poetry." *Dial* 24 (1898): 217–18.

Morris, George Perry. "Wanted—Poetry, Not Verse." *The Writer* 18 (1906): 195–96.

Morris, Joan. Introduction. *After the Ball.* 1974. Elektra/Nonesuch Records, 1987.

Moses, L. G. "Indians on the Midway: Wild West Shows and the Indian Bureau at World's Fairs, 1893–1904." *South Dakota History* 21 (1991): 205–29.

Mott, Frank Luther. *A History of American Magazines, 1741–1850.* Cambridge: Harvard University Press, 1938.

Munkittrick, R. K. "Never Despair." *Century* 44 (1892): 800.

———. "The Present Style." *Century* 41 (1890): 158.

Munsey, Frank. "Impressions by the Way." *Munsey's* 30 (1903): 151–52.

———. "Impressions by the Way." *Munsey's* 33 (1905): 187–88.

———. "The Publisher's Desk." *Munsey's* 11 (1894): 111–12.

Nasaw, David. *Going Out: The Rise and Fall of Public Amusements.* New York: Basic Books, 1993.

"The Need of Poets." *Outlook* 86 (1907): 53–54.

Nelson, Cary. *Repression and Recovery: Modern American Poetry and the Politics of Cultural Memory, 1910–1945.* Madison: University of Wisconsin Press, 1989.

———. *Revolutionary Memory: Recovering the Poetry of the American Left.* New York: Routledge, 2001.

New Indexed Miniature Guide Map of the World's Columbian Exposition at Chicago, 1893. New York: Rand-McNally, 1893.

Newbolt, Henry. "Admiral Death." *McClure's* 11 (1898): 296.

Newcomb, John Timberman. "The Footprint of the Twentieth Century: American Skyscrapers and Modernist Poems." *Modernism/Modernity* 10 (2003): 97–125.

———. "*Poetry*'s Opening Door: Harriet Monroe and American Modernism." *Little Magazines and Modernism.* Eds. Suzanne Churchill and Adam McKible. Forthcoming.

Norton, Charles Eliot. "Review." *Putnam's Monthly,* September 1855. In G. Clarke, *Walt Whitman: Critical Assessments.* Vol. 2. 5–6.

Norworth, Jack. "Take Me Out to the Ball Game." Music by Harry von Tilzer. *Hurrah for Our National Game: Jewels from the Baseball Diamond, 1858–1913.* Newport Classic CD, 1994.

"Of Editors and Their Critics." *North American Review* 183 (1906): 696–98.

Ohmann, Richard. "History and Literary History: The Case of Mass Culture." *Modernity and Mass Culture.* Ed. James Naremore and Patrick Brantlinger. Bloomington: Indiana University Press, 1991. 24–41.

Okker, Patricia J. *Our Sister Editors: Sarah J. Hale and the Tradition of Nineteenth-Century American Women Editors.* Athens: University of Georgia Press, 1995.

Ollivant, Alfred. "Death in Battle." *McClure's* 15 (1900): 96.

Orvell, Miles. *The Real Thing: Imitation and Authenticity in American Culture, 1880–1940.* Chapel Hill: University of North Carolina Press, 1989.

Ostriker, Alicia Suskin. *Stealing the Language: The Emergence of Women's Poetry in America.* London: The Women's Press, 1986.

"Our 'Forty Immortals.'" *The Critic* 15 (April 12, 1884): 169.

Park, You-Me, and Gayle Wald. "Native Daughters in the Promised Land: Gender, Race, and the Question of Separate Spheres." *American Literature* 70 (1998): 607–33.

Pattee, Fred Lewis. *The New American Literature, 1890–1930.* New York: Century, 1930.

Payne, William Morton. "Recent Poetry." *Dial* 22 (1897): 92.

Peabody, Josephine Preston. *Fortune and Men's Eyes.* 1900. Boston: Houghton Mifflin, 1911.

———. "Modern Life and Modern Poetry." *Poet-Lore* 14 (1902): 56–69.

———. *The Wayfarers.* Boston: Copeland & Day, 1898.

Pease, Donald E. "New Americanists: Revisionist Interventions into the Canon." *Revisionary Interventions into the Americanist Canon.* Ed. Donald E. Pease. Durham, N.C.: Duke University Press, 1994. 1–37.

Peck, Harry Thurston. "The Migration of Popular Songs." *The Bookman* 2 (1895): 97–103.

Petrey, Sandy. "The Language of Realism, the Language of False Consciousness: A Reading of *Sister Carrie*." *Novel* 10 (1977): 101–13.

"Philister." "The Passing of the Man-Poet." *Dial* 26 (1899): 329.

Poe, Edgar Allan. *Poems*. Ed. E. C. Stedman and George E. Woodberry. New York: Scribner's, 1895.

"Poetry in General and in Particular." Review of *The Nature and Elements of Poetry* by E. C. Stedman. *Atlantic Monthly* 73 (1904), 702–04.

"A Poets' Pantheon." *Munsey's* 21 (1899): 472–73.

Poirier, Richard. *A World Elsewhere: The Place of Style in American Literature*. New York: Oxford University Press, 1966.

"Prize Topical Poems: The Result of the Competition for April." *Munsey's* 31 (1904): 25.

"Prize Topical Poems: The Result of the Competition for February." *Munsey's* 30 (1904): 727.

"Prize Topical Poems: The Result of the Competition for May." *Munsey's* 31 (1904): 310.

"Prizes For Topical Poems." *Munsey's* 30 (1903): 320.

Publisher's Weekly 45.1148 (January 27, 1894): 184–85.

Reese, Lizette Woodworth. *A Wayside Lute*. Portland, Maine: Thomas Mosher, 1909.

"The Rejection of Poetry." *Dial* 36 (1904): 353–55.

"Review." *Boston Intelligencer,* May 3, 1856. In G. Clarke, *Walt Whitman: Critical Assessments*. Vol. 2. 37.

"Review." *Crayon,* January 1856. In G. Clarke, *Walt Whitman: Critical Assessments*. Vol. 2. 28–30.

"Review." *The Critic* [London], April 1, 1856. In G. Clarke, *Walt Whitman: Critical Assessments*. Vol. 2. 31–35.

"Review." *New York Daily Times,* 1856. In G. Clarke, *Walt Whitman: Critical Assessments*. Vol. 2. 40–47.

Review of *The Black Riders* by Stephen Crane. *Munsey's,* July 1895. In Weatherford 65, *Stephen Crane: The Critical Heritage.*

Rhoades, Lillian Ione. *The Story of Philadelphia*. New York: American Book Company, 1900.

Rice, Wallace. "Francis Brooks." *The Poems of Francis Brooks*. Ed. Wallace Rice. Chicago: R. R. Donnelley, 1898. v-xviii.

———. "A Philistine View of Poetry." *Dial* 26 (1899): 362.

Riggs, Thomas Jr. "Prometheus 1900." *American Literature* 22 (1951): 399–423.

Ripley, George. Review. *New York Daily Tribune,* 1850. In G. Clarke, *Edgar Allan Poe: Critical Assessments*. Vol. 2. 247–49.

Roberts, Kate. "Fireside Tales to Fireside Chats: The Domestic Hearth." *The Arts and the American Home, 1890–1930*. Ed. Jessica H. Foy and Karal Ann Marling. Knoxville: University of Tennessee Press, 1994. 44–61.

Robinson, Edwin Arlington. *The Children of the Night*. 1897. New York: Scribner's, 1905.

Roche, James Jeffrey. "Personal Tributes to Dr. Holmes." *The Writer* 7 (1894): 164.

"Romance vs. Reality." *Munsey's* 11 (1894): 92.

Roosevelt, Theodore. Review of *The Children of the Night* by Edwin Arlington Robinson. *Outlook* 80 (1905): 913–14.

Rose & Snyder. "Take a Car." New York: F. A. Mills, 1905.

Russell, Charles Edward. *Thomas Chatterton; The Marvelous Boy: The Story of a Strange Life,* 1752–1770. New York: Moffat, Yard, 1908.

Rydell, Robert W. "A Cultural Frankenstein: The Chicago World's Columbian Exposition of 1893." *Grand Illusions: Chicago's World's Fair of 1893.* Chicago: Chicago Historical Society, 1993. 141–70.

Saltus, Edgar. "The Colossal City." *Munsey's* 32 (1905): 787–93.

———. *Love and Lore.* New York: Belford, 1890.

———. "New York from the Flatiron." *Munsey's* 33 (1905): 381–90.

———. *Poppies and Mandragora.* New York: Harold Vinal, 1926.

Santayana, George. *The Complete Poems of George Santayana: A Critical Edition.* Ed. William G. Holzberger. Lewisburg, Penn.: Bucknell University Press, 1979.

———. *A Hermit of Carmel and Other Poems.* New York: C. Scribner's Sons, 1901.

———. Letter to Wallace Rice, March 3, 1905; Wallace Rice Papers, Midwest Manuscript Collection, Newberry Library, Chicago.

———. *The Letters of George Santayana.* Ed. Daniel Cory. New York: Scribner's, 1948.

———. "Marginal Notes." Review of *Civilization in the United States,* edited by Harold Stearns. *Dial* 72 (1922): 554–68.

———. *Sonnets and Other Verses.* New York: Duffield, 1894.

———. "Thomas Parker Sanborn." 1889. *George Santayana's America: Essays on Literature and Culture.* Ed. James Ballowe. Urbana: University of Illinois Press, 1967. 46–47.

Savage, Philip Henry. *Poems.* Ed. Daniel Gregory Mason. Boston: Small, Maynard & Co., 1900.

Schlereth, Wendy Clauson. *The Chap-Book: A Journal of American Intellectual Life in the 1890s.* Ann Arbor: UMI Research Press, 1982.

Schwartz, Hillel. *Century's End: A Cultural History of the Fin de siècle—from the 990s through the 1990s.* New York: Doubleday, 1990.

Scollard, Clinton. "Recent Books of Poetry." *Critic* 42 (1903): 229–37.

Shapiro, David. "William Cullen Bryant and the American Art Union." *William Cullen Bryant and His America.* Ed. Stanley Brodwin and Michael D'Innocenzo. New York: AMS Press, 1983. 85–95.

Sherman, Frank Dempster. *Poems of Frank Dempster Sherman.* Ed. Clinton Scollard. Boston: Houghton Mifflin, 1917.

Shi, David E. *Facing Facts: Realism in American Thought and Culture, 1850–1920.* New York: Oxford University Press, 1995.

Shields, Sophie K. *Edwin Markham: A Bibliography.* Staten Island, N.Y.: Wagner College, 1952.

Shulman, Robert. *The Power of Political Art: The 1930s Literary Left Reconsidered.* Chapel Hill: University of North Carolina Press, 2000.

Simmel, Georg. "The Metropolis and Mental Life." *On Individuality and Social Forms.* Ed. Donald N. Levine. Chicago: University of Chicago Press, 1971. 324–39.

Small, Miriam Rossiter. *Oliver Wendell Holmes.* New York: Twayne, 1962.

Smith, Barbara Herrnstein. *Contingencies of Value: Alternative Perspectives for Critical Theory.* Cambridge, Mass.: Harvard University Press, 1988.

Spofford, Harriet Prescott. *Art Decoration Applied to Furniture.* New York: Harper's, 1877.

Stedman, Edmund C., ed. *An American Anthology, 1787–1900.* Boston: Houghton Mifflin, 1900.

———. *Poets of America.* Boston: Houghton Mifflin, 1885.

———. "Proem to an American Anthology." *Century* 60 (1900): 303.

Sterling, Andrew B. "Meet Me in St. Louis, Louis." Music by Kerry Mills. New York: F. A. Mills, 1904.

Stetson [Gilman], Charlotte Perkins. *In This Our World.* Boston: Small, Maynard, 1899.

Stevens, Wallace. *Collected Poems.* New York: Knopf, 1954.

Stevick, Philip, ed. *Imagining Philadelphia: Travelers' Views of the City from 1800 to the Present.* Philadelphia: University of Pennsylvania Press, 1996.

Stickney, Trumbull. *The Poems of Trumbull Stickney.* Ed. William Vaughn Moody, George Cabot Lodge, and John Ellerton Lodge. Boston: Houghton Mifflin, 1905.

Stidger, William L. *Edwin Markham.* New York: Abingdon Press, 1933.

Stone, Herbert S. Letter to Harriet Monroe, January 2, 1895. Harriet Monroe/*Poetry* Papers, University of Chicago. Box 1, Folder 11.

Stowe, Harriet Beecher. *House and Home Papers.* Boston: James Osgood, 1864; 1872.

Stringer, Arthur. "In the Open." *McClure's* 22 (1904): 126.

Susman, Warren I. "'Personality' and the Making of Twentieth-Century Culture." *New Directions in American Intellectual History.* Ed. John Higham and Paul K. Conkin. Baltimore: Johns Hopkins University Press, 1979. 212–26.

"F. T." "Mr. Lowell's Poems." *Living Age* 124 (1875): 387–96.

Tawa, Nicholas E. *The Way to Tin Pan Alley: American Popular Song, 1866–1910.* New York: Schirmer Books, 1990.

Tebbel, John, and Mary Ellen Zuckerman. *The Magazine in America, 1741–1900.* New York: Oxford University Press, 1991.

Thomas, Calvin. "Have We Still Need of Poetry?" *Forum* 25 (1898): 502–11.

Thomas, Edith M. "Anima Urbis." *American Women Poets of the Nineteenth Century.* Ed. Cheryl Walker. New Brunswick, N.J.: Rutgers University Press, 1992. 378.

———. *The Dancers and Other Legends and Lyrics.* London: Brown, Langham, 1903.

———. *Fair Shadow Land.* Boston: Houghton Mifflin, 1893.

———. *In Sunshine Land.* Boston: Houghton Mifflin, 1895.

Thompson, F. L. "Communication: The Claims of Lyric Poetry." *Dial* 24 (1898): 286–87.

Thurston, Michael. *Making Something Happen: American Political Poetry between the Wars.* Chapel Hill: University of North Carolina Press, 2001.

Tichi, Cecilia. *Shifting Gears: Technology, Literature, Culture in Modernist America.* Chapel Hill: University of North Carolina Press, 1987.

Titherington, Richard H. "The Good Gray Poet." *Munsey's* 14 (1895): 138–46.

"The Tomes of Yesteryear." *Munsey's* 30 (1903): 153.

Tompkins, Gilbert. "The Making of a Popular Song." *Munsey's* 27 (1902): 745–48.

Tompkins, Jane. *Sensational Designs: The Cultural Work of American Fiction, 1790–1860.* New York: Oxford University Press, 1985.

Tompkins, Juliet Wilbor. "Plain Little Ann." *Munsey's* 16 (1896): 76–79.

———. "The Winning Touchdown." *Munsey's* 15 (1896): 470–75.

Towne, Charles Hanson. *Manhattan.* New York: Mitchell Kennerley, 1909.

———. "Night in Wall Street." *Munsey's* 32 (1905): 892.

———. "A Song of City Traffic." *Munsey's* 32 (1905): 793.

———. "The Street Lamps." *Munsey's* 32 (1905): 629.

"To Write a Summer Poem." *Munsey's* 11 (1894): 539.

Trachtenberg, Alan. *The Incorporation of America: Culture and Society in the Gilded Age.* New York: Hill & Wang, 1982.

Tribble, Evelyn B. *Margins and Marginality: The Printed Page in Early Modern England.* Charlottesville: University of Virginia Press, 1993.

Upson, Arthur. *Collected Poems of Arthur Upson.* Ed. Richard E. Burton. Minneapolis: Edmund D. Brooks, 1909.

"The Value of Poetry." *New Haven Register. The Writer* 17 (1904): 189–90.

Vanderbilt, Kermit. *American Literature and the Academy: The Roots, Growth, and Maturity of a Profession.* Philadelphia: University of Pennsylvania Press, 1986.

Van Wienen, Mark W. *Partisans and Poets: The Political Work of American Poetry in the Great War.* Cambridge: Cambridge University Press, 1997.

Vogel, Dan. *Emma Lazarus.* New York: Twayne, 1980.

Waddell, Elizabeth. "Why Minor Poets." *The Writer* 18 (1906): 150–51.

Wagenknecht, Edward. *John Greenleaf Whittier: A Portrait in Paradox.* New York: Oxford University Press, 1967.

Wald, Alan M. *Exiles From a Future Time: The Forging of the Mid-Twentieth-Century American Left.* Chapel Hill: University of North Carolina Press, 2002.

———. *The Revolutionary Imagination: The Poetry and Politics of John Brooks Wheelwright and Sherry Mangan.* Chapel Hill: University of North Carolina Press, 1983.

Walker, Cheryl. *Masks Outrageous and Austere: Culture, Psyche, and Persona in Modern Women Poets.* Bloomington: University of Indiana Press, 1991.

———. *The Nightingale's Burden: Women Poets and American Culture before 1900.* Bloomington: University of Indiana Press, 1982.

Wallach, Glenn. *Obedient Sons: The Discourse of Youth and Generations in American Culture, 1630–1860.* Amherst: University of Massachusetts Press, 1997.

Warde, Beatrice. *The Crystal Goblet: Sixteen Essays on Typography.* Ed. Henry Jacob. London: Sylvan Press, 1955.

Warman, Cy. "The Search for Gold." *McClure's* 14 (1900): 580.

———. "Will the Lights Be White?" *McClure's* 9 (1897): 861.

War Poems, 1898. San Francisco: Murdock Press, 1898.

Warner, H. E. "Will Poetry Disappear?" *Lippincott's* 63 (1899): 282–88.

Watson, William. "Song's Apostasy." *Atlantic* 94 (1904): 178.

Weatherford, Richard M., ed. *Stephen Crane: The Critical Heritage.* The Critical Heritage Series. London: Routledge and Kegan Paul, 1973.

Weigley, Russell F., ed. *Philadelphia: A 300-Year History.* New York: Norton, 1982.

Wells, Carolyn. *Idle Idyls.* New York: Dodd, Mead and Company, 1900.

Wertheim, Stanley, and Paul Sorrentino, eds. *The Crane Log: A Documentary Life of Stephen Crane 1871–1900.* New York: G. K. Hall, 1994.

Wharton, Edith, and Ogden Codman Jr. *The Decoration of Houses.* 1902. Ed. Henry Hope Reed and H. Stafford Bryant Jr. New York: Norton, 1978.

Wheeler, Lesley. *The Poetics of Enclosure: American Women Poets from Dickinson to Dove.* Knoxville: University of Tennessee Press, 2002.

Whipple, Edwin P. "The First Century of the Republic." *Harper's Monthly* 52 (1876): 514–33.

White, Morton, and Lucia White. *The Intellectual Versus the City.* Cambridge, Mass.: Harvard University Press and MIT Press, 1962.

Whitman, Walt. *Leaves of Grass.* Philadelphia: David McKay, 1900.

Whittaker, Frederick. *A Complete Life of General George A. Custer.* 1876. Vol. 2. Lincoln: University of Nebraska Press, 1993.

Whittier, John Greenleaf. *Complete Poetical Works.* Boston: Houghton Mifflin, 1894.

————. *Snow-Bound: A Winter Idyl.* Cambridge: Ticknor & Fields, 1866.

Whittle, Amberys R. *Trumbull Stickney.* Lewisburg, Penn.: Bucknell University Press, 1973.

"Why Are Manuscripts Rejected?: A Symposium." *The Bookman* 43 (1916): 262–86.

Wiggin, Kate Douglas. "The Best Books for Children." *Outlook* 69 (1901): 870–76.

Wilkerson, Marcus M. *Public Opinion and the Spanish-American War: A Study in War Propaganda.* Baton Rouge: Louisiana State University Press, 1932.

Williams, Raymond. *Marxism and Literature.* Oxford: Oxford University Press, 1977.

Wilson, Christopher P. *The Labor of Words: Literary Professionalism in the Progressive Era.* Athens: University of Georgia Press, 1985.

————. "The Rhetoric of Consumption: Mass-Market Magazines and the Demise of the Gentle Reader, 1880–1920." *The Culture of Consumption: Critical Essays in American History, 1880–1980.* Ed. Richard Wightman Fox and T. J. Jackson Lears. New York: Pantheon, 1983. 40–64.

————. "Stephen Crane and the Police." *American Quarterly* 48 (1996): 273–315.

Wilson, Daniel. *Chatterton: A Biographical Study.* London: Macmillan, 1869.

Wilson, Harold S. *McClure's Magazine and the Muckrakers.* Princeton, N.J.: Princeton University Press, 1970.

Wilson, Rob. *American Sublime: The Genealogy of a Poetic Genre.* Madison: University of Wisconsin Press, 1991.

Wisan, Joseph E. *The Cuban Crisis as Reflected in the New York Press, 1895–1898.* New York: Columbia University Press, 1934.

Wit, Wim de. "Building an Illusion: The Design of the World's Columbian Exposition." *Grand Illusions: Chicago's World's Fair of 1893.* Chicago: Chicago Historical Society, 1993. 41–98.

Witherbee, Sidney J., ed. *Spanish-American War Songs: A Complete Collection of Newspaper Verse during the Recent War with Spain.* Detroit: Sidney J. Witherbee, 1898.

Wortham, Thomas. "William Cullen Bryant and the Fireside Poets." *Columbia Literary History of the United States.* Ed. Emory Elliott. New York: Columbia University Press, 1988. 278–88.

Zboray, Ronald J. "Antebellum Reading and the Ironies of Technological Innovation." *Reading in America: Literature and Social History.* Ed. Cathy M. Davidson. Baltimore: Johns Hopkins University Press, 1989. 180–200.

Ziff, Larzer. *The American 1890s: Life and Times of a Lost Generation.* 1966. Lincoln: University of Nebraska Press, 1979.

INDEX